STORIES
FROM THE
FIELD

STORIES FROM THE FIELD

A Guide to Navigating Fieldwork in Political Science

Edited by Peter Krause and Ora Szekely

Columbia University Press
New York

Columbia University Press
Publishers Since 1893
New York   Chichester, West Sussex
cup.columbia.edu
Copyright © 2020 Columbia University Press

Library of Congress Cataloging-in-Publication Data

Names: Krause, Peter, 1979–editor. | Szekely, Ora, editor.
Title: Stories from the field : a guide to navigating fieldwork in
    political science / edited by Peter Krause and Ora Szekely.
Description: New York : Columbia University Press, 2020. | Includes
    bibliographical references and index.
Identifiers: LCCN 2019044327 (print) | LCCN 2019044328 (ebook) |
    ISBN 9780231193009 (hardback) | ISBN 9780231193016 (trade paperback) |
    ISBN 9780231550109 (ebook)
Subjects: LCSH: Political science—Research—Methodology. |
    Political science—Fieldwork.
Classification: LCC JA86 .S796 2020 (print) | LCC JA86 (ebook) |
    DDC 320.072/3—dc23
LC record available at https://lccn.loc.gov/2019044327
LC ebook record available at https://lccn.loc.gov/2019044328

Cover design: Nthabiseng Kamala

CONTENTS

III. MAKE A PLAN . . . THEN BE READY TO TOSS IT

IV. CREATIVELY COLLECTING DATA AND EVIDENCE

V. DEVELOPING LOCAL KNOWLEDGE

VIII. STAYING SAFE AND HEALTHY

ACKNOWLEDGMENTS

A s with any book—and certainly any book involving 44 contributors—there is a long list of people whose help and hard work we would like to acknowledge. First, we would like to offer our sincere thanks to the contributors to this volume. We are beyond delighted to have been able to share these insightful stories more broadly, and we are very grateful to our contributors for agreeing to share them with us. Academics are not, as a rule, particularly keen on explaining to the world at large how our particular brand of sausage gets made. Our publications are generally the perfectly pruned and polished final products of the research process, in which the years of sweat, uncertainty, and countless mistakes are barely visible. This book, we hope, will serve as a corrective and complement to this aspect of our discipline. We are deeply grateful that our contributors were willing to share some of the less glamorous parts of their lives as field researchers in the interest of encouraging readers who may think that their own struggles and doubts are theirs alone. As an added benefit, we're also thrilled to preserve some frankly fantastic stories for posterity.

We are also grateful for all of the support we received in bringing this project into the world. We thank the Northeast Middle East Politics Working Group, where the idea for this book first arose and many of whose members were early supporters and contributors. We are thankful for the insights provided by two anonymous reviewers of the manuscript, who provided painstaking comments that greatly improved the book, as well as to the friends and colleagues of all of the contributors (including both of us) who read and offered feedback on the individual chapters. At Columbia University Press, our editor, Caelyn Cobb, was incredibly enthusiastic about this project from the beginning, and provided us with invaluable support through what was at times a logistically complicated process, as did her staff. (This was particularly true because we were both away on field research ourselves during the early stages of the project, and often in different time zones, making coordination even more challenging than usual.) We'd also like to thank Nthabiseng Kamala at Boston College Media Technology Services for helping to draft our cover design, all of the research assistants in the Political Violence Project at Boston College who edited drafts of the manuscript throughout the process, and the Clark University Political Science Department's Harrington Fund. We also want to acknowledge the families, friends, partners, children, and others who provide an important tether to home for researchers in the field. Their love and support—from Skype calls after difficult interviews, to cups of coffee provided while analyzing data at home, to those much-needed reminders to take a break and go for a walk—make all the difference. And of course, we want to offer our sincerest gratitude to our interview subjects, survey respondents, experimental participants, and all the other people who have shared their experiences, perspectives and expertise with us and our colleagues over the years.

Finally, we'd like to end with a special note of thanks to those whose work makes our work possible: our fixers, translators, interpreters, drivers, security officers, research assistants, survey enumerators, and all of the other folks whose skill sets so often go unacknowledged but without which academic field research would grind to a halt. We cannot thank you enough, but we can commit to ensuring that your work receives the credit it deserves. As a first step in that process, this book is dedicated to you. Thank you.

Peter Krause, Boston, MA
Ora Szekely, Providence, RI
January 2020

STORIES
FROM THE
FIELD

INTRODUCTION

LEARNING THROUGH STORIES

PETER KRAUSE AND ORA SZEKELY

This book began as a conversation during lunch at a small conference on Middle Eastern politics in May 2018. A group of us began swapping stories about our experiences doing fieldwork in countries across the region. Some stories were funny, some were shocking, and some were touching—but the most striking thing was how readily each story led the group directly to asking questions, giving insightful advice, and sharing the kind of knowledge that can only be gained through hard-earned experience. In that moment, we felt that this type of vibrant discussion should not be limited to irregular, fleeting exchanges among small numbers of academics: *Someone*, we thought, *should really be writing this down*. That belief became the basis of the book you are now reading.

As we set about putting this book together, we were guided first and foremost by the belief that the best way to learn how to do fieldwork is to hear directly from those who have done it. Unfortunately, scholars rarely systematically share their personal stories and lessons in print, limiting their reach to conversations with trusted colleagues or words of advice shared with graduate students during office hours. This book pulls back the curtain, making available to all honest stories and insights from forty-four scholars who have made fieldwork a central part of their research.

High-quality fieldwork certainly shares some common practices, but solutions to dilemmas that all of us face in the field vary a great deal across locations, topics, and researchers themselves—far more than they do in controlled lab experiments. There is no single ideal blueprint for success-ful fieldwork. Excellent fieldwork is done by individuals who make very different decisions about how they gather information, how they interact with the society around them, and to what extent positivist or interpre-tivist approaches guide their work. Following the example of those par-ticularly effective interviews that give the interviewee the agency to drive parts of the conversation, we gave our contributors agency in shaping this text. The result is a "bottom-up" methods book: we as editors provided the idea but the contributors largely selected the content. We asked our con-tributors to share with us what they considered their best, most insightful stories and lessons from the field: the ones they tell their grad students and colleagues, the ones they'd like to go back and tell their younger selves. Beyond suggesting some broad themes—methods, logistics, eth-ics, and personal perspectives—we left the rest up to them. We did not ask or assign contributors to discuss certain topics or methods, nor did we ask them to take particular positions on contested issues.

What we did do was purposely approach scholars from a variety of backgrounds who had done high-quality field research. We are thank-ful that the vast majority of these scholars agreed to participate. This book includes contributions from scholars who focus on North and sub-Saharan Africa; Central, East, and South Asia; eastern and western Europe; Central and South America; North America; and the Middle East. Our contributors work on diverse topics ranging from political economy to international conflict and civil war, and from civil society and social movements to gender politics. We also ensured that we included contributors who represent a healthy range of academic ranks, genders, and national and ethnic backgrounds. This was especially important to us because we recognize the ways in which the identities carried by research-ers, and the lived experience they bring with them to fieldwork, shape their experiences in the field. We hope these perspectives will help readers relate the insights included here to their own experiences.

THE UNORTHODOX NATURE OF THIS BOOK

Our unique approach to assembling this book yielded chapters that were both unorthodox and quite effective in their style and substance. In response to our request to simply tell engaging stories from their own experiences that distilled their most important advice, contributors offered insights not normally seen in methods books, or in any academic books for that matter. Rather than describing how to do everything right, the stories included here provide insight into what researchers do when things go wrong, sometimes quite suddenly, or when complicated ethical or logistical issues arise. Instead of a step-by-step guide to designing a survey, one chapter explains how to handle enumerators in Iraq who were themselves filling out the very surveys they were supposed to distribute. Instead of instructions on how to conduct content analysis, another chapter provides insights on interpreting American politicians' doodles in the margins of classified documents. Instead of an explanation of the best identification strategy, we received advice on how to cook chickens with the wives of rebel leaders in Sierra Leone. Even chapters centered on more "conventional" topics, such as interviewing, discuss how to safely interview sex traffickers in Lebanon and Russia, how to embed with fascist militias in Italy, and how to talk to terrorists—in person or online, your choice.

What we have here—in style and in substance—is therefore the opposite of most academic work. We tell our students (and ourselves) not to write a novel but, instead, to "put the bottom line up front." But that's not how the field research process works, despite our desire to make it seem neat and tidy in our publications. As Nadya Hajj, Daniel Posner, and Marc Trachtenberg all note in their chapters, planning in fieldwork is important, but plans change. As Richard Fenno explains, you "soak and poke," you stumble around and discover things you didn't even know you were seeking.[1] As these pages attest, even the most respected academics in our field experience uncertainty and sometimes make mistakes. These chapters are presented according to a logic of discovery—not to the classic logic of explanation. With the story first and the takeaways last, you travel with the authors through their challenges, not knowing the end result.

There is much to be gained by thinking and feeling through those struggles alongside the authors rather than hearing the lesson up front, devoid of the sweat and stress that earned it in the first place. These academics are not distant two-dimensional figures; they are real three-dimensional people. Furthermore, as each chapter's focus is a story from the field—from a period before the research itself was published—these chapters can be read as prefaces to some of the most interesting books and most productive careers in political science. Readers come to understand why Stathis Kalyvas decided to study Greek history and write *The Logic of Violence in Civil War*, how David Laitin first acquired local knowledge in Africa, and how Erica Chenoweth has worked to reconcile her interactions with both governments and grassroots activists as she published groundbreaking research on nonviolence. In demystifying the process by which such important research took place, our hope is to encourage readers to think ambitiously and creatively about their own research.

One of the advantages of the "how the sausage gets made" approach is that stories that honestly reflect the complexities of the research process can serve as a starting point for conversations about research ethics, both inside and outside the classroom. Many of the chapters included here involve complicated and difficult ethical challenges that the authors address openly and honestly. Although research ethics are often presented as a simple set of guidelines based on abstract hypothetical scenarios, the real world experiences shared here demonstrate that in practice these questions require a lot of careful thought, and that the best answers aren't always easy, obvious, or universally agreed upon. Contributors also demonstrate the ways in which norms and guidelines have had to evolve over time to keep pace with the changing nature of field research, particularly with regard to new technologies of communication and data storage, as well as research conducted online.

We should note that these issues stood out to us in part because, in addition to our experience as field researchers, Ora Szekely, coeditor of this book, spent six years as a member of her university's institutional review board (IRB), charged with authorizing and overseeing research on human subjects. In this role, she observed firsthand the range of questions that this type of research can raise, and the complexity of answering them. Questions such as "How do power disparities shape the nature of informed consent?" and "How do our own identities shape the ways in which our research participants engage with us?" have always been an important part of constructing an ethical research design. Meanwhile, the evolving natures of technology, the research process, and even "the field" itself generate new questions, such as "Are online spaces public or private?" and "How do we most effectively protect digital data?" There is no universally correct set of answers, but we hope these stories spark conversations about these and other questions, help readers think through ethical issues, and give them the tools to develop their own sets of guiding principles.

HOW TO USE THIS BOOK

Faculty and students who are preparing to go into the field, sharpen their skills for the future, or teach about fieldwork can all make great use of this book. Moreover, the book contributes to our intradisciplinary conversation more broadly in that it serves as a companion to the existing publications of each contributor. Reading these chapters side by side with the books and articles that resulted from the fieldwork they describe provides fascinating context for the authors' work and a soup to nuts guide to designing, organizing, and conducting one's own research. To facilitate this process, the publications that resulted from each fieldwork story are listed at the end of each chapter.

We also hope this book will be read as a complement to the growing number of excellent books on research methods, including more formal theoretical guides to field research. These stories add insight on issues and skills that graduate and undergraduate coursework rarely covers, including how to travel securely in conflict zones, how to handle conversations on sensitive topics, and how to eat and drink socially (and safely) when in the field. Readers will learn from our contributors' mistakes, as many of these chapters serve as humble entries in the "failure CVs" that scholars have begun to post publicly, with narration and lessons-learned attached.

For professors teaching classes on research methods and fieldwork, this book can be effectively assigned to, and happily consumed by, both graduates *and* undergraduates. As those who have taught or taken research methods courses know, overly dry or instructional textbooks can make it challenging to capture students' attention and imagination. Furthermore, it can be challenging to find relevant sections among long academic books and articles when there is a limit to the number of pages one can assign for each class meeting. Our hope is that this book will provide a way of addressing these issues. The chapters included here are engaging, practical, and written in an accessible narrative style with no unnecessary jargon—a style that we think students (and other readers) learn from particularly well. Furthermore, the fact that they are generally only a few pages long ensures that there are no wasted words, and a chapter can easily be assigned and read alongside any other content for a given course.

Finally, we encourage readers to use these chapters as conversation starters. Everyone relates to compelling personal stories, and even though the chapters are bite-sized, the issues and questions they raise are not. Instead of (or alongside) a forty-page article discussing research design or ethics, professors can assign a chapter from this book that covers almost any topic or region of the world. Each chapter's focused nature assures it can be read quickly—including during class time—and it can spark reflection and discussion, both inside the classroom and out. For students, there is no reason to wait to take a class on fieldwork to read this book. For the ever-growing number of students planning to travel abroad, this book can help you prepare for these experiences and learn how to engage in more meaningful ways with the places where you live and study, as well as with the people around you.

In short, treat this book as a guidebook. Underline it, bookmark it, annotate it, and throw it in your bag on your way out the door. We hope it provides comfort and guidance when you face inevitable, unexpected challenges in the field (or at least something interesting to read while you're waiting for that border guard to come back with your passport).

WHAT'S TO COME: THE OUTLINE OF THE BOOK

Whether it involves stepping off a bus at two in the morning in an unfamiliar city or discovering that you're going to be sharing a hotel room with some exciting local wildlife, field research often begins with a sense that you have been tossed into the deep end. In that spirit, this book's first part addresses some universal themes, including the power of personal relationships, the impact of bias, and the role of emotions, in stirring chapters by Ian S. Lustick, Zoe Marks, and Richard A. Nielsen. The book then pulls back out for a more orderly, thematically organized progression, filled with engaging and dynamic stories. After we welcome you to the field, the book progresses as one would through the fieldwork process: designing the research and deciding where to go, dealing with the unexpected upon arrival, collecting evidence and developing local knowledge, grappling with issues of identity and ethics, and staying safe and healthy.

In part II, "Designing Your Research and Deciding Where to Go," five contributors provide valuable insight on the first steps in the fieldwork process. Stathis N. Kalyvas details the serendipity that drove him to conduct fieldwork on the Greek Civil War, and how the inductive process forced him to rethink his assumptions about the dynamics of political violence. Christina M. Greer details the process of designing and carrying out a survey with a social services employees union to analyze the distinct identities of African, Caribbean, and Black Americans in New York City. Krista E. Wiegand discusses the personal challenges of navigating institutional review boards as she shifted from interviewing Hezbollah members to interviewing Filipino government officials after being placed on government watch lists. Stephen M. Saideman describes various strategies for conducting effective fieldwork in countries where he doesn't speak the language—Brazil, Chile, Japan, and South Korea—from working with local scholars to hiring student researchers. Finally, Fotini Christia offers sharp personal insights on how she built connections with journalists and expats, remained disciplined in structuring her surveys and field experiments, and navigated being the "third gender" as a Western woman conducting fieldwork in war-torn Afghanistan.

Like military engagements—where plans go out the window at the first whiff of grapeshot—part III cautions readers who are heading into the field to "Make a Plan . . . Then Be Ready to Toss It." The six chapters in this part progress from contributors making smaller (and happier) adjustments to their research question or personnel . . . to full-scale exit and reentry with an entirely new approach for those who hate conducting fieldwork. Nadya Hajj "lets go and lets Ali" by allowing her Palestinian interviewees to not simply answer her questions, but also teach her what questions she didn't even think to ask. Daniel N. Posner tells of a similar experience in Zambia and Malawi, where he changed the focus of his dissertation once he realized that the perceptions of the people there were far different than what he had assumed from afar. In a related vein, Kristin Michelitch recounts the adjustments that she and her collaborator needed to make while doing research on the effects of listening to the radio on voter behavior in rural Mali. Sometimes flexibility in the field means learning how to cope when, due to identical names and the need to set appointments over the phone, you interview the wrong people. In the case of Bethany Lacina, preparation to learn her interviewees' backgrounds helped mitigate otherwise trying situations with Indian politicians and military generals. Such mistakes are innocent, but how should you cope when local research partners are intentionally dishonest or corrupt? Matthew Franklin Cancian and Kristin E. Fabbe explain how they resolved a sensitive situation involving one crooked enumerator team that threatened to harm their reputations and sink their survey in Iraq. Finally, it is important to remind ourselves that not everyone enjoys the fieldwork process. Amelia Hoover Green openly admits to being a fieldwork-hater, providing an honest and engaging tale of how she nonetheless revamped her entire approach to be effective, if not elated, in the field.

In part IV, "Creatively Collecting Data and Evidence," seven excellent chapters cover a range of new twists on the classic methods of interviews and archival research. Jessica Stern details how she developed her approach to interviewing terrorists over time, touching on the psychological costs involved in this work, as well as the impact her identity as a woman had on interviewing (mostly) violent men. Marc Trachtenberg and Lindsey O'Rourke each spin tales of sifting through countless documents in the archives, reminding us that not all fieldwork focuses on talking to others. Trachtenberg details how "stumbling around in the archives" can nonetheless lead to great discoveries if you have a solid understanding of the issue area. O'Rourke explains how notes and drawings on archival documents—sometimes obtained via Freedom of Information Act (FOIA) requests—can provide unique insights into the minds of politicians who scribbled them long ago. Even fieldwork based on interviews can involve a great deal of innovation, as Keith Darden's chapter detailing his experience acting as an informal taxi driver in Ukraine demonstrates. Mia Bloom and Ayse Lokmanoglu also used less traditional research methods in their online field research on jihadi propaganda. Their retelling of interactions with jihadi fighters, spokespeople, and sometimes suitors confirms that, in today's world, "fieldwork" need not require physical travel, although it can still involve significant risk. Valerie Sperling relates how sometimes the most insightful data collection is the least planned, as she learned about anti-Americanism and gender roles in Russia by interacting with local shopkeepers and cold-calling the numbers of risqué ads on the local sidewalk—for research purposes, of course. Robert Ross provides another fresh angle on collecting evidence in the field through his experiences interviewing Chinese academics abroad, who provide both windows into China's security policy and examples of its suffocating nature.

In part V, "Developing Local Knowledge," six contributors detail how they came to know their fieldwork location and its people in unconventional ways. Wendy Pearlman makes an articulate case for "field-being": simply living and interacting in the field in noninstrumental ways. Her own

experience doing so with communities in the Middle East has led to enduring relationships and deep knowledge that cannot be acquired through
quick, overscheduled visits. What better way to get to know an area than
by walking all over the place? That's exactly what Paul Staniland does, and
his stories of strolling without a fixed destination through fieldwork sites
in South Asia productively demonstrated his outsider status while revealing key social and political dynamics on the inside. David Laitin provides
a simple but effective standard for sufficient local knowledge that all can
strive to meet—the "onion principle." Until one has the ability to buy onions
(or other products) at the going market rate for locals, one lacks the ability
to effectively navigate the manipulations of the area and do quality fieldwork. Food- and drink-based pathways to knowledge are not uncommon
in the field. John McCauley explains how getting drunk on *dolo* for two
days with village elders in Burkina Faso served as an unexpected vetting
process that ultimately built trust and gained him and his team the necessary access to conduct research there. Will Reno addresses the importance
of local knowledge when doing research in insecure environments, specifically discussing the need to find a trusted local host with an effective private
army to do field research in Mogadishu. And Amaney Jamal reflects on the
importance of fieldwork—as distinct from data collection in the field—as a
means of developing local knowledge and networks.

In part VI, "Seeing and Being Seen: Identity in the Field," five contributors offer intimate tales of how their personal and professional identities affected their fieldwork. Laia Balcells tells of the draw of studying a
civil war in her home country of Spain, and describes the emotional toll
and ethical challenges of remaining objective despite her Catalan identity. Enze Han explains how his Han Chinese identity generated a mix of
indifference and animosity among minority communities he interacted
with in Inner Mongolia and Xinjiang, forcing him to consider his own
subjectivity and positionality for the first time. Melissa Nobles set out to
research a Brazilian democracy that supposedly had no racial discrimination, only to find that no one wanted to assert a "Black" identity for
themselves (or for her). She related how her own Black and American
identities played a key role in how she was able to access and perceive
the society during a period of ethnic awakening. Desmond King relates
how often Americans were surprised that a non-American like him was
researching the politics of race and the federal government in the United

States. Although his outsider status raised initial questions, it ultimately provided him with more intimate access to archives and interviewees on this sensitive topic. Finally, Peter Krause explains how chosen identities—such as institutional affiliations, political agendas, and personal candor—can help transcend differences in born national and religious identities between people in the field, whether they are former Irish militants or skeptical Algerian archivists.

In part VII, "Being Ethically Accountable," six contributors grapple with the ethical challenges they faced while conducting fieldwork, from funding sources, to relationships with governments of all stripes, to a researcher's accountability as a participant observer. Erica Chenoweth describes the tensions when studying violence and nonviolence and, relatedly, engaging with both governments and grassroots activists. She shares the questions that inform her own personal code of conduct, which can help others prepare for the moral and ethical conundrums that are inevitably present in political research. Zachariah Cherian Mampilly challenges the notion of a distant, othered "field," relating searing personal experiences at home that nonetheless bear the marks of research in uncomfortable territory. He then raises tough ethical questions about the close relationship between governments and scholars of security issues, challenging whether the latter fully appreciate their impact on the former. Marc Lynch reminds us that even at the moment of greatest hope and openness in the field, things can change, and change quickly. As political winds blow to and fro in Egypt and the broader Middle East, he demonstrates with heavy examples that scholars have a serious responsibility to protect their sources, even if prominent journals say otherwise. One would expect that embedding with a fascist militia in Italy would be replete with ethical challenges, and Alessandro Orsini pulls no punches in detailing them. Faced with threats if he failed to turn over his manuscript before publication, he explains how he responded in light of the responsibility scholars have to each other. Emil Aslan Souleimanov describes the responsibility he had to his interviewees, in this case Chechen ex-militants. He thinks through the importance of trust and interpersonal relationships, and the ethical implications thereof, in the context of his research. Finally, Ora Szekely considers what it means to be perceived in particular ways by one's research participants, and the particular discomfort of accidentally ending up on Hezbollah's satellite TV news coverage.

In part VIII, four contributors offer their advice for "Staying Safe and Healthy," based on their harrowing experiences living in conflict zones, interacting with criminals, and getting violently ill. Sarah Zukerman Daly details the uneasy feeling of not knowing who was in control when she stepped into conflict zones in Colombia. Nonetheless, she offers sharp advice for how to identify trusted allies in the field, even as she honestly details some of her own slips in judgment. Carla B. Abdo-Katsipis knew that there would be safety concerns when she approached members of a sex trafficking ring in Lebanon. Even though she had to be flexible about meeting the involved parties on their terms, she explains how she was still able to maintain safety on her terms. The United States is "the field" for many, and the challenges of health and safety do not disappear inside its borders. Ravi Perry describes a series of serious health episodes that forced a reappraisal of how he cared for himself while covering elections in Ohio. Vipin Narang brings this section to a close with a simple message: drink the tea—even if it's lukewarm and gives you "Delhi belly," as it did Vipin. Because of that tea, Vipin gained unique knowledge about India's nuclear strategy, which he argues was worth the slight risks to his health.

We couldn't assemble such a large, impressive cast of scholars and not have them offer "One Last Thing Before You Go." If we're lucky, most of us have a few good mentors throughout our lives. This chapter is a chance to have forty-four of them offer you their best short piece of fieldwork advice in one place, separate from their chapter stories. Think of it as stopping by during the office hours of all of our contributors one last time before setting off into the field. Except that in the case of this chapter, gaining the insight will take you far less time and effort, and you can take it with you to read and reread in the field.

Finally, we conclude by asking, What does it mean to do fieldwork? Here, we draw out some of the overarching themes in this book and ruminate a bit on the broader lessons to be learned from our contributors' insights regarding the practice of field research.

Everyone loves a good story, and we all enjoy hearing about others' research experiences in the field. But the stories shared here are more than just gripping anecdotes. They represent both an important source of shared knowledge about practical research methods in the field and an invaluable way of illustrating methodological, logistical, and ethical concepts that, in the abstract, can seem dry and distant. We hope this book provides useful advice and sparks good conversations, and that one day you will have your own stories from the field to share. We're all ears.

NOTE

1. Richard Fenno, *Homestyle: House Members in Their Districts* (Glenview, Ill.: Scott Foresman, 1978).

I

WELCOME
TO THE
FIELD

1

FIELDWORK AND EMOTIONS

IAN S. LUSTICK

▸ FIELDWORK LOCATION: ISRAEL/PALESTINE

T here is nothing like being in the field to teach the comparative political scientist about politics. No matter how well equipped one might be by instructors, the "literature," prior theorizing, or a rich conceptual repertoire, a genuine encounter with politics plunges the researcher into an ocean of observations that can be as mysterious and confusing as they are potentially instructive. Indeed, the encounter with the field is so saturated with learning opportunities that what can be registered by the thin cortex of the researcher's brain—where cognition, cogitation, calculation, and rational deliberation occur—is wholly insufficient. Learning, especially in the field, also requires emotional engagement, as well as the ability to notice and track the character of that engagement.

I have conducted fieldwork in Israel/Palestine regularly (if not always conventionally) since 1969. In this chapter, I share three specific episodes— on a Mediterranean beach, on a bus ride to Masada, and in a West Bank collective taxi—that taught me as much as they did precisely because of the emotional reactions they triggered in me.[1]

A DAY AT THE BEACH: SADNESS, SHAME, AND INSIGHT

In the late summer of 1969, I was a junior at Brandeis University, spending six months at a branch of that university located in Jerusalem known as the Jacob Hiatt Institute. One weekend, I traveled with my girlfriend, also a Brandeis student, from Jerusalem by "tramp" (hitchhiking), collective taxi, and hiking to what in those days was a relatively inaccessible but not too distant beach on the Mediterranean—*HaHof HaYarok* (The Green Beach)—south of the city of Netanya. We had been in the country for only two months. Our Hebrew was poor. We brought some food and camped out under a rudimentary shelter on the beach, watching a rider gallop along the surf as the sun set. We spent the next day sunning and swimming. There were no services at the mostly deserted beach, although someone was acting as if he were a lifeguard. We struck up conversations with a large family having a picnic—a family that included four men about our age, or a bit older. It was exciting because, for the first time, we found Israelis ready to respond to our broken Hebrew, in Hebrew, rather than seeing us as an opportunity to practice their broken English. While we were getting Hebrew lessons from them, we were giving swimming lessons to them. None of the men could swim, and we were gently showing them how.

They brought out food to share. It being the 1960s, I had brought my guitar. Soon we were sitting on the beach, and I was playing and singing. We were all eating watermelon. As we ate and talked, we learned, to our surprise, that these people were Arabs—from Nazareth, the largest Arab town in Israel. One of the men proudly described his work as a teacher. We explained, of course, that we were students from the United States—Jewish students. This led to some basic political and historical questions being raised about, well, why did the Jews come to this country anyway? As part of our response, I played the song "Dona Dona," a Yiddish folk song translated into English about slaughtered calves and why, metaphorically, Jews had fled, or should have fled, from Europe. "Only those," goes one verse, "who treasure freedom, like the swallow, have learned to fly."

We spent a wonderful afternoon in this way, perhaps understanding about 50 percent of what we were trying to say to one another, until it began to be time to think about leaving. We agreed that they would give us a ride to the main road, and that we would come to Nazareth soon to visit them. But as we were packing up, they discovered something was amiss with their car. While they were tinkering with the engine, I was approached by the lifeguard (or security guard, I was not sure who he was, really). He asked me to come with him to the part of the beach about fifty yards away near the parking lot.

Standing there was an older couple from France. They and the life-guard had been watching us with growing concern and now alarm. "Do you know," he said to me, "who those people are that you are with? Do you realize they are Arabs?"

"Yes," I said, "they're from Nazareth. One of them is a teacher."

"And I bet," he continued, "that they have offered you a ride."

"That's right, they have," I responded. "They'll drive us to the main road where we can tramp or take a bus."

"Look," he said, "don't do it. Don't do it on any account. This couple here," he said, motioning to the older folks, "have offered to drive you to a bus station."

The older couple approached us with expressions of deep worry on their faces. "Please, come with us, right now," the man said, with what sounded like a Yiddish accent. "Don't worry. Just say goodbye and we'll leave."

"But we already agreed to go with them. They're fine people. We spent the day with them. There's no problem."

"Look," the lifeguard said, again. "You don't understand. They are Arabs, they will kill you and rape your girlfriend. It happened recently to tourists who accepted a ride from Arabs."

"That's ridiculous," I told him, "and it would be terrible if suddenly I told them we had changed our minds."

I went back to talk to my girlfriend, who was wondering what this was all about. As I told her, we noticed that our Arab friends were eyeing us with distress and perhaps anger. "He's telling you not to go with us," one cried to us, "because we are Arabs." We didn't know what to do, but we leaned toward sticking with the plan to leave with our friends. But then the lifeguard and the older couple again called us over. When we told him we were staying, they raised the stakes.

"You," said the lifeguard, talking directly to me, "you might take the risk. It's your life, but how can you put your girlfriend in danger."

"Exactly," said the older man, "you must think, what would her father say? What would you tell him if something happened to her."

And that's when my fear overcame my judgment—when my ignorance took its toll on my humanity. She and I looked at each other. Then I looked at the lifeguard. "OK," I said, "we'll go with you." When we went to gather our things, our Arab friends showed that they were hurt and deeply upset.

They knew exactly what had happened, and they knew we had chosen to distrust them, to think the worst of them.

"You don't believe I'm a teacher, do you?" cried the teacher. "And you'll never come to visit us either."

"Yes," I said, "we do and we will, but we just have to go now, we can't wait for your car to be fixed." We moved quickly to the car of the older couple and got in. Torn between fear and guilt, we left our swimming students and our Hebrew teachers insulted and abandoned.

Our trip back to Jerusalem was quiet and sad. A part of that sadness—born of fear and ignorance—has never left me. And the teacher was right. We lost the paper with their names and address. As quickly as we realized we had made a terrible mistake, we also realized there was no way to apologize or make things better, no way to ever make contact with these people again.

All I could do was learn from the experience, and I believe I did. Most of what I learned was from what I felt—how trapped I felt into acting brutally toward people who had offered nothing but friendship and assistance; how ashamed I felt to see how my ignorance and fear could be manipulated by others; how tempted I felt to avoid the shame by believing that we had actually been in danger; how frustrated I felt that structures of inequality could produce dilemmas and cruelties that the best of intentions could not overcome; and how much anger could be generated in a situation where injustice and inequality is hidden, not discussed, and remains unacknowledged.

In the years that followed, I determined that studying the Arab minority inside of Israel was just too difficult and too painful a problem for someone like me at that time, a person who believed in a "Jewish and democratic state." Instead, I focused entirely on Israel's occupation of the West Bank and Gaza. My first publication was a paper I wrote that semester in Israel titled "What the West Bank Arabs Think."[2] And when I returned to the country in 1973 for dissertation research, my topic was the impact of the occupation on Palestinian politics in the West Bank and Gaza Strip and the possibilities created for peace based on an independent Palestinian state.

But the field can be as cunning as history. In the midst of my work in the West Bank, in October 1973, the Yom Kippur/Ramadan War erupted. Continuing my research on the military government in the West Bank and Gaza was impossible. Searching for another topic, I was led, ineluctably, to the military government that had ruled Arab citizens of Israel from 1948 to 1966, and then to the larger question of how Arabs citizens of the country were controlled and manipulated by state and parastatal institutions operating on behalf of "Jews," not "Israelis." That was the project that became my dissertation, and then my first book—*Arabs in the Jewish State: Israel's Control of a National Minority*.

I did not dedicate the book to those Arabs on the beach, although I wanted to do so. Publishing a book on this topic in the United States was so controversial that almost every major academic press in the country refused to review the manuscript. Even my eventual publisher, the University of Texas Press, insisted on careful control of what was said in the preface and acknowledgments so that, as much as possible, my credentials as a Jewish Zionist could protect the press against pressures that threatened to prevent publication even after the contract had been signed and revisions completed. I always hoped that somehow those Arabs on the beach, or perhaps their children, might know of what came, in part, from what they suffered that day. The sadness associated with the groundlessness of that hope is another emotion triggered by that episode, no less instructive than the others.

THIS LAND IS MINE, HOW THRILLING

Later during that half year in Israel/Palestine, I had my first encounter with the radical irredentism that Israel's victory in the Six-Day War of 1967 had triggered, especially among young religious Jews. My first reaction to hearing such ultranationalist talk was revulsion. I was, after all, a stalwart liberal, a fierce opponent of the Vietnam War. I was a Jewish nationalist—but a liberal Jewish nationalist, committed to imagining Jews as a peculiar nation precisely because of their universalist values—and anxious to infuse, à la Martin Buber and Franz Rosenzweig, real human meaning into Jewish rituals and practices more commonly imagined as narrowly parochial.

But one day, traveling through the West Bank from Jerusalem to the Dead Sea and Masada, I felt something strong and peculiar, indeed shocking. This land I was seeing, this really was where my people had been born; where the patriarchs lived; where the Kingdom of David was established; and where the Maccabees had fought the Syrian Greeks. How wonderful it was, how marvelous, that after all the centuries of wandering and suffering and persecution, after the Holocaust, we Jews had gained something so special. "OK," I said to myself, "I realize it was taken from Arabs, and that by strict terms of justice it should be relinquished, or at least shared. But why not," I thought, "why not just this once, shouldn't Jews get something for themselves, maybe even a bit more than they deserved—to rule this land, to inhabit it as a Jewish country? How simply wonderful that would be!"

The feeling did not last long, and I can no longer conjure it up. But for years I could, and I can still at least remember having it. That I could experience so powerful an emotion helped me understand how Gush Emunim settlers—those who formed the vanguard of the more than 700,000 Jews now living east of the 1949 armistice line—feel all, or at least much, of the time. That feeling, and the memory of that feeling, helped tremendously in research for my book on what Gush Emunim settlers believe, how they think, and how they feel about the land they have taken from others. Without it, my book *For the Land and the Lord* would not have been written. I simply would not have been able to talk calmly to the people I was studying, to read their intricate and voluminous internal debates, or to understand how love and dedication can coexist and even dominate one's knowledge of the injustice one is committing.

NATIONALISM AND HOMOSOCIALITY IN A COLLECTIVE TAXI

The third episode occurred some years later. I was traveling back to Jerusalem from Nablus in a collective Arab taxi, having spent the day talking with activists in the "Palestinian National Front"—a communist party–linked organization, banned by the Israeli military government, that in the early and mid-1970s was committed to building a nonbelligerent but independent Palestinian state alongside Israel.

The car was a Mercedes. I was seated next to the window on the passenger side in the middle row of three rows of seats. My Arabic was not good, but I was looking forward to listening to what the seven middle-aged Palestinian men in the car would be talking about. It was obvious that I was an American, or at least not an Israeli.

We started out on the hour and a half drive down the mountain spine of the West Bank shortly before sunset. It was a twisting, dramatic road, with spectacular views, usually driven at hair-raising speed and with as much brash disdain for other drivers as possible. In those days, we could be fairly confident of making the trip uninterrupted by Israeli checkpoints, police, or army patrols.

But this trip turned out to be different from any other. The driver had the radio tuned to music. There was no talking. We were driving south. The sun began to set, drenching the hills and the inside of the car in a wonderfully eerie, reddening light. But it wasn't the light per se, or the silence of the passengers and driver, or the controlled rocking of the car that started to feel unusual. It was their combination with the music. It was "Arabic music"—pure instrumental, no singing, with a steady, throbbing beat. It was heavy, masculine, melancholy, and powerfully erotic. I felt myself completely engulfed by the music, its effect deepened by the lengthening shadows, the red sky, and the silence of the men in the car with me. It seemed that the eight of us were in a kind of time warp, or space ship, completely separated from the rest of the world. We seemed as riders in a camel caravan, moving through a mysterious and awesome terrain, experiencing a force and a presence as intimate and real as it was ineffable.

But was I just imagining this? How could I feel what these men, so different from me, were feeling? Maybe this mood, these sensations and emotions, were just in my head, products of a naïve Orientalist fantasy. The others were quiet, perhaps because they had things on their mind—jobs, money problems, family issues, politics, aches and pains. Who knew? All I knew was that I had never felt anything like this before, and I had never felt so close to a group of people who were, in fact, complete strangers.

As we approached Ramallah, darkness spread over the landscape. The music stopped. The car was quiet for several minutes. Then the man beside me turned and spoke, in accented but clear English: "Now," he said, "you know what it is to be an Arab man."

And perhaps I did. And if I can't still feel what I felt then, I can remember feeling so, and that has connected me to the Middle East—its peoples and its predicaments. So has the fear and shame that surged within me at *HaHof Hayarok*, and the memory of those emotions. The same is true of the swelling attachment and love for the "Jewish" Land of Israel that sprang up within me on that ride to the Dead Sea, and my memory of these feelings. To this day, these connections enliven my study of politics in the region and help me understand both the fascination and the confusion of my students.

I read my old field notes and was amazed at the detail I had accumulated, and how little of it I recall. But the emotional realities I experienced—they have never left me.

———

Ian S. Lustick *is professor and Bess W. Heyman Chair of Political Science at the University of Pennsylvania.*

PUBLICATIONS TO WHICH THIS FIELDWORK CONTRIBUTED:

- Lustick, Ian S. *Arabs in the Jewish State: Israel's Control of a National Minority.* Austin: University of Texas Press, 1980.
- ———. *For the Land and the Lord: Jewish Fundamentalism in Israel.* New York: Council on Foreign Relations, 1988.
- ———. *Paradigm Lost: From Two-State Solution to One-State Reality.* Philadelphia: University of Pennsylvania Press, 2019.

NOTES

1. I am grateful for conversations with Hilary Lustick, an education leadership scholar, whose analysis of the role of emotion in her own research helped me see more clearly its role in mine. For a useful survey of work on emotion and fieldwork, see Dimitrina Spencer, "Introduction: Emotional Labour and Relational Observation in Anthropological Fieldwork," in *Anthropological Fieldwork: A Relational Process,* ed. Dimitrina Spencer and James Peter Davies (Newcastle: Cambridge Scholars, 2010), 1–47. See also Liora Nutov, "Researcher Emotions as Data, a Tool and a Factor in Professional Development," *Qualitative Report* 22, no. 12 (December 2017): 3260–67.
2. Ian Lustick, "What the West Bank Arabs Think," *Jewish Frontier,* June (1970), 13–19.

2

COOKING SOUP AND KILLING CHICKENS

NAVIGATING GENDER AND FOOD-AS-FIELDWORK IN WEST AFRICA

ZOE MARKS

▸ FIELDWORK LOCATION: SIERRA LEONE

In Sierra Leone, everyone has a unique recipe for groundnut soup.[1] I learned this while traveling in the provinces to interview participants in the country's ten-year civil war. As I visited people's homes, I gradually learned to cook Sierra Leonean food with my hosts and interlocutors, including several former wives of the rebel leader Foday Sankoh. Cooking with women from the Revolutionary United Front (RUF) was a privilege. In spending time with them, they told me stories about the war and shared their present-day experiences, educating me in the material realities of their daily life and subtly shifting the power balance of my research. As experts of their domain, navigating cooking pots and coal fires, they gained control over the context and content of our visit. Groundnut soup, a ubiquitous Sierra Leonean dish, gradually became a crucible for forging connections and better understanding the lives of the people I met.

There was no obvious connection between cooking and my research. I was in Sierra Leone to examine how insurgency changes over time and to understand how the RUF was able to sustain a decade-long civil war despite minimal support and largely coercive recruitment. Yet the social ebb and flow of eating and waiting defined my experiences around the country as I met hundreds of interviewees through diverse gatekeepers. The twelve months I spent traveling, lodging, eating, and passing time with RUF interlocutors was essential to my learning who they are as people and how they experienced insurgency. As I sought care and reciprocity in research-based relationships, cooking emerged organically as a practice alongside other more (or less) sophisticated methods. As a result, my dusty field notes include scattered shopping lists and recipes alongside descriptions of rebel strategy and tactics, laws and orders, and harms and hardships witnessed and survived.

My experiences in Sierra Leonean kitchens underscored the strength of some cultural taboos, even as I researched why fighters had blithely and wildly broken other norms. Watching boys kill chickens and women prepare them for stew helped me understand more viscerally how men and women can be socialized for particular forms of violence. Attending to the social side of social science research—through food—helped me to better understand the personal and gendered experiences of war and its aftermath. Creating and sharing something as simple as a pot of soup with interviewees also made carrying and sharing their heavy stories more manageable.

Cooking together is a bridge between common courtesy (always offer to help your hosts) and practicality (meet your interlocutors where they are). For me, it was also a deliberate act of feminist solidarity, physically stepping out of the privileged realm of men talking politics with a foreign researcher, in order to physically step into the world of women. In Sierra Leone, as elsewhere, women are busy preparing food, chasing children, and working. Joining them provided a poignant window into how gender, power, labor, and money affected their lives in intimate, ordinary ways. Moving between gendered spaces enabled me to listen to and learn from women who also lived through the war and were instrumental to the rebel group's survival. Other scholars have written about this not-quite-ethnography as immersive fieldwork[2] and ethnographic interviewing.[3] Successful embedded research requires equal parts of spontaneity and patience on the part of the researcher—taking advantage of both moments, what Lee Ann Fujii describes as "accidental ethnography,"[4] and long periods that Mats Utas, Clifford Geertz, and others call "deep hanging out."[5] In Sierra Leone, my hanging out happened while waiting: for phone calls, for people to show up, for the rain to stop, for transport to arrive, for rice to be served. Offering to help with whatever tasks busied the people around me was an easy way to make myself useful, learn new skills, and build connections.

Much like the adaptive life history interviews I conducted, cooking in Sierra Leone has no crisp instructions, units of measurement, or timers—you adjust as you go. Women showed me how to "buy buy" (Krio for shop/buy) oil, seasoning, smoked fish, and other ingredients at the market, where they are sold in standardized volumes that roughly translate into cooking quantities. A cup of peppers is not the same volume as a cup of rice—and you can buy either small cups or large cups—but all are sold at common prices. After learning the markets, I learned the magic combinations of MSG and seasoning used for various soups and sauces, and how to identify flowering basil by the roadside. I studied carefully how to chop onions with no cutting board, slicing the thinnest slivers off the peeled top into a wooden mortar. These experiences strengthened my conversational skills in Krio, Sierra Leone's English-based lingua franca, so I could build rapport and navigate sensitive interviews alone. Throughout Africa there is legitimate distrust of researchers, health professionals, legal teams, and others that dates to the colonial era when wealth was gained by taking people's knowledge, products, and land. Similar patterns of extraction without accountability continue today. Sierra Leonean culture is warm and welcoming, but circumspect about divulging the whole truth to strangers, a practice compounded by political systems built on ubiquitous and powerful secret societies.[6] Speaking Krio, cooking with women, and staying with interlocutors' families provided a way for me not just to overcome distrust but to earn trust.

MAMMY B.

When I first met her in eastern Sierra Leone in 2009, Mammy B. was a wisp of a woman hiding behind a brilliant smile.[7] I assumed she had always been thin. Having known her for ten years now, I've come to understand that when she said things were very hard for her back then it was because her postwar husband withheld money for food. The day I arrived on her doorstep with one of her friends from the war, she welcomed us with big hugs followed by a long stretch of nostalgic catching up. Over the following weeks, we visited often and took local trips together to visit mutual friends and other interviewees. On the day we set aside for her interview, she insisted on cooking for us, so we agreed on groundnut soup—a budget friendly crowd-pleaser—and sent her son with a small fistful of bills to buy the ingredients. Thus began my first cooking lesson from one of the former wives of Foday Sankoh

(1937–2003), the founder of the rebel group. Cooking with Mammy B. was the first time I saw a strong woman delegate killing a chicken to a young boy, and it was the first lesson I had in how to char, boil, pluck, and dismember the bird.

As an interviewee, Mammy B. was quick to talk about her past and equally quick to move on to other subjects. Over a small coal fire under a hot midday sun, she told me how Sankoh met her years before in a similar setting and had fallen in love with her beauty. She laughed about how little changed in her life after they were married because he was often away. He would send food and gifts between visits, and she said she was happy she could provide for her family during the early years of the war. As the RUF faced growing scarcity and insecurity, so did she. She navigated most of the conflict alone with their son because Sankoh was imprisoned and his other wives were scattered across the country. Like other women I interviewed, much of her wartime experience was spent doing what we were doing—cooking, chatting, tidying, and waiting.

Cooking with Mammy B. in her sparse compound a day's walk from the former RUF headquarters provided a stark illustration of the tradeoffs that characterized life in rebellion. Under duress in the war, she partnered with a man who had power and status, but his protection and resources waned with his political power. By the time I met her, Mammy B. had even fewer options, having married a man with modest resources who did not provide for her family. She glowed with pride when discussing her son, but when he ran off to do chores, she whispered about the challenges they faced and the social weight of postwar stigma. Bereft of her wartime support networks and social status, Mammy B. struggled to find enough money and food for them. Cooking together helped me navigate the tensions of asking delicate questions and discreetly providing material support, while also demonstrating respect publicly and privately for the wife of the former "leader of the revolution." It gave us time alone, away from men, in which she told me things she did not want other members of the RUF to overhear. In later years, she left her husband and moved to the city. Now our visits are characterized by urban bustle, not rural idyll, and though our conversations and visits revolve around similar characters, the story has changed. Her new home reflects the ways her postwar life continues to evolve as she pursues a better life for her son and herself.

AUNTIE F.

Just a couple of weeks after my interviews with Mammy B., in a town where the paved Freetown highway once ended, I met Auntie F., another wife of a top rebel leader.[8] She lived with her children on a leafy compound with a garden her mother tended at the back. There were friends and neighbors around, but no male partners. Auntie F. is a woman who smiles with her eyes and laughs with her belly. When she and I sat down together, she was quick to dive into the stories she thought most important—how she and the Commander had met, and her opinions of his other wives. She also carved out space to share heartaches and grief about the hardships of war and lost family and friends.

She was warm and took to me with ease, and I tried to reciprocate in kind as a gracious guest. I had a few interviews in town that day, and the last person I met with was a friend of hers who wanted to meet in F's house. When he and I finished talking, my interlocutor that day (the former head of RUF security) reappeared to join us. I knew from their languid postures and social norms that the men would sit in the parlor trading war stories until food appeared before them. As a foreigner and a visitor, my status dictated that I, too, should stay—and my research mandate was to absorb their reminisces. But I had written down war stories all day. I knew their arc and explanatory limits. I excused myself to join F., her mother, and a gaggle of children at the back of the house where I could put down my notebook and set one foot (albeit never both) out of the research exchange.

Freed from the constraints of data collection, I asked Auntie F. if she would teach me to make groundnut soup. She deferred to her mother, translating her Mende-language[9] instructions for me and interpreting her movements. She laughed at what I knew—for example, to wait for the deliciously crusty rice at the bottom of the pot to be served—and what I didn't know, how to open a tin can with a knife. After we ate, Auntie F. said she wanted to show me something and asked me to wait in the parlor. She returned with a smile on her face but no more twinkle in her eye and pressed into my hand two photos: one of her wartime husband, and one of their son. "He looks *just* like his father!" she exclaimed, passing the photos to me and then to her wartime companions as she painfully related how he had disappeared with his father in Liberia. We spent only one day together, but by crossing out of the stilted interview structure and into the

FIGURE 2.1 Auntie F. cooking in her mother's kitchen.

domestic realm that day, I saw more closely the strength of her family ties, the fragility of their material possessions, and the abundance of their farm and garden. I also sensed that this was a temporary interlude for F., who was not much older than I. As the former wife of a powerful man, she had cultivated hopes and dreams bigger than what the town at the end of the road had to offer. I later heard that she moved to the provincial capital, but by the time I visited her new home there, she'd already crossed the border and moved to Liberia. She was searching for her son.

MAMMY I.

Mammy I. is an important grandmother. She has little patience for the teenagers and infants causing a ruckus in her sunset years, and even less patience for white strangers who come knocking at her door speaking elementary Krio. When we met in 2009, she was dismayed by my surprise visit, so similar to those of lawyers for the Special Court for Sierra Leone, the war crimes tribunal. Her home was no sanctuary, crowded as it was by neighbors, family, and a menagerie of useful animals. But it was a domain in which she could assert control over a stressful life. I visited twice— once leaving a message, then, introducing myself and being given a date to return—before she invited me on the third visit to sit across from her in the two-chair parlor. She asked me not to record and not to take notes, but agreed to an interview when she learned the scope of my project. Then, she asked me what I wanted to know.

She was arguably one of the most important and powerful women in the rebellion, but her perspective on its political project was hard to pin down. One minute she was blustering and scowling, proclaiming she alone opened and operated the transborder supply routes that kept the RUF going during its hardest years. In the next minute, she presented herself as a discreet and reluctant revolutionary, caught like so many others in a system she did not design. As Mammy I. told me in sparse terms about the timeline of RUF trading between eastern Sierra Leone and Côte d'Ivoire, she leaned into a large plastic bowl balanced in her sturdy lap. Wrapped in a well-worn but stately *lappa* (fabric tucked like a skirt around the waists of women of all ages), she relentlessly cut into a clean-plucked chicken carcass.

"When did you first learn about the RUF?" I asked gingerly. She swiftly chopped off the chicken's head and answered.

"How often did you cross from Guinea to Liberia and Ivory Coast?" She leaned back and pointed its claws at me. "Where did the money come from?" The crudely sharpened blade sawed back and forth in the palm of her hand, releasing one foot and then the other into the bowl.

"What did they do with the supplies you brought?" Her hands snapped its wings backward and sliced down the chest. "Whom did you trust?" She pulled the innards out and dumped them in another bowl at her feet.

"Did you meet the leader personally?" She scattered the kittens that appeared near her ankles to investigate. "Were there any other women with your position?" She cracked the back of the bird to better split open its thighs.

"Did they pay you?" With a thud the long kitchen knife came down on the leg joints. She said as much with her movements as with her words.

Working methodically, she looked up only periodically to scrutinize my face in the shadows as she weighed the value of each response she gave. She never paused in her task. Watching the dull blade, I saw that her firm grip was more powerful than the knife in pulling apart the bird. Between my deliberate questions and her brusque answers, the exchange became a metaphor for how she had survived the war: with restraint, she wielded simple tools, using force and precision to transform mundane trading activities into realms of extraordinary power.

Finally I asked, "What, if anything, do you hope for in the future and what worries you most about the present?" Mammy I. didn't look up, and she didn't respond. She pulled a rag from under the heavy plastic bowl now weighed down with chicken meat. She wiped her hands and adjusted her seat, seemingly tired of my questions. I wish I could remember exactly what she said, but I can only paraphrase from my field notes: "I am an old woman now. The war is done, but still we struggle. I want to live in peace."

She hoisted her bowl, along with her lappa, and turned toward the door. "Come visit me again sometime," she added with a nod. And I did.

THE MEN AT KISSI ROAD

Toward the end of my doctoral fieldwork, I spent many days in and around a compound in Eastern Freetown, where a small clutch of former RUF commanders and intelligence officers—all men—lived communally. It was an overcrowded property with no water, toilet, or electricity. The latrine out back had collapsed, and one of their wartime enemies lived next door, but poverty kept the dozen or so families pushed together. Everyone knew each other's business, and everyone knew me. In the days leading up to my departure, I told the men whose stories I'd been documenting that I wanted to cook for them. Many months of letting other people cook for me had left me with a fierce urgency to reciprocate, and I had some village chickens from the provinces that needed to be regifted before I left. Although I stopped eating meat when I was ten, I had encountered so much death during fieldwork—from bushmeat,[10] to war stories, to malaria—that I thought it was time to confront its visceral reality by killing the chickens I had been tending. The morning of our small party, I swaddled one of my flapping chickens in cloth and bundled her, head out, into a black plastic bag tucked in the back seat of my sun-bleached two-door Suzuki.

At Kissi Road, I triumphantly handed the bird to one of my friends before going off to the market with Haja, one of the women neighbors in the compound, to "buy buy" the rest of the supplies. In retrospect, it was an ill-conceived feast. Despite months of participant observation in kitchens, I had decided to cook *attieke*, a dish I had never seen prepared and woefully underestimated the labor intensiveness of making. When I returned from the market to start cooking and declared that I wanted to kill the chicken myself, I was met with a stern "no." The men called over a twelve-year-old boy, Haja's son, and told me he would kill the bird for me. I insisted that I wanted to do it, "it's important for me to learn," I pleaded, surprised by their refusal. "Absolutely not," said men who had otherwise shown infinite patience sharing with me personal stories and hidden histories. One of the men finally looked at me exasperated and said, "You're a woman. Women can't kill animals."

For a moment, I felt time stop as I replayed in my head the past two years of studying women's experiences in the RUF. Suddenly I saw more clearly the power of social taboos—and their transgression—in Sierra Leone. As everyone agreed that I would not be allowed to kill the chicken, I realized what cultural consensus felt like as it played out in everyday situations. Perhaps most important, I realized how easily social norms can enforce compliance. I asked some follow-up questions and was intrigued by the limits of my friend's vague explanation about motherhood and protecting women's fertility. But I also let it go. We compromised, and I was allowed to watch as he cut the neck of my chicken. Holding it down, he told me to watch out for blood, and I inched backward into the wall of the house. When it was over, I let Haja's son clean it while I focused on slicing the onions and waited to fry my remarkably lean bird. Hours later, when the food was finally ready, my friends praised the chicken—a true country fowl!—that had been given to me by Auntie F.'s mother, and they shared their helpings with the younger boys who waited in the wings for leftovers. Not a word was said about my movement in and out of gendered spaces—cooking with Haja or eating with the men—nor my navigation between friend, confidant, and researcher. Everyone had been observing one another and participating in the relational nature of interview research all along.[11]

REFLECTIONS

Cooking groundnut soup with Auntie F. and Mammy B. provided a bridge out of political violence and legacies of war into the material reality of their present-day lives. It built mutual rapport and offered insight into household roles and family networks: who came to eat, who was served first, who did the chores, who gave instructions, how much meat was in the pot, and how many spoons there were for serving. The stories they shared and the ease with which we passed time showed a marked contrast to the authority Mammy I. displayed during my visit. Watching this grandmother of the erstwhile revolution butcher a chicken provided an embodied experience of the power and physical potential of women, themes I'd studied extensively through interviews. I saw how she translated her emotions into a methodical and mundane task, which helped me better grasp how anger and revenge could propel methodical and mundane violence. This was underscored in many of my interviews with former fighters in which they described being given drugs that "made you see a person like a chicken." By making room for cooking during fieldwork, I better understood this metaphor as over and over again I saw that chickens were small things that could be killed by someone's son at the back of the house. I also better understood the extent of social rupture in which women and men, boy and girls, could kill not just chickens but fellow citizens.

For all the lucid stories and insights I gained cooking with interlocutors, the political economy of hospitality in Sierra Leone remains obscured to me in many ways. I have tried over the years to pay for my share and to subsidize my hosts' families on top of that. But I suspect I will always come out a debtor for the generosity of time and spirit with which people have greeted me. I once planned to write a cookbook featuring the food and stories of women from the war. They enthusiastically walked me through staple dishes, and I took a few lengthy photo essays. But I never wrote the cookbook. After returning to the UK, I worried that it reified gender stereotypes, amounted to little more than a self-indulgent travelogue, or fed foodie exoticism, even though the opposite was what had so affected me. Maybe cooking and eating together in Sierra Leone simply felt too intimate to be measured, translated, and shared.

Over time I have come to appreciate that the afterlife of fieldwork cannot be contained within the parameters of its premise as a well-defined research exchange. Moving between the present and past, analysis and experience, has turned my interviews into relationships and my data into memories. When I sit down to write, I often feel trapped between the obligation to share and a duty to protect what's sacred. Perhaps, if Sierra Leone taught me anything, it is that meals—like stories—are meant to be shared, and it is largely by sharing that they become sacred.

GROUNDNUT SOUP

Recipe adapted from Fatmatah Mansaray, Chairlady, RUF Party Women's Wing

The original dish serves 100–130 people; this is adapted for 6–8. Tofu, shrimp, fish, or vegetables can be substituted for meat—add more or less as your budget and preferences allow:

- 2 small white onions, finely chopped
- 1/4 c. fragrant hot chilies, diced or whizzed in a food processor (tiny *nenekoro* are hard to find outside West Africa, but a mix of scotch bonnet, red, and green bird's eye chilies work well)
- 1/2–3/4 c. vegetable oil (this helps bind the peanut butter and can be ladled off at the end if desired)
- 3/4–1 c. groundnut paste (all natural smooth peanut butter)
- 4–5 garden eggs,[12] sliced in half moons (substitute 1 small or 3 Japanese eggplants)
- 1 small tin tomato paste (3 tablespoons)
- 2–3 *maggi* or *jumbo* cubes (or 2 chicken and 1 beef stock cubes)
- 1–2 teaspoons "white maggi" (MSG)—optional
- salt (to taste)
- 3–4 sprigs of *patmenji* (basil)
- 10 c. water
- 1 small village chicken—killed, cleaned, cut, boiled, seasoned (with salt, black pepper, and maggi), and fried in hot oil
- 1–2 small firm white fish (e.g., snapper or tilapia)—cleaned, cut in chunks, seasoned (with lime juice, salt, black pepper, and maggi), and fried in hot oil.

Heat the vegetable oil in a large soup pot and add the onions and peppers, cooking covered, stirring occasionally, until translucent—about

15 minutes. If using garden eggs, while onions and chilies cook, peel and slice the garden eggs, then heavily salt and leave to sit for ten minutes; rinse and wash away the bitter seeds, draining the half moon pieces (eggplant can just be peeled and chopped). Soften the groundnut paste/ peanut butter in one cup of water before adding it to the pot with two quarts of water. Bring to a boil. Add garden egg slices and leave to boil until the groundnut paste is fully emulsified and the foam at the top of the pot has disappeared—this takes about thirty minutes, keep a close eye on the pot as the foam likes to boil over! Stir in the tomato paste, maggi/stock cubes, and seasoning, as well as any fish, chicken, other protein, or additional vegetables. Add roughly torn basil leaves and salt to taste; add water, or conversely, boil with the lid off to reduce the liquid. Serve over rice.

——

Zoe Marks *is lecturer in public policy at the Harvard Kennedy School.*

PUBLICATIONS TO WHICH THIS FIELDWORK CONTRIBUTED:

- Marks, Zoe. "Sexual Violence in Sierra Leone's Civil War: 'Virgination,' Rape, and Marriage," *African Affairs* 113, no. 450 (2013): 67–87.
- ——. "Sexual Violence Inside Rebellion: Policies and Perspectives of the Revolutionary United Front of Sierra Leone," *Civil Wars* 15, no. 3 (2013): 359–79.
- ——. "Women in Rebellion: The Case of Sierra Leone." In *Oxford Handbook on Women, Peace, and Security.* ed. Jacqui True and Sara Davies, 489–500. New York: Oxford University Press, 2018.

NOTES

1. I am tremendously grateful to the many people who taught me to cook and love Sierra Leonean food, and who shared their time for the stories in this chapter. Special thanks go to Fatmatah Mansaray, with whom I updated the recipe, and Erica Chenoweth, Chisomo Kalinga, and the editors for their invaluable feedback on previous drafts.
2. Edward Schatz, *Political Ethnography: What Immersion Contributes to the Study of Power* (Chicago: University of Chicago Press, 2013).
3. James P. Spradley, *The Ethnographic Interview* (Long Grove, Ill.: Waveland Press, 1979).

4. Lee Ann Fujii, "Five Stories of Accidental Ethnography: Turning Unplanned Moments in the Field Into Data," *Qualitative Research* 15, no. 4 (2015): 525–39.

5. Mats Utas borrows the phrase "deep hanging out" from Clifford Geertz, who inadvertently coined James Clifford's term in his book review: Clifford Geertz, "Deep Hanging Out," *New York Review of Books*, October 22, 1998; Mats Utas, *Sweet Battlefields: Youth and the Liberian Civil War* (Uppsala, Sweden: Department of Cultural Anthropology and Ethnology, Uppsala University, 2003).

6. Mariane C. Ferme, *The Underneath of Things: Violence, History, and the Everyday in Sierra Leone* (Berkeley: University of California Press, 2001).

7. *Mammy* (pronounced with a soft "a") is a Krio term of respect for a woman with social status. I use initials throughout to protect her and others' anonymity.

8. *Auntie* is a Krio term of respect for a woman with social status; this was how F. was introduced to me by her fellow ex-combatants.

9. Mende is one of Sierra Leone's many languages, spoken by about a third of the population, primarily in the country's south and east.

10. Bushmeat refers to local game meat, such as small deer (duiker), large rodents (grasscutter), monkeys, and wild cats, all caught in the fields or forests primarily using traps. In Sierra Leone, like most parts of the world, forests are a common source of meat for people living in rural areas and provide delicacies for those in urban areas.

11. Hanif Abdurraqib, introduction to *Prince: The Last Interview*, by Prince (London: Melville House, 2019), vii–xiii; and Lee Ann Fujii, *Interviewing in Social Science Research: A Relational Approach* (New York: Routledge, 2017).

12. A kind of small, bitter eggplant.

3

RECITE!

INTERPRETIVE FIELDWORK FOR POSITIVISTS

RICHARD A. NIELSEN

▸ FIELDWORK LOCATION: CAIRO, EGYPT

The first word the angel Jibril spoke to the Prophet Muhammad was a command: "Recite!"

❧

May 30, 2011. It is my first day in Cairo. I have no fixer, no translator, and no connections.[1] I definitely have no *wasta*, the social currency of reciprocity that often gets the job done in Egypt. Naturally, the newscaster Arabic from class isn't getting me far, and although I've theoretically learned some of the local dialect too, it is unfamiliar in my mouth and my ears. Finding my hotel takes several hours of questioning strangers on the street; I leave a trail of confused and amused Egyptians behind me. I am here to study Muslim clerics, but I have no plan other than to walk into mosques and see what happens. This does not seem like an auspicious start.

A few hours later, I have planted myself on the floor at the back of the mosque in al-Husayn Square. The mosque is an imposing building in the heart of Old Cairo that commands the busy square in front of it, with shoppers streaming by on their way to wander the maze of Khan al-Khalili bazaar. This is no mere neighborhood mosque. It has existed in some form for eight hundred years and is one of the holiest sites in Egypt. But I don't know this when I walk in. Instead, I'm at the al-Husayn mosque because it is across the street from where I would really like to sit, at the renowned al-Azhar mosque/university complex. I want to test the waters first.

I sit at the back, cross-legged on lush green and gold carpet dappled with stylized leaves and punctuated by row upon row of marble columns soaring up to meet the roof arches. I watch pilgrims filing in to visit the shrine believed to be the final resting place of Imam al-Husayn's head. I start sketching. Then I sneak a few photographs. Are cameras allowed here? I accept a piece of bread from someone offering food to worshipers. I haven't spoken to anyone, but I don't really want to. I just want to observe without being singled out.

Someone takes an interest in me. First, some glances at my notebook. Then at my camera. Then perhaps at my blond hair. More at the notebook. He moves closer. Now insisting that I stand: "What are you doing here? What do you want? American spy?" Is this serious? He looks serious. The young man is maybe twenty, wiry and shorter than I am, clean-shaven, wearing a traditional dark gray ghalabiyya, and holding a Qur'an. I start to think that I've made a mistake. It has been three months since the January revolution, and a vigilante spirit has taken hold; neighbors protecting neighbors as the state recedes.

I try to explain that I am a student interested in Islam. There are more questions. I can't understand. A small crowd is gathering. The young man presses me for answers, looking increasingly displeased. It is becoming a scene. This does not seem like an auspicious start.

FIGURE 3.1 Inside the al-Husayn mosque. Are cameras allowed here?

Desperate, I offer to recite the Fatiha—the evocative opening chapter of the Qur'an—as a token of my sincerity. I've just barely memorized it during my layover in Frankfurt. The moment the offer leaves my lips, I regret it. I am likely to mess up.

Yet as soon as I begin, the change is palpable.

Bismillah ar-Rahman ar-Rahim
Al-hamdu lillahi rabb al-'alamin
Ar-Rahman ar-Rahim Maliki yawm id-din

Under pressure I forget the beginning of the next line, and the same skeptical young man is now eagerly supplying the missing syllables, urging me to succeed.

Iyaka na'abudu wa iyaka nasta'in
Ihdina sirat al-mustaqim
Sirat alladhina an'amta 'alayhim
Ghayr al-maghdub alayhim wala ad-dalin

I finish to exclamations of "ya ustaz!" (O teacher!) and "ma sha' allah!" (look what God has wrought!). The group has grown during the recitation, so I am surrounded now by what feels like a dozen men of varying ages, mostly young, their piety evident from prayer marks on their foreheads. More onlookers remain seated close by. Cell phones appear. I now face a dozen cameras, for which I perform the Fatiha again. This time, I recite more confidently. The crowd begins to disperse, evidently assured that I am not a threat. Have some mistakenly concluded that I'm Muslim? I'm not sure. The earnest young man writes his phone number and name in my field notebook: Nasir, the Arab name for "one who gives victory." He insists that I call him the next day so that he can show me around. There are no more questions about whether I am an American spy.

It would neatly tie together a great story if Nasir had become a key interlocutor during my time in Egypt. He certainly could have been. He was a twenty-two-year-old religious student, precisely the demographic I was hoping could give me an entrée into the world of al-Azhar. But we met once or twice and then drifted apart. Nasir lost interest when it became clear I wasn't going to convert to Islam, and I found another set of friends at al-Azhar. Fieldwork relationships are complicated, and fieldwork stories often have loose ends.

🍃

I have never heard reciting scripture endorsed as a research method for political scientists. Let me endorse it for you now.

Why should political scientists memorize and recite scripture? If you want to understand how pious people think, act, mobilize, protest, vote, and generally do politics, you would do well to understand their religious practices. If memorizing holy texts is a central ritual, then memorize those texts!

Memorizing and reciting portions of the Qur'an has had at least three essential effects on my research. First, it is impossible to understand the layers of meaning in the speech of religious actors if you do not have some command of key holy texts. After memorizing the thirty-one shortest chapters of the Qur'an, I began to hear them quoted everywhere. References to them abound in phrases that had previously escaped my notice. I began to understand sermons better. I learned to pray properly because Islamic prayer incorporates Qur'an recitation. I began to pick up on mistakes: the prominent cleric Yusuf al-Qaradawi stumbling over some words while quoting a verse on his Aljazeera show and getting some help from his cohost.

The most advanced Muslim scholars memorize the entire Qur'an, often as children. At my best, I had one-sixtieth of the Qur'an memorized, and certainly not as well. If this small portion opened new rhetorical worlds to me, I strongly suspect that there are at least fifty-nine more layers of meaning that I'm missing out on by not having memorized the rest.

Second, I memorize and recite scripture as a practice of participant observation[2] that allows me to gain interpretive insight. Most political scientists are trained in a strictly positivist orientation, where learning happens by observing. But there is also such a thing as learning by doing. Religion, in fact, often relies heavily on learning by doing, which is one reason merely observing religion without practicing it has sometimes led political scientists to adopt impoverished views of the role of religion in political life. I can't claim any formal training in methods of participant observation. Instead, I found myself drawing on my childhood years of Mormon Sunday School to develop a research philosophy of learning by doing—paying attention to how I felt, thought, and behaved during and after my memorization. I know why Qur'an reciters cup their hands to their face: feeling the tone from your mouth buzz into your ear via your hand helps you stay on tune in a crowded space. I know why religious students at the teaching mosques memorize their textbooks, because I know what it feels like to engage with an authoritative text through memorization rather than critique.

The intellectual tradition most associated with this mode of learning is *interpretivism*; defined by Timothy Pachirat as "humans making meaning out of the meaning making of other humans."[3] Although interpretivism is not mainstream in American political science, I found that the interpretive practices I adopted in my fieldwork[4] were essential to helping me produce solid *positivist* political science in my book *Deadly Clerics*.[5] In it, I make the case that Muslim clerics, including jihadist clerics, understand themselves to be academics. When jihadist preacher Anwar al-Awlaki discusses his influence on the Fort Hood shooter, he calls Nidal Hassan "my student." When the leader of ISIS, Abu Bakr al-Baghdadi, faces questions about his qualifications to lead, he releases an academic biography. And when jihadist ideologue Abu Muhammad al-Maqdisi wants to defend his place in the jihadi firmament, he touts his high citation count.

This interpretive move of trying to see jihadists as they see themselves was the genesis of my argument that clerics are far more likely to become jihadists when their academic ambitions in mainstream Islamic legal academia are blocked. The rest of the book supports this claim through a combination of standard positivist approaches: regression analysis and case studies. But I did not merely use interpretive ethnography to understand the context before proceeding with the "real" analysis. Without the interpretive insight, the regressions would have been totally different. To my knowledge, variables such as "Does this person have a PhD in the Islamic Sciences?" and "Does this person report having memorized the Qur'an on their CV?" have not appeared in any other regression analysis of jihadists. As a result of my experience integrating interpretive and positivist methods, I share with Lisa Wedeen the optimistic view that "interpretive social science does not have to forswear generalizations or causal explanations and that ethnographic methods can be used in the service of establishing them. Rather than taking flight from abstractions, ethnographies can and should help ground them."[6]

Third, memorizing the Qur'an has helped me build respectful relationships in the field. Striving for friendship and rapport with those you meet in the course of your research is its own reward, and it is an essential ethical posture for fieldwork. And by maintaining a disposition of respect, I find that other good things tend to follow. My interlocutors in Cairo seemed to sense that my efforts to understand Islam were sincere, and they responded far more generously than they might have if they thought I had ulterior motives. In a separate incident from the one I described here, an Egyptian told me that "I couldn't be CIA because they could never memorize the book of God."

I have ambiguous feelings about advertising that I have memorized parts of the Qur'an to put my interlocutors at ease. Is it patronizing? Sacrilegious? Manipulative? Yet when I have been on the receiving end, I found similar researcher behavior endearing rather than off-putting. While in graduate school, I was part of a Mormon history reading group with about twenty other Mormons and ex-Mormons. Max Mueller, a non-Mormon scholar of American religions, came to one of our sessions to talk about his book project[7] and won my trust in part because of his mastery of Mormon lingo and slang. The content of his memorization was not holy scripture—in part because Mormons don't memorize the Book of Mormon the way Muslims memorize the Qur'an—but it performed the same role. I appreciated the high price he had paid for near-native fluency in the specialized language of Mormonism.

Chances are, memorizing the Qur'an is not exactly what you need for your fieldwork. It turned out to be an asset for me when working with Muslim clerics, but your mileage may vary. Even if you are working in a Muslim context, don't intentionally get into risky situations expecting that rattling off the Fatiha will get you out! And as is often the case, who you are influences how people react. Things might have played out differently if I were a woman, for example.

So what can you do?

See through your interlocuters' eyes, hear through their ears, and speak with their idiom if you can. This may save you from deeply misunderstanding the meaning and purpose of what they do.

The Mukhtaba al Azhar was much, more welcoming. They tried to first direct me to the Mushiekha, but I said I already been there: Mushiekha, but I said I wanted to study the said I wanted to study the fatwas from old sheikhs of al azhar and that seemed fine.

Then on my way out, I noticed that to the right as you come in, there is an office for the Azhar other project. I'll have to check it out Monday. I'll have to check it out the muktaba is closed Friday and Sat.

جامع الازهر

FIGURE 3.2 My sketch of the inner courtyard of the al-Azhar mosque. The sketch conveyed to them that I respected something they loved.

Be open to what Lee Ann Fujii calls "accidental ethnography"—the observations that you make about the places you are when you're not "on the clock" executing your research plan.[8] My encounter on my first day in Cairo was the product of a dozen accidents. My inability to plan for my fieldwork landed me in the mosque. A chance encounter led to a confrontation. A desperate recitation led to its productive resolution. Perhaps my poor planning made me especially open to accidental fieldwork, but I think even those executing the most fully planned field activities should remain open to serendipity.[9]

Figure out how to respect what the people you are studying value. This, I think, was the key reason Qur'an memorization meant so much to my interlocutors in Cairo. As pressure to publish relentlessly ramps up for junior scholars, there is a temptation to employ smash-and-grab fieldwork tactics: get in, run the experiment/survey/regression, get out, write it up. This mode of research makes it all too easy to treat our interlocutors in the field instrumentally rather than respectfully.

Memorization isn't the only way to credibly convey your genuine respect. I like to sketch, and although I make my fieldwork sketches for myself, I find that they are quite popular with those I am interviewing. Several students at the al-Azhar mosque, for example, were quite taken with a sketch I made of the inner courtyard, and they subsequently invited me into their study circle. Like Qur'an memorization, the sketch conveyed to them that I respected something they loved.

Building a relationship with your interlocutors is an essential skill for the field, and understanding them is a precondition for doing good work. I can't tell you how to do it. Your field site is different from mine, and people value different things. Instead of religious practices, it may be an appreciation of tradition, a shared struggle, a counterculture, or something else entirely. But everyone makes meaning out of their life. Your fieldwork will be more successful if you can figure out how they construct that meaning and find ways to convey to them that you understand. No matter how positivist your research design, figuring out how other people make meaning out of their lives is an interpretive task.

Richard A. Nielsen *is associate professor of political science at the Massachusetts Institute of Technology.*

PUBLICATION TO WHICH THIS FIELDWORK CONTRIBUTED:

- Nielsen, Richard A. *Deadly Clerics: Blocked Ambition and the Paths to Jihad.* Cambridge: Cambridge University Press, 2017.

NOTES

1. Thank you to Bernardo Zacka, Marsin Alshamary, Chappell Lawson, Sarah Par-kinson, Peregrine Schwartz-Shea, Gabriel Koehler-Derrick, Jillian Schwedler, and Timothy Pachirat for inspired comments. I am forever indebted to my friends from the field, especially Diaa', who guided me around Cairo arm in arm.

2. A note about terminology: the term *participant observation* denotes the research practice of learning about a culture through participation and observation at close range. Participant observation is often used synonymously with *ethnography*, which Spradley defines as "the work of describing a culture": James P. Spradley, *Participant Observation* (Long Grove, Ill.: Waveland Press, 2016,) 3. But I see use-ful daylight between the two. Ethnography has become laden with expectations about the duration and depth of a researcher's cultural immersion. People will look at you askance if you claim to do ethnography with less than six months at a field site. Participant observation eludes the weight of these expectations. You can practice it in mere minutes by asking, What am I seeing, hearing, touching, tast-ing, and smelling that might help me understand how the humans constructing this culture make meaning out of their lives? For me, the mental shift this question evokes can transform a profoundly mundane situation into a fieldwork episode teeming with possibilities for insight.

3. Timothy Pachirat, "We Call It a Grain of Sand: The Interpretive Orientation and a Human Social Science," in *Interpretation and Method: Empirical Research Meth-ods and the Interpretive Turn*, ed. Dvora Yanow and Peregrine Schwartz-Shea, (New York: Routledge 2006), 426–32. For more, see Lisa Wedeen, "Conceptualiz-ing Culture: Possibilities for Political Science," *American Political Science Review* 96, no. 4 (December 2002): 713–28, https://doi.org/10.1017/S0003055402000400; Edward Schatz, *Political Ethnography: What Immersion Contributes to the Study of Power* (Chicago: University of Chicago Press, 2013); Dvora Yanow and Peregrine Schwartz-Shea, eds., *Interpretation and Method: Empirical Research Methods and the Interpretive Turn* (New York: Routledge, 2015).

4. I conducted fieldwork in Cairo in May–June 2011 and April–May 2012. The imme-diate aftermath of the 2011 Egyptian revolution was an exceptionally open time to be wandering around religious institutions in Cairo asking questions. I have only returned to Egypt for fieldwork once since the 2013 regime change (in April 2019) because I fear it is no longer safe to study Islamism with the methods I'm describ-ing here. I wish I could have spent longer in Cairo, but extended field excursions are for the childless or the well-to-do, and I was neither. Grants from various

sources covered my travel, but not my family's, so I went alone and kept it short. If, like me, you have constraints that make long stays impossible, take several short trips to the field and try to make every moment count.

5. Richard A. Nielsen, *Deadly Clerics: Blocked Ambition and the Paths to Jihad* (Cambridge: Cambridge University Press, 2017).

6. Lisa Wedeen, "Reflections on Ethnographic Work in Political Science," *Annual Review of Political Science* 13, no. 1 (2010): 255–72, at 257. https://doi.org/10.1146/annurev.polisci.11.052706.123951.

7. Max Perry Mueller, *Race and the Making of the Mormon People* (Chapel Hill, N.C.: UNC Press Books, 2017).

8. Lee Ann Fujii, "Five Stories of Accidental Ethnography: Turning Unplanned Moments in the Field Into Data," *Qualitative Research* 15, no. 4 (2015): 525–39.

9. For a meditation on the role of serendipity in research, see Timothy Pachirat, *Among Wolves: Ethnography and the Immersive Study of Power* (New York: Routledge, 2017), https://doi.org/10.4324/9780203701102.

II

DESIGNING
YOUR RESEARCH
AND DECIDING
WHERE TO GO

4

FIELDWORK BY DECREE, NOT BY DESIGN

STATHIS N. KALYVAS

▶ FIELDWORK LOCATION: GREECE

The story of how I got to conduct the fieldwork that ended up in my 2006 book, *The Logic of Violence in Civil War*, illustrates the significance of chance, randomness, and serendipity in conducting research.

It all goes way back to 1988, when I was accepted to the graduate program in political science at the University of Chicago. At the time, Chicago had a policy of accepting (many) more students than it could fund, and then effectively conducting a grueling and stressful funding selection process in-house. As I was admitted with no funding, my only option was to accept a Fulbright scholarship that I had been awarded in Greece. This scholarship was good for just one year and also came with the so-called two-year home requirement, a provision intended to stem the brain drain to the United States. It basically obligated you to return to your country after obtaining your PhD. Say what you want about Chicago's policy (which the university phased out a few years later), but without it I would not have been admitted in the first place. I am grateful to have been given the opportunity to take Chicago's offer and eventually receive funding from the university.

Fast forward a few years. After completing my studies, getting my PhD, getting a first job at Ohio State, and a year later moving on to NYU, I had to face the music. The two-year home requirement had been in the back of my mind, but with a tenure track job at a good university, I thought

I would find a way to bail myself out. How wrong I was. When the moment came for me to switch status and apply for permanent residency (the "green card"), I was told by NYU's International Office that it would be pretty much impossible unless I managed to obtain a waiver from the relevant agency (in this case, the United States Information Agency [USIA]). I did scramble to apply for a waiver pursuing a number of different legal paths, but eventually I learned that all of my applications had been rejected by the USIA.

I had no option but to leave the country.[1] So one night in the fall of 1997, I packed my suitcases as the chairman of the department wished me "a nice exile," and I flew back to Greece on a two-year leave of absence with a year off my tenure clock and no salary. I had to scrap my main project at the time (a study of polarized politics) because I couldn't conduct its demanding library research in Greece and the internet was still in its infancy. I could finish a couple of papers, but with time on my hands, I began to seek new research possibilities.

A conversation I had with former Chicago PhD classmate Roger Petersen in New York just before my departure sparked my interest in studying conflict. Roger was a pioneer in the study of civil conflict. I still vividly remember reading his dissertation proposal on an announcement board at Chicago. His creative combination of rational choice theory (imparted by Jon Elster), network analysis (inspired by John Padgett), and security studies (John Mearsheimer's contribution) to explain the choices of Lithuanian peasants during and immediately after the Second World War caught my imagination: this was methodological eclecticism at its best applied to a fascinating topic. At the time, however, I was working on a completely different (and equally fascinating) topic, the emergence of Christian Democratic parties. Roger then moved to Saint Louis to take a job at Washington University, and we got quite out of touch—remember, this was before the internet! I only saw him again a couple of years later, when he came to NYU while on sabbatical. I shared with him my predicament and asked him about his research, which resulted in a conversation that rekindled my excitement. I had been curious about the Greek Civil War, partly because I knew very little about it, and this conversation got me thinking about using my time in Greece to conduct a small project to learn about it. Reading Roger's work,[2] I was particularly attracted by his "on-the ground" perspective, and I thought it would be a good idea to do something along those lines. However, unlike classic ethnographies I had read and admired a great deal,[3] Roger managed to combine interviews with a strong theoretical agenda and a compelling research design—an unusual combination reminiscent of another book that had caught my imagination, my advisor David Laitin's *Hegemony and Culture*. It was around that time that I read Diego Gambetta's, *The Sicilian Mafia*, a book that helped me absorb this type of research.[4] This book resonated with an earlier experience I had had as an undergraduate student, working as an enumerator for a large psychological and medical survey conducted in the Greek countryside. I had discovered that I loved hearing people talk and, most important for the case at hand, that people exhibited a propensity for relating their experience. In short, many streams converged in quite a subconscious way during that time.

After returning to Athens and embarking on this odd two-year exile, the first thing I did was consult some established Greek historians of the period about my idea. They were quick to disabuse me: "Don't even think about interviewing survivors," they said, "most won't talk, and those who would will lie." Of course, they had interacted only with important figures, political and military leaders or leading intellectuals, rather than with ordinary people. With few exceptions, historians had very little interest in the experiences of country folk and were extremely suspicious, if not outright dismissive, of oral testimonies and local research. Anthropologists were much more open to these approaches, but they were equally suspicious of any inclination toward theorizing systematic empirical patterns and quite disdainful of approaches that took rationality seriously.[5] As for political scientists, steeped in the study of elections and parties, they were openly puzzled about why anyone would want to embark on such a wild topic.

But where to start? Again, Roger's experience inspired me; he had stumbled on his own research by chatting with immigrant Lithuanian families in Chicago while working as a salesman of Eastern European household goods. The initial challenge was to locate "ordinary people" who could share their experiences of the civil war. I began by asking my friends to tell me about their grandparents, and I quickly realized that most of them had indeed had all kinds of traumatic experiences that I had never suspected. I began meeting with them without really knowing what to ask and discovered that they loved to talk and had a lot of stories to tell, although they were utterly confused about details, dates, and the sequence of events. It all sounded fascinating and bewildering at the same time, full of intriguing details that were hard or even impossible to make sense of, or verify.

That experience convinced me that the only way to make sense of these stories was to focus on a particular geographic area, to minimize the "noise" and try to triangulate this baffling mass of information. Using my network of friends' grandparents and proceeding by snowball sampling, I did a few pilot trips in several areas of Greece. In one of them, I stumbled into a former classmate of mine at the University of Athens who had become a judge in the provincial town I was visiting. I went ahead and asked him whether he knew if the courts kept archives from the civil war period—there were few open state archives covering that period then. He took me to the basement of the court building, where lo and behold tens of unopened, huge bags full of papers were rotting away. Once I had opened some of them, I realized that the material they contained was precious. Although judicial documents incorporate all kinds of biases, they also contain extremely valuable and detailed information. At this point I had my first research epiphany: I would focus my fieldwork on this particular region; perhaps this could even turn into a bigger project than I had initially planned!

The research question I had set out with was pretty straightforward: How do individuals pick sides in civil wars? Once I started interviewing people and mining the archives, I came to the realization that many people's "choices" were in fact endogenous to a variety of complex factors and would be extremely difficult to disentangle. I also realized the important role violence played in that process, something that had not occurred to me because my understanding of civil wars at that point focused on their political rather than their military aspects. Hence, having realized the importance of violence as an important independent variable of political behavior, I gradually opened up to thinking of it as my dependent variable.

Armed with increasing local knowledge generated from the intensive archival research I was conducting, I began structuring my interviews around the details of the events that had taken place in that region rather than the set of vague, preconceived notions I had been carrying around in my head. For example, influenced by Barrington Moore and Theda

Skocpol, I had thought that civil wars were fundamentally instances of mass mobilization—uprisings—with people coming together around a set of grievances to challenge the existing regime.[6] Indeed, this is what social movement theory and the theory of social revolutions—and also the historiography of the Greek Civil War—had taught me. Yet what I was finding pointed to a much more complex, sequenced process whereby violence often came *before* mobilization and triggered it endogenously, as well as ultimately molding the political identities that would come to define the conflict. It took me some time to come to the realization that the "data" I was collecting was forcing me to question my own assumptions. Once I became fascinated by the transformative power of violence—a fact that I had not anticipated—I completely reframed my research question. Instead of asking how people made their choices, I decided to focus on the logic of violence and how it constrained and even generated people's choices. It was extremely difficult for me to publish papers at this stage because this idea was not widely understood or accepted; it required a theoretical and conceptual apparatus that was just not obvious. I needed to build a theory of insurgency and nest within it a theory of violence. In other words, I had to write a book. That was going to take a long time, a lot of effort, and require considerable confidence in my ability to carry it to fruition—at a time when my tenure review was coming up. In the end this gamble paid off, but there is no denying the professional risk it entailed. However, I was so taken by the project that I did not hesitate. And here I have to thank my other doctoral advisor, Adam Przeworski, for encouraging me to undertake such a risky project. No matter how strongly one feels about a project, encouragement from a mentor or trusted senior colleague can be essential.

How about hypotheses? I was taught that the way to do research began with theory and was followed by the formulation of hypotheses, the gathering of data, and the testing of these hypotheses, leading to the confirmation or falsification of the theory. But I was doing everything in reverse: I started with fieldwork to collect data without a clear idea of what exactly I was seeking. In turn, the fieldwork forced me to ditch not only my initial insights but also my original research question. I had to formulate a new question, generate a new theory, which I then had to test with new data and more fieldwork. Fortunately, I could stagger my fieldwork in small increments. Six months into my exile, I applied for postdocs and was lucky to get one at the European University Institute in Florence. This gave me the time and ability to work on the theory, which I was able to "pilot," as it were, by writing a study of the dynamics of violence in the then ongoing civil war in Algeria that had begun in 1992.[7] The postdoc also gave me time to put together a much more coherent grant proposal than I would have been able to write before this process began, which ultimately funded the bulk of my fieldwork.[8] In addition, traveling back and forth to the field was much easier flying to Greece from Italy rather than from New York.

Needless to say, I redesigned my fieldwork and tweaked my research design to reflect all of these developments. Instead of studying a region in a purely ethnographic way, as I had originally planned, I decided to combine ethnography and quantitative data collection. I would research the local history of every village in the region with the aim of generating a data set that would enable me to test my hypotheses locally yet systematically. At the time, most comparativists tended to dismiss local studies as "case studies," at best, or parochial, at worst—indeed, I still occasionally run into descriptions of *The Logic of Violence in Civil War* as a study of the Greek Civil War. By using homicides and villages as my unit of analysis, I was able to combine the local and the large-N into what is now known as a "subnational" research design, thus spearheading what would become known as the "micro-turn" in conflict studies, at a time when cross-national, macro-level studies dominated the field.[9] Needless to say, this was incredibly labor-intensive. I had to visit more than sixty villages and identify informants in each of them. After I was done, I replicated my study in another region of the country and built another data set covering the entire territory of Greece using a variety of published (mostly local) sources to run additional tests. At the same time, I collected a considerable number of qualitative observations from a broad cross-section of conflicts worldwide. Following publication of my book, I discovered the existence of a unique data set, the Hamlet Evaluation System, which had been designed and used during the Vietnam War and had a logic compatible with that of my study. I was thus able to conduct additional out-of-sample empirical tests.[10]

It is important to add here that this empirical strategy was anchored in a robust theoretical structure. Initial fieldwork produced several intuitions that were subsequently filtered through broad comparative reading;

in turn, the intuitions that survived this filtering provided the foundations for a theoretical model that led to fully formed empirical characterizations and hypotheses.

The takeaway of this story ought to be obvious by now. Field research (and research more broadly) is a highly dialectical processes that requires constant movement between theory and data. I find the current trend of overengineering and isolating research design, theory, and empirical research by means of watertight procedures (such as preregistration, preanalysis plans, etc.) to be potentially limiting, perhaps even counterproductive— as is the imposition of complicated and ever-expanding standards for the collection and handling of qualitative evidence. What makes fieldwork potentially so rewarding and meaningful is its simultaneously structured yet fluid quality, the fact that it can open us up to a hitherto unsuspected reality. In short, rather than trying to fit fieldwork (and empirical research more broadly) into what is effectively a Procrustean bed, we should allow our research to guide us.

I am aware that this recommendation might sound heretical, tantamount of caving in to our own implicit biases. The absence of a watertight separation between theory and research design, on one hand, and data collection, on the other, is increasingly considered inappropriate at best, potentially dishonest at worst. I understand the logic of such a view and accept that it might make sense when dealing with certain types of mostly narrowly framed data collection and estimation procedures—most notably surveys and experiments. Nonetheless, I believe it is important to allow enough room for fieldwork, and empirical research more broadly, to guide the process of theorization—and, in turn, for theorization to allow us to distill empirical complexity into empirical "essence." More often than we like to believe, our empirical and theoretical priors tend to be crude and potentially misleading approximations of the phenomena we study. As a result, sophisticated empirical research is often designed on the basis of underlying theoretical assumptions and empirical scope conditions whose validity is far from given.

Instead of trying to force these phenomena into these priors, we have much to gain by allowing the field to guide us: at the very least by allowing us to correct faulty assumptions, but sometimes by pushing us to reorient our research and open new theoretical vistas. Elizabeth Kolbert recounts the story of how, during the 1980s, scientists were able to successfully revise the causes of the destruction of many organisms sixty-five million years ago, most famously the dinosaurs, an event known as the "Cretaceous-Tertiary extinction." This revision was triggered by the work of a geologist, Walter Alvarez, who had originally embarked on a study of how plate tectonics led to the emergence of the Italian peninsula. In the process of his research, he came across a thin layer of clay containing an unusually diverse and large number of uncommon fossils. This discovery suggested to him that they had disappeared abruptly, eventually leading him to question the then dominant theory that posited the gradual disappearance of organisms, known as "uniformitarianism." In turn, this led to the formulation of an alternative theory, that of the catastrophic consequences of an asteroid impact. As Alvarez told Kolbert, "Here you have a challenge to a uniformitarian viewpoint that basically every geologist and paleontologist had been trained in, as had their professors and their professors' professors, all the way back to [Charles] Lyell."[11] In short, this unexpected fieldwork finding totally unrelated to Alvarez's initial research project could have been dismissed as an irrelevant and minor anomaly. Instead, it led to a major theoretical innovation.

As I discovered by entering the field by decree rather than design, theoretical and empirical discoveries force us to acknowledge that we often know less than we think we do. Rather than heading too narrowly to what is already established, this example suggests that we have much to gain by being open to the unexpected and the unknown.

———

Stathis N. Kalyvas *is Gladstone Professor of Government at the Department of Politics and International Relations at University of Oxford.*

PUBLICATION TO WHICH THIS FIELDWORK CONTRIBUTED:

- Kalyvas, Stathis N. *The Logic of Violence in Civil War*. New York: Cambridge University Press, 2006.

NOTES

1. Now a much easier option consists of getting a bridge type of visa and "serving" the two home years in small segments, mostly during summers.

2. Roger D. Petersen, *Resistance and Rebellion: Lessons from Eastern Europe* (Cambridge: Cambridge University Press, 2001).

3. James C. Scott, *Weapons of the Weak: Everyday Forms of Peasant Resistance* (New Haven, Conn.: Yale University Press, 2008); James C. Scott, *Domination and the Arts of Resistance: Hidden Transcripts* (New Haven, Conn.: Yale University Press, 2008).

4. David D. Laitin, *Hegemony and Culture: Politics and Change Among the Yoruba* (Chicago: University of Chicago Press, 1986); Diego Gambetta, *The Sicilian Mafia: The Business of Private Protection* (Cambridge, Mass.: Harvard University Press, 1996).

5. The limited research that existed at that time tended to privilege the highly ideologized experiences of activists rather than the experiences of ordinary people; e.g., Janet Hart, *New Voices in the Nation: Women and the Greek Resistance, 1941–1964* (Ithaca, N.Y.: Cornell University Press, 2018).

6. Barrington Moore, *Social Origins of Dictatorship and Democracy: Lord and Peasant in the Making of the Modern World* (Boston, Mass.: Beacon Press, 2015); Theda Skocpol, *States and Social Revolutions: A Comparative Analysis of France, Russia, and China* (Cambridge: Cambridge University Press, 2015).

7. Stathis N. Kalyvas, "Wanton and Senseless?: The Logic of Massacres in Algeria," *Rationality and Society* 11, no. 3 (August 1999): 243–85, https://doi.org /10.1177/104346399011003001. I considered conducting fieldwork in Algeria, but this proved impossible due to the situation on the ground in this country.

8. Thanks to the Harry Frank Guggenheim Foundation for their support!

9. Lars-Erik Cederman and Manuel Vogt, "Dynamics and Logics of Civil War," *Journal of Conflict Resolution* 61, no. 9 (October 2017): 1992–2016, https://doi .org/10.1177/0022002717721385; Lars-Erik Cederman and Kristian Skrede Gleditsch, "Introduction to Special Issue on 'Disaggregating Civil War,'" *Journal of Conflict Resolution* 53, no. 4 (2009): 487–95.

10. Stathis N. Kalyvas and Matthew Adam Kocher, "The Dynamics of Violence in Vietnam: An Analysis of the Hamlet Evaluation System (HES)," *Journal of Peace Research* 46, no. 3 (May 2009): 335–55, https://doi.org/10.1177/0022343309102656.

11. Elizabeth Kolbert, *The Sixth Extinction: An Unnatural History* (New York: Henry Holt, 2014), 70–91.

5

CONDUCTING 1,500 SURVEYS IN NEW YORK CITY (WITH GREAT UNCERTAINTY AND A LIMITED BUDGET)

CHRISTINA M. GREER

▸ FIELDWORK LOCATION: NEW YORK CITY

When I was in graduate school, I decided to write a dissertation on urban centers and the complexities for Black communities therein. I had entered my doctoral program in political science fully prepared to continue research I had begun as an undergraduate, comparing crime and public policy in urban centers. At my first meeting with the director of graduate studies, I told him about the research I had conducted in Boston and Baltimore. I proudly explained how I had learned about, and successfully executed, various aspects of qualitative methods and snowball interviewing. I also eagerly told him how I perceived my role as a researcher in urban spaces—as a Black American interacting with other Black Americans from diverse geographic locales and varying socioeconomic statuses. What were the ties that bound us? Would racial identity be enough to solicit honest and candid responses? Would my outsider status prevent my respondents from being forthcoming, or would that status serve me well as I inquired about details pertaining to their city, institutions, and historical practices?

I was fully prepared to establish my intellectual foundation as a scholar of politics in American urban spaces. The director heard me out and then bluntly replied, "Cities are dead." There was not an ounce of my being that agreed with that statement. At that moment, I realized that an equal dose of flexibility and conviction would be necessary for me to survive and thrive in this profession. These types of statements and interactions are more common than we would like to believe. If you find yourself interested in a "dead topic," you may want to think about the projection of the field. Are your interests really in the dustbin of academia, or are they merely out of fashion for the moment? If the latter is the case, by the time you have conducted your research and begin to establish yourself within your respective field, you may find yourself at the forefront of new and emerging debates. Urban politics has seen a resurgence in the past few years, and nothing is more encouraging than knowing that you followed your academic instincts and anticipated or created new ways of thinking about "dead topics." Essentially, graduate school is the nesting ground where you establish and sharpen your intellectual instincts. There will be times when you falter, and the advice of seasoned scholars should be carefully considered. However, if a burning question is inside you that you feel must be analyzed and answered, then you must follow that feeling. You may need to shift the focus ever so slightly, but the kernel of truth that you know to be real must be interrogated.

I switched gears over the course of my tenure in graduate school so I could follow my first intellectual passion while simultaneously writing from a framework that was more mainstream and widely accessible to leaders within the discipline. I began to craft a research agenda that focused on the distinct identities of African, Caribbean, and Black Americans in New York City. Many scholars had compared Caribbean and Black American populations, but very few social scientists at the time had compared all three large Black ethnic groups. That is, people who had immigrated voluntarily from countries throughout the Caribbean and the continent of Africa as compared to Black Americans who were descendants of individuals involuntarily brought to these shores and forced into chattel slavery for centuries. Social scientists who had conducted research on Caribbean and Black American attitudes and interactions had largely focused on qualitative analyses to support their emerging and robust theories. As I attempted to build on this research by adding Africans as a third comparative group, I also felt it necessary to conduct quantitative analyses to support my claims. I then did what any graduate student in the social sciences who is interested in quantitative methods would do: I went straight to the National Election Study (NES) and the General Social Survey (GSS). These two large data sets sample roughly two hundred fifty "blacks" in each iteration, which rarely yielded any statistically significant results when I attempted to disaggregate the data by ethnicity. Even when aggregating the data over several years, there were often barely enough Black ethnics in the sample to adequately test my hypotheses.[1]

Next, I looked at the National Black Election Study (NBES); clearly this robust study, conducted by some of the leaders in racial politics, would include questions about race *and* ethnicity for Blacks in America. I initially scanned the codebook and found nothing. I didn't panic, I assumed my "control-F" search needed to be a bit more specific. As I searched for the words *ethnic, ethnicity, Africa, Caribbean, West Indian*, and so on and consistently yielded no results, the panic set in. I then printed out the codebook; surely the NBES would have questions about Black immigrants because at least 10 percent of the Black population in the United States is foreign born, to say nothing of second and third generation Caribbean and African groups. I was wrong. The NBES had not asked any questions pertaining to Black ethnicity. It was then that I realized I would have to conduct my own quantitative research from scratch.

Before I embarked on research on something that seems so obvious and necessary, natural doubt crept into my psyche. If ethnic distinctions within the Black community are so obvious to me as a researcher, why had no one previously conducted quantitative research analyzing them? Had I stumbled upon an innovative dissertation and research topic, or was I destined to travel down a dead end? These are the types of questions that inevitably seep into my consciousness at the beginning of a research project each and every time.

My first challenge was how to gather data. I could not rely on preexisting data sets as my peers had done. Therefore, I had to go beyond the traditional data sources and think more creatively about where I could collect consistent and robust data.[2] I had a relationship with the Social Services Employees Union (Local 371 in New York City), and the president of the union allowed me to use his eighteen thousand member population as the basis for my research. I secured a small amount of funding from my department and university, but it was clear that I would need to be not only the intellectual driver behind the research questions but also the coordinator of the survey in the field. Because I was conducting the survey in 2005 with a relatively older union population, I chose to conduct the survey via mail and not online. I made this decision for two reasons. First, the digital divide is real. I was surveying a largely Black population, and I knew that many members did not use computers the way many young graduate students did. Second, the research was conducted in 2005. Smartphones were barely a thing, and computer use was not as prevalent as it is today.

The cost of conducting the survey through the mail far exceeded costs for an online survey. I received grants for the external and internal envelope stamps and the envelopes of different sizes. These minor details were so necessary. Placing an envelope inside of an envelope required business envelopes of two different sizes. Stamps and labels had to be affixed, and the weight of the outgoing survey could not exceed the weight of mailing a normal letter. However, an introductory letter outlining the research and the institutional review board notification; a three-page, double-spaced, stapled survey; and a cover letter with a return envelope affixed with a stamp and address label—all included in a regular envelope which also had a stamp and address label affixed—came in just under weight. I had not thought about these costs when deciding to conduct my mail-in survey. Had I included just one more stamp or staple, each survey would have had an additional thirty-cent mailing cost. That may not seem like a lot, but when sending out three iterations of fifteen hundred surveys . . . I will let you figure out the math. Essentially, it is expensive to conduct original research. It is also important to keep in mind that many prestigious fellowships and grants are subject to a home institution "fee," which can mean that up to 30 percent of the grant you receive goes toward the general university overhead fund. There are hidden and unexpected costs to conducting original research: paying for survey construction, hiring research assistants to help with field experiments, traveling to archives, and more.

Once I finally got the survey out into the field, completed surveys slowly began to be returned. I will never forget what it felt like to open the first survey and see the multiple-choice questions answered. Not only was I looking at people's attitudes toward immigration, government spending, participation, and other Black ethnic groups, but I had also begun to create original data. I was officially a social scientist. What I did not anticipate were the personal notes that accompanied the surveys. Respondents of countless surveys wrote me a note of thanks. Some were glad these questions were finally being asked, others were glad they were finally being acknowledged. Many wished me luck in my research endeavors, and a few respondents even included coupons for regular grocery items to "keep me going" as I finished my studies. There was something very familial about the personal notes from my respondents. It reminded me of political scientist Michael Dawson's larger idea of "linked fate," which I was exploring in my dissertation.[3] What was it that connected Black respondents to me, my survey, and ultimately to my success in graduate school and beyond? For them, the survey was more than just questions about their attitudes toward political participation and policy issues; it was a rare acknowledgment that they and their truths and their stories mattered. My survey was a vehicle for them to be seen in a country that often ignores and devalues the experiences of the "others."

After conducting my surveys in the field, I followed up with qualitative interviews with union leadership and rank and file members. As I interviewed older Black union workers, many asked if I had relatives from outside of the United States. Many of my Caribbean respondents were excited to hear that my paternal grandmother was from the Bahamas. I had not planned on sharing that piece of personal history with my respondents, but almost every Caribbean or African respondent inquired whether I was something other than "just Black." In many ways their questions confirmed some of the theories of racial solidarity and ethnic distinction I dissected in the project. I wondered how forthcoming some of my respondents would have been had I not been able to tell them about my deceased grandmother whom I had never met from a country I hadn't visited since I was in elementary school. Still, the family connection was enough to serve as a seal of approval and increase my response rate.

If I had not had the "grandmother card" at my disposal, I often wondered whether my Black immigrant respondents would have been so generous toward me and so honest in their responses. I may never know. What I do know is that research can serve as a means not only to explore new ideas but to shed light on communities and populations who are often pushed into the shadows. I was able to collect enough data to ultimately have statistically significant findings and responses that would help inform my subsequent qualitative interviews. Through my survey collection, I discovered that Caribbean immigrants, not Black Americans, were the least likely to believe in the American dream. I uncovered some of the minor distinctions between Black ethnic groups that threatened to obstruct collective action and substantive coalition building. And I developed a theory of Black ethnicity directly tied to a diasporic under-standing of race and linked fate. My survey collection enabled me to bet-ter understand the nuances and complexities of Blacks in America, using questions I thought important, timely, and pertinent. That is the power of data collection. An intellectual vision, a methodological plan, and a touch of flexibility can change how we view the world and the groups we care about.

Christina M. Greer *is associate professor of political science at Fordham University.*

PUBLICATION TO WHICH THIS FIELDWORK CONTRIBUTED:

- Greer, Christina M. *Black Ethnics: Race Immigration and the Pursuit of the American Dream.* New York: Oxford University Press, 2013.

NOTES

1. The Collaborative Multiracial Post-Election Survey (CMPS) did not exist when I began my dissertation or when I finished my manuscript. The CMPS is a recent data set that provides postelection content from a multiracial, multiethnic, multi-lingual set of more than ten thousand respondents. This cooperative data source has provided a space for current (and future) scholars of race, ethnicity, and pol-itics (REP) to contribute to a collective and ask and share questions of interest to their particular research interests.

2. Mark Q. Sawyer, *Racial Politics in Post-Revolutionary Cuba.* Cambridge: Cam-bridge University Press, 2005.

3. Dawson's theory of linked fate argues that blacks across the class spectrum will have a shared racial identity that transcends class status. Most surprising to schol-ars was Dawson's analysis of the strong ties that wealthier blacks felt toward the less economically stable members of their racial group. My research sought to bet-ter understand this concept and the potential complications ethnicity may pose to Dawson's theory: Michael C. Dawson, *Behind the Mule: Race and Class in African-American Politics.* Princeton, N.J.: Princeton University Press, 1994.

6

HEZBOLLAH WILL TAKE YOUR DATA

HOW TO PLAN FOR RESEARCH
AMONG INSURGENTS

KRISTA E. WIEGAND

▸ FIELDWORK LOCATION: LEBANON

I n 1995, I conducted my first field research and inadvertently ended up interviewing terrorists. I was working on my master's thesis at American University, studying the role of national and religious identity in the Lebanese Civil War. I had traveled to Lebanon to conduct interviews and surveys in the field, even though Lebanon was still tense and a travel ban was in place. Incredibly, I received approval from the institutional review board (IRB) to conduct both surveys and interviews in Lebanon. I had a very supportive thesis advisor, an Israeli peace activist and scholar who was confident that I could do the field research in Lebanon. I was trying to figure out how national, religious, and regional identity played a role in the Lebanese Civil War. There was no local polling company at that time, nor any logical way to pursue a randomized survey, so I set about trying to get a good variety of surveys from different religious groups. In postwar Lebanon, the religious and regional divisions were still quite sharp: Lebanese Christians were living in East Beirut and to the north, along the coast and into the mountains up from Jounieh and Byblos; Druze were living in the mountains east of Beirut; and Muslims were living in West Beirut and south of the capital, along the coast and in the Bekaa Valley near Syria.

A friend's mother arranged for me to meet with a professor she knew, who helped me contact others who were willing to be interviewed. The internet was still in its infancy, especially in Lebanon, and email was not a good way to contact people. Land lines were unreliable because they required an infrastructure that had been destroyed in the war. Calling cell phones and personal connections were the only means of communication; as a result, I relied solely on my friends' friends and their friends. The people I knew were educated Christians and Sunnis who had fled during the war and were returning to Lebanon. At first, I relied on their contacts and asked people at the beach clubs, mountain cabins, restaurants, and cafés to fill out my surveys, which were in English and translated into Arabic. In this fashion, I was able to acquire about two hundred completed surveys, eventually compiling some interesting patterns and data about the role of identity in Lebanon.

I now had an overwhelming number of surveys from Sunnis, Maronite Catholics, Greek Orthodox, and Druze, but I had very few Shia respondents. To get access to Shia respondents, my friend Pierre asked his car mechanic in south Beirut, a Shia, to distribute my surveys around his neighborhood among Hezbollah and Amal supporters, and to return them to me a week later. A few days later I learned that my surveys had been confiscated by Hezbollah, and I was not certain which office or branch of the organization had them. I asked my friend to arrange a meeting with the people who had confiscated them, so I could persuade them to return my surveys. As a graduate student with limited funds, it had cost me a lot to photocopy the fifty or so surveys I had given to the car mechanic.

I went to an office in Dahieh, a suburb in south Beirut, with my friend Pierre, and we met with a handful of people from Hezbollah for a couple of hours. I would not recommend visiting such a group without prior arrangements and safety considerations, and without weighing the pros and cons. They proceeded to interrogate me about whether I was in the CIA, why the U.S. government was pro-Israeli, and what I—an American woman who was not married to a Lebanese man—was doing in Lebanon. I did my best to explain that the CIA does not hand out surveys to collect information, but in the end I was unable to recover my surveys. As a consolation prize, they gave me a beautiful rosewood Qur'an stand made in Iran, for my use when (if) I decided to convert to Islam.

The meeting had been intimidating, but it led me to want to learn more about Hezbollah. A few years later this became the major research topic for my PhD years at Duke University. Two years later, with the travel ban lifted, I returned to Lebanon for a year to teach political science courses at Notre Dame University–Louaize, and I got to know Lebanese society and politics much better. The focus of my doctoral research at Duke was territorial disputes, political violence, nationalism, ethnic conflict, and the Middle East.

In the summer of 2000, I heard that the Israeli army (IDF) and the South Lebanese Army (SLA) had suddenly withdrawn from the southern occupied part of Lebanon where they had been since 1982. I knew I had to travel there as soon as possible to see firsthand what the until recently occupied border region and disputed territory of Shebaa Farms were like. News reports indicated that Hezbollah now controlled the entire southern region, which had been abandoned by the IDF and the SLA. I realized I needed permission from Hezbollah to travel in the south of Lebanon.

I went online to Hezbollah.org (a website that has since been taken down), as well as to several other renamed sites, and clicked on "Contact Us." I sent an email requesting permission to travel in the south of Lebanon for research reasons, and I received a response instructing me to contact an official when I arrived in Beirut the following week. I was able to secure travel funding from Duke with a vague research proposal about observing the transition in the south of Lebanon, but I had no plans for the field research I would do when I arrived there. I traveled to Beirut only a few weeks after the Israeli withdrawal, and because I was not planning to conduct any interviews, I did not seek IRB approval for anything.

When I arrived at Hezbollah's Central Information Office in the southern suburb of Haret Horeik with my friend Joe, who would help me with my request for travel papers, I was caught off guard. First, my passport was taken to register in their records, and second, I was brought into a room to meet with Sheikh Attalah Ibrahim, director of information for Hezbollah, for the interview I had supposedly requested. On the spot, I had to come up with questions to ask him about Hezbollah policies and strategies, not sure how far I could go when asking about the organization's positions on Israel. I came up with questions on the fly, asking about Hezbollah's plans in the south of Lebanon, how the "liberation" had been celebrated by all Lebanese (regardless of religious identity), and how Hezbollah was participating in Lebanese politics. The sheikh spoke with my male friend Joe in Arabic, never making eye contact with me, and the two of them had long exchanges that Joe, not a professional interpreter, summarized the best he could for me. I felt uncomfortable but knew that the cultural norm for religious Shia men was not to shake hands or look directly at women they did not know, and I needed to not take it personally. Sometimes, field research turns into something unanticipated, and it was important for me to be culturally sensitive and ready for a conversation that would turn into an interview.

Instead of getting travel permission, I was instructed to visit Hezbollah's district office in Nabatiya, near the former southern border. Along with my friend Joe and his mother, who had come along because she was curious about seeing the south of Lebanon, I was shown into a reception room for coffee and another meeting. There was none of the hype that most journalists write about, none of the tension that people assume is present among members of a group like Hezbollah, whether labeled "guerillas," "terrorists," or "resistance fighters." Rather, they were politely curious about my interest in them and my reasons for wanting to visit the "liberated areas." They immediately accepted my brief explanation for my interest in the south of Lebanon. Whether they believed it or not was irrelevant, as I soon realized. In concluding our meeting, the Hezbollah district head instructed a man named Ahmed to serve as our guide, take us anywhere we wanted to go in the formerly occupied zone, and answer all my questions.

We spent ten hours with Ahmed, with Joe driving more than three hundred miles, all within the formerly occupied zone. I visited IDF posts that had been imploded as the IDF soldiers were withdrawing, drove past vast areas of burned trees and bushes and as yet undiscovered land mines, and visited with United Nations peacekeeping forces who were still located in the region despite Hezbollah's takeover. Again, without any original intention of interviewing a Hezbollah fighter, I had an incredible opportunity to ask all sorts of questions about why Ahmed had supported Hezbollah during the war and again in 2000, as well as all about Hezbollah politics. Ahmed had been a bodyguard to the head of the military wing of Hezbollah, and he had been captured by the IDF in 1994. He had spent eleven years in a prison in Israel and had only been released a few months earlier, as part of a German-mediated agreement to swap Israelis and Lebanese, alive and dead. This "field research" taught me more in one day than I could ever learn from books, or even from conducting interviews with Hezbollah officials in Beirut.

Two years later, in the summer of 2002, while studying Arabic at American University of Beirut, I had planned to follow up with Hezbollah officials about what was going on in Lebanese politics and the changes made in the south of Lebanon. I had to cancel my interviews, however, because the U.S. embassy had contacted my Arabic professor, asking her to "keep an eye on Krista since she is on a CIA watch list." In the post-September 11, 2001 atmosphere that included passage of the PATRIOT Act, I immediately realized that I should not pursue any further contacts with Hezbollah. The organization had been listed as a terrorist group by the U.S. government. I was extremely frustrated, but at the same time I was unwilling to risk being interrogated by U.S. officials who, under the PATRIOT Act, did not have to provide me with a lawyer. I was stunned when I was told of my status, but I was not surprised because I had been "randomly" selected for security checks with my luggage when flying, as well as interrogated by Irish authorities on a family trip to Ireland about why I had so many Lebanese, Syrian, and Jordanian stamps and visas in my passport. Eventually an airline representative told me flat out that I was on a flight watch list and that it was not random that I had been selected for extra security checks.

My visit in 2002 was my last visit to Lebanon or anywhere in the Middle East until 2011. Conducting interviews with Hezbollah had become difficult, so I turned my work toward disputes in East Asia, where I would not get into trouble for my research. It was another eight years before I felt comfortable writing and publishing an article and then my book about Hezbollah and Hamas, which included my field research in Lebanon. I didn't know how I was going to use my earlier interviews, but they found their way into my book *Bombs and Ballots: Governance by Islamic Terrorist and Guerrilla Groups*. Although I did not have IRB approval, I decided the risk was worth it because the people I spoke with were from Hezbollah's media groups. I recommend seeking IRB approval for any field research trip, even when interviews are not anticipated. It is much better to obtain IRB approval before any field research so that the research can be used in dissertations, articles, or books. I also recommend that scholars understand the risks and the political situation of the country in which they are planning to conduct research. I felt comfortable in Lebanon because I knew many locals who helped guide me away from certain areas and counseled me to avoid talking to certain types of people.

From my research in Lebanon, I learned that spontaneous opportunities would appear for which I was not prepared. I had to make an ethical choice regarding conducting interviews without IRB approval or foregoing them altogether. In the end, I decided to use these interviews in my publications because, in both cases, Hezbollah officials had granted me the interviews by choice, not by my request, and gave me their names with no requests for confidentiality. After the 2006 July War between Hezbollah and Israel, I was not even sure that the people I had spoken with in the main office and district office of Hezbollah were still alive.

I did not conduct field research again until 2017, this time as a Senior Fulbright Scholar in the Philippines. I interviewed government officials, bureaucrats, scholars, and journalists about the South China Sea dispute. Even though my interviews in the Philippines were much more organized, sometimes they were spontaneous, and I had to decide whether to ask the person to sign my IRB consent form giving me permission to use the information in my research. In the Philippines, I learned that I needed to have my IRB consent forms, interview questions, and my notebook with me at all times. I learned that I should be fully aware of cultural norms and not be afraid to ask questions that might generate controversy. Although very different in context, my field research experiences in both Lebanon and the Philippines were similar in that I faced unforeseen circumstances, which presented both ethical challenges and great opportunities.

Krista E. Wiegand *is associate professor in the Department of Political Science and director of the Global Security Program at the Howard H. Baker Jr. Center for Public Policy, at the University of Tennessee, Knoxville.*

PUBLICATION TO WHICH THIS FIELDWORK CONTRIBUTED:

- Wiegand, Krista E. *Bombs and Ballots: Governance by Islamic Terrorist and Guerrilla Groups.* New York: Routledge, 2010.

7

WHEN THE LINGUISTIC LIGHTWEIGHT GOES ABROAD

RELYING ON SHARP STUDENTS

STEPHEN M. SAIDEMAN

▸ FIELDWORK LOCATIONS: BRAZIL, CHILE, GERMANY, JAPAN, SOUTH KOREA

My work has mostly been what I call "medium-n" analyses: I examine a number of case studies, often from multiple regions. Although my linguistic skills are not great, I usually end up researching a number of cases that would bedevil any scholar who is not fluent in four or five or six languages. My current project focuses on approximately sixteen case studies, asking both legislators and military officers about their civil-military relations. Coauthors have covered some of the cases, but I am responsible for the cases in Brazil, Chile, Germany, Japan, and South Korea—five languages. When doing a project on NATO, I could conduct most of the interviews in English. However, similar to my experience working on Hungarian and Romanian cases for a book on irredentism, wars of unification that did and did not occur in the 1990s, this time that was impossible.[1] Instead, I have relied on various kinds of translators. In this chapter, I explain how I select translators, some of the challenges involved, and how I addressed them.

In these five countries, I generally followed two strategies: work with a partner or hire students. I did not choose a third strategy—delegate to others the job of interviewing. I could have hired professional translators, and did so for a few interviews in Japan, but I could not afford to do this for all of the case studies. I also prefer to hire people who have a good understanding of the political system because they can both help arrange interviews and give me feedback along the way. For most of the work in

Japan, I relied on an academic who served as my partner in some of the research. The challenges that arose in this partnership are the same ones that apply to coauthoring: varying time commitments and pace of work, different senses of what is needed, and so on. As these are well known, here I focus on the process and challenges of hiring students.

For each case study, I contacted people I knew or that friends knew who could recommend students to me. By accident more than on purpose, three different kinds of students assisted me. In Brazil, I worked with graduate students who researched Brazilian politics and were very plugged-in to the politics and society of Brasilia. In South Korea, I was referred to a couple of students who were finishing their graduate work in interpretation. In Chile, I worked with two advanced undergraduate students who were from families steeped in politics. Each group of students helped to arrange interviews, often drove me to the interviews, and then served as interpreters. They also translated the consent forms and other documents as needed. I tried to pay the same rates in each country—the going rate for research assistance in my home country—but the interpreter students in South Korea had their own rates (somewhat higher than those I tend to offer). Offering less than what I would pay my own graduate students would seem to be an ethical breach but paying more was less problematic. To be clear, I only give coauthor credit to research partners. For translators and/or fixers, I not only pay them appropriately but also acknowledge them in every publication that results from their work. This leads to a key piece of advice—start writing the acknowledgments section as you do the research so you do not have to search through your emails later to figure out how to spell a name from five years earlier.

One of the challenges is that I cannot really say whether any of the translation was wrong or of poor quality because I did not understand the languages being spoken. My comfort level did vary because the professionally trained interpreters took notes and provided longer responses than those who were untrained. To compensate for variations in interpretation quality, I tried to get as many interviews as possible to triangulate not just the interview subjects but also the translations. Over the course of the interview period (between one and two weeks usually), I found that the translators became more comfortable, learning how to phrase my questions better in their native language and how to phrase the answers.

Not being able to speak the local language is not just a challenge for the actual interviews; it also complicates the logistics of getting to the interview. Most of the interviews for my current project involved people who work in a national capital, and one might think getting around would not be so problematic—and you would mostly be correct. Many transit systems have English as a second language, and Uber/Lyft—whatever flaws they have—allow one to get a ride from one spot to another without having to tell the driver where one is going. Because of the language problem, it was more difficult to use a taxi if I was not with my interpreter. In general, I prefer subways because they have reasonably good maps and one can GPS/Google-map from the subway to the interview location.

However, two complications arose over the course of this project. First, buildings in Tokyo do not have street names or numbers.[2] This is not just a problem for wayward academics from North America but for Japanese citizens as well. When arranging an interview, one must ask how to get to the right building from a specific exit from the subway system (which is easy to navigate, unlike Tokyo's train stations). While working in Japan, it is imperative to rent a smartphone or have one that can be used in Japan because GPS is absolutely required to address the absence of street names and building numbering.

The second complication was the fact that Chile's capital is in Santiago, but its Congress resides in Valparaíso, a town on the coast about an hour or so from Santiago. This involved two practical problems: arranging interviews and traveling there. We had to save specific days for interviewing people based in Valparaíso because it was not feasible to go back and forth given the traffic problems that might occur. In some countries, it was pretty easy to line up a series of interviews back-to-back in a specific location, but the politicians of Chile were not so cooperative. We had to expend significant time and effort to get to Valparaíso for one interview with the hope of landing a second one. The first time we tried, we failed to get any other interviews. An effort to get an additional legislator to meet with us in Santiago also failed.

On my last day in Chile, with a flight late at night, my interpreters and I went to Valparaíso one more time to meet with one legislator. This went both really well and quite poorly. It went really well in that the interview took place right before a vote, and the politician's aide then stationed us outside the chambers and corralled two additional interview subjects. We got what we needed thanks to coincidence and the generosity of this one aide.

Brazil was much, much easier because most of the government is within walking distance of the rest of the government. The only hang-ups I had there were trying to get a ride back from a military base on the edge of town (my interpreters came to the rescue) and impeachment. I had to cancel my first trip to Brazil because the people I wanted to interview were too busy impeaching their president to talk to me. I went the next year, and I was lucky to leave Brasilia just as protests broke out when people learned that the new president had bribed people during the impeachment vote of the previous year.

What went poorly? Getting back to Santiago. One of my interpreters drove us down in her mother's car. On the way back to Santiago, we stopped to get gas. Her car was a diesel. It was a full-service station, and unfortunately those putting in the fuel did not bother to read the big "DIESEL" label on the gas cap. Oops. This meant we could not start the car for fear of damaging the engine. The car was pushed into a neighboring garage where mechanics took the fuel tank out, emptied it, cleaned it, and reattached it. Luckily, the mechanics had the time to do the work. We had to wait for a couple of hours, which then meant our return to Santiago was in rush hour. But we did make it back. Not quite as perilous as fieldwork in a danger zone, but it could have been a major problem if I could not get back to fly home.

Why not stay at home and subcontract interviewing entirely? Given my use of principal-agent theory, I am too well aware that I am not great at delegating. When I work with my own research assistants in Canada, I often give instructions that are vague or difficult to follow, so asking folks elsewhere to do the interviewing for me could be problematic. Plus other principal-agent dynamics could kick in as well—how do I know my researchers are doing what they say they are doing? (See chapter 13 by Cancian and Fabbe for a discussion on this issue.) More important, during these interview trips, I learn as I go along and can adapt and adjust the questions. I learn of new institutions or informal behaviors or examples that I want to ask about in subsequent interviews. A subcontractor could do that, but this person probably will not be driven to ask the same questions that come from my theoretical perspective and from my curiosity. I have repeatedly found myself in these interviews going in directions I had not expected. I simply do not trust that someone else would follow the same paths.

Doing fieldwork requires flexibility as well as grant money and good contacts. I feel guilty asking professors I do not know for assistance, but I try to pay it forward when people need help in Ottawa or in areas in which I have come to develop some expertise or contacts. When in the field, one must adjust on the fly and be calm when miscommunication happens or inconveniences arise. This project would not be possible if I did not have the grant money, if I did not lean on my network for contacts, and if I did not roll with the punches. Some trips produce more results than others, some interviews are utterly useless, and some are extremely useful. There is no one set formula for making this kind of research work. The only way it can work is to be decent to those with whom you work and to those who need your help because you will surely need assistance someday—and karma is a thing.

———

Stephen M. Saideman *is Paterson Chair in International Affairs at Carleton University and director of the Canadian Defence and Security Network.*

PUBLICATIONS TO WHICH THIS FIELDWORK CONTRIBUTED:

- Saideman, Stephen M., and Philippe Lagassé. "When Civilian Control Is Civil: Parliamentary Oversight of the Military in Belgium and New Zealand," *European Journal of International Security* 4, no. 1 (2019): 20–40.
- ——. "Public Critic or Secretive Monitor: Party Objectives and Legislative Oversight of the Military in Canada," *West European Politics* 40, no. 1 (2017): 119–38.

NOTES

1. To be clear, I have not done any work in conflict zones, so my experiences are probably not helpful for those going into more dangerous situations. For an excellent discussion of those issues, see, in addition to other chapters in this book, Kate Cronin-Furman and Mille Lake, "Ethics Abroad: Fieldwork in Fragile and Violent Contexts, *PS: Political Science & Politics* 51, no. 3 (2018): 607–14, doi:10.1017/S1049096518000379.

2. Every address has three sets of numbers—reflecting the quadrant in the neighborhood that the building is in and then the subquadrant, and so on—but it is not an easy system to use. Many businesses automatically send directions to anyone interested in visiting them.

8

NAVIGATING DATA COLLECTION IN WAR ZONES

FOTINI CHRISTIA

▸ FIELDWORK LOCATION: AFGHANISTAN

I began doing research in Afghanistan in 2004 while still a graduate student in the middle of writing my dissertation. A couple of years after the fall of the Taliban, Afghanistan was pristine territory for social science, and it was not yet overrun by foreign academics. The Afghan war was then known as "the good war" when compared to a violently disintegrating Iraq, and pundits as well as locals were optimistic about peace because change felt palpable. Even in those early days, there was no valor or glamour associated with being in Afghanistan. Although a difficult setting in which to do research as a foreigner and as a woman, it proved to be a great learning ground for meaningful fieldwork in tough places.[1] The lessons from the Afghan countryside inspired some of my most exciting early work and have stayed with me for life, enabling do-no-harm policy relevant research in other war-torn, hard-to-access areas such as Iraq and Yemen.[2]

BUILDING CONNECTIONS WITH JOURNALISTS AND EXPATS

My first realization, a mere few hours after setting foot on the ground in Afghanistan, was the importance of building connections with journalists and expats. Insightful and well informed, even when not social-scientifically minded, they can be a great resource for research. Journalists combine a good understanding of the local context with a broad network of influential acquaintances, and they do not see academics as competition given our vastly different publishing horizons. Rather, they appreciate the rigorous nature of our work, and they saved me a great deal of time and effort by making introductions, offering helpful suggestions on an array of logistical arrangements, and explaining how red tape worked in Kabul. I am still grateful to the United Nations staffers who, on my first trip to Afghanistan, rented me a room in their house on Kabul's Butcher Street that was meant to serve as their safety bunker. It was the best bargain in town, and it came with a lot of advice on how to navigate a then unfamiliar terrain. Their frequent offers for a car ride or a meal, generous in and of themselves, came with information that helped tremendously in figuring out how to optimize my data collection strategy.

I also got phenomenal insight, better than any book on Afghanistan I had ever read, from expat area experts who had lived in the region for decades. Their nuance was unparalleled and offered some really creative views on whom to interview and how, what survey questions to ask, and how to come across as an overall savvy researcher in this context. My meetings with true connoisseurs of Afghanistan and its people, such as Michael Semple and the late Nancy Dupree, were memorable in that regard. Some influential policy-related pieces resulted from these interactions that not only deepened my interest in the area and attracted positive attention to my work but also proved integral to later thinking on my research.

Friends or acquaintances with local connections to share also turned out to be invaluable. I remember chaperoning an Afghan friend in meetings with aspiring suitors, who were so keen to impress her that they would offer to help out her researcher friend (me!), providing hard-to-get contact details for potential interview subjects. This Jane Austen-esque interaction didn't just show me the importance of local acquaintances; it also showed me the value of understanding local gender politics and how being a woman in such a field setting, as insightfully noted by other academics doing research in the Muslim world, could be a strength at times and a weakness at others.[3]

BEING THE "THIRD GENDER" AS A WESTERN WOMAN IN AFGHANISTAN

Some of the best advice I got was to keep my head low and covered and to be cognizant of the gender dimension in everything I set out to do in Afghanistan. Afghan women are treated as second-class citizens, but Western women working in Afghanistan are seen as a third sex, with access both to the Afghan male and female worlds that are more often than not segregated. Being able to interact with both Afghan men and women for my research allowed me to see not only the large gaps between the spaces the two genders occupy but also the several points of contact and what they meant for research on topics that transcend gender, such as local governance and development.

For instance, for a project on community driven development across the Afghan countryside, the gender dimension was critical as an outcome variable and from a measurement perspective. Specifically, we needed to do large-scale data collection involving surveys in villages with both male and female members of households. That required having female enumerators for female subjects and male enumerators for male subjects. Our enumerators also had to be able and willing to travel with us for extended periods of time in the Afghan countryside because our sample covered five hundred villages in a diverse set of ten Afghan districts dispersed across the country. The enumerator recruitment process was very cognizant of gender; we had to make sure that the women we hired as enumerators had escorts who were male relatives. That meant we needed to come up with mother-son, wife-husband, daughter-father, or sister-brother teams of enumerators. We looked for pairs that allowed us to optimize on enumerator quality. We often had to recruit women first because they were harder to find; then we tested whoever was available among their father, brother, son, or husband to see who best fit the requirements to serve as the counterpart male enumerator. Although these gender demands made for a challenging recruitment process, the familial relations they entailed helped the team sustain high morale and performance in the field, even in the toughest of places in rural Afghanistan.

As an individual researcher, being a woman helped me to relate and connect with interview subjects who were willing to interact and share stories because they perceived me as less threatening than male colleagues. I have no doubt that several warlords whom I interviewed for my dissertation were keen to meet with me, not just because of their interest in my research topic but also partly because I was a Western woman academic, not a usual sighting in Afghanistan at the time. From the set of influential warlords who were initially too busy to meet me, I learned how to best present my research project. It was through such initial conversations that I became more aware of the importance of appropriately presenting myself and my work. The ultimate intent of writing a dissertation is to turn the work into a published manuscript, so I told my subjects I was working on a future book. They could readily recognize that, and they often explicitly ask to be referenced. It was also important to highlight the academic nature of the project, as well as my institutional affiliation.

For the harder-to-access elites, an approach that always worked involved, as other researchers have noted, dropping some names of prominent individuals who had already granted me access.[4] It was easier to first secure interviews with more marginal elites who may have fallen out of power but who, at some point, had played a major role in terms of rivalry and competition to contemporary power players in the field. These people readily grant interviews, and they had more time to talk about the past and the glorious times in which they may have been involved. Once I secured their version of the story, the more influential public officials who may have originally been too busy to meet due to other obligations became available.

DISCIPLINE IN DATA COLLECTION AND WORKING WITH LOCAL RESEARCHERS

One aspect of fieldwork involves going with the flow and reaching out to build connections with locals and expats to figure out exactly how to position yourself and your work; another aspect requires being very organized and systematic. Specifically, in Afghanistan, and in all other war zones where I have carried out research since then, I never failed to notice the importance of discipline during the data collection process. There are codified and straightforward ways to do surveys or experiments, but people often get sloppy with their field notes. It is important to keep everything organized and systematic: take detailed field notes, along with photos, and transcribe them as consistently and as often as possible. It is field notes that offer rich context and allow a researcher to figure out how to gather, organize, and present the rest of the data collected from the field. They bring great color but can be easily confused or left out if not kept and documented in a rigorous way.

Discipline is even more important when leading a team of local researchers in the field. Enumerators require a lot more training than is usually programmed or budgeted, need to be followed in the field to test both their capacity to collect data and their knowledge of the survey and research instruments, and need to be monitored closely. Irrespective of how professional they are, the quality of work they will produce for you—that is, the quality of data they collect—is directly correlated with your level of involvement, dedication, and oversight in the data gathering process.

Beyond making sure that the financial incentives for enumerators are structured appropriately, I found that being closely involved in enumerator training and appealing to their national pride worked wonders. Specifically, indicating how the data they were collecting would contribute to research and important knowledge for their country and, in turn, potentially help improve living conditions, highlighted the importance of gathering data accurately and with attention to detail. They were all also very keen to be personally acknowledged as part of the data collection team in any academic work published from this data collection effort, something that was on offer as an extra incentive to create accountability for the data collected. Ultimately, training local enumerators is a way of giving back beyond the specific research project and findings, by building capacity and skill. And this giving back to the field site, either through policy pieces that effectively communicate the findings and impact of the academic work or through building local research capacity, is both the right thing to do ethically and an undoubted enabler of future research.

———

Fotini Christia *is professor of political science at Massachusetts Institute of Technology.*

PUBLICATIONS TO WHICH THIS FIELDWORK CONTRIBUTED:

- Christia, Fotini, and Michael Semple. "Flipping the Taliban: How to Win in Afghanistan," *Foreign Affairs* 88, no. 4 (July-August 2009): 34–45.
- Christia, Fotini. *Alliance Formation in Civil Wars.* Cambridge: Cambridge University Press, 2012.
- Christia, Fotini, Andrew Beath, and Ruben Enikolopov. "Empowering Women Through Development Aid: Evidence from a Field Experiment in Afghanistan," *American Political Science Review* 107, no. 3 (August 2013): 540–57.

NOTES

1. On the relevance of fieldwork, see Soledad Loaeza, Randy Stevenson, and Devra Moehler, "Symposium: Should Everyone Do Fieldwork?," *APSA-CP Newsletter* 16, no. 2 (2005): 8–18.

2. For an excellent discussion on qualitative research in war zones, see Elisabeth Jean Wood, "The Ethical Challenges of Field Research in Conflict Zones," *Qualitative Sociology* 29, no. 3 (September 2006): 373–86, https://doi.org/10.1007/s11133-006-9027-8.

3. Jillian Schwedler, "The Third Gender: Western Female Researchers in the Middle East," *PS: Political Science & Politics* 39, no. 3 (July 2006): 425–28, https://doi.org/10.1017/S104909650606077X.

4. Schwedler, "The Third Gender," 425.

III

MAKE A PLAN . . .
THEN BE READY
TO TOSS IT

9

LET GO AND LET ALI

NADYA HAJJ

▸ FIELDWORK LOCATIONS: PALESTINIAN REFUGEE CAMPS
IN LEBANON, JORDAN, AND SYRIA

During my graduate school methodological training with the late, great Americanist Randall Strahan, I encountered David Collier's *APSA-Comparative Politics* newsletter on "Data, Field Work, and Extracting New Ideas at Close Range."[1] I was struck by Collier's attention to the role of data-rich country studies that could serve as a source of new ideas and hypotheses. Collier's insights built on sociologist Alejandro Portes's insistence that researchers who are experts in one case can play an influential role in "extracting new ideas at close range."[2] These scholars are deeply engaged with both theory and the close analysis of cases. This combination of traits gave some field researchers a superpower I coveted because they had "an unusual capacity to see the general in the particular."[3] However, reading about the existence of the superpower is not the same as possessing it. In this short piece, I describe how my research project shifted from close analysis of a refugee community to a broader comparative assessment of how institutions form in anarchic settings. Reading scholarship extensively before beginning field research, listening carefully to interviewees, and letting go of tightly controlling the interview process helped me acquire the superpower of extracting general ideas from specific cases.

By 2012, I had spent almost eight years living in Palestinian refugee camps in Lebanon, Jordan, and Syria. The genesis of the Palestinian refugee condition began in 1948 when approximately 750,000 Palestinians fled to Jordan, Syria, and Lebanon, where refugee camps were established to house them. In Lebanon, 53 percent of the Palestinian population still live in these camps.[4] Since 1948, camps have transformed from tented spaces to landscapes filled with cement apartment homes and a hive of entrepreneurial endeavors. Much of my research was centered in Nahr al Bared refugee camp (NBC), located near the port city of Tripoli in northern Lebanon. NBC was built in 1951, but it was destroyed in 2007 during a battle between Lebanese military forces and a non-Palestinian group known as Fatah al-Islam. Shortly after its destruction, the international aid community and Lebanese government agreed to reconstruct it. For a time, displaced NBC residents lived in temporary dwellings in the nearby Beddawi refugee camp.

Over the years, I traced the shifting political and economic conditions for NBC residents. I had conducted hundreds of interviews using methodologically reliable and valid questions that the institutional review board (IRB) deemed ethical. I was the foremost expert on entrepreneurial activity and business growth in the construction sectors of Palestinian refugee camps. However, moving beyond my rich descriptive study to contribute to a new idea or general theory in comparative politics seemed far out of reach. On May 18, 2012, I had concluded my seventieth interview with yet another NBC refugee business owner who had temporarily relocated to Beddawi refugee camp following the 2007 conflict that destroyed his original business and home. He was awaiting approval on a business grant application and the reconstruction of his home in the new NBC. Out of sheer frustration with the stalled direction of my research project, I went rogue. I put down my IRB approved script, took a big gulp of cardamom coffee, and asked Ali, "Is there anything else I should have asked you but didn't?" Over the course of eight years we had developed a rapport, and his next comment revealed that he felt he could candidly challenge me. He looked me in the eye and said,

> You know, you have interviewed me more than four times since 2004. You know so much about my business and even my family history. I know you care. But every time you ask the same questions, and I say the same things. But lately things have changed in NBC. After the 2007 conflict there, I feel differently about things, but your questions don't get

at that change I feel. You need to loosen up and just listen to me. I wonder why you didn't ask me how I feel about the upcoming move to the newly rebuilt Nahr al Bared 2.0?

He went on to say,

> Of course, I want to return to the new NBC. But it will be very different there, and most of all I will feel dispossessed for a second time. Do you know why? It is because I won't own my new place there, like I did before! I used to own a home in the camp that I was proud of—we worked for sixty years to scrape together a life. Now we can't own, rent, or sell part of our new home.

I was puzzled and asked myself, "What did he mean he *owned* his home in the refugee camp?" Ali rummaged around in a box and produced a tattered property title. It was a formal legal title that established the owner's right to use, sell, protect, and benefit from the ownership of his home. Probing him further, he said there were repositories of file cabinets stuffed with property titles lining the walls of camp committee (CC) offices in refugee camps throughout Lebanon.

The existing scholarship on institutional formation did not anticipate that a refugee community would undertake the risk and cost associated with property right creation. As a student of political science, I was well versed in the predictions of Spontaneous Order folks and New Institutional Economics regarding the necessary conditions for property rights formation. The former presumed that informal property rights were the only likely outcome in nonstate settings, and the latter required the presence of a state for the creation of formal property rights. I had held tightly to their assumptions that refugees would have neither the motive, means, nor long time horizon to incentivize the formation of property rights. In turn, I constrained my field research and never asked refugees about property rights. However, Ali's comment sparked a "first principles" way of thinking. A first principle is a basic assumption that cannot be deduced any further. Over two thousand years ago, Aristotle defined a first principle as "the first basis from which a thing is known."[5] I began to ask the more basic question of how refugees construe order in the absence of a state apparatus such that they could facilitate stability and growth.

For the first time, I was able to see how the rich particulars of refugee camp industry and growth might connect to a general theory of institutional formation in comparative politics. "Let go and let Ali" became my new motto for releasing control of the research process with my carefully crafted questions and opening myself to the unexpected lessons that Ali and other refugees could teach me.

I thanked Ali and hopped in a taxicab back to NBC's committee office. The CC office might have looked like a boring meeting room to an unwitting observer, but it was, in fact, filled with proof positive that legal titles establishing ownership of the right to use, sell, and protect an investment or asset had developed in the most unlikely of political economic spaces: a refugee camp. The file clerk at the CC permitted me closer inspection of the titles. His cigarette burning down to a nub and the hazy smoke filling the room only added to the moment, pregnant with the drama of field research.

Like Indiana Jones tearing through cobwebs and finding the Holy Grail, I squeaked open a metal file cabinet drawer and discovered hard copy evidence of property titles in refugee camps all across Lebanon and Jordan. It was as if an unknown historical artifact had been unearthed. Property rights are not supposed to exist in Palestinian refugee camps. At least, the existing scholarly record did not predict their presence. After all, why would a marginalized community living in uncertain political economic conditions go to all the trouble and effort of crafting institutions that lay claim to assets in a refugee camp? Yet my unscripted routine interview with a Palestinian refugee led to the discovery of formal legal titles inside refugee camps strewn across Lebanon and Jordan. This discovery triggered a new understanding of the potential for institutional innovation and evolution in transitional political space, places that lack a stable sovereign state with the legal jurisdiction to define and enforce institutions. This new idea of communal resilience and institutional innovation in challenging political spaces became the driving force behind my research agenda.

By "letting go and letting Ali," I was able to develop the superpower I had always coveted. Although I had prepared well for field research by letting the existing scholarship inform my first round of questions, future iterations of research questions evolved to respond to the dynamic nature of the interview process. I also shifted to thinking about the first principles motivating the creation of order in anarchic spaces. After years of developing trust and rapport with refugees, I learned to lean on their expertise to inform the questions I asked. After all, they are the experts on the ground and are most aware of real-time shifts in political economic conditions. In fact, releasing firm control of the interview process led me to discover a trove of property titles that were crafted and enforced by Palestinian refugees. This was a totally unexpected finding based on my careful reading of the literature on institutions. The mantra of "letting go and letting Ali" helped connect my specific knowledge of businesses and growth in Palestinian refugee camps to a general comparative political theory of institutional formation in transitional spaces.

Nadya Hajj *is associate professor of Peace and Justice Studies at Wellesley College.*

PUBLICATIONS TO WHICH THIS FIELDWORK CONTRIBUTED:

- Hajj, Nadya. *Protection Amid Chaos: The Creation of Property Rights in Palestinian Refugee Camps.* New York: Columbia University Press, 2016.
- ——. "Institutional Formation in Transitional Settings," *Comparative Politics* 46, no. 4 (July 2014): 399–418.

NOTES

1. David Collier, "Data, Field Work, and Extracting New Ideas at Close Range," SSRN Scholarly Paper (Rochester, N.Y.: Social Science Research Network, 1999), https://papers.ssrn.com/abstract=1757215.
2. Collier, "Data," 5.
3. Collier, 4.
4. "UNRWA | United Nations Relief and Works Agency for Palestine Refugees," UNRWA, accessed April 10, 2019, https://www.unrwa.org/.
5. Aristotle, *The Metaphysics* (Mineola, N.Y.: Courier Corporation, 2013), 1013a14–15.

10

BE PREPARED (TO GO OFF SCRIPT)

DANIEL N. POSNER

▸ FIELDWORK LOCATIONS: ZAMBIA, MALAWI

I arrived in Lusaka, Zambia, in June of 1993. It was my first time in Africa, and I wanted to hit the ground running. I had just six months in the field, and I wanted to make the most of my time. I had a clear, well-developed research topic and a notebook full of questions I was eager to spring upon people as soon as I got off the plane. Yet I recall those first days as being immensely frustrating. Nobody I spoke with had the slightest interest in answering my questions. I wanted to investigate how Zambia's recent transition to democracy had affected the character of interethnic relations in the country. But all that anyone wanted to talk about was the historic referendum that had just taken place in neighboring Malawi, a country about which I knew little. As I learned, Malawi had long been one of the most closed and repressive countries in Africa. So when the country's long-time dictator, Kamuzu Banda, allowed a referendum on the continuation of one-party rule—and lost—it was natural that people in Lusaka wanted to talk about it. In hindsight, I can see that this obsession with Malawian affairs made complete sense, but at the time it was exasperating.

However, what began as a source of annoyance quickly became an opportunity. Having followed a mentor's advice to seek out journalists, I befriended a British/Australian couple who were working as stringers for the BBC and the Associated Press. Both were deeply involved with the Lusaka-based Malawian opposition—one of them had stage-managed the triumphant return to Malawi of exiled opposition leader Chikufwa Chihana a few months earlier. They invited me to sit in on strategy sessions on the porch of their bungalow in Lusaka with dissidents, several of whom would go on to be ministers in the new Malawian government and leaders in parliament. Thanks to these connections, a few weeks later I found myself in a motorcade with Chihana and his entourage barnstorming villages in rural Malawi to rally support for the opposition. The experience was totally exhilarating, and it taught me a huge amount about campaigning, local politics, and political change. It also provided an introduction to the role of ethnicity in Malawian politics, which would later provide a useful counterpoint to the way ethnicity manifested itself in politics across the border in Zambia (and the germ of an idea for a paper built around a comparison of ethnic politics in the two settings).

Once the excitement of the Malawian referendum had died down in Zambia, I finally did get to ask the questions I had been planning about the impact of democratic politics on cross-group interactions. I interviewed politicians, activists, journalists, academics, and people on the street, and there was near unanimity among them that ethnic politics had intensified since the return of multiparty elections. But the examples people gave to substantiate their views perplexed me. Several of the people I interviewed pointed to the fact that Bembas had been appointed to all of the key positions in the cabinet. But others pointed to the control of the highest political positions by a different group, Luapulans. Still others identified Lundas or Chishingas as the ones occupying the most important posts. What in the world was going on?

I came to realize that people in Zambia viewed the country's ethnic politics through different lenses. Although everyone was keeping score of which groups were being favored, the scorekeeping was done with reference to different ethnic categories. Some who looked at the country's politics saw it through the lens of (what Zambians referred to as) "tribe." Others saw the country's politics through the lens of language group memberships. The upshot was that Zambians could look at the same set of cabinet members, judges, diplomatic appointees, senior civil servants, and other key officeholders and make different—although equally accurate and correct—claims about which group was receiving preferential treatment. To complicate things further, some language communities spanned multiple provinces, which meant that distinctions were sometimes made between members of the same language group who happened to trace their roots to different provinces, and some of the labels (for example, "Bemba") were applied to both tribes and broader linguistic groups. Even when people used the same labels, they sometimes had in mind different groups of beneficiaries.

The more I came to understand the complexity and multidimensionality of ethnic categories in Zambia, the more I began to wonder whether I was asking the wrong question. I had chosen Zambia as a field research site because its ethnic diversity and recent transition to competitive multiparty politics made it an ideal place to study how democratization affected intergroup relations. But it began to dawn on me that the more interesting question was why, when Zambians reflected on the role ethnicity was playing in the country's new multiparty era, they saw the country's ethnic landscape and performed their mental accounting of which groups were favored and disfavored in such different ways. Before tackling the question I thought I had come to Zambia to try to answer, I began to wonder whether I needed first to understand the conditions under which people viewed the country as divided among seventy-odd tribes, four to five language groups, or a still different number of provinces or regions. Before studying whether conflict across group lines had intensified, I needed to understand why conflict was perceived to be taking place along one line of social cleavage instead of another.

Looking back, I am grateful that I had the flexibility to change course and pursue this new research question. The dissertation and book I ultimately wrote were much more theoretically interesting because I allowed myself the opportunity to shift gears and adjust to a new set of stimuli. My engagement with Zambia had been limited to secondary sources, and my sense of what was critical to investigate was based on theoretical accounts of African politics that had been written and inspired by events many years earlier. The question I had thought important from afar was less compelling once I hit the ground and began talking to people, observing what was happening, and reflecting on the events of the day.

My experience taught me some additional lessons. Many students arrive in graduate school knowing exactly what they want to study. Sometimes they know not just the question they want to answer but the part of the world in which they want to work and the specific research design they want to implement. This is generally a bad idea.[1] From my first experience with fieldwork in Zambia, I learned that going into the field wedded to a particular question is generally a bad idea too. Fieldwork is not just about testing a set of hypotheses developed in advance; it is also about identifying which hypotheses are most worth testing.

The lesson is not, of course, that one should do purely inductive research or that it's OK to go to the field without having read everything that has been written about one's case or having reflected on candidate research topics and hypotheses that might be worth testing. Nor is it that one should not bother to write a prospectus or draft survey questions or experimental protocols in advance. It is simply that one should be *flexible* in order to maximize the chance that the time and energy one devotes to data collection is applied to the most important questions. My experience taught me that those questions may not become apparent until one has spent time marinating—"soaking and poking," as Richard Fenno advocated—in the environment one is studying.

The importance of flexibility is also illustrated by my experiences in Malawi. Had I been too committed to my main research topic, and not been willing to take advantage of the serendipitous timing of my arrival in Lusaka and the connections I happened to make with people in the Malawian opposition, I would have missed out on an enormously important source of insight into how politics operates on the ground and an extremely useful exposure to the contrast between how ethnic politics worked in Zambia and Malawi.

Back in the day, when students of developing countries usually had just one opportunity to do their fieldwork—often through a Fulbright or other year-long fellowship—taking this lesson to heart was harder to do. Flexibility of the sort I am advocating is challenging when one has just one shot to collect the data and wrap up the fieldwork. But graduate students today often have the opportunity to undertake multiple trips to the field. My experience suggests the critical importance of consciously structuring at least the first of those trips to maximize opportunities for identifying new questions. These questions may be more interesting and relevant to the issues of the moment than the ones that seemed compelling from a distance. Such flexibility can put researchers in a position to take the fullest possible advantage of serendipitous opportunities that may arise. One should go into the field prepared, but one should also be prepared to go off script.

Daniel N. Posner *is James S. Coleman Professor of International Development in the Department of Political Science at the University of California, Los Angeles.*

PUBLICATIONS TO WHICH THIS FIELDWORK CONTRIBUTED:

- Posner, Daniel N. "The Political Salience of Cultural Difference: Why Chewas and Tumbukas Are Allies in Zambia and Adversaries in Malawi," *American Political Science Review* 98, no. 4 (2004): 529–45.
- ——. *Institutions and Ethnic Politics in Africa.* New York: Cambridge University Press, 2005.

NOTE

1. Even worse is when students arrive knowing—or thinking they know—what the *answer* is, viewing their graduate education as an opportunity to acquire the skills to "prove" their position in a more academically acceptable way.

11

RADIO GAGA

EVOLVING FIELD EXPERIMENTS IN MALI

KRISTIN MICHELITCH

▶ FIELDWORK LOCATION: MALI, BETWEEN MOPTI AND TIMBUKTU

I n 2010, my colleague and coauthor Jaimie Bleck and I were interested in the effect of initial exposure to the national state radio station, the Office of Radio and Television in Mali (ORTM), on people's political engagement surrounding the upcoming March 2012 Malian elections. Although Mali had been heralded as one of the most stable and competitive democracies in sub-Saharan Africa, village chiefs were also known to largely "gatekeep" political information and otherwise influence opinions and vote choice of villagers. However, over the last couple of decades, radio towers emitting ORTM had been spreading from the capital city of Bamako out to rural villages. Inspired by the seminal work of Daniel Lerner, Lucian Pye, and Eugene Weber on mass media expansion, we wondered whether access to radio would increase autonomous and pluralistic political engagement among villagers.

Our approach was simple.

Step 1: For a natural experiment, locate areas with no radio emissions, as well as contiguous areas that had just received radio emissions but where people did not yet widely own radios.

Step 2: In a field experiment within the radio emission area, randomly assign some men and women to receive solar crank radios to boost exposure and others to receive a placebo item as yet undetermined (eventual answer: flashlight).

Step 3: Collect novel outcome data related to political identity, knowledge, opinions, and behaviors.

Of course, this approach did not go according to plan.

Our main article[1] is frequently used by colleagues teaching field experimental methods as an example par excellence of experiencing major disruptions of the original research plan—a coup and a rebel insurgency. However, this is a tale of facing and adapting to many different fieldwork challenges, from Mother Nature, to putschists, to gender dynamics in a cross-cultural team.

A NATURAL EXPERIMENT BLOWN AWAY BY THE WIND

We had already jettisoned the natural experiment before arrival in Mali in December 2011. It was literally blown away by the wind. What seemed feasible sitting at our desks in the United States—to locate a sharp division among otherwise similar villages that were both inside and outside the boundary of ORTM emissions—proved impossible. There were no media maps. We discovered this by hiring research assistants to drive around villages between Mopti and Timbuktu on motorcycles with a radio, trying to tune in to ORTM. These reconnaissance missions revealed that due to "winds off the Sahara" some villages got ORTM all the time and others got it some of the time. We'd have to drive much farther north to find an area receiving no ORTM emissions, but doing so would mean traversing the north-south divide in Mali, planting us firmly in the territory of a different ethnic group—the Tuareg.

Not only would the causal identification in such a natural experiment be confounded by ethnicity (the northern Tuareg are seminomadic traders and herders oriented on the Sahara, whereas the southern Bambara and Peuhl engage in farming and herding in the Sahel), but we deemed the security situation too precarious. Citing neglect from the southcentric state, the Tuareg had repeatedly rebelled to form their own state. Directly prior to our fieldwork, armed Malian-born Tuareg mercenaries had been returning home from fighting in Libya (following Muammar Gaddafi's fall), and grievances about the lack of public service provisions were bubbling up again to create a low-intensity secessionist movement (more on that later).

With the natural experiment literally blown away by the wind, we moved on to Step 2, our field experimental design.

HOW TO GIVE A RADIO (TO A WOMAN)

We identified a group of ten villages that received consistent ORTM but where people had not yet obtained radios. Because of potential for spill-over within a village, we decided to randomly assign treatment at the village level. Recruitment at the village level began with visits to the village chiefs (*dugutigis*) to pay customary respects (in the form of kola nuts) and obtain consent for the research team to enter. Within each village, we would hold a public lottery and randomly select extended family households (*dus*). However, we were a bit stuck when it came to the next part. Would we then randomly invite one person in each du to participate in the research and receive a radio (or flashlight)?

It might seem straightforward to most people—just give people radios or just give people flashlights. However, we anticipated that it would be tricky to give a radio to a woman and interview her about political opinions in this rural context. Indeed, women are often excluded from research in similar contexts because of the difficulty and expense. But we were committed to including women, both because we had theorized heterogeneous treatment effects by gender and because we are committed to making sure we afford women the same opportunities as men, even if it requires substantial effort. To find a solution, we knew it was absolutely essential to conduct qualitative work—focus groups and interviews—in out-of-sample villages to hone the entire research design. We did so closer to Bamako, where ORTM had been broadcast longer and many people had already obtained radios.

Elderly male patriarchs (*dutigis*) of the dus or other male family members often dominated the household radio. We heard stories of some dutigis carrying the batteries for the radio in their pocket so other household members couldn't "waste" the batteries. Furthermore, we were warned that dutigis may insist that opinions be collected from the dutigi, the public face of the family, who provides the opinions on behalf of the du. When dutigis consent to allowing a junior household member to give opinions, they may also hover and influence the opinions expressed.[2]

We asked the out-of-sample villagers, "How can we give radios so they won't be commandeered by the dutigi or other male family members?" First, the fact that we had solar, crank radios alleviated the concern about battery hoarding—radio use was "unlimited" due to the renewable energy, which is very important in nonelectrified villages. Second, we would definitely need to give a radio to the village chiefs, which could be used together with the dutigis in the "old men's lounge," a communal space where the dugutigi and dutigis spend large portions of the day communing. Third, participants suggested that the best strategy to ensure women's access was to give two radios (or flashlights) per du: one to a man and one to a woman. That way, there would be a device for men and a device for women, who often work separately due to gendered divisions of labor. If the dutigi disagreed with the random selection, we would simply replace the du with another du. The recipient of the device would have the "job" of maintaining the device on behalf of the family (in the case of the radio, to make sure it was charged by cranking it or leaving it in the sun). Finally, we would need to hire female enumerators to interview female respondents, and we would need to convince their families that the enumerators would be treated respectfully while traveling in a mixed-gender team.

This strategy worked amazingly well. Although it was challenging, we were able to recruit both female and male enumerators who could travel with our team. Being women ourselves undoubtedly aided in the confidence that the female enumerators would be properly and respectfully treated on the road. Dugutigis and dutigis were agreeable to the random selection. The public lottery for selecting dus (as well as the presence of white American women in the village) was somewhat of a spectacle for the dutigis. We welcomed this distraction, which quelled their desire to helicopter over our respondents and alleviated the need for enumerators to shoo them away. Finally, our follow-up research determined that the radios were by and large maintained by the randomly selected respondents.[3]

LADIES, PLEASE STOP COOKING

After a two-week training of a sprightly troop of novice enumerators, we finally hit the road to enumerate the baseline survey and deliver the radios and flashlights in the ten villages. We were camping in some of the most beautiful terrain in the world—red desert, clay villages with thatched roofs accessed by four-by-four, pirogue, and donkey cart. Without electrification this far into the desert, the stars in the sky were the brightest I'd ever seen. I had my tent, sleeping bag, headlamp, food bars, etc. My creature comfort is a hot shower, so I would take a bucket of hot water with a small scoop behind a village wall to "shower," using darkness as my privacy.

The days were long and hard for everyone, but exciting. Our enumerators got along fantastically. The enumerators seemed to feel empowered by doing the job, often the first formal money-making opportunity they'd ever had.

We were a bit like a big happy family on a road trip. Each night we would, per Malian style, eat with our enumerators from a common bowl in "eating teams." Each gender had a common bowl. The carbs—rice, couscous, or the like—would be spread throughout the bowl, and the good stuff (meat, vegetables, and sauce) was in the center. Eating was done with the right hand only, and this hand needed to stay in one's own area of the bowl. The person with the most status within each gender distributed the good stuff into your sector of the bowl for you to eat.

Yet these dinners became the source of controversy. We needed to bring in food supplies to every village to feed the team, and we hired village women to cook Malian cuisine. However, we found that our female enumerators kept cooking the food for the research team while the male enumerators took their leisure by playing soccer or relaxing.

As good feminists, we were very much against our female enumerators working a "second shift" and doing additional unpaid work. We protested day after day for them to stop cooking. However, day after day the ladies kept cooking, each time with a slightly different excuse.

LADIES: The village women here don't know how to cook properly, we are much better cooks and you must eat a tasty meal!

US: We will make sure to hire the best village women and we are fine if the meal is mediocre—you can't be cooking after working, you need your rest!

LADIES: The village women do not wash their hands, we will all get diarrhea!

US: We will provide them soap and instruct them to use it prior to the cooking. Please stop cooking, you need your rest!

LADIES: We were done early with work so we decided to cook, it doesn't bother us, don't worry!

US: You can't keep cooking like this. See, you all and the male enumerators are treated the same and paid the same and have the same expectations from us. We don't want you to cook. Please stop cooking!

We slowly came to understand why the female enumerators kept cooking. We knew that cooking was traditionally a woman's job in Mali. However, we did not realize the depth of power women held by cooking. Namely, men control scarce household financial resources, but women control scarce household food resources. Even though the men's common bowl might appear to have the same or better morsels than the women's bowl upon meal presentation, women could preemptively divert some good morsels to their mouths during the cooking process—a first-mover advantage known to any good cook. In this context, women did not want to give up their source of power (and extra food) to the village women.

WHAT? A COUP? AND AN INSURGENCY?

We left Mali, heading back to our respective universities, excited about the upcoming election and the idea that men and women with greater exposure to ORTM would have more political knowledge, more opinions, a larger plurality of opinions, greater national identity, and a host of other outcomes. We hired research assistants to keep a journal of what was said on the radio to hone our measurement of outcomes and sat back to watch the election events unfold.

One evening, I got a call from Jaimie. There had been a military coup in Mali. On March 21, 2012, low-ranking soldiers staged a coup, disgruntled by the inadequate arms and supplies they had to battle the northern insurgents. The first thing they did was take over ORTM and the state TV station, even before taking over the presidential palace. They additionally cited corruption of the *classe politique*, and overall poor performance in delivering public services to the people of Mali. A trio of insurgent groups—the secessionist National Movement for the Liberation of Azawad (MNLA), the Islamist hard-line group Ansar Dine, and the terrorist organization Al Qaeda of the Islamic Maghreb (AQIM)—capitalized on the political chaos and marched out to occupy the north and declare an independent state, with our study area ambiguously on the border of state and rebel controlled territory. The villages remained unoccupied by either side, but they were only twenty-five to fifty kilometers away from towns that the rebels and army held.

What to do? First and foremost, it was shocking and disturbing—people that we knew were facing additional hardship in a context in which life was already hard. Civil servants such as teachers fled south, tourism evaporated, travel to markets was stymied, and people were fearful.

Should we and could we continue the research? If we did, we would need to adapt the research to focus on the effect of putschist-controlled radio on attitudes toward the coup and the status of democracy as a whole. People had examined media effects under consolidated authoritarian regimes in the past. If we could collect some outcome data, it would be an important opportunity to understand media effects from a "long-term" media exposure with good causal identification directly in the wake of a transition. We decided, yes, we would put in any additional amount of effort necessary to try to collect some outcome data as long as it was safe and respectful for both enumerators and participants.

It was challenging and stressful to monitor the situation and ascertain whether and when it would be OK to recommence with research activities. After things had come to somewhat of a political standstill between the new junta and the insurgency, local people were able to safely move around the study area. We decided it was safe to collect outcome data in May and again in July. Jaimie held a training in Bamako, and her Malian-born husband, Drissa, accompanied the enumerators to the villages for enumeration. Knowing the villagers' food availability had declined, we "paid" respondents for participating in the final surveys by bringing in a cow for slaughter to each village, and enumerators distributed the meat to respondents and their families.

Our discoveries turned out to be professionally rewarding, resulting in multiple publications and visibility among colleagues.[4] However, the professional success of the project juxtaposed against the unfortunate circumstances for Malians often put me in an odd emotional space. Presenting the work at conferences and have audiences amped up about the "unique opportunity to conduct novel research" felt weird. Of course, both can be true—research can be interesting, and the object of study can be unfortunate. Nonetheless, I felt bad that some of our personal success was in any way related to unfortunate circumstances for our respondents and ordinary Malians as a whole. It is easy for others to view your data as data, but you know your data as real people facing real political events.

LESSONS FOR BUDDING FIELDWORKERS

These are just some of the many exstoriences from that fieldwork—an exstorience is a portmanteau joining the words "story" and "experience": a situation that is easier to tell as a story than to actually live through. The first takeaway lesson is that you will attract funding with Plan A, then quickly move to Plan B, to Plan C, to Plan D, sometimes even before arrival, eventually winding up on Plan X. This happens for lots of reasons, from wind to a military takeover of the regime. You will need to switch gears and sometimes couch your research in entirely different scholarship.

The second lesson is that you need to vet everything qualitatively in out-of-sample areas, especially experimental interventions that represent an intent to introduce change in a society. We felt ethically fine giving people solar crank (and thus sustainable) radios as an intervention—radios already existed in Mali and were considered desirable to own. However, even something as simple as giving a radio or a flashlight required a lot of qualitative research. Do not make the mistake of believing that your intervention or sampling strategy is obvious and needs no vetting.

Third, you will find yourself in conundrums where your own norms are challenged in diverse contexts, and it will take time to get to the bottom of these differences. There is no one answer here on what to do. Try to be gracious and work with people rather than steamrolling or waving away others' contentions because they conflict with your values.

Fourth, you need to carefully consider the safety of both participants and enumerators in your research, especially under difficult political conditions. You can't rely on the institutional review board (IRB) alone to make ethical calls. The IRB considers participant safety, but often they are unfortunately not familiar enough with your context and research to require a sufficiently high bar. Furthermore, even if the IRB is not looking out for enumerator safety, that doesn't mean you shouldn't be. Especially if your research occurs in difficult political contexts, it will be your responsibility to make good ethical calls with a commitment to never put enumerators or participants in harm's way.

Finally, other people will not understand the physical, mental, and emotional hoops you will jump through for your field research, often while simultaneously juggling "regular" job duties. Nonetheless, there is no amount of book reading you can do that replaces the number of insights and discoveries that are often gleaned through your exstoriences working directly with the actors you study.

——

Kristin Michelitch *is assistant professor of political science at Vanderbilt University.*

PUBLICATIONS TO WHICH THIS FIELDWORK CONTRIBUTED:

- Beck, Jaimie, and Kristin Michelitch. "Capturing the Airwaves, Capturing the Nation? A Field Experiment on State-Run Media Effects in the Wake of a Coup," *Journal of Politics* 79, no. 3 (2017): 873–89.
- ——. "The 2012 Crisis in Mali: Ongoing Empirical State Failure," *African Affairs* 114, no. 457 (2015): 598–623.
- ——. "Is Women's Empowerment Associated with Political Knowledge and Opinions? Evidence from Rural Mali," *World Development* 106 (June 2018): 299–323.

NOTES

1. Jaimie Bleck and Kristin Michelitch, "Capturing the Airwaves, Capturing the Nation? A Field Experiment on State-Run Media Effects in the Wake of a Coup," *Journal of Politics* 79, no. 3 (2017): 873–89.
2. In our *World Development* publication, we show that bystander presence during survey enumeration is more common for female respondents throughout sub-Saharan Africa.
3. Bleck and Michelitch, "Capturing the Airwaves."
4. Jaimie Bleck and Kristin Michelitch, "2012 Crisis in Mali: Ongoing Empirical State Failure," *African Affairs* 114, no. 457 (2015): 598–623; Jaimie Bleck and Kristin Michelitch, "Is Women's Empowerment Associated with Political Knowledge and Opinions? Evidence from Rural Mali," *World Development* 106 (June 2018): 299–323, https://doi.org/10.1016/j.worlddev.2018.01.006.

12

CROSSED WIRES

INTERVIEWING THE WRONG PEOPLE

BETHANY LACINA

▸ FIELDWORK LOCATION: INDIA

This is the story of the two times that I interviewed the wrong person. The first one I will blame on the phones. I had been interviewing members of the Indian parliament and other members of the Indian political elite.[1] It was going pretty well. I had quadrupled my consumption of milky tea and biscuits. I was filling up notepads with subjects' reminiscences and hot takes.

Begging for interviews was in some respects easier than I expected. MPs generally had not only their office phone numbers but also their home and mobile phone numbers on the parliamentary website. (The government of West Bengal took the opposite tack. The state government website did not list a single phone number, not even a general line.) Indian MPs also mostly answered their own phone, and always answered their own mobile.

My real problem was my fraught relationship with my mobile phone. There were all kinds of technical oddities. Numbers had to be dialed differently for cell phones, land lines, long-distance land lines, and long-distance cell phones. Properly dialed calls were frequently dropped. I found it difficult to hear over any connection. Any ambitions I had of making calls in Hindi were quickly abandoned. At the time, I had communicate-with-a-street-vendor fluency, mostly because street vendors are masters of nonverbal cues. But over the distortion of a phone line, I could barely understand things said to me in English let alone another language.

I came to dread the customary phone greeting. Nobody identified themselves or their office when picking up the phone. Instead, the speaker would offer "Hello" or "Namaskar" or sometimes just "Ji?" (yes?). When I got someone on the line, I would antagonize them for the first minute by shouting back and forth about whether we could hear each other. Then I would further antagonize the speaker by not being entirely certain with whom I was speaking. I eventually established a rhythm of how to ask whether I was speaking to such and such a person. But being transferred remained fraught.

ME: May I speak to Mr. Singh?
UNIDENTIFIED VOICE: Just a moment.
UNIDENTIFIED VOICE: Hello?

Had the transfer gone through? Was I still speaking to Mr. Singh's secretary or to the man himself? It had gone both ways for me. I had talked to secretaries in the inappropriate second person and to politicians in the inappropriate third person. It could be difficult to distinguish between a dropped call and a brush-off. One way to say "no" to a bothersome caller is to transfer the call like a hot potato between assistants and finally let the whole thing lapse. Was I getting the runaround, or was it just bad phones?

I had one near-catastrophe because of phone problems. I was trying to reach a retired general who worked at a think tank. Unbeknownst to me, this think tank also enjoyed the affiliation of an economist whose name differed from that of the general only in the final vowel. The economist's last name ended with the "ai" (as in "chai"). The good soldier's last name terminated in the "ay" (as in "Bombay").

I called the think tank, asked the secretary to connect me to Mr. Bombay, and then went through my request to set up an appointment. I congratulated myself on another interview landed, not realizing I had been connected to Mr. Chai. I should have been tipped off by his jolly remark that "I'm more of an economist myself, but I'll be happy to talk to you." I thought the general was being precious about his Renaissance man interests. Fortunately, I figured out the ai/ay gaff between the time I arrived at the office and the beginning of the interview.

I was not so lucky on the Sunday of my second case of mistaken identity. My interview that day was with a notorious man. Call him Mr. Morgan

Thomas Mitchell from constituency X. Mr. Mitchell had lost both his legs in an explosion when his old insurgent buddies tried to assassinate him. Such events raise questions that are difficult to phrase in a delicate manner: "So tell me about the time you broke with your coalition partners and restarted a civil war," or "How'd you get so good at bombing trains?"

We had originally planned to meet on Wednesday at the MP's office. Instead I met a secretary who told me to go to the MP's residence on the following Sunday. This put me in a pretty good mood. If Mr. Mitchell was important enough to have a secretary who screened his appointments, who knew what fascinating political facts he would have for me?

On the ill-fated Sunday, I made my way to the guest house maintained by Mr. Mitchell's home state. The same secretary showed me in and then sat down to take a phone call. I assured him that I knew I was a bit early and that I was happy to wait. I pulled out my newspaper. Then the secretary—who, to clarify, was not in a wheelchair and appeared to have had no amputations—said, "Well, shall we start?"

My mind raced: Is he going to do the interview for the MP? Is he the MP? How can that be? He is clearly not a double amputee. Is it possible that this is some kind of a con job; have I been lured into an interview with an impostor? And who would try to impersonate someone who did not have legs and not attend to that detail? Perhaps this is a kidnapping situation given that MP Mitchell was obviously involved with some intense people.

In short, I was totally flustered. In the best case scenario, this guy was the MP. I had been talking to him about "Mr. Mitchell" consistently for two meetings now. He must be wondering what could possibly be wrong with me. Also, I had prepared to interview someone whose military career had led to his opponents hiring his estranged supporters to blow him up. My questions were pretty specific to that sequence of events. Events that the man before me had evidently not experienced. After an excruciating hour or so, I stumbled back into the Delhi sunlight. I went home in a daze, wondering with almost idle curiosity what had just happened.

It turned out there was no blaming this case of mistaken identity on the phones. There were two parliamentarians from constituency X from the same party with rather similar names. One was Morgan Thomas Mitchell and the other was Thomas Morgan Mitchell. And, well, Mr. Thomas Morgan Mitchell was still recovering from the rather nasty attempt on his life.

Mr. Morgan Thomas Mitchell and I had just enjoyed some sweet tea, Ritz crackers, and a low-quality discussion of Indian federalism.

After all my anxiety over dropped phone calls, awkward greetings, and muffled names, I had gotten my wires crossed without the help of any technology. My mind had skimmed right past the difference between two MPs' names, and I had gone to interview the wrong one. Is there a lesson in all of this? Obviously, you should be more detail-oriented when it comes to names than I was. However, you should also aim to be as detail-oriented as I was when it came to the history and characteristics of my interviewees. Meeting with the wrong people was problematic and a bit awkward, but far worse mistakes would have occurred if I did not know they were not who I wanted to talk to when we met face-to-face. I could have asked embarrassing or insulting questions to my interviewees, or—even worse—I could have unknowingly included their responses in my work as if they were the correct people. That did not happen because I read up extensively on my interviewees before meeting them, which not only allows a researcher to ask sharper, more in-depth questions, but also to sniff out incorrect statements and, in my case, mistaken identities.

I suppose I never would have accidentally interviewed a civilian economist or a non-double-amputee if I had made all of my interview requests in person. That course of action also would have resolved my anxieties about India's phone system. After all, is it not a fieldwork rite of passage to go to people's offices and sit for weeks at a time, until the guru is finally willing to teach you? "Just show up" and "just keep waiting" must be two of the most common bits of fieldwork advice students receive.

Simply showing up is a tool that is becoming less and less useful. The sit-and-wait method exploits a couple of advantages that were more reliable in the past than they are now. First, just showing up is less useful in a world where more people have mobile technology and can be on the move throughout the workday. These tools make people schedule themselves more tightly and occupy time that might otherwise have been free. For example, in *Home Style*, Richard Fenno mentions that many useful conversations happened when he was riding in a car with a politician[2] because the respondent had nothing else to do. In a world of cellular data plans, Wi-Fi, laptops, and tablets, that kind of interview opportunity is gone.

Second, the sit-and-wait strategy trades on the novelty of having an academic or a foreigner around. Cultural globalization has done a lot to erode that novelty. American political scholars have found that fewer elites are willing to talk with political scientists as the number of requests grows exponentially. In other field sites as well, elite respondent fatigue is a real possibility. Most important, in the just-show-up method, the researcher is betting that he or she can loiter indefinitely without trouble. Development, bureaucratization, and worries about violence mean that more and more official places have security guards, guest passes, and other conditions that simply do not allow for loitering. Also, permission to loiter depends on a researcher's race, gender, and other identities. As field researchers become more diverse, loitering becomes a less universally useful strategy.

When I did my field research more than ten years ago, Indian MPs were on the cusp of becoming people who you needed to access through formal channels. Many of the places that they went on official business were closed to the public. They spent limited time at their offices because they did not need to be there. I probably could have adopted the just-show-up strategy and had about the same amount of success. I doubt that is true now.

At the planning stage of your fieldwork, consider the risk of low elite response rates even in countries that were very amenable to research a few decades ago. Remember that archives are an option when you are studying elites (see also chapter 17 by Lindsey O'Rourke for more on this topic). Using archives may mean switching your focus to less recent events, but the improvement in data quality may be worth it. Also, check the archives even if you are dealing with a government that is known for secrecy. Some of the things I found in India's archives were probably not supposed to be declassified but slipped through when parts of the bureaucracy were merged or moved offices.

Be on the lookout for anything that will strand people with nothing better to do than talk to you. I had some of my best interview days during power failures, floods, and general strikes. Hopefully, you will have a phone to play with while you wait, preferably one with a video chat option.

Bethany Lacina *is associate professor of political science at the University of Rochester.*

PUBLICATIONS TO WHICH THIS FIELDWORK CONTRIBUTED:

- Lacina, Bethany. *Rival Claims: Ethnic Violence and Territorial Autonomy Under Indian Federalism*. Ann Arbor: University of Michigan Press, 2017.
- ——. "How Governments Shape the Risk of Civil Violence: India's Federal Reorganization, 1950–56," *American Journal of Political Science* 58, no. 3 (2014): 720–38.
- ——. "India's Stabilizing Segment States," *Ethnopolitics* 13, no. 1 (2014): 13–27.

NOTES

1. Excellent pieces on interviewing political elites include Richard F. Fenno, "Observation, Context, and Sequence in the Study of Politics," *American Political Science Review* 80, no. 1 (March 1986): 3–15, https://doi.org/10.2307/1957081; Sharon Werning Rivera, Polina M. Kozyreva, and Eduard G. Sarovskii, "Interviewing Political Elites: Lessons from Russia," *PS: Political Science & Politics* 35, no. 4 (December 2002): 683–88, https://doi.org/10.1017/S1049096502001178; and appendix of *Peaceland: Conflict Resolution and the Everyday Politics of International Intervention*, by Séverine Autesserre (Cambridge: Cambridge University Press, 2014).

2. Richard F. Fenno, *Home Style: House Members in Their Districts* (New York: Little, Brown, 1978).

13

"YOU DON'T KNOW WHAT YOU'RE GETTING INTO"

DEALING WITH DISHONESTY IN THE FIELD

MATTHEW FRANKLIN CANCIAN AND KRISTIN E. FABBE

▸ FIELDWORK LOCATION: IRAQ

"You don't know what you're getting into; or who you're getting into it with!" the recently fired survey team leader yelled as Matthew walked back to his car. Interpersonal conflict is never enjoyable, but it can be especially uncomfortable in a foreign conflict zone. This fight occurred underneath the barrel of an (unmanned) armored reconnaissance vehicle in the Kurdistan region of Iraq in 2017 as we were conducting a survey of Kurdish fighters (called *peshmerga*, meaning "those who face death" in Kurdish) and their attitudes toward outgroups. Outright violence was unlikely, but tensions were certainly high as both of our cars exited the peshmerga's base, with the fired team's car behind Matthew's. Matthew let out a huge sigh of relief when they turned in another direction instead of following his car out into the Iraqi desert.

Why did we have to fire Team Four and create this tension? Although Team Four (one of four teams working on our project) had been submitting the requisite number of electronic surveys during their first week of enumeration, the metadata provided by Qualtrics, the survey software we were using, indicated that about half of the surveys, which were designed to take thirty minutes, had been completed by this team in under five minutes. Judging from the time stamps on each survey, it seemed that the team was doing legitimate surveys in the morning, but then two of the team members were rapidly clicking through surveys in the afternoon, faking plausible answers to make the agreed quota without doing the hard work of interviewing soldiers.

Kristin had recently departed to neighboring Turkey to work on a separate project, so I (Matthew) was trying to monitor all four teams on my own, dropping in randomly and unannounced to verify the work they were doing. Kristin was monitoring remotely, watching surveys come in via the Qualtrics software in real time, but she could not be in front of the computer all the time. I was only one person and couldn't be everywhere all the time. Therefore, we had been careful to institute a number of safeguards against enumerator deception, and we felt confident that we had found a real case of cheating with Team Four. For example, each of the four team leaders was required to submit a photo of himself arriving and leaving the work sites every day. The reticence of Team Four's leader to do so was a hint that something was amiss. Each team was also required to submit their location via WhatsApp. Assuming that their research site was in an area with cell phone coverage (which they usually were despite the ongoing war), we could confirm that they were traveling to their assigned military bases. I was living at a hotel in the central part of the research area, and these WhatsApp pin drops enabled me to visit a random site every day, unannounced, to ensure that the work was proceeding as reported. We had noticed that the wayward team went back to the same base every day for the first four days, whereas the other teams were constantly moving to new locations as assigned. On a lengthy phone discussion reaching into the wee hours of the morning (one of many that summer), Kristin and I discussed the evidence and decided that Team Four had to be fired.

The hard work, however, fell on my shoulders. Although I had visited the other three teams in the first days of monitoring the project, it was now time to visit Team Four, whom we had identified as survey scammers, and confront them.

Enumerating surveys is hard work wherever it is done: you have to approach strangers, convince them to spend their time with you, and then ask potentially intrusive questions. None of our enumerators had themselves been peshmerga fighters. Furthermore, there was an ongoing war between the Kurds and the Islamic State of Iraq and Syria (ISIS), which made for a tense political environment. Beyond the political and social challenges, the brutal Iraqi summer often pushed daytime temperatures over 110 degrees. On one day in Sinjar, the thermometer peaked at 122 degrees. If they were lucky, the enumerators would be able to conduct their work in an air-conditioned room in a base headquarters building. Often, however, they had to settle for a shady patch of dirt in a rudimentary outpost somewhere on the base. It was understandable that some of the enumerators would succumb to the temptation to fake surveys.

On the way to confront Team Four, I explained to my driver that I was going to fire the team. The driver, himself a retired peshmerga, suggested that I say there was some technical difficulty with the survey and that the whole thing was being shut down. Kristin and I had discussed taking this less-than-honest route on our phone call the night before, but we had decided that this particular part of Iraq was too small and that we would probably get caught fibbing. What if someone from Team Four knew someone from Team One? We couldn't be sure, and we didn't want to get caught lying. So I dismissed my driver's suggestion and decided to confront the team with the knowledge of their misdeeds. The driver's advice, however, turned out to be sage.

I finally located Team Four around noon, and they were just finishing their two hours of legitimate surveys. As the peshmerga they had been interviewing left, I initiated the difficult conversation. As soon as I asked Team Four how long they thought a survey *should take*, they realized that the jig was up. Instead of taking the discovery in stride, however, the team leader got angry and began yelling. I had not anticipated a confrontation and had to make a snap decision; I decided to ask calmly to see all the tablets to verify the number of surveys that had been done. Once all the tablets were physically in hand, I told the team that they were fired. It was at this point, as both parties walked back to their cars, that the leader of Team Four yelled out the threat that began this chapter.

On the drive back to the hotel, I received a conciliatory phone call from Hiwa, one of the team members. Several hours later, Kristin received a call and an email from the angry team leader himself, who tried to blame the episode on me. Kristin didn't buy it. First, she trusted me—as it turns out, working long hours in a war zone will make you fast friends. Second, having seen the evidence of cheating for herself, she knew that the leader of Team Four was now resorting to a futile strategy of trying to drive a wedge between us. That was not going to work. She decided to ignore further emails and phone calls for the time being. Then, in yet another late-night phone call, we discussed the incident, deciding that we needed a real strategy for mending the rift. The leader of Team Four was obviously immature and dishonest, but he was also politically connected, and we were concerned. The conciliatory phone call from Hiwa provided an opportunity.

We arranged a meeting for several days hence, when Hiwa and I would both be in Erbil. In the meantime, Team Four's leader had made a more explicit threat over email about what would happen if the wages for the "work" they had already done were not paid. On the day of the meeting, Hiwa proposed that he and I meet under the auspices of a relative of a prominent Kurdish politician, Sherif, at a popular hookah bar.

When I arrived at the bar, Sherif and Hiwa were seated in the company of two female students from a local university. "Which one of them is cuter?" Hiwa asked me, gesturing to the girls (who also spoke English). I decided to dissimulate. "They are both sweet in their own way, like apples and oranges." I was trying to dodge the question without offending anyone. This received an approving laugh from Sherif, who then told Hiwa and me to retire to deal with our business at a separate table, alone.

What was going on? Clearly bringing along Sherif to the meeting was a signal of power, but its strength was ambiguous. Were Hiwa and Sherif just drinking friends, or was this a legitimate node of influence that Hiwa could use if we didn't make amends with Team Four? We had mooted the idea of not paying the team anything on a phone call prior to the meet-up. We decided it would be better to play it safe and conciliate them, offering to pay for the legitimate surveys rather than playing hardball. Refusing to pay at all would have risked further infuriating Team Four's leader and alienating Hiwa, who seemed to be trying to make nice. We reasoned that playing hardball would probably lead to a battle of influence between the academics and the renegade team. For example, there would have been a competition between us to reach decision makers within the peshmerga to stymie or allow the research to proceed. We wanted to conduct our research, not waste time waging a feud. So in the corner of a Kurdish hookah bar, I and Hiwa exchanged conciliatory words and some cash.

Then came a twist that I really wasn't expecting: Hiwa offered to continue the research together with the two other team members who had not forged surveys. Was there a legitimate rift within Team Four, where the left hand didn't know what the right was doing? Furthermore, why did they want to continue doing the research? As it was an economically trying time, perhaps they needed the money. However, we believed they had been instructed by someone to keep an eye on us foreigners and to make a report. In Iraq, like many other countries in the region, there is a strong informant culture, and one is never quite sure who is making reports to whom.[1] Were they working for one of the political groups that had sanctioned our research, just to ensure that we were doing what we said we would? Or were they working for a foreign group, believing that we worked for the American government? Or were they simply cash-strapped students who wanted another chance after they had dropped the ball the first time?

Whatever the case, recalling the driver's wise words, I told Hiwa I would call them if we decided to continue working in their province. Of course, we would continue, but I decided to equivocate. When I returned to Sherif, Apple, and Orange, Sherif greeted the news of the deal well. The next day, Kristin received a conciliatory email from the former leader of Team Four. We had lost some money and some time, but a major crisis was averted.

Within a few days, things were getting back on track. Our main local partner, who had recruited the other three survey teams but not this one, agreed to raise a new team in the now unmanned province. The new team leader was named Jihad; although it is a common name, it is a word that conjures negative associations for many Westerners. In contrast to the less sensationally named members of Team Four, however, Jihad was as honest as the sun was hot in an Iraqi summer. Moreover, he was an energetic and serious scholar who pushed his team to do an excellent job catching up, and the survey wound up being a success.

A few conclusions are in order, first, about avoiding survey falsification and, second, about how to navigate foreign power structures. Even in difficult conflict zones, many legitimate local scholars want to do good research and take pride in their work. We know many! But one can never be too cautious when it comes to survey monitoring, regardless of location.[2] A host of electronic tools exist now to help verify enumerator compliance that did not exist even five years ago; we used Qualtrics and WhatsApp, but the options for researchers will surely multiply.[3] Every researcher who wants to run a survey successfully should consider using tools like these if possible. It also is good practice for researchers to describe the safeguards they employed in any articles they write. Beyond that, however, there really is no substitute for physically visiting and monitoring a survey site unannounced. Showing up, seeing Team Four's legitimate morning interviews, and then watching the peshmerga leave for the day ultimately confirmed what was happening with the wayward team beyond reasonable doubt. Have a stress-management plan (that doesn't involve alcohol) in place if you have to do the uncomfortable work of firing people who both need the money and could harm you. Although my experience as a Marine had toughened me up a little, I still took a few days off to relax with friends in the mountains following the Team Four showdown.

Second, it is often hard to predict who will be the most reliable partners. The Western-educated leader of Team Four turned out to be duplicitous, whereas Jihad was someone we could trust with our lives. To this day, we don't know what to make of Sherif's presence at our final peace conference with Team Four; maybe it was a tacit threat as we feared, but Occam's Razor would argue that the meeting could just be coincidental. These interactions aren't just about logistics; with reflection, they can inform your research.[4] Further illustrating the problems of identifying the ranks and roles of individuals, formal permission from the government was all we needed in some areas, but that counted for little in other areas; a call from an acquaintance cleared us through a check point when a letter from the minister of peshmerga affairs failed. In summary, researchers in conflict zones need to keep an open mind about everyone they meet—an open mind that the person could be an ally or an obstacle.

––––––

Matthew Franklin Cancian *is a PhD candidate in political science at MIT.*
Kristin E. Fabbe *is an assistant professor at Harvard Business School.*

PUBLICATION TO WHICH THIS FIELDWORK CONTRIBUTED:

- Cancian, Matthew Franklin, and Kristin E. Fabbe, "Empathetic Enemies: Victimized Combatants and the Politics of Revenge and Forgiveness" (work in progress).

NOTES

1. See, for instance, Wendy Pearlman, "Narratives of Fear in Syria," *Perspectives on Politics* 14, no. 1 (March 2016): 21–37.

2. Blaydes and Gullim point out special difficulties posed by religion in surveys in the Arab world, whereas Benstead argues that the problem is generalized: Lisa Blaydes and Rachel M. Gillum, "Religiosity-of-Interviewer Effects: Assessing the Impact of Veiled Enumerators on Survey Response in Egypt," *Politics and Religion* 6, no. 3 (September 2013): 459–82; Lindsay J. Benstead, "Survey Research in the Arab World: Challenges and Opportunities," *PS: Political Science & Politics* 51, no. 3 (July 2018): 535–42, https://doi.org/10.1017/S1049096518000112.

3. For more on electronic surveying, see Lindsay J. Benstead, Kristen Kao, Pierre F. Landry, Ellen M. Lust, and Dhafer Malouche, "Using Tablet Computers to Implement Surveys in Challenging Environments," *Survey Practice* 10, no. 2 (March 2017): 2781, https://doi.org/10.29115/SP-2017-0009.

4. See Sam D. Sieber, "The Integration of Fieldwork and Survey Methods," *American Journal of Sociology* 78, no. 6 (May 1973): 1335–59, https://doi.org/10.1086/225467.

14

SUCCESSFUL FIELDWORK FOR THE FIELDWORK-HATER

AMELIA HOOVER GREEN

▶ FIELDWORK LOCATION: EL SALVADOR

I got nothing, zero, no research whatsoever done on my first trip to El Salvador. I had hoped to achieve fluency in Spanish, settle into an apartment, and start doing interviews with ex-combatants from that country's civil war (1980–1992). I had planned to spend six months in El Salvador, followed by six months in Sierra Leone. Instead, I found myself struggling to get out of bed. After six weeks of immersion in Spanish, public transit logistics, and self-loathing, I came home convinced that I would have to give back my grant money and drop out of graduate school. I hated fieldwork.

Almost a year later I went back to El Salvador. I completed more than forty interviews in less than a month. I got great material. I still hated fieldwork. I never made it to Sierra Leone.

In this chapter, I provide a comparative reflection on those first two trips, now both nearly a decade in the past. If this were a piece of positivist research, I'd have to report a nonfinding: my hatred of fieldwork did not vary and, therefore, can't explain why my 2009 trip succeeded whereas my 2008 trip failed. But hating fieldwork did affect nearly everything about my research, from sampling, to methods, to ethical calculations—although I don't mention hating fieldwork in the resulting publications. My 2008 and 2009 trips illustrate what it means to hate fieldwork, how I succeeded despite hating it (and why I felt I had to), and some ways that hating fieldwork changed my research. There are some questions and field locales where it's possible to hate fieldwork and still succeed. Whether one (and by "one" I mean "I") *should* still do fieldwork is a different question.

TWO EXPERIENCES OF HATING FIELDWORK

Ten years ago, on my twenty-seventh birthday, I lay in bed with yet another fever-and-sore-throat, trying to rouse myself to go celebrate. As usual in the evenings, I was alone in my stuffy little room, staring fixedly at my laptop, where—also as usual—ESPN.com was failing to load the Twins highlights. As I remember it, I sat up and croaked with quiet melodrama: "I hate this." I smooshed a couple of lanes of the ant highway on my windowsill, flicked off the fluorescent ring light, lay back down, and considered skipping my own party.

I'd been in San Salvador for about a month at that point. My Spanish, already passable, was improving; my hosts were kind and interesting; I was nurturing new friendships among my classmates at the Frente Farabundo Martí para la Liberación Nacional (FMLN)-affiliated Center for Exchange and Solidarity ("el CIS"). Each week I made my way to more and more of the places I'd been trying to visualize for two years: the chapel where Archbishop Oscar Romero was martyred; the Ministry of Defense; the cathedral; El Playón, where death squads dumped their victims; and the Universidad Centroamericana (UCA), site of the 1989 Jesuit massacre. I took hundreds of pictures and jotted dozens of pages of notes, playing the part of the intrepid researcher.

I was, all the same, utterly miserable and entirely unproductive. Every day I contemplated the list of people I should call about interviews and found some reason not to pick up the phone. The notes I took were mostly meaningless. I made vague noises about "working" and shut myself in my room for hours on end, knowing that I should do something different but unable to figure out what. Nothing I did felt easy or right or hopeful. None of my clothes fit because I'd lost too much weight. I obsessed over my changing body, sometimes inordinately delighted by the continued weight loss and sometimes fully convinced that my clothes didn't fit because I was *gaining* weight. I hadn't received any eating disorder treatment for a year, and suddenly my whole brain was a sea of red flags.

Later that birthday evening, having dutifully arrived at a bar, drunk exactly one Pilsener with CIS pals, and taxied home to my tiny turquoise bedroom to weep and read Stephen King, I wrote in my journal:

I am a motherfucking grown-up!
I don't have to do things I hate!

I felt calmer after reminding myself that I could let myself out of my self-made trap. I began to consider that I could, and perhaps should, leave the field (in both senses). I should leave El Salvador if I was miserable and not really working; I should leave political science if I couldn't hack fieldwork. In a long string of emails, I told my dissertation supervisor everything, expecting and accepting that this was the end of my fledgling career. She told me to come home and not make any rash decisions.

Ten months later I was back. At some point, I handed the now extremely grubby and tattered list of interview contacts off to Erika Murcia, a Salvadoran CIS friend who had become my research assistant, fixer, translator, and general savior. Erika made the phone calls I dreaded (that is, all the phone calls). I installed myself in a hostel that had air conditioning and hot water, within walking distance of a rich-people mall with sub-Arctic climate control, fancy coffee, and an English-language bookstore. Usually a taxi picked me up from the fancy hostel at 8 A.M.

Nearly every day, nearly all day, I listened to ex-combatants' experiences. I did not ask about violence against civilians because I assumed I would get few honest answers, but many Salvadoran ex-combatants seemed eager to get their secrets out under the promise of confidentiality. Consequently I heard a shocking amount about the cruelty and banality of war. It rained hard most afternoons, so I got used to listening to answers shouted over the sound of a deluge on a tin roof. Interviews began to fall into organized patterns, some of which actually matched my theoretical priors. The clothes I'd brought to San Salvador became lightly but ineradicably mildewed.

In the evenings, exhausted, I'd crank up the air conditioning, plop down on my bed, and eat saltines for dinner while audio files transferred from my digital voice recorder to my computer. After chatting briefly with my partner or my mom, I'd leaf through the day's interview notes and lock the pages away, dutifully complying with the protocols approved by my university's institutional review board (IRB). I was usually asleep by 8:30 P.M. When I got sick, I had my very own tiny bathroom with a cool, bleach-smelling tile floor. On one sick day, I realized that I felt like I was catching a break. A rather detached-sounding internal voice noted, *apparently I'd rather have uncontrollable diarrhea than do this job.* I still hated fieldwork. It was confusing because I was *succeeding* at fieldwork.

For years after those first two trips, I knew that I hated fieldwork and frequently declared that I hated fieldwork, without fully understanding what that meant. It certainly doesn't mean anything objective; it's not the sum total of physical discomfort, illness, bad weather, terrifying traffic, crime, language barriers, and troubling revelations. It isn't necessarily even related to being good or bad at fieldwork. It's also not quite the same as experiencing poor mental health while in the field, either—although I'd be the first to admit that the two are related in my case.[1]

Looking back at the worst of the worst times, the most ragged and splotchy of the journal entries from each trip, I've decided that, for me, the defining feature of fieldwork-hatred is needing to force myself to do everything, from oozing out of bed in the morning to locking up my notebook pages at night. This brings on a sort of existential exhaustion that neither sleep nor buckets of coffee can cure. (I tried both.) Forcing it also implies faking it, constantly. I was faking when I ordered my coffee in the morning, faking when I chatted with taxi drivers—and, I think, sometimes faking my interest and empathy with interview respondents.

DOING IT ANYWAY

At this point a reasonable reader might ask why I went back to El Salvador a second time, let alone all the other times since. Other readers, particularly those in the middle of their own dissertation research, may understand immediately. The structure of (U.S.) PhD training in political science is one reason someone might *need* to do fieldwork despite hating it. Machismo is another. In my graduate program, it seemed impossible to be a "good comparativist" without a stock of fieldwork adventure stories, whether the adventures served the ostensible purpose of the trip or not. Sometimes, though, fieldwork is really and truly necessary. I wanted to learn about the experiences of low-level combatants in the Salvadoran

Civil War, and I wanted to learn about these experiences in great detail. I could not do the project without some qualitative interviews.

But how is a newbie researcher to tell the difference between necessity, on one hand, and machismo or mere convention, on the other? Compliance with machismo and convention had been an utter disaster, but my questions demanded at least some time in the field. Finally, I realized that I was doing semistructured interviews with strict protocols to protect confidentiality, a procedure that already limits reinterviews. This was not ethnography; it didn't need to be ethnography. My dissertation advisor's rightly classic book on Salvadoran insurgency relied on long-term ethnographic research.[2] Without realizing it, I had been working from the assumption that I should literally follow in her footsteps. But I didn't have to do so.

Realizing I wouldn't be an ethnographer meant I could think of my interviews as part of an empirical strategy designed to measure, carefully, a particular set of outcomes—rather than as an attempt to understand the full range of respondents' experiences as fighters. Of course, I relied on some ethnographic principles in collecting and analyzing interview data. My sense of my own positionality, and my awareness of the stakes involved in recounting one's memories of such a critical period to a white American woman from a fancy university, fundamentally shaped the final analysis. But I was free, at least analytically, to conduct interviews that asked directly and primarily about respondents' experiences of the institutions I was interested in: recruitment, military training, political education, and disciplinary procedures. My interviews, and my visits to El Salvador, became shorter and more efficient.

Having abandoned the idea of long-term, immersive, ethnographic fieldwork, I scheduled several short trips, with breaks in between. Looking back at the first, failed trip, I thought concretely about specific things I hated: being too hot to sleep at night, mosquito bites, not being able to hang out on the internet, cold-calling for interviews, figuring out public transit, not having my own bathroom, my mediocre Spanish. On my return trips, I stayed in the aforementioned air-conditioned room with a private bath, ate breakfast at the bakery across the street, outsourced phone calls to Erika, hired her to translate when necessary, and drove around in taxis every day. Your mileage may vary, as they say. But on this trip and others, I found that my budget evened out: per-day expenses were much greater, but I accomplished a lot more each day. The way I have talked about these decisions in the years since is to "prioritize what gets you through the day."

Necessity is the mother of invention, and the necessity I experienced pushed me to consider nonfieldwork information sources about combatant experiences in the Salvadoran Civil War, two in particular. First, I worried that some potential interviewees, particularly those with less formal education, might be put off by an in-depth interview (perhaps especially with me). I commissioned Erika to administer a structured questionnaire in veterans' service offices around the country during the fall of 2009. Erika collected 260 responses from all over the country; I never left home. Second, I realized rather belatedly that many of the Salvadorans living in the United States were ex-combatants. At the time, I was living in San Francisco, a center of the sanctuary movement—yet I hadn't spoken with any of the thousands of Salvadorans there, owing to my previous myopic focus on having an "authentic fieldwork experience." I began seeking interviews at home. Ultimately, I interviewed more than one hundred Salvadoran ex-combatants, as I had initially hoped, about a quarter of them in the Bay Area.

I finally decided not to travel to Sierra Leone, both because I judged that I could write a good dissertation on the basis of subnational variation in El Salvador alone and because I worried that I'd be too miserable to function in Sierra Leone. In the end, the dissertation confined my interest in the Mano River wars to a short chapter where I breezily discussed a host of extension cases. In my 2018 book, I similarly focused on El Salvador—but I fleshed out the Sierra Leonean and Liberian cases in a long chapter. Here I relied extensively on other people's fieldwork and, as with the Salvadoran case, on existing quantitative data on violence. Would fieldwork have yielded better, or at least more detailed, results? Probably. Was it possible for me to do that fieldwork? Probably not.

THE METHODS, AND ETHICS, OF HATING FIELDWORK

Some of the methodological implications of fieldwork-hating are already clear, particularly the push toward triangulation and my deep reliance on a brilliant and tenacious research partner. Others surprised me. For example, I was a young, white, American woman who smiled a lot and didn't speak fluent Spanish—a credulous-looking person. Rightly or wrongly, I occasionally used my identity and appearance to create an impression of harmlessness as a way of gaining access. In the new, nonethnographic era, however, I quickly realized that I needed to balance the impression of naïveté I created by signaling that I knew a lot and would be difficult to bullshit.[3] This I did by listening for locations, unit designations, and other specifics in the introductory section of the interview, and then name-dropping key events or people that were likely to be relevant. This produced more specific answers and avoided the usual recitation of pablum that frequently interviewed ex-combatants tend to deploy with inexperienced researchers.

It does not feel good to hate such a big part of one's job. It feels even worse to consider that hating a big part of one's job may lead, or may have led, to unethical research practices. But I'm writing about hatred; hatred has inescapable ethical stakes. First, doing research that is likely to get the right answer, as opposed to research that merely accomplishes the doing of research, is an ethical imperative. In nearly any research-ethics framework, but particularly in the framework that informs human subjects research at U.S. universities, this is so because beneficence requires that we balance the potential harms of research against the putative benefits.[4] If the benefits are illusory because the research is incorrect, no balance is possible. To whatever extent my accommodations to fieldwork-hatred lowered the quality of my findings, or transformed fieldwork into mere hoop-jumping, that is an ethical failing. I have thought a lot about this, and I feel mostly confident that my results are not based on errors introduced by fieldwork-hatred, or on systematic errors more generally.

A second ethical quandary looms larger for me. I believe researchers who depend on people's expertise and do not pay for respondents' time have an ethical obligation to provide some benefit to those people, not just to the world at large in the form of increased knowledge. The best researchers that I know form lasting relationships at their field sites, returning again and again and providing support to individuals and community organizations via their work and resources. Both by design and because my visits were so brief, I don't remember most of my interview respondents' names. More important, and more relevant to the discussion of hating fieldwork, it is not clear to me that my work in El Salvador provided any sort of net benefit to any of the people or communities with whom I formed temporary relationships. I was careful to provide resources short of payment; I expressed respect and consideration. And I believe I did no significant harm.[5]

I did, however, ask people to tell me about critical moments in their lives. And sometimes, when I was hearing about critical moments in a respondent's life, I was thinking about how soon I could possibly take a nap. I suspect that this is sometimes true for everyone who does fieldwork; no one is superhuman. At the same time, those of us who hate fieldwork run a higher risk of "faking it" in the wrong moment. That risk is compounded, in my view, by the fact that fieldwork-haters are less likely to reinterview, and less likely to stay connected over time. It's an uneasy thing to acknowledge.

Will I ever do fieldwork again? This is what I've been asking myself since my last visit to El Salvador in 2015. I have yet to come to any firm conclusions. Increasingly, I find myself drawn to work that I can do (mostly) from the comfort and safety of home: big data sets, methodological work, and so on. I also have a broader network of colleagues than I did in graduate school, many of whom love fieldwork. I can imagine collaborating with these folks on future projects to minimize field time (and to minimize people in the field having to put up with a fieldwork-hater). I believe, on balance, that my research will benefit the people and communities who helped me during my visits to El Salvador. I'm still not sure I will go back.

I'm not sure my experiences should be instructive. But for those seeking instruction, here are the key points:

- Even fieldwork-haters can do effective fieldwork. Not all excellent fieldwork is ethnography.
- Prioritize what gets you through the day. Be honest about what you need, and even about what you want. Get plenty of rest.
- Consider the methodological and ethical implications of your fieldwork-hatred. Hating fieldwork doesn't necessarily imply ethically or analytically dubious research, but it does imply some extra responsibilities.
- Almost everyone feels pressure to like fieldwork. Not everyone actually does. You are not alone. Find colleagues and friends with whom you can be honest. You can do this.

Amelia Hoover Green *is associate professor of politics at Drexel University.*

PUBLICATIONS TO WHICH THIS FIELDWORK CONTRIBUTED:

- Hoover Green, Amelia. "The Commander's Dilemma: Creating and Controlling Armed Group Violence Against Civilians," *Journal of Peace Research* 53, no. 5 (2016): 619–32.
- ——. "Armed Group Institutions, Combatant Socialization and Violence Against Civilians: Evidence from El Salvador," *Journal of Peace Research* 54, no. 5 (2017): 687–700.
- ——. *The Commander's Dilemma: Violence and Restraint in War.* Ithaca, NY: Cornell University Press, 2018.

NOTES

1. I've written about mental health and the academy more generally; see Amelia Hoover Green, "Academia, Mental Health, and the Cult of Productivity," *Duck of Minerva* (blog), April 28, 2017, http://duckofminerva.com/2017/04/30702.html.
2. Elisabeth Wood, *Insurgent Collective Action and Civil War in El Salvador* (Cambridge: Cambridge University Press, 2003).
3. This falls under the category of "strategic positionality," compare with Victoria Reyes, "Ethnographic Toolkit: Strategic Positionality and Researchers' Visible and Invisible Tools in Field Research," *Ethnography* (October 2018), https://journals.sagepub.com/doi/abs/10.1177/1466138118805121.
4. Department of Health and Human Services, "Belmont Report: Ethical Principles and Guidelines for the Protection of Human Subjects of Research," 1979, https://www.hhs.gov/ohrp/regulations-and-policy/belmont-report/index.html.
5. But, on the (in)sufficiency of "do no harm," see Catriona Mackenzie, Christopher McDowell, and Eileen Pittaway, "Beyond 'Do No Harm': The Challenge of Constructing Ethical Relationships in Refugee Research," *Journal of Refugee Studies* 20, no. 2 (June 2007): 299–319, https://doi.org/10.1093/jrs/fem008.

IV

CREATIVELY
COLLECTING
DATA AND
EVIDENCE

15

HOW TO INTERVIEW A TERRORIST

JESSICA STERN

▸ FIELDWORK LOCATIONS: SOUTH ASIA, THE NETHERLANDS

I confess at the outset that I was not trained to interview terrorists nor, indeed, to interview anyone. My doctorate is in public policy, and the research methods part of our curriculum included econometrics and statistics, not ethnographic interview techniques. No doubt there were elective courses I could have taken had I known the direction my curiosity would take me, but I did not.

I started out doing what I was trained to do—policy analysis of national security issues. After some time in government, I received a fellowship to write a book on terrorism with chemical, biological, radiological, or nuclear weapons (or CBRN, the then-fashionable term). Even if I had wanted to do the kind of quantitative analysis I was trained to do, the terrorism data available to researchers in the 1990s were notoriously bad. The focus was almost exclusively on transnational terrorist incidents, and the variables were limited to the name of the group, its claimed ideology, the choice of weapon and target, and the numbers injured or killed. I felt compelled to understand entirely different issues from the sort that might be illuminated by the existing data. I wanted to know *why*. . . . Why did terrorists want to kill people with these weapons? Why, more fundamentally, did individuals want to become terrorists? A novel idea came into my head. If I wanted to explain terrorists' motivations, why not simply ask them?

In doing this, I was following my curiosity, not my training. There were very few scholars working on terrorism at that time, and it was difficult to find a mentor. I had to teach myself on the job.[1] I started out with interviews of American neo-Nazis who had acquired chemical or biological agents. People would ask me, "How did you find these people?" I found them in entirely haphazard ways, and it sometimes took a long time. To find Americans, I would often start by looking them up in the phone book. Sometimes I would start through people who knew the perpetrator: a neighbor, a person quoted in the media, or the local police. Often, it takes months to arrange an interview. (It took me four years to get access to the man I'm currently writing about.) In Gaza, I was staying with a doctor, who knew the doctor who was then leading Hamas. In Pakistan, I happened to meet a young reporter working for a pro-jihadi newspaper who introduced me to his contacts. That man became my guide, although he didn't always accompany me.

People also ask, "How do you get them to talk?" What I quickly discovered was that getting them to *stop* talking was often the larger challenge. I learned that terrorists relished the chance to talk to a woman who is eager to listen. I was genuinely and insatiably curious about their motivations—a state of mind that cannot be faked. Despite my lack of training, I felt my way into an interview technique that has seemed to work. I will try to describe it here.

LESSON 1: GENDER MATTERS

First, I believe it helps to be a woman. I was seen as less threatening, as a person who required solicitousness. In addition, many men love to talk about themselves, especially to women. This is especially true for lonely men, as the neo-Nazis often were. But this desire to talk about themselves was also true for religious conservatives in South Asia and the Middle East.

When among religious militants, I covered my hair and most of my body. But I need to clarify this woman thing. I cannot say they saw me exactly as a woman, nor did they see me as a man. Despite my ambiguous gender, their perception of my vulnerability was a great benefit (and perhaps, ironically, may have kept me safe). For example, I had been trying to interview Fazlur Rahman Khalil, the leader of the Pakistani jihadi group Harkat ul Mujahideen, for more than a year by the time I finally met him in 2000. He was a friend of bin Laden's, and a signatory of bin Laden's 1998 fatwa ordering attacks against America. Harkat members' numbers were found on the phone used by bin Laden's trusted courier after bin Laden was killed by U.S. military personnel in 2011.

I had asked my guide to arrange this interview for me. It took him a while. I suspect that it was a question of whether Pakistan's intelligence agency, the ISI, wanted him to meet me. I went to the interview alone. We met at one of the group's offices in Islamabad. Khalil went through a series of statements at the start of the interview that I could have written myself. "The group had no camps in Afghanistan. If Afghanistan shut down the training camps, that would have been a very good thing, if such camps had existed. The group had no relationship with the ISI." I assumed he said this because he feared we were being recorded. Khalil spoke as if at a press conference, as many terrorist leaders do on first meeting. Eventually, we got through these well-rehearsed lies and were able to turn to topics about which he had less incentive to deceive me. It came into my mind to ask "Are you married?," a question for which he was clearly unprepared. He smiled. He told me he had just taken a second wife. She was in their home, nearby. Without thinking, I asked if I could meet her. Suddenly, in his eyes, I became a woman, or at least, more woman than man. I believe he surprised both of us when he said yes. He certainly surprised his guards. Soon after this, I was taken to his home, an enormous mansion. There I discovered that he had met his young wife in Saudi Arabia, where he frequently traveled to raise funds for the jihad. This visit would not have been possible were I a man. One of Khalil's former followers would tell me, shortly after this, that he had left Harkat, not so much because of changes in his thinking but because he realized that Khalil and the other leaders were making money off the naïveté of their followers. Khalil's mansion, and his taking on a second wife, were evidence of his business acumen.

LESSON 2: LISTEN CLOSELY TO EVERYTHING, NOT JUST ANSWERS TO YOUR PLANNED QUESTIONS

Second, listen closely to everything you hear—not just the information you're seeking. Before the 9/11 attacks, it was possible for Americans to meet with all kinds of terrorists, even the jihadis who were part of

Osama bin Laden's International Islamic Front. Although I rarely asked about such things, my subjects told me surprising details about their secret lives that were not generally known at that time. For example, I learned where operatives purchased weapons (sometimes from their enemies); that some explicitly anti-Shi'ite groups were fund-raising and spending time in Iran; that some of the militants I met called themselves "Harkat" or "Jaesh operatives" when in Pakistan and "Al Qaeda" when in Afghanistan; that groups who were ostensibly enemies would sometimes collaborate, teach each other, or loan out their operatives or expertise.

I also learned a good deal about why. I discovered that there were many underlying motivations for becoming a terrorist (beyond righting a perceived wrong), among them the desire for money, camaraderie, revenge, dignity, or a sense of purpose (which Michelle Dugas and Arie Kruglanski call a quest for significance[2]). I did not use rigorous methods for sampling: I only spoke with terrorists whom I intuited were not going to kill me—a ridiculously unsafe (as well as unscientific) practice that I can no longer condone or recommend. My convenience sample was selected on the basis of whom I happened to meet. Nonetheless, I discovered a number of things that were not generally known, and not knowable from existing data sources. Some of my colleagues called this work "journalistic," which they did not mean as a compliment.

LESSON 3: BE PSYCHOLOGICALLY PREPARED

Third, you need to be psychologically prepared. A psychologist who accompanied me on my first in-person interview said to me, "You have to be able to find the terrorist within yourself."[3] I'm not sure how he knew this. He was working as a pollster and, as far as I know, had never interviewed violent men. His advice sounded absurd, even incomprehensible, when he first offered it. I did not experience myself as a violent person. I even skipped the violent parts of *War and Peace*. But over time I came to understand what he meant and realized he was right. I've learned to listen and watch and feel my way into my interviewee's story. I strive not to judge, not even for a moment, while I am with the subject. Often, but not always, the terrorist's grievance is easy to understand, and I can sympathize with him. I have learned to follow his moral or spiritual or political logic, even if that logic would seem twisted to the person I am outside the room. It is the terrorist's actions—his *means* for pursuing his goals, delib-erately targeting noncombatants—that are barbaric, a violation of ethical norms as well as law. So I keep my thoughts and feelings focused on his goals, not his methods for achieving them. But even when the thought of terrorist acts is in the room between us, I can almost always defer judgment. I feel my way into his feelings. This trick—concentrated obser-vation while suspending judgment—is essential to this kind of work.

LESSON 4: RECOGNIZE YOUR LIMITATIONS REGARDING SURVEILLANCE

Many of my interviews for *Terror in the Name of God* were cleared by my university's institutional review board (IRB). I always asked my subjects to help me change their names and identifying details. Other than leaders, who usually wanted to be made more famous, they were mostly happy to have their views deidentified. My operating assumption was that any intelligence agency that wanted to monitor me or prevent me from car-rying out the interviews would be able to do so, and I also assumed that my interviewees felt the same. I am not a trained operative, and I knew the limits of my tradecraft. I also assumed that whatever I did to protect my data would never be good enough because the individuals I was inter-ested in were also of interest to various intelligence agencies. This became especially clear when I found two men rifling through my things in my hotel room in Lahore. Together, the IRB and I decided that encrypting my communications would only make me look more like a spy and thus more worthy of being spied *upon*. The terrorist groups I was focusing on at the time were not enemies of their own governments but of other govern-ments. In retrospect, this all seems a bit cavalier. But we were all feeling our way with regard to a type of research that was new to my IRB.

A U.S. government agency at one point had some "suggestions" for me. I made it clear that I could not take any such suggestions because it would make me feel entirely unsafe. I suppose I should say that it would be unethical to do so, but I don't really believe that because my subjects had deliberately targeted civilians.

What would I do if any of my subjects were nonviolent civilians who were of interest to intelligence agencies? In that case, I would probably find a different topic to research.

LESSON 5: IRB EXEMPT RESEARCH STILL RAISES ETHICAL ISSUES; GET HELP IF YOU'RE PERPLEXED

Due to changes in IRB requirements, my current research on high-level war criminals has been deemed IRB exempt because it focuses on specific leaders who are not meant to be representative of all leaders or all war criminals. (The same is true for some of the terrorist leaders I've interviewed.) But there are still ethical issues to consider. Should I share with interviewees that I assume we're being recorded when I meet with them in prison? (I do.) For many of the interviews that take place in prisons, I have to take notes by hand, without a recording device. Should I let them read how I've described them and our conversation in advance of publication? (I sometimes do.) Should I identify the name of a wartime rapist who told me that the remorse he pantomimed for the court was a successful ploy to achieve a lighter sentence? He "had sex" with twenty-five Muslim girls, he said, not just the five he was accused of raping. If I identify him, I could be subpoenaed and he could be rearrested upon his release.

The 2019 revision of the IRB definition of "research" makes oral history and biography explicitly exempt, so qualitative researchers are left to consider moral dilemmas such as these on their own. I was uncomfortable addressing these issues without a lawyer, and I sought advice both from the director of my university's IRB and a university attorney. I also consulted an ethicist about some questions regarding revealing information about a high-level U.S. government official who is now deceased. Although there are no absolute right or wrong answers, I was much more confident, for example, using the real name of the rapist after consulting these experts.

In retrospect, talking to terrorists in the field—even prior to 9/11—was stupidly dangerous. After the 9/11 attacks, and after I had a child, I was no longer willing to subject myself to this level of risk. But I had intuited my way into an interview style that has served me well ever since. I begin by trying to figure out what the subject wants and which topics he might feel compelled to lie about. Subjects usually hope to use an interview as part of their marketing strategy, so I try to get the marketing material out of the way. For example, a terrorist leader or war criminal will need to provide a compelling political rationale for whatever crimes he committed or oversaw. He will speak about fear, and the need for defense, never offense. And I listen. But I have also found that subjects are less likely to lie if you ask them personal questions—such as "what are you most proud of" or "what are your favorite books"—which can be quite revealing and are more closely related to why. Much of the time, the subject will not know the answer to these questions when we first sit down to speak, and both of us learn from the conversation.

I would later train as an academic candidate in psychoanalysis. The training gave me words for what was happening in an interview between the subject and me and, more important, what was happening in my own mind. By that time, however, I'd already developed my own technique through hundreds of hours of practice.

Now that I'm older and wiser, and have been treated for the PTSD I didn't know I had, I only interview subjects who have renounced violence or who are incarcerated. But the interview style I developed for active militants still seems to work. I recently finished a series of twelve, four-hour interviews with a single subject—a man convicted of genocide, Radovan Karadzic. My subject is a renowned liar and a master manipulator, but his motivations and his strategy for mobilizing violence are nonetheless plain to see in my research notes.

Here is what I recommend to young scholars wanting to learn how to do this kind of close interviewing of violent individuals. You have to do enough internal work to bear knowing the violence within yourself (even if that violence manifests itself in the form of negative reviews or nasty footnotes rather than in armed combat). You will need help—someone to monitor your return from the altered state you will inevitably enter into and back to your normal self. Make sure you're safe (in other words, do what I say, not what I did when I was young and foolish). I'm not entirely sure that this style of interviewing can be taught; it may be based, at least in part, on an unusual reaction to fear. (Sometimes, but not always, what I fear the most is the presence of evil, or so I've come to believe.) Don't go into the work with the illusion that you're going to get clear answers to a set list of questions. And be ready to learn unexpected things. You may learn more than you want to know.

———

Jessica Stern *is research professor at the Pardee School of Global Studies at Boston University.*

PUBLICATIONS TO WHICH THIS FIELDWORK CONTRIBUTED:

- Stern, Jessica. *Terror in the Name of God: Why Religious Militants Kill.* New York: HarperCollins, 2003.
- ——. *Denial: A Memoir of Terror.* New York: HarperCollins, 2011.
- ——. *My War Criminal: Personal Encounters with an Architect of Genocide.* New York: HarperCollins, 2020.

NOTES

1. I did approach two anthropologists when I first realized I was able to do these interviews, but both of them discouraged me from further study with the argument that my intuitive approach, however untutored, seemed to be working—why take the risk that a more scholarly approach would adversely affect the outcome?
2. See Michelle Dugas and Arie W. Kruglanski, "The Quest for a Significance Model of Radicalization: Implications for the Management of Terrorist Detainees," *Behavioral Sciences & the Law* 32, no. 3 (2014): 423–39, https://doi.org/10.1002/bsl.2122.
3. The psychologist was Steve Kull, a friend of a friend who was curious enough to accompany me to Texas.

16

STUMBLING AROUND IN THE ARCHIVES

MARC TRACHTENBERG

▸ FIELDWORK LOCATION: PARIS, FRANCE

I spent 1971—all twelve months—in Paris doing the research for my doctoral dissertation. In terms of the mechanics of doing research, it was a different world back then. For example, photocopying was very expensive, so I had to hand copy most of the passages I thought I might want to use. And I didn't even know before I arrived which sources I wanted to examine. The published guides to the archives didn't tell you much, and the more detailed finding aids were all in Paris. Looking back now, it is clear that I didn't know what I was doing.

That point applied not just to the logistics of research but to more substantive matters as well. I was working on the reparation question after the First World War. Germany had been required by the peace treaty worked out in 1919 to pay compensation to France for the damage done during the war, and this issue played a very important role in international politics in the immediate postwar period. I had selected (or actually, more or less drifted into) that topic for some general reasons. It seemed to me that too much of the work on the origins of the Second World War had focused on Hitler and on the 1930s, and it seemed to me that the 1920s had been neglected. I thought the line between the 1920s and the 1930s had been overdrawn and that people had not paid as much attention as they should have to what we would now call "structural" factors. At the time, I had not heard of that term. It was clear that there had been a struggle over the Versailles system, not just in the 1930s but, even more important, in the period right after World War I, and that struggle had focused on the conflict over reparations. I was in the Berkeley PhD program in history, and at that time grad students were required to have an outside field. I had chosen economics. Therefore, I thought I had the background to study the reparation issue. Without knowing much about the availability of evidence, or about how recently it had been released, I assumed that there would be enough material to support a dissertation on this topic.

Before I arrived in Paris, I had learned what I could about the topic from published sources, and I had absorbed what was then the standard view: reparations were obviously beyond Germany's capacity to pay; the "vengeful" French had taken a hard line on the question; and Britain and the United States approached the issue in a much more reasonable and conciliatory manner. My goal, when I began my research, was to try to figure out why the French had behaved in that way. In dealing with that issue, I just stumbled around, looking at whatever sources I could find that seemed to have some bearing on the topic.

The Klotz Papers, at the Bibliothèque de Documentation Internationale Contemporaine in Nanterre, just outside of Paris, was one such source. Louis-Lucien Klotz was the finance minister in the Clemenceau government, the government that negotiated the peace treaty in 1919. I had already learned that Clemenceau had been contemptuous of Klotz— the "only Jew I ever met who has no capacity whatever for finance," he called him—and that his key advisor on reparation and related issues was Louis Loucheur, the minister of industrial reconstruction. But given Klotz's position, his papers certainly seemed worth looking at.

And what a surprise they contained! They had the records of the peace conference commission responsible for working out the terms of the reparation settlement; Loucheur was the French representative on that group. The British delegates had suggested some very large figures, and Loucheur clearly thought they were preposterous and that much lower figures were in order. The Germans, in his view, could pay about $30 billion. The British figures were four times larger, and Loucheur commented that "we leave to the poets of the future the task of finding solutions."[1] I remember how startled I was when I read this. Could it be that we had all been sold a bill of goods? Was the standard view about the vindictive French and the more moderate Anglo-Saxons simply a myth?

I had found a loose thread in the fabric of the conventional wisdom, and once I started to pull on it, it unraveled very quickly.

But the point is that this was something I had just stumbled into. I had not started out with the goal of proving anything of the sort. I was not even trying to test the conventional view, which I basically shared when I began my research. And that was not the only time I came across key pieces of evidence more or less by accident.

I remember another case, also in an archive just outside of Paris, fit into that pattern as well. I was trying to understand NATO strategy in the 1950s, and I had learned, especially from my friend Bob Wampler, that an important decision had been made at the end of 1954 to adopt a strategy for the defense of Europe that placed heavy emphasis on nuclear weapons. Specifically, this was the decision to adopt a NATO document called MC-48, and I wanted to find out as much as I could about that document and the thinking that supported it. Wampler had gotten some terrific material from the British archives, and I wanted to see what I could find in the archives of the French ministry of defense at Vincennes. The key source there was the papers of General Clément Blanc, the French army chief of staff at the time. I found some remarkable material on MC-48 in that collection, which I used in an article on the subject, first published in French in 1996, and then republished (with some changes) in English in 2012 in *The Cold War and After*.[2]

As I found out when I went back to that archive, I had been given a file in the Blanc papers that was not supposed to be provided to researchers; it had been given to me by accident. The reason it was still classified was quite clear: the key thing about MC-48 is that it rested on the assumption that if the decision to launch a major nuclear attack was to be effective, it had to be made very quickly, and that meant the military authorities would play the central role in making that decision. The French government, understanding the great political sensitivity of this issue, naturally wanted to keep the public from finding out what had been decided. Documents showing that this was the government's goal were actually in the file. It was quite understandable why French governments, even after the end of the Cold War, wanted to keep people from knowing about all this.

I know of other examples where people have been given important documents by accident when doing archival research. A former student of mine, working in the Taylor Papers at the National Defense

University, was given important documents on the mistaken assumption that he had a security clearance and would not use them in anything he published. Those documents showed how Secretary of Defense Robert McNamara bullied the Joint Chiefs of Staff into taking a position on the issue of deploying nuclear missiles in Europe that varied enormously from their real position.

Is it right to use material obtained in this way? I personally don't have any problem with it. I tend to view historians like me as being engaged in a kind of game with people who determine which documents we're allowed to see. Their goal is often to keep us from "getting the dirt" on policy makers. That's why they use the term "sanitized" to refer to documents in which key passages, containing the "dirt," have been deleted before being released. Our goal, on the other hand, is to get the "dirt"—that is, the full truth. In playing that game, we naturally use whatever assets their inefficiency provides for us.

Sometimes we have to develop new methods for that very purpose. One of the main things I ended up doing, when I was writing my book on the 1945–1963 period, was to collect variant versions of the same document: versions declassified differently in different repositories, or different accounts of the same meeting such as U.S. and British accounts of Anglo-American meetings. These accounts were found by doing work in both British and American archives, and the comparisons are often quite illuminating. They show the nature of the bias incorporated into the body of declassified material by virtue of the fact that declassification is a politicized process; once you identify the bias, you can control for it when working out your own interpretation.[3] The point here is that the methods you end up using are not just the ones you learned in graduate school—certainly not just ones you learn in a "methods course." They're methods you develop to deal with particular problems you encounter as you do your work.

Again, these are things you more or less just stumble into. You can never tell what obstacles you may encounter. Nor can you tell what strokes of luck you'll have. At one point, I needed to do some work on the American nuclear strategists, and I wanted access to some of the old material at the Rand Corporation in Santa Monica. I also needed to do some interviewing, and it turned out that people were very accommodating. Fred Kaplan had recently published his book, *The Wizards of*

Armageddon,[4] which many of the people I needed help from did not like. They thought Kaplan was very smart, but he was not particularly sympathetic to what they did. They were ready to help me because there was a good chance I'd redress the imbalance and provide a more positive view of what they had done.

I had another stroke of luck with the Kennedy tapes from the Cuban Missile Crisis. I happened to run into McGeorge Bundy, formerly Kennedy's national security advisor, at a conference at Columbia. He told me in passing that the Kennedy Library had just released transcripts of the tapes of the meetings held at the beginning of the Cuban Missile Crisis in October 1962. Why hadn't I heard about this? The *New York Times* had published a story about the release of the transcripts a bit earlier but had not treated it as very important. The *Times* instead quoted the chief archivist at the Kennedy Library as saying the new material contained "no surprises," that "it doesn't change anything. There is nothing new of substance."[5] Still, I thought the new material would be worth a look, and indeed there were some major surprises in the October 16 tapes.

At the time, I didn't plan on using that material in anything I was writing. I was much more interested in the Berlin crisis and European issues than in the Cuban crisis. But a friend of mine, Steve Van Evera, was taking over as editor of *International Security*. He said the first issue to be published under his editorship was very important, and he asked me if I had anything he could publish. I said I had come across some terrific material related to the Cuban Missile Crisis and could work something up, which I did. But that draft was not publishable; it was discursive, unfocused, and without any real point. Steve then had me work with his friend John Mearsheimer, whom I had not previously met, and John told me exactly how to restructure the analysis so it spoke directly to questions of interest for security studies people in political science. That restructuring worked, and John's contribution was so great that I asked him if he would like to be listed as coauthor. He said no, that this article would be important for me, that it would in fact establish my reputation in the field, and he didn't want to dilute the effect. I'll always be grateful to him for that.[6]

So what's the bottom line here? You try to be systematic when you're doing your work. You try to have some kind of plan for tackling the topic you're interested in. But like war plans—which, as the saying goes, don't survive first contact with the enemy—research strategies should never be viewed as straitjackets. You might try to be systematic, but you will always be amazed at the hit-or-miss process of archival research. You have to be ready to adjust your strategy to whatever obstacles or opportunities turn up. *On s'engage, puis on voit* (you throw yourself in, and then you look around). That is how Napoleon said you had to approach battle. In real life, of course, it's important not to overimprovise, and when tackling a problem in international relations, it's important to think hard about how you propose to proceed. As Dwight Eisenhower declared, "plans are worthless, but planning is everything." And that applies not just to military planning but also to planning a research project in the archives or otherwise: in doing research, you really need to be more flexible than you might think.

––––

Marc Trachtenberg *is research professor of political science at the University of California, Los Angeles.*

PUBLICATIONS TO WHICH THIS FIELDWORK CONTRIBUTED:

- Trachtenberg, Marc. *Reparation in World Politics: France and European Economic Diplomacy, 1916–1923.* New York: Columbia University Press, 1980.
- ——. *The Cold War and After: History, Theory, and the Logic of International Politics.* Princeton, N.J.: Princeton University Press, 2012.

NOTES

1. See Marc Trachtenberg, *Reparation in World Politics: France and European Economic Diplomacy, 1916–1923* (New York: Columbia University Press, 1980), 59–60; Marc Trachtenberg, "Reparation at the Paris Peace Conference," *Journal of Modern History* 51, no. 1 (March 1979): 24–55, https://doi.org/10.1086/241847.

2. See Marc Trachtenberg, "La formation du système de défense occidentale: les États-Unis, la France et MC 48," in *La France et l'OTAN, 1949–1996*, ed. Maurice Vaïsse, Pierre Mélandri, and Frédéric Bozo (Paris: Editions Complexe, 1996); republished, with some changes, in English translation in Marc Trachtenberg, *The Cold War and After: History, Theory, and the Logic of International Politics* (Princeton, N.J.: Princeton University Press, 2012), 143–49.

3. See Marc Trachtenberg, "Declassification Analysis: The Method, and Some Examples" and "Declassification Analysis: More Grist for the Mill," http://www.sscnet

.ucla.edu/polisci/faculty/trachtenberg/decl/grist.htm. These were posted on a website I created as an online supplement to my book: Marc Trachtenberg, *A Constructed Peace: The Making of the European Settlement, 1945–1963* (Princeton, N.J.: Princeton University Press, 1999).

4. Fred Kaplan, *The Wizards of Armageddon* (Stanford, Calif.: Stanford University Press, 1991).

5. Fox Butterfield, "Library Releases Cuban Crisis Tapes," *New York Times*, October 27, 1983.

6. See Marc Trachtenberg, "The Influence of Nuclear Weapons in the Cuban Missile Crisis," *International Security* 10, no. 1 (1985): 137–63. The editors also asked me to select some key excerpts from the documents for publication and write an introduction to the documents, which was published in that issue as well.

17

DETAILS IN THE DOODLES

DOCUMENTING COVERT ACTION

LINDSEY A. O'ROURKE

▸ FIELDWORK LOCATION: UNITED STATES NATIONAL ARCHIVES, WASHINGTON, D.C.

Unlike many of the contributors to this book, my field research does not require traveling to distant locations or navigating treacherous political environments. As a scholar focusing on U.S. foreign policy, my research trips have been centered on the decidedly more mundane environment of U.S. governmental archives, particularly the National Archives and Records Administration, the National Security Archive, and several presidential libraries. To date, most of my archival research has been conducted for my dissertation, which was recently published as my first book, *Covert Regime Change: America's Secret Cold War.* In it, I investigated the causes and consequences of U.S.-backed covert regime change attempts, such as assassinations, coups, arming foreign dissidents, and secretly meddling in democratic elections. The biggest challenge I faced was that, by definition, states try to conceal their role in covert operations. To take the subject outside the realm of conspiracy theory, I had to uncover hard evidence that the U.S. government was actively trying to overthrow the targeted states. To that end, my archival research goal was to uncover primary source evidence confirming each of the sixty-four covert regime change attempts in my data set.

When I embarked on the project, my biggest fear was of investing time in the laborious process of conducting archival research without a guarantee that I would uncover sufficient information of value, thereby wasting precious time in a publish-or-perish discipline. Particularly at first,

I often felt that my fears were coming true. I spent countless days chasing down dead ends. Many of my Freedom of Information Act (FOIA) requests were rejected outright. At other times, I would finally get my hands on a long sought-after document, only to discover that it had been redacted (i.e., key "sensitive" parts were blacked out) at precisely the point of interest for me. Some days, after eight hours of trying to decipher files that had been photocopied into oblivion, I would leave the archives with my brain feeling like mush. Over time, however, I came to deeply love and enjoy the process, and there were many days when I could hardly bring myself to leave after uncovering a crucial lead or a valuable document.

Won over by my experience, I have become an avid proponent of archival research in political science. Because it can illuminate, in granular detail, aspects of the policy-making process that are usually opaque, archival research greatly assists the process of generating and refining theories, avoiding theoretical dead ends, testing alternative hypotheses, and demonstrating a theory's causal mechanism at work. In my own research, for example, one commonly held belief is that Washington engaged in so many covert regime changes during the Cold War because the Central Intelligence Agency (CIA) acted without oversight and that its reckless meddling provoked America's interventions. As Senator Frank Church (D-ID) famously warned in 1975, the CIA was a "rogue elephant" rampaging out of control. Given the prevalence of this view, I expected to find more evidence for it before embarking on my research project. Once in the archives, however, it quickly became apparent that the executive branch—not the CIA—was the driving force behind the covert interventions. Although the CIA did exercise some leeway in determining how to conduct an operation, I found no evidence that it ever launched a covert regime change without presidential orders to do so. Thankfully, discovering this early on allowed me to better focus my research efforts and adjust my theoretical predictions accordingly.

Moreover, whether intentionally or not, archival documents and contemporaneous recordings, such as the White House Tapes (a collection of the secret tapings made by six U.S. presidents between 1940 and 1973, housed at the University of Virginia), often reveal a different story than the one in the memoirs and public statements of policy makers.[1] This phenomenon was perhaps most famously demonstrated in 1971 when a collection of top-secret Department of Defense reports on the Vietnam

War—known as the Pentagon Papers—was leaked to the press. The Pentagon Papers reveal that each of the four preceding presidential administrations had misled the U.S. public about their actions in Vietnam and continuously escalated America's involvement in the region despite serious misgivings about the wisdom of these actions.[2] The Pentagon Papers are particularly incisive in their scrutiny of U.S. behavior, but they are not abnormal in that regard. I have often been struck by the extent of candor policy makers have shown when discussing their doubts regarding certain policies in confidential memos and private conversations when compared to their confident public assessments.

My favorite thing about archival research was coming across handwritten notes, pen marks, or doodles on a document that revealed it to be an original. Unlike the post hoc recollections politicians share in interviews and memoirs, these notes reflect the private, unfiltered, contemporaneous reactions of policy makers to a particular document. There's something about seeing these marks that enables me to make a personal connection to the individuals involved. It's an irrational feeling—one that I imagine is akin to what drives memorabilia collectors to spend millions purchasing Babe Ruth's bat or Marilyn Monroe's dress. Historical figures can sometimes feel like abstractions, but seeing the original documents presented to them and knowing the decisions they made based on these documents drives home for me that they were real, fallible people, with limited information, making decisions that had ramifications outside of their control and understanding. Perhaps naïvely, I left the archives with more sympathetic views of certain politicians than I had when I entered. Even when documents detail leaders taking an action I consider to be a grave mistake, I have often been struck by the tragic nature of their decision-making process. Far more often than not, their misguided actions seem to be driven by common character flaws, such as inattention, myopia, or hubris, rather than by anything approaching malice. Indeed, I have found a lot of truth in the sentiment summarized by Margaret Thatcher's press secretary, Bernard Ingham: "Many journalists have fallen for the conspiracy theory of government. I do assure you that they would produce more accurate work if they adhered to the cock-up theory."[3]

At other times, the handwritten notes and doodles feel like an insight into the personality of their author.[4] John F. Kennedy's doodles, for instance, strike me as the work of an anxious and methodical mind.

He preferred small geometric figures, particularly sailboats, and when grappling with a difficult problem, he would write the same word over and over—"Vietnam," "Cuba," or "Iraq"—often with boxes around them as if to visually illustrate America's Cold War strategy of containment. Ronald Reagan, by contrast, preferred drawing cartoons and animals, and he is said to have shared autographed doodles of cowboys, horses, and football players with White House visitors. Befitting a five-star general who took up painting to relax, Dwight D. Eisenhower doodled everything from bucolic landscapes, to nuclear weapons, to caricatures of his staff. In fact, the most memorable doodle I came upon in my research was by Eisenhower. On a White House memo from June 28, 1954—the day after Jacobo Arbenz, the democratically elected president of Guatemala was ousted during a U.S.-backed coup—Eisenhower twice wrote "Guatemala" in the margin of a White House conference schedule for the morning, possibly to add it to the meeting's schedule. This addition would not be particularly noteworthy if not for the remarkable doodle accompanying it. The drawing depicts a lean and muscular man—shirtless—whose contented face bears an uncanny resemblance to Eisenhower himself (albeit younger than his sixty-three years). Beside him is a gunboat floating in water and the words "internal security"—possibly a reference to the next task facing the newly installed Guatemalan regime of consolidating its political control over the country. Of course, one can only speculate what compelled Eisenhower to doodle that figure the morning after a foreign government was toppled on his orders, but it certainly conjures up an image of strength and masculinity.

My practical advice for people considering archival research is as follows. First, do as much prep work as possible beforehand. Most archives have specific rules about the number of boxes of documents you can request at one time, set times for the archivists to pull files, rules for copying documents, dress codes, and so forth. It's also important to have a good sense of the key political actors for your research topic so you can focus on their collections of papers. Toward this end, many archives have helpful online finding aids and subject guides. The footnotes of previous scholarly works on the topic also provide locations where researchers have found relevant archival materials in the past. Because compiling lists of documents to request can be quite time consuming, do not waste

THE WHITE HOUSE

WASHINGTON

LEGISLATIVE LEADERSHIP CONFERENCE

MONDAY, JUNE 28, 1954 --- 8:30 AM

1. Symington Amendment to the Extension of Trade
   Agreements Act   (Secretary Dulles)

2. Report on Status of Legislation in Senate Finance
   Committee (Senator Millikin)

3. Senate Report (Senator Knowland)

4. House Report (Speaker Martin)

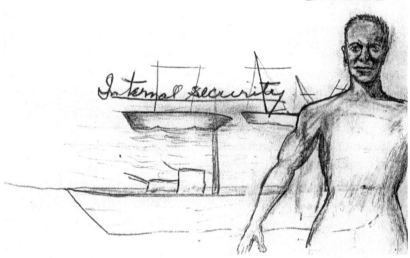

FIGURE 17.1 Eisenhower "Guatemala" doodle on June 28, 1954, White House Memo (Box 1, folder "Legislative Meetings 1954, May-June [3]" of the Legislative Meeting Series, of the collection, EISENHOWER, DWIGHT D.: Papers as President; Eisenhower Presidential Library, Abilene, Kans.).

precious time in the archives on this task. Limit your time in the archives to work that can only be done in the archives.

Second, when in doubt, ask for help. I have found archivists to be incredibly helpful and generous with their time. Because of their expansive working knowledge of the collections, they have often suggested unexplored locations to check when I thought I had reached a dead end.

Third, take meticulous notes as you work. You may find a document that seems so incredibly perfect that, of course, you assume you will remember it later. But the truth is, after eight hours of staring at files, things blur together. Monday's amazing find will be Friday's old news. Unless you diligently keep track of key documents as you come across them, it will be difficult to find them again later.

Fourth, I recommend saving digital copies of your photographs or scanned documents arranged in folders according to their location in the archives (e.g., folder and box) along with your relevant research notes to facilitate easy access later. It is easy to amass a huge trove of files when conducting archival research, and you'll thank yourself once it comes time to recall and cite these documents if you saved them in an organized fashion in the first place. Also, back everything up! I have heard horror stories of scholars losing vast amounts of work when their laptop crashed or their bag was stolen. Fortunately, this danger is now completely avoidable thanks to Wi-Fi and cloud storage services such as Dropbox, Google Drive, or Box.

Fifth, do not try to make sense of everything that you read while at the archives. If you read everything closely as you come across it, you are likely to spend valuable time lost in the weeds. Instead, skim everything, save anything that seems like it could be remotely valuable, and piece together the documents once you are back home. It is better to err on the side of getting too much material than not getting enough, especially because documents you grab can also be used for future projects.

Sixth, the same document may be redacted differently in different collections. If, for instance, you found that a certain memo from the State Department to the White House was redacted in an obstructive way in the State Department files, it may be worth tracking down the same memo in a White House collection to see if it was declassified differently there, allowing you to access more of the document by itself or by combining the two versions.

Seventh, do not expect the FOIA process to move quickly. In its current form, FOIA statutes allow U.S. citizens to request the release of government documents from more than one hundred federal agencies and numerous state agencies, varying by state law. Each agency has its own procedure for filing FOIA requests either online or by mail, but most of these procedures are easily accessible on the agency's website. Once a FOIA request is received, the relevant agency determines what to release. Requested documents can be redacted in part or denied in whole according to nine exemptions, including whether declassification of the document would threaten U.S. national defense or reveal private information about U.S. citizens. Despite the promise the FOIA process offers to increase government transparency, FOIA offices are often understaffed, underfunded, and plagued by massive backlogs. In 2017 alone, for instance, the Department of Justice recorded more than 111,344 backlogged FOIA requests.[5] In my experience, it usually takes weeks for government agencies to acknowledge receipt of a FOIA request, and months or years for them to answer it. (In general, the more specific the request, the quicker it will be answered.) I have dozens of outstanding FOIA requests that are more than five years old. Although I do not want to dissuade anyone from filing a FOIA request—it is an incredibly valuable tool for researchers—scholars working with short time constraints should be aware of its limitations.

Eighth, for scholars who may feel prohibited from conducting archival research by the cost of travel or family obligations, it is becoming increasingly easy to conduct archival research online. While writing my dissertation, for instance, I spent hours combing through declassified CIA documents using the CIA Records Search Tool (CREST). At the time, researchers could only access the CREST database from several computers located at the National Archives and Records Administration (NARA) in College Park, Maryland. Although the CREST system was a useful resource, the setup could be quite frustrating. If you made the trek out to College Park only to find that the computers were already in use—too bad. When the computers were free, and you found something of interest, you could not download or email the file. You could print it on the pastel blue paper provided by NARA to distinguish printouts from actual archival documents, but then you had to reassemble and scan the documents at home. Thanks to that cumbersome system, I still have boxes of blue paper in my basement! Fortunately, things are much easier today. In January 2017, the entire CREST collection was made publicly available online on the CIA's electronic reading room. Searches that would have required a trip to the archives can now be done online instantly, at any time.

The same holds true for many other archival collections, so it is definitely worthwhile to investigate the possibility of online research if a trip to the archives is out of reach. At the same time, scholars should keep in mind the potential drawbacks of online research. Because many online collections are limited in their scope and accessed via keyword searches, results are limited to what's available and the researcher's skill in doing this kind of search. This can make it more difficult for scholars to understand the full context of a document, and it decreases the likelihood of surprise discoveries that come from browsing through an entire box of files.

Finally, I have found archival documents to be a great teaching aid. In my experience, having students evaluate a key primary source document stimulates class discussions and ties theoretical concepts to real historical events. You generally can't bring students to your fieldwork site, but you can immerse them in its history by putting archival documents in their hands.

To encourage students to incorporate archival documents in their own work, many universities house special collections of donated papers from influential alumni. Flagship state universities, in particular, often have massive collections of local and state government documents. For easily accessible online collections of U.S. foreign policy documents, I recommend the State Department's Foreign Relations of the United States (FRUS) series, the Declassified Documents Reference System (DDRS), the Digital National Security Archive, the CIA's Electronic FOIA Reading Room, the Presidential Recordings collection at the University of Virginia, and the American Presidency Project at UC Santa Barbara.

I would be lying if I said that archival research is always fun. Parts of the process—redacted documents, denied FOIAs, illegible photocopies—can be frustrating. But there is also the thrill of the hunt during archival research, and the moments of tedium are more than offset by the delight that comes from uncovering a crucial new document . . . or an unexpected great doodle.

_____

Lindsey O'Rourke *is assistant professor of political science at Boston College.*

PUBLICATIONS TO WHICH THIS FIELDWORK CONTRIBUTED:

- O'Rourke, Lindsey A. *Covert Regime Change: America's Secret Cold War*. Ithaca, N.Y.: Cornell University Press, 2018.
- Downes, Alexander B., and Lindsey A. O'Rourke. "You Can't Always Get What You Want: Why Foreign-Imposed Regime Change Seldom Improves Interstate Relations," *International Security* 41, no. 2 (Fall 2016): 43–89.

NOTES

1. "The Secret White House Tapes," Miller Center, University of Virginia, January 10, 2017, https://millercenter.org/the-presidency/secret-white-house-tapes.
2. "Report of the Office of the Secretary of Defense Vietnam Task Force," 1969, National Archive, https://www.archives.gov/research/pentagon-papers.
3. Bernard Ingham quoted in Andrew McKenzie-McHarg and Rolf Fredheim, "Cock-Ups and Slap-Downs: A Quantitative Analysis of Conspiracy Rhetoric in the British Parliament 1916–2015," *Historical Methods: A Journal of Quantitative and Interdisciplinary History* 50, no. 3 (2017): 156–69, https://www.tandfonline.com/doi/abs/10.1080/01615440.2017.1320616.
4. For an extensive and amusing overview of the doodles of American presidents, see Cabinet Magazine and David Greenberg, *Presidential Doodles: Two Centuries of Scribbles, Scratches, Squiggles, and Scrawls from the Oval Office* (New York: Basic Books, 2007).
5. "Summary of Annual FOIA Reports for the Fiscal Year 2017," Office of Information Policy, U.S. Department of Justice, 2017, https://www.justice.gov/oip/page/file/1069396/download.

18

MY STINT AS A UKRAINIAN TAXI DRIVER

KEITH DARDEN

▸ FIELDWORK LOCATION: UKRAINE

I n the sweltering July of 2009, I spent several weeks driving the pit-
ted roads in rural areas of southwestern Ukraine. The campaign for
the January 2010 presidential elections that ultimately brought Viktor
Yanukovych to power was already in full swing. I was in the country to try
to understand the persistent regional divides in Ukraine—the very ones
along which Ukraine would later cleave through secession and war when
Yanukovych was forced out of office in February of 2014.

The specific puzzle that brought me to this part of Ukraine was a sharp
discontinuity in voting patterns along an imaginary line spanning much
of the country that ran through northern Odessa province. Villages that
were walking distance apart across this line differed from one another in
no obvious socioeconomic characteristics, but they voted very differently.
To the south of the line, large majorities supported Russophile parties
and candidates. To the north, those candidates and parties received marginal support. It was something of a Ukrainian Mason-Dixon line, and
my hypothesis was that this split had to do with a cultural divide that
was the legacy of the boundary between the Ottoman Empire and the
Polish-Lithuanian Commonwealth.

My initial research plan had been twofold. First, I was going to collect polling station–level voting data—information that at the time was
not available on the internet or in Kyiv—from the districts within a
narrow band on either side of the Kodyma creek, which served as the

eighteenth-century boundary between Ottoman and Polish territories. Second, I wanted to do some semistructured interviews with people from villages on either side to see whether there were differences in underlying cultural attitudes, language use, or other variables that had not been measured in any existing data sets. But I also wanted to understand why people voted the way that they did, and that created a whole host of problems I hadn't anticipated.

The main problem was that asking people about voting was a sensitive topic. People generally wouldn't talk. One respondent disclosed to me that vote-buying was common in these parts of Ukraine, but that was revealed after we had split a couple bottles of bad Moldovan cognac in a local tavern. In general, voting and vote-selling was something people were nervous about discussing, particularly with a foreigner. They had some experience with international election monitors, and they often feared the local administration, who did not want any reports of election violations coming from their districts. I could provide no assurances to get them to talk. The usual boilerplate language assuring respondents of their anonymity didn't persuade anyone. Respondents knew they weren't *really* anonymous because I had found them, and I typically knew their names and addresses. In a rural post-Communist context, where people had no concept of neutral scholarship and were not inclined to trust strangers anyway, the risks of disclosing information about illegal voting practices—and particularly vote-buying—were greater than the reward (zero). Plying them with cognac or vodka didn't seem like a viable research strategy over the long term. It would probably lead to a biased sample of hard drinking males, and it might end badly for any number of reasons. The institutional review board (IRB) definitely wouldn't approve. How do you get people to talk about sensitive topics when they don't trust you, and they have no reason to trust you to keep their information anonymous because (unlike a university's IRB) they have no concept of social scientific research?

The solution, it turned out, was my faithful rental car: a cheap black four-cylinder Hyundai with Odessa city plates. In the Ukraine of 2009, there were no ride-sharing services, scant few taxis in rural areas, infrequent and inconvenient buses, and most people did not own cars. To get around between villages and towns in the area, people would stand by the roadside with their hand out until a driver stopped. They would tell the driver where they were headed, and if it was on the driver's way, everyone would agree on a price and the driver would take you there. It was similar to an informal ride-sharing or taxi service in which everyone participated.

So I started picking up rides. At first, I thought this would make my limited time in the field more productive. Given the poor quality of the roads, it could take several hours to go a hundred kilometers. If I could squeeze some interviews in on my drives between districts and polling stations, I'd get more done. Moreover, I thought it would be an easy way to approach people—one that didn't involve being a creepy foreigner knocking on doors or stopping people in the fields. Plus the car kept me safe from stray dogs, which were ubiquitous in the countryside. It seemed like a great idea.

And it was. When I was just a taxi driver—a chance encounter and a limited, anonymous transactional relationship—people were suddenly happy to talk: about themselves, their families, and . . . most important . . . about the elections—who they voted for and why, and about the vote-buying that was going on all around us. Other than the different circumstances of our meeting, I approached people in the same way, identifying myself as a professor from Yale University in the United States who was studying Ukrainian elections, and I asked them if I could pose a few questions. But on the drive, people were far more forthcoming. Not everyone was offered money for their vote, but they all knew of the practice. In fact, they knew quite a bit. For example, the going rate for a vote at the time ranged from 20 to 50 Hryvnia (4–10 USD), but 20 or 30 was pretty standard, and the people who managed the vote-buying were called *agitatory* (agitators). Each party or candidate had its own agitator, who was generally a local person. The respondents had no shame about taking money to vote, but they often took offense when I asked whether they actually voted for the candidate they had been paid to vote for. Of course! They kept their word. There was no way to monitor compliance, but apparently there didn't need to be. At the end of the interviews, I invited them to ask any question they might have of me, and I made it clear that they could rely on me to answer entirely truthfully because we would never see each other again. This seemed like appropriate compensation for the information they shared with me, but only a few people took advantage of it.

The breakthrough came a couple of weeks into this stint as a Ukrainian taxi driver when I picked up a middle-aged woman and her teenaged daughter heading to a town about twenty minutes away. It was a bit off my path, but I took them anyway because the long drives were yielding great material. After chatting for a bit and getting some background information (how many generations her family had lived in this area, for example), I asked if I could question them about the election. I started with my usual question about whether they had ever been approached by an agitator. The woman became very excited and said proudly that she, herself, was an agitator for one of the two main political parties, indeed, the one that was dominant in that particular region.

Over the course of the drive she explained to me how the entire system worked. The agitators were given a fixed budget and a district to cover, but it was up to them to choose how to spend their money to get the best results in the election. Her strategy was to go door-to-door and talk to people to get a sense of whether they had any strong prior feeling about any of the candidates. If they had strong feelings at all, she simply thanked them for their time and moved on. If they were uncertain or indifferent, she would offer them money to vote for her candidate, and they were generally quite happy to accept. Agitators were evaluated based on the election results from their districts, and they could be hired for future campaigns if they were effective. It was a remarkable interview.

In the end, the cultural legacies of empire certainly mattered. They shaped voters' basic orientation toward Russia, which became quite important in Ukrainian elections in the twenty-first century. But these basic inclinations were buttressed by substantial provincial-level political machines that were effectively buying the votes of the undecided, and solidifying and sharpening the differences between electoral districts on opposite sides of the historical imperial divides. Without my time behind the wheel, I would have missed half of the story.

Why did interviews in the car work so well? When it comes to getting people to share private information with you, anonymity is better than trust. These interactions were perfect because they were purely anonymous—and more important—the respondents *knew* it was anonymous because they knew exactly the circumstances under which we had met: a chance encounter. I had not selected them. They had ultimately chosen to get in my car. And they knew perfectly well that unless they chose to share their identifying information with me, I would not have it. I had no power over them because I didn't know who they were, and no harm could come from talking to me. Under those circumstances, people proved very willing to talk.

We tend to think that repeated contact, intimacy, and relationships get people to be more likely to bare their souls. The presumption of the "ethnographic interview,"[1] or most serial interviewing techniques, is that familiarity and trust are the keys to knowledge.[2] But trust is not the key to all forms of knowledge. Children lie to parents. Husbands lie to wives. The more intimate we are with someone, the more we care what they think about us, and the more we try to shape their perception and varnish their image of us. Perhaps for certain topics, the more intimate we are with our respondents, the less we will really learn. To be sure, in some circumstances neither brevity nor anonymity are possible. For example, if we are seeking to understand particularly complex processes that are long in the telling, follow-up interviews and intimacy may be required.[3] But sensitive facts are more likely to be revealed to the anonymous stranger. The fleeting encounter— the mythic conversation with the cab driver—may not be of much use if you are the passenger, but it's a great tool if you're in the driver's seat.

***

Keith Darden *is associate professor in the School of International Service at American University.*

PUBLICATION TO WHICH THIS FIELDWORK CONTRIBUTED:

- Darden, Keith. "Imperial Footprints: Colonial Legacies, Party Machines, and Contemporary Voting" (in progress).

NOTES

1. James P. Spradley, *The Ethnographic Interview* (Long Grove, Ill.: Waveland Press, 1979).
2. The notion that familiarity and trust are critical tools goes back to the anthropology of Margaret Mead and Bronislaw Malinowski. For more recent treatments, see Robert S. Weiss, *Learning From Strangers: The Art and Method of Qualitative Interview Studies* (New York: Simon & Schuster, 1995); Benjamin L. Read, "Serial Interviews: When and Why to Talk to Someone More Than Once," *International Journal of Qualitative Methods* 17, no. 1 (December 2018): 1–10, https://doi.org/10.1177/1609406918783452.
3. Lee Ann Fujii, *Interviewing in Social Science Research: A Relational Approach* (Abingdon, UK: Routledge, 2017).

19

CONDUCTING FIELDWORK IN A VIRTUAL SPACE

EXPLORING ISIS's ENCRYPTED MESSAGING ON TELEGRAM

MIA BLOOM AND AYSE LOKMANOGLU

▶ FIELDWORK LOCATION: ISIS ENCRYPTED ONLINE PLATFORM

Terrorist groups have embraced the internet. For many groups, online space is the default platform for recruitment, strategic communication, and fund-raising. ISIS has retained a "first-mover (or most-innovative-mover) advantage in the media realm."[1] Seized ISIS materials reveal that online videos constitute a first step toward recruitment, followed by contact, online involvement, and eventually physical emigration to the "Caliphate."[2] Interviews with captured operatives reveal that 77 percent of active lone shooters become "self-radicalized through Internet forums and other forms of media."[3] As ISIS lost all of its territory in the former Caliphate, the shift to the virtual space has provided a new lease on life. Online propaganda was such a fundamental part of ISIS's raison d'etre that a 2018 Soufan Center report explained the privileged position accorded the media personnel (videographers, producers, and editors) who crafted it:

> The group paid members of its media team nearly seven times the salary of an average foot soldier. Even more striking, recruits with a background in production, editing, or graphic design were being afforded with the rank of emir, a clear signal of their value to the organization.[4]

The Telegram platform played a crucial role in showcasing this material as well as in recruiting and coordinating ISIS attacks in Europe and rest of the world.[5] It was used to organize *ghazawat* (media raids), a digital attack to spread hashtags and messages and make them go viral. These raids hearken back to the classical period of military raids in the desert, except they are now done within the safe space of Telegram and launched into open and accessible internet platforms.[6] For example, in 2016 Rachid Kassim urged his three hundred Telegram followers to carry out what prosecutors have termed "terrorisme de proximité,"[7] which resulted in several attacks including the killing of a couple in Magnaville, two teen jihadis killing 86-year-old Father Jacques Hamel in Rouen, an attack involving an explosive-laden vehicle near Notre Dame in Paris, and the shooting of a police officer in Les Mureaux via his Telegram channel "Sabre de la Lumière."[8]

Telegram is a free, cross-platform app with invited chat rooms and channels that permit public-public, public-private, and private-private communications for more than one hundred million users. It allows users to engage in secret chats and to share messages, documents, videos, and photos. When messages are deleted on one end of a chat, they disappear on the other end. A user can set a "self-destruct timer" that also deletes the message once it is viewed. The "end-to-end encryption [means] nobody but the sender and recipient can read the messages."[9] These security features, cross-platform construction, and secret chat option offer a secure environment for interaction between ISIS and its network. However, "the general public remains relatively uninformed about the complex ways in which many jihadists maintain robust yet secretive online presences."[10] For most, the language barrier is a challenge because the majority of ISIS and jihadi Telegram networks operate in Arabic. For others, securing access to the network can be tricky.

For the past three years we have conducted *virtual field research* on ISIS encrypted networks.[11] On the Telegram app, ISIS manipulates an environment rich with addictive properties, creating online spaces that encourage group identity, shared opinions, and dominant ideologies, while exploiting an individual's need to be a part of the group.[12]

Moving our field research to the virtual space brought with it several challenges. The first was getting our university to approve the research through its institutional review board (IRB). By definition, much of the material we captured in screenshots was posted by people using anonymous or pen names. Because of the built-in public nature of online posting and the anonymity of participants, we applied for and were able to get an IRB waiver for the research project. However, the caveat was that we would observe but not participate in chat rooms. It was crucial that we maintained a safe environment for research and did not end up accidentally radicalizing others if we posted graphic materials or disseminated ISIS communications. We also hoped to avoid a midnight visit by the FBI, who might be monitoring jihadi communications and trace our IP addresses.

Nevertheless, this research raises particular ethical challenges, in part because it is relatively new. The "Belmont Report" was published in 1979,[13] a time when anonymized social media could not have been foreseen, and this protocol does not address issues of digital ethnography. Our research followed the strictest IRB guidelines, and the authors anonymized all identifiable information in the distribution of data in all presentations and publications. It was a priority to ensure the safety of both the subjects and the researchers in pursuit of the spirit of the "Belmont Report."

Academic researchers may fail to grasp the intricacies of the online space, and we are limited in what we can observe because of the graphic nature of the material and the 24/7 postings across every time zone in the ISIS global network. The ideal scenario for this research would be to follow the research protocols laid out by Martyn Frampton, Ali Fisher, and Nico Prucha,[14] who have created unique algorithms to "auto scrape" all content across tens of thousands of channels. They then analyze the captured materials using big data tools. In contrast to what Frampton, Fisher, and Prucha are doing, we hand-collected all of the materials and engaged a number of coders to ensure intercoder reliability. To date, we have more than 20,461 unique images, postings, or other content, and we are creating a searchable database that will be available to researchers in the future.

Individual collection of data adds an additional nuance and layer to the research that provides insight into the behavioral dynamics of the social media platforms and how the platforms sustain user engagement. These behaviors indicate a "social media addiction" that cannot be observed or measured when automated scraping of data is employed. For instance, no observations can be made of users' reactions when channels become unavailable or how the platform exploits participants' "fear of missing out." Individual researchers can observe how participants in the chat group sustained or increased their screen time when organizations employed the addictive strategies of varying channel content while at the same time limiting access if participants did not engage within a predetermined time period. If participants do not join within the time limit, they experience an emotional loss of having missed out. Being able to observe these behaviors is necessary to understanding the big picture of how terrorist organizations construct emotional and psychological dependency.

Collecting the content from the channels and chat rooms became exceptionally challenging once ISIS "admins" (channel administrators) became worried about "lurkers" such as journalists, academics, think tank researchers, and security personnel who might monitor the platform for reasons other than subscribing to the radical jihadi ideology. The admins for the channels keep track of accounts that do not post or engage other members in chats. This eventually brought us to the attention of the admins.

To observe the platform, you must join a channel or a chat by clicking on a dedicated link within a designated period of time. This is usually limited to a maximum of thirty minutes, but for some of the more exclusive channels the time limit might be only ten minutes. Participants in these groups can contact one another (including researchers who are only observing the channel) through direct messages. In previous versions of Telegram, members of a chat could call the number associated with others' accounts. One day in June 2017, after joining two new links (while sitting in the office where we conducted all of our research), one of the project laptops began to ring. We had not realized that the newly updated version of Telegram could be used for direct communication (like WhatsApp or Skype). When ISIS calls, it is probably best not to answer. We managed to quickly post an Arabic direct message to the member who had called that "I was busy and being monitored at my workplace." However, this blatant excuse placed the account in the admin's sights for increased scrutiny. Shortly thereafter, a series of threats was posted that included photoshopped screen shots of one of our Twitter accounts and called Dr. Mia Bloom a "drunkard and an alcoholic" (see figure 19.1).

Although it was mildly amusing that Bloom was not considered "slave market worthy" (this was more compliment than insult), the images of beheadings directly messaged to Bloom were far less entertaining.

FIGURE 19.1 ISIS photoshopped image of Mia Bloom's Twitter account.

At first glance, field research in the virtual world might appear to place the researcher far from danger. One is not located in a conflict zone and, seemingly, is not at risk. However, some ISIS social media fanatics will issue specific threats, may call for your assassination, or publish private or identifying information about you ("dox you"), and provide their network with the details of where you live and work. We explain later in this essay how one amateur journalist had to be remanded to federal protective custody after trying to use his anonymous account on Telegram to "interview" ISIS supporters. One has to weigh the gravity of any threat against the assumption that fantasists online routinely issue hollow threats from the safety of their parents' basement.

Nevertheless, it is crucial that researchers take precautions before conducting this type of research. The platform assumes that the user will use a pen name, but you should not use your own personal mobile device, nor should you include any personal details in your account. There is a fine line between engaging in deceit or concealment and safeguarding oneself during high-risk (virtual) field research. The story of how our team was found out illustrates this dilemma (see figure 19.2).

> **FORWARDED FROM AL-TĀSNI | NEWS**
> **@UKHTMUAQIYAH**
>
> Mia M Bloom I know you are in my channel and
> you as per your twitter bio "Writer, terror analyst
> bourbon lover I tweet about SUICIDE TERROR,
> WOMEN TERRORISTS &ISIS."
>
> Women terrorist ! but will you write about these
> women who gathered at water wells and got
> bombed and shredded to pieces? No you wont!
> Because you're shameless bitch your blood is as
> halal as american and canadian soldiers
>
> P.S don't change @ it wont help you like last time.
> I will find you again   👁 1   7:24 AM

FIGURE 19.2 Threatening Telegram message to Bloom.

ETHICS: THE IMPORTANCE OF CONFIDENTIALITY AND ANONYMITY

As you begin to conduct virtual research on Telegram, there is no step-by-step instruction booklet or "Telegram for Dummies" guide that you can use. The skills required to maintain access to the platform are an illustration of what Michael Kenney terms *techne*, or on-the-job training.[15] At the outset, many errors and mistakes are likely.

First, we recommend using an approved virtual private network (VPN) to protect the location of the researcher because Telegram includes the location in the user profile. The institutions from which the research is conducted should be able to provide approved, possibly air gapped,[16] laptops with a secure VPN that is automatically launched with each login to the Telegram application. The laptops we use for research are dedicated project equipment that contain no personal information, to protect the researchers.

Second, the phone used to create the unique Telegram account should not contain any personal information. After purchasing a prepaid mobile device, the researcher should create a unique Telegram account exclusively for the purpose of research. For example, if you use your own cell phone number or if you have ever posted an image of yourself connected to that number, it will be archived by Telegram and is difficult to delete. Changing your name or photo doesn't automatically erase the archived information, and you have to manipulate the app on a mobile device (not a laptop) to ensure that you delete all previously posted information and images associated with that account. Laith Al Khouri, the Middle East and North Africa director of Flashpoint, noticed these mistakes and alerted our Minerva research team at Georgia State University to the potential danger of creating an account under someone's real name and then trying to make it anonymous after the fact. This was probably how Dr. Mia Bloom's profile was discovered.

Attempting to befriend people in chat rooms poses an additional danger because ISIS admins are suspicious of lurkers, assuming them to be spies or government agents. In one case we observed, an eager journalism student who wanted to write about his experiences on the platform was doxed by members of the chat room who posted his email account, cell phone number, and home address. They also revealed his Facebook, Twitter, and Instagram accounts and called for his beheading. This situation became sufficiently alarming that the FBI intervened and provided the amateur journalist with federal protection. In short, although this research might sound "cool" to the outside observer, it can be dangerous if appropriate precautions are not taken.

In virtual field research, researchers face unique risks. The content ISIS generates on its channels includes graphic images that are shocking, upsetting, and often intended to horrify.[17] We advise researchers not to view or collect materials prior to meals and to avoid viewing content before going to bed (so as not to induce nightmares). Taking many breaks and having a secondary research project to switch from the graphic images to more mundane materials may forestall posttraumatic stress disorder (PTSD) for some researchers. We have observed the unintended consequences of sustained research on this platform may lead to psychotic breaks or antisocial behavior. Having an on-staff mental health professional is recommended for this type of work. We bring in a psychologist every year to offer support and advice for students who might be disturbed by the images and deliberately do not code the many violent videos we find on the platform. We leave these to other researchers with stronger stomachs. Like scholars who focus on sexual grooming or child pornography, we provide a dedicated private computer for use on these projects. This is preferable to using public machines, lest a passerby glances at your computer and glimpses executions, maiming, or immolation.

Furthermore, virtual research requires patience and many hours of screen time. Amarnath Amarasingam has reported that the life span of most ISIS Telegram channels averages two hundred days.[18] One needs to constantly add new channels to maintain access in case channels are shuttered or an account is flagged and access is lost for lack of engagement with others (for not posting or answering questions because of IRB limitations). The channel and chat invitation links are time sensitive, and if you are not logged on to the platform, you probably will miss the narrow time window to add new groups or chats. ISIS relies on this to sustain user engagement; anyone on the network is required to monitor the platform 24/7. Links expire and others might be shut down. Joining back up or monitoring duplicate channels is one way to assure the continuity of the research over the period of analysis. Even skipping one day could translate into a loss of access because some admins note how regularly an individual account logs on and might kick off an account if their online presence is irregular.

As a long-standing member of a group or a channel, your account may be flagged for direct communication. The interaction is generally succinct and in Arabic. Often it is no more than a salutation to ascertain whether the account holder is a lurker, or worse, a researcher observing and reporting on ISIS activities. Most of these approaches entail a brother (or sister) posting a direct message saying "hello how are you?" or posting ISIS specific emojis. Our IRB prohibited engagement, but we were allowed to post an emoji in some situations to prevent losing access to a network after we had lost access to several dozen channels by not participating or responding to direct messages. The contacts happened infrequently, and we could deter further conversation by posting something meaningless such as a ninja jihadi or an image (gif) of a short prayer. However, in some cases the communication was more personal. One of our original accounts designated by the word *Umm* (meaning "mother of" and signifying that it belonged to a female) received a few offers of marriage or requests to move to Syria (Sham) even though the account contained no images or any supplementary information other than that the account holder was a woman (see figure 19.3). For all other problems that might arise, we suggest consulting the latest privacy guidelines from the Electronic Frontier Foundation.[19]

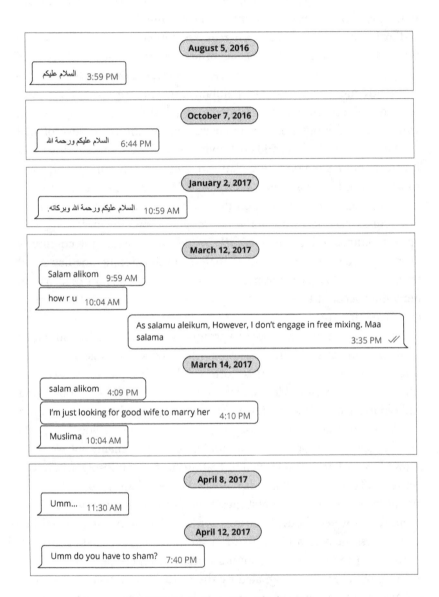

FIGURE 19.3 Chat with a jihadi suitor.

ETHICS: DATA COLLECTION AND DISTRIBUTION

The ethics of data collection are complicated by the fact that many of the existing protocols were written with medical research in mind—forty years before the appearance of social media—and are a poor guide for ethical online research. Every research team needs to address ethical concerns prior to data collection and distribution. Digital ethnography and social media research are shifting in real time, and updated research guidelines are needed that include online anonymized data collection. The European Union has taken several initiatives, beginning in September 2018, implementing new regulations to limit the dissemination of terrorist content from the internet.[20] The United Kingdom Counter-Terrorism and Border Security Act has made it illegal to view content deemed to support violence and terrorism.[21] However, these new regulations have created a backlash from both the public and academic researchers who argue that these restrictions limit freedom of expression and hinder future potential research.[22]

More broadly, virtual field research on violent extremist social media raises a number of questions that we encourage researchers to consider: What does it mean to provide anonymity to subjects who themselves have anonymized their identities on social media? If the users themselves chose names for their "public" social media persona, is additional anonymization necessary? In the case of members in ISIS Telegram channels, are keeping the identities of the participants ethical and safe?[23]

DATA COLLECTED

The propaganda we collected includes battlefield reports, photo reports, videos, magazines, and discussions about lone actor attacks in the West. Some chat rooms publish a membership list (and indicate who is currently online), allowing members to engage one another in secret chats and allowing administrators to monitor and police the network. This opens additional research opportunities to conduct field experiments and ascertain the extent of online social media addiction in the future.

From the outset, ISIS's "virtual world" pushed its narrative online to recruit, sow fear, and spread its propaganda to audiences worldwide. Now that ISIS has been dislodged militarily from Iraq and Syria, the virtual world is the new battlefield from which to coordinate lone actor attacks against Western targets while expanding its influence on its affiliates in the Middle East and Southeast Asia. Today this virtual world is the only arena in which the Islamic State can promote its strength and endurance.[24]

The platform has provided us with the ability to distinguish between attacks directed by ISIS and attacks merely inspired by the group. We were able to do this by monitoring the observable variations in the recounting of events. For example, attacks in Dhaka (July 2016) or Tehran (June 2017) were posted live to Telegram in real time as they unfolded, whereas attacks in San Bernardino (December 2015) or Orlando (June 2016) were presented with different degrees of detail and information well after the fact. This research has yielded a breadth of data about the inner workings of the ISIS network. It shows how ISIS governed as a proto state in Iraq and Syria and provides unique insights into its Caliphate strategy for expansion and shifts to the affiliates.[25]

Conducting fieldwork in the virtual space of violent extremist organizations is increasingly emerging as a popular area of research, whether it is for jihadi groups, extreme right-wing organizations, or new bad actors such as incels. New ways of conducting this research unfold on a daily basis with the emergence of new platforms, apps, and technology. It is important to acknowledge and highlight the potential benefits and pitfalls of using new media to research violent extremist organizations. Political science, criminology, and sociology appear to be heading toward codifying field research in the virtual space, but it is crucial to protect the researcher and the subjects of our research. Be extremely cautious and, for the time being, follow ethical guidelines to the best of your ability.

———

Mia Bloom *is professor of communication at Georgia State University.*
Ayse Lokmanoglu *is a graduate student at Georgia State University.*

PUBLICATIONS TO WHICH THIS FIELDWORK CONTRIBUTED:

- Bloom, Mia, and Chelsea Daymon. "Addicted to Terror? Charting the Psychological Qualities of ISIS Social Media," *Orbis* 62, no. 3 (2018): 372–88.
- Bloom, Mia, Hicham Tiflati, and John Horgan. "Navigating ISIS' Preferred Platform: Telegram," *Terrorism and Political Violence*, 2017 (online publication) 10.1080 /09546553.2017.1339695.

- Winkler, Carol, and Ayse Lokmanoglu, "Communicating Terrorism and Counter-terrorism." In *The Handbook of Communication and Security*, ed. Bryan C. Taylor and Hamilton Bean. New York: Routledge, 2019.

NOTES

1. Daniel Milton, *Communication Breakdown: Unraveling the Islamic State's Media Efforts* (New York: Combating Terrorism Center, U.S. Military Academy, October 2016), 1.
2. Joby Warrick, *Black Flags: The Rise of ISIS* (New York: Anchor Books, 2016).
3. Joel A. Capellan, "Lone Wolf Terrorist or Deranged Shooter? A Study of Ideological Active Shooter Events in the United States, 1970–2014," *Studies in Conflict & Terrorism* 38, no. 6 (2015): 407, https://doi.org/10.1080/1057610X.2015.1008341.
4. "IntelBrief: The Islamic State's Enduring Narrative," *The Soufan Center* (blog), September 11, 2018, https://thesoufancenter.org/intelbrief-the-islamic-states-enduring -narrative/.
5. Seth Cantey and Nico Prucha, "Online Jihad: Monitoring Jihadist Online Communities," *Online Jihad: Monitoring Jihadist Online Communities* (blog), 2019, https://onlinejihad.net/.
6. Nico Prucha, "IS and the Jihadist Information Highway—Projecting Influence and Religious Identity via Telegram," *Perspectives on Terrorism* 10, no. 6 (2016): 48–58, http://www.terrorismanalysts.com/pt/index.php/pot/article/view/556.
7. "Did Jihadist Rashid Kassim Lure French Youths to Plot Attacks?," *BBC News*, September 15, 2016, https://www.bbc.com/news/world-europe-37340697.
8. Stacy Meichtry and Sam Schechner, "How Islamic State Weaponized the Chat App to Direct Attacks on the West," *Wall Street Journal*, October 20, 2016, https://www .wsj.com/articles/how-islamic-state-weaponized-the-chat-app-to-direct-attacks -on-the-west-1476955802.
9. Rhiannon Williams, "What Is Telegram: The New WhatsApp? The Telegraph," *Telegraph*, February 25, 2014, http://www.telegraph.co.uk/technology/news/10658647 /What-is-Telegram-the-new-WhatsApp.html.
10. Laith Alkhouri and Alex Kassire, "Tech for Jihad: Dissecting Jihadists' Digital Toolbox," *Flashpoint*, July 2016, https://www.flashpoint-intel.com/wp-content /uploads/2016/08/TechForJihad.pdf.
11. The research was supported by the Minerva Research Initiative, Department of Defense Grant No N00014-16-1-3174; any opinions, findings, or recommendations expressed are those of the authors alone and do not reflect the views of the Office of Naval Research, the Department of the Navy, or the Department of Defense.

12. Mia Bloom and Chelsea Daymon, "Addicted to Terror? Charting the Psychological Qualities of ISIS Social Media," *Orbis* 62 (2018): 372–88.

13. Department of Health and Human Services, "Belmont Report: Ethical Principles and Guidelines for the Protection of Human Subjects of Research," 1979, https://www.hhs.gov/ohrp/regulations-and-policy/belmont-report/index.html.

14. Martyn Frampton, Ali Fisher, and Nico Prucha, "The New Netwar: Countering Extremism Online," *Policy Exchange*, 2017, https://policyexchange.org.uk/wp-content/uploads/2017/09/The-New-Netwar-1.pdf.

15. Michael Kenney, "Beyond the Internet: Mētis, Techne, and the Limitations of Online Artifacts for Islamist Terrorists," *Terrorism and Political Violence* 22, no. 2 (2010): 177–97.

16. An "air gapped" device is one that has never been connected to the internet.

17. Cyanne E. Loyle and Alicia Simoni, "Researching Under Fire: Political Science and Researcher Trauma," *PS: Political Science & Politics* 50, no. 1 (January 2017): 141–45, https://doi.org/10.1017/S1049096516002328.

18. Amarasingam Amarnath, "Jihadism on Telegram: A Large-Scale Study of Recent Trends and Group Dynamics," presented at the Vox-Pol Conference, Amsterdam, Netherlands, 2018, https://www.voxpol.eu/wp-content/uploads/2018/08/VOX-Pol-Conference-Programme-1.pdf.

19. "Privacy," *Electronic Frontier Foundation*, accessed April 9, 2019, https://www.eff.org/issues/privacy.

20. European Commission, "State of the Union 2018: Commission Takes Action to Get Terrorist Content Off the Web," September 12, 2018, http://europa.eu/rapid/press-release_MEMO-18-5711_es.htm.

21. "Counter-Terrorism and Border Security Act 2019—UK Parliament," accessed April 9, 2019, https://services.parliament.uk/Bills/2017-19/counterterrorismandbordersecurity.html.

22. "UK Counter-Terrorism Law Would Restrict Freedom of Expression," *EDRi* (blog), September 26, 2018, https://edri.org/uk-counter-terrorism-law-would-restrict-freedom-of-expression/.

23. We also question the assumption that the sources of research funding inherently prejudice research. Please refer to chapter 33 by Erica Chenoweth and chapter 34 by Zachariah Cherian Mampilly in this book for extensive discussions on the issue of government funding and research.

24. "IntelBrief."

25. Aisha Ahmad, *Jihad & Co.: Black Markets and Islamist Power* (Oxford: Oxford University Press, 2017).

20

ALL THE SIGNS ARE THERE

INCIDENTAL DISCOVERIES DURING FIELDWORK ON GENDER DISCRIMINATION IN RUSSIA

VALERIE SPERLING

▸ FIELDWORK LOCATION: RUSSIA

In July 2014, Lisa McIntosh Sundstrom and I were conducting interviews in Moscow and St. Petersburg with human rights activists, feminist activists, LGBTQ activists, and lawyers who worked with all three types of groups. Our research "puzzle" at the time was this: Given that Russian citizens had sent tens of thousands of cases to the European Court of Human Rights (ECtHR), and that there was plenty of discrimination against women in Russia, why was the only Russian gender discrimination case that had reached the judgment stage at the Court brought by a *man*?

By any measure, ours was a productive trip. We interviewed about thirty people in three weeks and brought home a great deal of data about the various obstacles to bringing gender discrimination cases into the Russian courts (which is a required step before bringing such cases to the ECtHR), as well as the obstacles to successfully bringing these cases through the ECtHR. Our initial query and subsequent fieldwork grew into a book titled *Courting Gender Justice: Russia, Turkey, and the European Court of Human Rights*.

Russia had invaded Ukraine, annexed Crimea, and been struck with retaliatory sanctions by the United States a few months before our trip. So Lisa and I had wondered whether we would confront significant anti-American sentiment from our interviewees. We didn't. One male professor who had written an article about sexual harassment was reluctant to meet us, but ultimately agreed, seemingly because Lisa was Canadian, not American. In our interview, he told us that he believed President Putin had taken Crimea because President Barack Obama "forced" him to—by signing a deal with Ukraine's new pro-Western government to lease the naval base at Sevastopol (ending Russia's long-standing access to a warmwater port). That erroneous claim was as close to anti-Americanism as we got.

One afternoon we went into a one-room sewing store on the third floor of a low-key mall near the Sokolniki metro station to buy a spool of thread and a needle. Lisa had torn the knee of her pants in a mishap the previous day. On the door of the sewing store we encountered a sign that read: "Sanctions!!! To President Barack Obama and the members of his administration. You may not enter the store [. . .] or purchase goods [here], due to the tense political situation between Russia and the USA. It is pointless to appeal this decision!!!!!" I took a picture of the sign (see figure 20.1), which apparently embarrassed the proprietress so much that she gave Lisa the needle for free. The sign was intended for Russians,

FIGURE 20.1 Russian sewing store imposes sanctions on Barack Obama's administration.

not for a Russian-speaking American, whom I'm sure she never imagined would walk into her store. Doing that "daily life" errand revealed the resentment of American sanctions that we knew had to be out there (public opinion polls suggested as much), but we were not likely to encounter this resentment among our human rights-, feminist-, and LGBT-activist interviewees who tended, on the whole, to be fairly positively disposed toward the West.

Lisa and I also noticed a strange phenomenon in St. Petersburg. Namely, the sidewalks featured many stenciled ads offering apartments by the hour, "work for young women," and ads ostensibly posted by one woman or another (Anya, Olya, Camilla) offering unnamed services, but sometimes represented by a heart and a "+18" (see figure 20.2). I snagged a paper advertisement that offered "wife for an hour" services from someone named "Vika." Also offered were "dates" and "casual acquaintanceships." We didn't see any of these ads in Moscow; perhaps St. Petersburg, as a border area, expects more sex tourists (although why the ads were in Russian, then, we couldn't fathom).

FIGURE 20.2 Sidewalk ad in St. Petersburg: "Call Anya (if you're over 18)."

With our fieldwork completed, I was in the St. Petersburg airport heading to London to meet my partner and child for a long-awaited vacation. I had some time to kill and some extra credit on my Russian SIM card, so I decided to do some additional "research" by responding to these intriguing ads. I called two. The "wife for an hour" number was answered by a woman who told me (when I asked) that what was on offer was *otdykh dlia muzhchin* (R&R for men). At first, I thought she'd said, "Footwear for men" (*obuv' dlia muzhchin*), but after a momentary delay I got it, thanked her, and hung up.

The second ad I called was for "Kristina." The conversation went like this (in Russian):

ME: Good day. I saw your ad. What's on offer?
HER [POLITELY]: What do you need?
ME: I don't need anything. I'm a foreigner, and I saw your ad on the sidewalk in St. Petersburg, and I was interested to know what was being offered.
   [Pause]
ME: Is it sex work? (*Eto intimnaia rabota?*)
HER: Yes, sex work. (*Da, intimnaia.*)
ME: Say, is that legal?
ME: Hello? Hello?

Our project was motivated by a feminist concern about women's access to justice when confronted with discrimination. Some of the same gender stereotypes that make sex work largely the province of women were at play in the employment discrimination cases described to us, and in the difficulty women faced in getting domestic violence cases taken seriously by police. Prostitution hadn't been a topic of our research because sex workers had—as far as we knew—brought no gender discrimination cases in either the Russian courts or from Russia to the ECtHR. Finding these ads—simply when walking around in St. Petersburg—reminded us that what you see when you're out and about, being an "accidental ethnographer," can be just as instructive as what you learn from a carefully planned interview.[1] Our project didn't incorporate these "found" materials. (I was in no position to incorporate the results of my brief telephone conversation because the call was not covered by my existing IRB clearance.) However, this material echoed the structural gender discrimination we had been hearing about from our activist interviewees and the difficulty women seeking redress for violations of their rights encounter both inside and outside of the Russian legal system.

One of the benefits of field research is exactly this sort of unexpected discovery, which can contribute to the broader knowledge of a researcher's area of study. Some of the things we learn on field research won't necessarily contribute to the project we're working on at the time—or even to a specific project at all. But all of these insights are valuable, even if they may not be what we expected to find.[2]

Valerie Sperling *is a professor of political science at Clark University.*

PUBLICATION TO WHICH THIS FIELDWORK CONTRIBUTED:

- Sperling, Valerie, and Lisa McIntosh Sundstrom, with Melike Sayoglu. *Courting Gender Justice: Russia, Turkey, and the European Court of Human Rights.* New York: Oxford University Press, 2019.

NOTES

1. Lee Ann Fujii, "Five Stories of Accidental Ethnography: Turning Unplanned Moments in the Field Into Data," *Qualitative Research* 15, no. 4 (2015): 525–39.
2. This echoes the point made by Wendy Pearlman in chapter 22 in this volume.

21

LEARNING FROM FOREIGN COLLEAGUES

ROBERT ROSS

▸ FIELDWORK LOCATION: CHINA

As an American scholar of China's security policy who regularly interacts with my Chinese counterparts, I never forget that their intellectual and political restrictions are far different from mine. Chinese scholars and policy intellectuals in universities and think tanks that specialize in Chinese security policy and U.S.-China relations work within the political constraints of China's one-party authoritarian system. The Chinese Communist Party expects that they will adhere to the party line and not challenge its policies. Failure to accept these constraints can be costly to a scholar's personal life and career development.

The concept of the independent scholar is not part of China's traditional intellectual culture. Rather, scholars at both universities and think tanks tend, for the most part, to consider themselves part of the Chinese state, with the responsibility and obligation to contribute to the "national interest," including to national security policy. On rare occasions this can lead a brave scholar to speak out against national policy, but the overwhelming norm is that our colleagues identify themselves as loyal members of the Chinese political elite. Moreover, insofar as we are foreign experts on own country's relations with China, the Chinese leadership has an interest in our perspective on those relations. Thus the assumption must be that our own comments and analyses will appear in a report our colleagues prepare on our meeting, or as part of a larger report prepared for the political leadership.

Foreign researchers of Chinese security policy do not address issues of domestic stability, including party policy toward ethnic minorities, dissidents, and local politics, so we do not threaten party authority and are of minimal interest to China's security bureaucracy. Moreover, if your research involves meetings with scholar-officials at ministry think tanks and universities—such as the China Institute of Contemporary International Relations (ministry of national security), the China Institute of International Studies (ministry of foreign affairs), Chinese Academy of Social Sciences (the state council), and the National Defense University (ministry of national defense)—you will be going directly to them; Chinese security agents do not need to follow you.

I do, however, assume that my hotel room is monitored. I assume that every hotel room in Beijing frequented by foreigners is monitored. I also assume that my email is read. But I do not find such activities overly alarming. If China's security ministry wants to spy on my conversations with my wife and children, so be it. Nonetheless, on short visits to China, I do not bring a computer. I use iPads and cell phones that I keep as "clean" as possible, but I still assume that they are "compromised." Clearly, this is a cause for some concern. But, insofar as I am a scholar and not a government official with access to classified material, I do not find this to be a cause of great concern.

Because the Chinese government monitors email and WeChat messages, I only conduct interviews in person. However, I do use email and WeChat to set up interview appointments prior to my arrival in China.

This research environment necessarily affects interview conditions in China, and I conduct interviews sensitive to these conditions. I limit my interview questions to topics relevant to my narrow field of study: Chinese foreign and security policy. I thus avoid gratuitous questions regarding past Chinese domestic incidents or contemporaneous domestic issues and party politics. My Chinese colleagues have no responsibility for these policies. But they will find such questions unfriendly and even potentially dangerous, and they will necessarily respond with a strong defense of party policy. Moreover, such questions may poison the atmosphere and will likely lead the interviewee to "clam up," thus rendering the interview useless.

We build long-term relationships with our Chinese colleagues, many of whom share our own complex thoughts on Chinese foreign policy and domestic politics. Over time, our Chinese colleagues become friends with whom we will have shared many experiences. Thus we should treat them with respect for their expertise and with consideration for the difficult conditions in which they work.

There are special conditions for Chinese scholar-officials working in institutions within government ministries. Chinese regulations often make it easier for these scholar-officials to meet outside of their institute, perhaps at a restaurant. Meetings outside an institute require less formal permission and less paperwork. In these circumstances, a Chinese researcher is almost always accompanied by another colleague from her or his institute. A similar procedure frequently exists for U.S. Embassy officials meeting with Chinese scholar-officials. These procedures reflect concern in both countries that officials are not compromised or are not incautious in their conversations. These conditions, however, need not diminish the value of an interview, although it may be difficult to scribble down notes while simultaneously enjoying what is almost always an exceptional Chinese meal.

Within these political constraints imposed by the China Communist Party, I feel free to ask my Chinese colleagues any questions, at any level of detail, that I believe are pertinent to my research on Chinese security policy, no matter how sensitive the issue may be in the Chinese system (e.g., the Taiwan issue). I pose such questions analytically rather than as an American nationalist challenging Chinese foreign policy. I assume that my Chinese colleagues understand Chinese political restraints much better than I do and that they can best decide how to respond to politically difficult or sensitive questions. I may also change the subject when it is clear that a certain line of questions is "inconvenient." Our Chinese colleagues do not take offense at legitimate research questions posed in a respectful manner, and among scholars, such situations need not affect a collegial relationship or the quality of an interview session.

Sensitive to the political conditions in China, I try to assure my Chinese colleagues that I will maintain the confidentiality of my sources; I do not even bother to ask whether I can tape an interview. I also assure my Chinese colleagues that no names will be used in my writings. In citations, I may refer to a source as "interview with Chinese policy analysts, Beijing, [month and year]," or "interview with a government policy analyst, Beijing, [month and year]." By omitting the exact date of the interview, we can minimize the likelihood of identification of our colleagues. This is not the preferred social science method for transparently coding interviews; but it tends to be the norm among scholars writing on Chinese security policy, and it is accepted by the leading journals on international security affairs.

Despite recognition that Chinese scholar-officials live and work in difficult circumstances, on some occasions well-informed and senior Chinese academic colleagues will respond evasively to every question, no matter how benign the question or how carefully we may pose it. Such reticence is unusual and probably reflects exceptionally strong political constraints that a particular scholar or government analyst may be experiencing at that time in her or his workplace. Nonetheless, such sessions are inevitably frustrating. Our time is valuable and our colleague knows that such evasiveness is not the norm and that she or he is not being helpful. Empathy is appropriate, but it can be difficult to conceal our frustration during these sessions.

At other times, our colleagues can be unreliable interlocutors. For example, one senior Chinese colleague did a complete reversal over two interviews I conducted six months apart. The subject was his preference for a Chinese maritime security policy. During the first interview, national policy was in flux, and this allowed a policy "debate" to develop among Chinese scholars and policy analysts. By the time of the second interview, however, the domestic context had fundamentally changed to support a particular policy preference. My colleague fell in line, rather than risk criticism, changing his position to conform to the emerging national policy consensus. Again, empathy is required, but we nonetheless tend to remember those colleagues who display such "political correctness" and understand that they may not be the most reliable subjects.

This experience also reminds us that we are most likely to observe "debates" among our colleagues when unexpected domestic or international developments create policy uncertainties. When this occurs and policy is in flux, there is greater political space for our colleagues to express their personal policy preferences. At other times, more stringent political conditions in China make most of our Chinese colleagues especially cautious and thus less forthcoming. Such are the political realities that our Chinese colleagues must accommodate. During these periods, interviews will, of course, be less rewarding than during more "normal" times.

Despite all of these constraints, interviews are uniquely valuable for research on Chinese security policy. Used in conjunction with primary sources such as government statements and officials' speeches, media reports, official and scholarly historical studies and document compilations, and journal articles and books by university and think-tank scholars, interviews can make a valuable contribution to the analysis of Chinese behavior. Interviews provide nuance, depth, detail, and richness to documentary analysis of Chinese perspectives on the policies of other countries, on trends in international security affairs, and on the underlying intentions that inform Chinese policy.

Interviews in China have made unique contributions to important security studies scholarship on contemporaneous and historical cases of U.S.-China relations, including on issues such as Cold War U.S.-China relations, Sino-Soviet relations, and Asian conflicts, and on contemporaneous Chinese policy toward the United States and Russia, Taiwan, Japan, the Korean Peninsula, and the South China Sea. Interviews have also contributed to important scholarship on past and present Chinese policy toward China's immediate neighbors in South Asia and Central Asia, as well as toward key regions of the Middle East and Europe.[1]

Research interviews are most useful for collecting data on Chinese policy that scholars can then use to shape and analyze their theoretically informed scholarship. Most of our Chinese think-tank colleagues do not view the world through theoretical lenses, and thus their responses to theoretically specific questions addressing cause and effect are not especially helpful. In any case, interviewee responses to questions on the value of a particular theoretical perspective cannot validate nor refute our theoretical propositions.

There has been growing concern that greater Chinese leadership opposition to research critical of China could lead to self-censorship as we seek to maintain access to China for fieldwork. I have not felt pressure to alter my research agenda or findings. But as an established scholar, I certainly have less to lose than a young scholar first making her or his way in China and in the field of Chinese politics.

Nonetheless, foreigners can write on subjects that Chinese cannot, and our scholarship often does not raise concern among Chinese officials. Chinese book stores are full of books by the great liberal thinkers in the Western canon and books on democracy. Moreover, contemporary scholarship in translation on Chinese security policy and U.S.-China relations is widely disseminated in China and, generally, these translations are accurate.[2] In this respect, specialists in Chinese security policy will experience less political pressure regarding access to research in China than our colleagues in comparative politics, who may specialize in elite politics and whose research may engage with sensitive issues in state-society relations.

Finally, collegiality requires us to recognize that our Chinese counterparts also have their own research agendas and that they have very full schedules. At times, they may simply not be able to find time to meet with us, despite their best intentions. More important, reciprocity requires that we allow time for our Chinese colleagues to pose questions to us that are part of their scholarship and research reports. To the extent that non-Chinese scholars can contribute to a Chinese scholar's own work, we develop a mutually beneficial relationship that can contribute to long-term cooperation between our academic communities.

———

Robert Ross *is professor of political science at Boston College.*

PUBLICATIONS TO WHICH THIS FIELDWORK CONTRIBUTED:

- Ross, Robert. *Negotiating Cooperation: The United States and China, 1969–1989.* Palo Alto, Calif.: Stanford University Press, 1995.
- ———. "The 1995–96 Taiwan Strait Confrontation: Coercion, Credibility, and Use of Force," *International Security* 25, no. 2 (Fall 2000): 87–123.
- ———. "China's Naval Nationalism: Sources, Prospects, and the American Response," *International Security* 34, no. 2 (Fall 2009): 46–81.

NOTES

1. See, for example, Avery Goldstein, "The Diplomatic Face of China's Grand Strategy: A Rising Power's Emerging Choice," *China Quarterly* 168 (December 2001): 835–64, https://doi.org/10.1017/S000944390100050X; Fiona S. Cunningham and M. Taylor Fravel, "Assuring Assured Retaliation: China's Nuclear Posture and U.S.-China Strategic Stability," *International Security* 40, no. 2 (October 2015): 7–50, https://doi.org/10.1162/ISEC_a_00215; Thomas Christensen, "Posing Problems

Without Catching Up: China's Rise and Challenges for U.S. Security Policy," *International Security* 40, no. 2 (2015): 7–50; Robert S. Ross, "China's Naval Nationalism: Sources, Prospects, and the U.S. Response," *International Security* 34, no. 2 (September 2009): 46–81, https://doi.org/10.1162/isec.2009.34.2.46; John W. Garver, *China and Iran: Ancient Partners in a Post-Imperial World* (Seattle: University of Washington Press, 2011).

2. China specialists M. Taylor Fravel, John Garver, Avery Goldstein, Alastair Ian Johnston, Michael Swaine, and I have had our scholarly books and articles translated and published in China.

V

DEVELOPING LOCAL
KNOWLEDGE

22

ON FIELD-BEING

WENDY PEARLMAN

▶ FIELDWORK LOCATION: THE MIDDLE EAST

I began my relationship with Middle East studies more than twenty years ago during a junior semester abroad in Morocco. My memories from that period are of the typically humbling mishaps of a young American abroad for the first time. I lived with a working-class local family that did not have hot water and bathed at a communal *hammam* once a week. When I joined, I elicited unforgettable scorn from the woman who helped me scrape off dead skin with a cloth mitt and quickly apprehended that I might not have done that before. I traveled to a peripheral city and stayed in a hostel, only later discovering that it was widely known to be a brothel. I began learning the Arabic alphabet and practiced reading street signs, my pride in sounding out F-a-n-t-a melting when I recognized the image of the tell-tale orange bottle below. And even my scarce knowledge of Arabic did me no good when I joined my classmates on a trip far into the Atlas mountains, where we were sent in pairs to spend a few days with Amazigh-speaking families. My partner and I performed an elaborate pantomime—consisting of bleating like sheep, repeatedly lifting our fingers to our mouths, and excitedly invoking the only word we knew ("No!")—to communicate to our hosts, somehow, that we were vegetarians.

I gathered more memories during subsequent years living in and among Arab communities: I spent a year volunteering at organizations serving Moroccan immigrants in Spain; made multiple return trips to Morocco as an Arabic language student; spent a semester at Birzeit University in the West Bank; interned at Palestinian human rights organizations in Ramallah and Gaza, and then spent another year doing Arabic language study at the American University in Cairo. This time in the region amounted to about two years between my BA and MA, and then another eighteen months between my MA and the start of my PhD.

Going back and forth delayed my doctoral studies considerably. When I began, I was the old lady in a cohort of stellar newly or nearly newly minted university graduates. During the prior year I did the interviews for what would become my first book, and I also got ideas that would inform my choice of a topic for my dissertation, which would become my second book. Even so, it was difficult then to account for what I had gotten out of the hours-turned-days-or-weeks devoted to watching Ramadan soap operas, playing with neighbor kids, looking through wedding albums, traveling on circuitous routes in shared taxis and mini-vans, and joining extended families for lunches that became dinners and then invitations to spend the night.

What I was doing across those years was not fieldwork. Indeed, I do not think I even knew the word *fieldwork* at that time. Nor was it ethnography or participatory observation, as I was not seeking information for any sort of research project. I would not even call it "deep hanging out," to invoke Clifford Geertz citing James Clifford.[1] Rather, it was just normal hanging out, but these accumulated experiences taught me much more about the Middle East than I realized at the time. Each was an installment in a lifetime investment in building an area studies expertise, and it all helped establish the foundation for the rest of my career studying this particular region. I would not trade that for the world.

As I cannot call this time fieldwork, perhaps it is best to think of it as "field-being." And field-being, I propose, deserves more appreciation then it currently receives as a part of the overall academic project of producing knowledge and understanding. Field-being can help us learn things in different ways than we do while conducting what is more conventionally understood as field research. In this regard, at least four salient distinctions come to mind.

First, and perhaps most basic, field-being is a crucial step in acquiring the proficiency in foreign languages needed to do credible research about societies that speak languages other than our own. In my experience, learning Arabic required both years of formal instruction and years of on-and-off living in the Arab world. I am fortunate that all of that preceded any attempts to do serious fieldwork.

Second, whereas fieldwork has us play the role of "researcher," field-being allows us to take on a diversity of other roles, each of which can give us a different perspective on the communities we seek to investigate. In my years in the Middle East, for example, I was a student, a friend, a coworker, a volunteer, an employee, a housemate, a tenant, a neighbor, and (as happens to many who spend much of their twenties abroad) a romantic partner. Each role introduced me to a distinctive environment and its own web of social relationships, assumptions, and norms. Each contributed to the personal, multifocal well of latent understanding from which I continue to pull in ways difficult to predict.

Third, in contrast to fieldwork (at least as it is usually done in political science), field-being invites us to follow rather than guide the disclosure of information, and this holds immense potential to expose us to things for which we might not even think to search. To return to my own experience, I spent considerable time immersed in Arabic-speaking settings long before I developed the capacity to express myself in that language. During that stage, the natural thing for me to do was keep quiet and concentrate on trying to absorb (or guess) what was being discussed around me. Unlike in the interviews that have now become a mainstay of my fieldwork, my typical role in those exchanges was that of a spectator, not that of a researcher actively trying to steer a conversation according to my goals. Research demands that we steer conversations purposefully, and there is no shame in that! But a lot can sometimes be gained by putting our agendas aside. And as a matter of principle, the more time we spend simply listening and observing, the more we earn a credible claim to be able to interpret, analyze, assess, and make meaning out of other people's worlds.

Fourth, whereas the value of fieldwork is conventionally measured in terms of data collected, the value of field-being might lay chiefly in the analytical intuitions honed. These somewhat intangible instincts about places, situations, and topics enable us to discern questions that are worth researching (because they matter to the people we research), help us identify nonobvious ways of exploring subjects, and enrich our ability to make sense of what we gather. In my experience doing interviews (as a part of fieldwork), I believe that intuition (built during field-being) has been far more useful to me than any preexisting list of questions or standardized guidelines about to how to ask them. Intuition strengthens the ability to read spoken and unspoken cues about what to probe more deeply or, alternatively, what to let go. Intuition, perhaps more than other kinds of knowledge, is gained experientially. And there is no better way to gain intuitions about a field site than by being there.

Students conducting fieldwork ought not to look at time in the field narrowly in terms of gathering data for a specific project, such as a dissertation. Rather, I encourage them to think of it broadly in terms of developing an enduring relationship with a place, language, or topic. In that regard, sometimes it is the episodes in the field that are unplanned or unsought, or perhaps not even understood or appreciated at the time, that prove most valuable as the years pass. Keep your eyes and ears open and absorb all you can. Nothing you hear or observe in the field is irrelevant in your quest to get to know a social universe different from your own.

As we move along in our lives and our professional trajectories, it can become increasingly logistically difficult to devote time to field-being, as opposed to fieldwork. Time is limited by teaching and service responsibilities, family duties, and the pressure to translate knowledge into publishable deliverables (professors' version of actionable intelligence). In whatever ways we can, however, it is worth trying to squeeze out time for field-being, or at least to cultivating the spirit of un-instrumentalized discovery that it represents.

Beyond our own thinking about "the field" as a place to be and not simply to work, we can encourage our students to take advantage of chances for field-being whenever possible. I am continually dismayed when I hear students, and especially undergraduates pondering post-graduation plans, refer to the idea of spending time abroad as "time off." "Time off *what*?" I usually respond. "Time off life?" My preprofessional undergraduates typically invoke this phrase with an apologetic tone, implying that going abroad after college is a digression from what they are *supposed* to do: go straight to graduate school and not delay the start of a high-powered career. If they depart from that path, they seem to feel that they need to justify it.

As educators, we should challenge that view. As long as it is safe and affordable, young people seldom go wrong by spending more time in other countries, languages, and cultures rather than less. Where they go and what they do matters less than simply getting there. We can encourage them, and remind ourselves that one need not be doing fieldwork to be in the field and learn.

———

Wendy Pearlman *is associate professor of political science at Northwestern University.*

PUBLICATIONS TO WHICH THIS FIELDWORK CONTRIBUTED:

- Pearlman, Wendy. *We Crossed a Bridge and It Trembled: Voices from Syria.* New York: Custom House, 2017.
- ———. *Violence, Nonviolence, and the Palestinian National Movement.* New York: Cambridge University Press, 2011.
- ———. *Occupied Voices: Stories of Everyday Life from the Second Intifada.* New York: Nation Books, 2003.

NOTE

1. Clifford Geertz, "Deep Hanging Out," *New York Review of Books*, October 22, 1998.

23

FIELDWORK ON FOOT

PAUL STANILAND

▸ FIELDWORK LOCATIONS: INDIA, SRI LANKA, SINGAPORE, THAILAND, MYANMAR, NORTHERN IRELAND

I'm a walker, and always have been. When I go to a new city, I get situated in my hotel or apartment and then immediately head out the door. This is a straightforward approach in Paris or New York; it can be a bit more complex in Srinagar, Yangon, or Belfast. Yet it has retained its appeal across fieldwork cities, in part out of a natural distractibility and restlessness; in part out of the loneliness that accompanies arriving in a new place; and in part out of a desire to avoid the haggling and hassles of finding someone to drive me to a destination of which I ultimately am not even sure.

But in large part I walk because it teaches me important things every time. The usual plan is to take a real paper map or guidebook and come up with a very rough goal—some tourist site or prominent attraction as a starting point. Walking is often supplemented by public transportation or a taxi/auto-rickshaw—Delhi, Bangkok, and Singapore, for instance, are sprawling cities with often prohibitive heat that makes walking everywhere a death wish.

Regardless of the precise way I get to where I want to walk, a certain sense of wandering is essential, unlike a trip for a meeting or interview for which the duration and target are clearly set. In recent years, a smartphone has become a valuable companion to a paper map, especially in places where formal maps are hazy guides to reality. A bottle of water, a snack, a book (paper or an ebook), digital camera, a local newspaper or two, and some pickpocket-proofed cash come along. The same black

Timbuktu messenger bag has accompanied me on every trip into the field since 2010; respectable enough for taking to interviews but durable enough for dust, rain, and rides in auto-rickshaws.

What does this give me, beyond something to do? In this chapter, I outline four benefits of fieldwork by foot: (1) understanding the lived experiences of war, (2) seeing how social and political cleavages manifest themselves on the ground, (3) identifying questions and puzzles as an outsider, and (4) learning to benefit from getting lost. The first two are specific to conflict environments; the third and fourth are more broadly valuable regardless of location.

THE LIVED EXPERIENCE OF CONFLICT

Walking makes clear the lived experience of people in an environment of war. In Colombo, Sri Lanka, at the height of the war with the Tamil Tigers (LTTE), barricades lined many streets, SMS alerts would occasionally let me know about bombs and security threats, security screening checkpoints were common, and armed police and soldiers on the streets were visible on every trip. A think tank I was affiliated with was on one of the common routes of the president's motorcade, and I spent many an afternoon commute home dripping with sweat waiting for streets to be reopened as members of the security forces kept vigil.

Srinagar, in Indian-administered Jammu and Kashmir, presented an even starker geography of conflict. In Colombo, the majority of the population could not plausibly be supporters of the LTTE—it was the Tamil minority that occupied the focus of the security forces. In Srinagar, in contrast, the majority of the population was potentially rebellious, creating a wider suspicion and more pervasive tension. Shutdowns and occasional militant attacks combined with massive levels of state security presence to create an urban environment dotted with checkpoints, fortified outposts, loitering police and paramilitaries, and Army and Home Affairs truck columns rumbling through the narrow, crowded streets. This became even more apparent on several occasions when I was in Srinagar for *hartals*— the shutdowns called for by separatist leaders that left the security forces as the primary population out on the streets.

Amid these smoggy displays of insecurity was the curious alternative world of Kashmir's tourism industry, with street vendors and houseboat operators seeking to win the cash of visitors. The two could never be separated, however; even along tourist-centric Dal Lake, security posts and Central Reserve Police Force detachments were inescapable.

In all of these contexts I was something of an irrelevance. Because I represented no security threat, I never felt the harsh glare of the state directly on me, making my experience very much unlike the lived experiences of the local population. But just navigating and keeping an eye on the visible manifestations of conflict created a visceral feeling of claustrophobia and uncertainty, even in me. The standard hassles of traffic, uneven sidewalks, stray dogs, and finding the next bathroom had layered atop them a set of constant low-level calculations. Where was I allowed to go? Where might a bombing or shooting, however rare, be most likely? Should I keep a distance from the security forces in case they were a target? Should I smile at checkpoints or look serious? What could I take photos of without getting in trouble? What kinds of documentation should I keep with me at all times, even when just out for a stroll? What would I do if there was a security incident?

I grew to be a jaunty, often wildly out of place, walker skirting around barbed wire with a messenger bag over my shoulder, both pretending a certain cluelessness and showing an all-too-genuine cluelessness in my interactions with the written and unwritten rules around me. It provided a glimmer of insight—admittedly still very distant—of what daily life must be like in these areas, and the frustrations and fears that accompany war.

By contrast, my fieldwork in Nagaland was primarily by car—long, bumpy rides through gorgeous but distant hills when not stuck in grinding traffic jams in India's Kohima and Dimapur, staying in a hotel on the outskirts of town, and seeing the sun set early every night. I never got a feel for the day-to-day of the place that I did in other places. I was on the same roads as the Army convoys, saw the Assam Rifles signs on the side of the road, and glimpsed police out of my car window, but I felt much more like an insulated researcher-tourist than a participant in anything approaching real life.

SOCIAL AND POLITICAL CLEAVAGES ON THE GROUND

Along with the security infrastructure in conflict zones, social cleavages become most visible when at ground level. Northern Ireland was my first conflict field site, and it was a remarkably walkable and accessible one as they go. I still remember with extraordinary detail my first walks through Belfast neighborhoods such as Sandy Row and ethnic interfaces along Donegall Pass. Later wanderings took me into various other neighborhoods all over the city. Although there was a security infrastructure of walls and cameras, it did not rival the active militarization of other conflict zones.

Instead, the challenge was knowing the political and social meaning of where I was—was this a Protestant neighborhood? Catholic? Neither, like downtown and South Belfast? Where was I going, and would I be getting myself into trouble by crossing from one neighborhood into another? In some places these were not issues, but in others they most certainly were, and I knew enough to know that I didn't know which was which. North Belfast was the hardest to navigate, with its bricolage of small ethnically defined neighborhoods, and I spent the least amount of time there. Urban ethnic segregation brought home a core reality of modern Northern Ireland—even if peace largely prevails, political cleavages map onto everyday life in an unavoidable and stark way. I was in Belfast for parts of two "marching seasons"—when Protestant lodges hold parades that can be sectarian flashpoints and sources of deep tension, and the geography of basic life can be further disrupted. Learning how to get around was more important because I was not ethnically identifiable. In South Asia, I was obviously a foreigner, but in Northern Ireland, other than being noticeably nerdier than the average person, I was indistinguishable from local citizens. I would not be automatically classified as politically unproblematic.

Friends, colleagues, and friendly passersby were essential sources of insight into how to navigate this landscape. Fieldwork's greatest value is immersion in a world different from one's own, a new set of referents, jokes, daily rhythms, and dangers. The transition from fancy coffeehouses in South Belfast to the Fall Roads or East Belfast, and getting from one to the other, became a matter of easy routine after a while, but it was certainly far from obvious during my first week. The social aspect of this learning makes clear how important it is to find people with whom to talk. Before setting out for a new city, I cast about ahead of time on social media and by reaching out to friends for contacts, whether they are professionally relevant or not. As an introvert who rarely strikes up friendships in chance encounters, having some friendly faces waiting for me is a huge help.

PRODUCTIVELY BEING AN OUTSIDER

The dusty pleasures of going on foot are not restricted to conflict zones. A crucial third benefit from walking is productively realizing how much of an outsider I am, and letting that guide my intellectual curiosities. It is easier to see puzzling interactions, curious signs, and unexpected buildings when on foot than when gliding by in a taxi.[1] This is not a feeling of alienation or loss, but instead one of abiding curiosity. My scholarly brain only works well when it sees puzzling things that challenge existing categories. I am far less skilled in almost all ways than almost every other political scientist, so finding interesting questions that drive new concepts, theories, and comparisons is the life blood of my work. This is why being an outsider can be profoundly productive rather than simply disorienting or uncomfortable.[2] Bringing a camera also keeps me looking out for unusual and distinctive sights, keeping an eye out for the interesting angle or striking contrast.

This is true even in the most seemingly sedate and anesthetized of environments. I came to really enjoy Singapore by combining its subway with walking, especially in Singapore's Little India and in the residential neighborhoods far from the glittering malls (which I was also quite happy to frequent). The richness and layered complexity of Singapore, from the way its markets work, to its cuisines, to its ethnic composition, were more apparent and tangible when it was literally all around me. I found myself driven to learn more when I got back to my guesthouse or when meeting friends: How exactly did the government assign people to public housing? Which roads were legacies of the British, and which came in the aftermath of independence? Why was there a shopping mall that had lots of Burmese people and restaurants? How many Bangladeshis live in Singapore, and when and how had that labor flow begun? Who precisely were these people driving fancy cars, and how did they relate to the grumblings I'd recurrently heard about both rich and poor foreigners moving to Singapore? A city that is often stereotyped as a boring, puritanical realm of air-conditioned conformity will always instead be a fascinating, complex, and incredibly rich political and social experiment to me, in ways good, bad, and simply interesting.

In Srinagar, this outsiderness drove a different set of questions than those about the nitty-gritty of insurgency and counterinsurgency that occupied my primary focus. I noticed a clear set of "middle-class" Kashmiris on my urban sojourns, found in comfortable coffee shops, glimpsed in nice houses in neighborhoods like Raj Bagh, and wearing stylish clothes and carrying nice phones. Who were these people, and more specifically, how did they make their money? This led to questions to my friends and interviewees about the political economy of Kashmir, the answers to which helped me move beyond standard clichés about Kashmiri tourism into a much murkier set of agricultural entrepreneurs, government employees, and, most interesting, politically connected families who benefited from the infusions of money that have accompanied Indian counterinsurgency. This element turned out to be crucial to my interpretation of why India was unable to fully stabilize Kashmir—some of the "development" funding provided by Delhi was essentially used to buy the quiescence of social constituencies and classes in ways that undermined governance, fueled local resentment, and made Delhi's proclamations of liberal democracy seem obviously, blatantly hypocritical. Sons of these social sectors would be among the leaders of the resurgent militancy of the mid-2010s. Despite having some degree of opportunity within the Indian system, they turned against what they perceived as the selling out, corruption, and opportunism of the comfortable classes.

THE PERILS AND PLEASURES OF GETTING LOST

Finally, there is a lot to be said for getting a bit lost. Living in Delhi was one of the most influential experiences of my life, for many reasons. But one of the things it helped me do was accept more chaos and going with the flow than is my natural inclination. Whether in Old Delhi, Civil Lines, the endless streets off Connaught Place, or even the leafy enclaves of South Delhi, there are many ways to get a bit turned around, even if not fully and irrevocably lost. Letting go was good for me. I had to negotiate with hard-charging rickshaw drivers in Hindi to get back to where I'd started; I saw parts of the city that I never would in an air-conditioned hotel car; and I experienced in a visceral way both the painful inequalities and vibrant microecologies of a vast and ever-growing metropolis. I spent a lot of time in central, chic Defence Colony, Pandara Park, and Jor Bagh. Even in these comparatively easy, upscale, and predictable locales, I wandered into back alleys and came upon scenes of suffering and celebration;

encountered unexpected parades, festivals, and weddings; and kept an eye out for new political posters and shifts in the rhythms of the neighborhood. No day was precisely the same. Some of these experiences were stressful and tiring; others genuinely relaxing. All of them made me a better person and researcher.

There are also sometimes more tangible rewards for getting lost. I remember a particularly bizarre and ill-fated trip to Fort in downtown Colombo to try out a guidebook-recommended restaurant in a hotel. The restaurant turned out to be closed, the area incredibly heavily fortified (including the Central Bank of Sri Lanka building that the LTTE bombed in 1996), and a beating sun made the entire expedition feel like an increasingly futile endeavor. But why take a taxi back home to sit alone watching satellite TV? So I kept walking, sweat filling every pore in my body—only to come across a famous bookstore I'd heard of but had never had a chance to visit. The combination of air-conditioning and interesting book purchases made the morning mostly worthwhile, especially compared to the alternative of just sitting around.

My bias toward walking endures, but recent fieldwork trips are ever-shorter and more focused as family and professional obligations limit the time I can spend overseas. And I feel that loss. A cab or even river taxi in Bangkok isn't quite the same as making a go of some walking. Delhi is a vastly easier city to get around in now that I have the money to hire a car for the day, but it is a less interesting and provocative one. So even now, when I get the chance to do fieldwork, I try to make a plan to get out into the world a bit. When I was recently in Delhi, for instance, I made it a goal · to take a nighttime walk down Sansad Marg or a quick late afternoon hop over to Lodi Gardens after a day of meetings and seminars. It can be a sweaty and dusty way to see the world, but it is also an immersive, addictive perspective on ways of living very different from my own.

Paul Staniland *is associate professor of political science at the University of Chicago.*

PUBLICATIONS TO WHICH THIS FIELDWORK CONTRIBUTED:

- Staniland, Paul. *Networks of Rebellion: Explaining Insurgent Cohesion and Collapse.* Ithaca, N.Y.: Cornell University Press, 2014.

- ——. "Armed Politics and the Study of Intrastate Conflict," *Journal of Peace Research* 54, no. 4 (July 2017): 459–67.
- ——. "Kashmir Since 2003: Counterinsurgency and the Paradox of 'Normalcy,'" *Asian Survey* 53, no. 5 (September–October 2013): 931–57.

NOTES

1. Although my work is not ethnographic, I very much agree with Lisa Wedeen's insistence that "There is never nothing going on": Lisa Wedeen, "Reflections on Ethnographic Work in Political Science," *Annual Review of Political Science* 13, no. 1 (2010): 255–72, https://doi.org/10.1146/annurev.polisci.11.052706.123951.

2. This is a way in which fieldwork can identify anomalies and outliers that drive concept- and theory-building. See Ronald Rogowski, "The Role of Theory and Anomaly in Social-Scientific Inference," *American Political Science Review* 89, no. 2 (June 1995): 467–70, https://doi.org/10.2307/2082443.

24

THE ONION PRINCIPLE

DAVID D. LAITIN

▸ FIELDWORK LOCATIONS: SOMALIA, NIGERIA,
CATALONIA, ESTONIA

My fieldwork exposure began as a Peace Corps volunteer in Somalia in 1969. Training involved four months of intense instruction in the Somali language, which facilitated subsequent research for my doctoral dissertation on the consequences of the official retention of colonial languages in independent Africa. That training, I am sure, sensitized me to the challenges field researchers face in interpreting data from their field sites, and it led me, in my second field endeavor in Nigeria, to articulate the "onion principle."

My family and I settled in Ile-Ife, Nigeria, in 1979 for a research project on the implications of religious change for political behavior. In that region of Nigeria—Yorubaland—about half the population had been converted to Christianity, the other half to Islam. The historical record revealed that these religious "treatments" in the nineteenth century were as-if random. My research strategy was to participate in religious life by going weekly to church and mosque (only a few hundred meters separated them) to observe the religious cultures in the two subcommunities. I was interested in seeing whether religious exposure could be linked to different political orientations. Another line of cleavage, which I have called "ancestral city" attachments dividing the Yoruba, was an alternative source that might condition political behavior. I chose a field site where religious groups were evenly divided and members of different ancestral cities were resident, and my wife and I set up a household in Ile Ife, which entailed becoming embedded in the local economy. A neighbor of ours, Roland Abiodun, a professor of humanities at the University of Ile-Ife (today's Obafemi Awolowo University) offered to guide me through the *oja oba* (the king's market) to help me purchase provisions. We first went to the stall of the onion merchant, a vibrant and commanding presence typical of Yoruba market women. I watched and listened as the bilingual dialogue progressed between local gossip and bargaining for his kilo of onions. The bargaining style was new to me. Several times Roland offered a price and our merchant quickly said *fun mi ni owo naa* (give me the money); but Roland didn't take that as his final offer, and then he went lower. After several iterations, Roland realized he had reached the bottom price and handed over four naira for his kilo. I followed suit. I gave her four naira and got my kilo of onions.

The next week on market day Roland could not join me, and I went alone. As I entered the market, our onion saleswoman spotted me in seconds and yelled "customer, customer, come here, to get your onions." Of course, I accepted her instructions. Upon arriving at the stall, the merchant revealed that for me there was no reason to bargain, and she would give me the four naira price right away. I was pleased that I was already accepted as a regular. Proudly, I visited Roland that afternoon and reported on my success. He smiled, a bit condescendingly, and told me that the market price for onions that week was one naira fifty kobo for a kilo. I was deflated. This anecdote became the source of a fieldwork guide-post for me and my students. I called it "the onion principle," summarized as a simple admonition: Do not write about a country unless you can buy onions at the market price.

The market was the locus of many tests of my local competence. At the oja oba, the bowls used to measure precisely a kilo of rice were typically raised at the bottom by a translucent wax, essentially a 20 percent tax for the unwary. When I quietly revealed to my rice merchant that I had been briefed about this fraudulent practice, a new bowl quickly appeared, and I never saw the waxed bowl again.

If I couldn't circumvent tricksters in the market, how could I do so at the church and the mosque, my two sites of ethnographic evidence? It was a challenge. In my interviews with church and mosque participants, as well as the circle around the *ooni* (traditional leader) of Ife, they would inflate their credentials, perhaps to secure a business relationship with an American or to have their exalted status proclaimed in a future book about their town. "Where was the wax at the bottom of their bowls?" I continually asked myself as I became more culturally adept. Tests of my skills in garnering local knowledge of Yoruba politics continued after I left Nigeria. Upon my return to Chicago, I was lucky to get into a cab with a driver from Abeokuta, a town close to where I conducted my field research. I had thirty free minutes to learn about religious and ancestral city divisions in a town that I had only briefly visited. Halfway through the Kennedy Expressway, the meter read nearly twice the price of a typical full fare. As I listened to his analysis of Ijebu/Egba relations in his home town, a rare chance for a complementary perspective, I said, "Femi, I must congratulate you on how you fixed your meter; this is not something many cab drivers can do." He looked back and smiled. "David," he said, "this meter is not for you; you can pay me anything that pleases you." His analysis of ancestral city politics in Abeokuta subsequently became much better grounded. Here I was able to pay for my cab ride at market price and get a less varnished account of local politics.

This corollary of the onion principle—consider all politicians in the same genre as market women—served me well in later research projects. One example comes from my study of the Catalan movement for "linguistic normalization," the program of ethnic entrepreneurs who demanded that Catalan rather than Spanish serve as the official language of the autonomous region of Catalonia. I went into this project believing that a deep-seated love of the language and the culture shared generally by the denizens of *els països catalans* (the Catalan countries) drove them to rally behind an expensive linguistic project that would enhance their ability to communicate with others by zero!

Should I buy this story? (Indeed, it was the story in my fellowship application to support the research, despite a warning from Juan Linz, who could see behind the smoke and mirrors of all Spanish politics.) In this case, I developed a degree of local knowledge by participating as a student in the *reciclatge* (recycling) program designed by the Catalan regional government to teach the Catalan language to the *administración periferica* (i.e., bureaucrats assigned from the political center to serve in Catalonia, and the support base for Barcelona's Espanyol football team). Relying on the primitive language skills I had then achieved, one day on the metro I noticed a well-dressed man reading *Avui*, the Catalan language newspaper that was a symbol of the normalization program but absent any serious journalism. Then I noticed that hidden inside the pages of *Avui* were the pages of *El País*, the Spanish-language paper for serious readers. This man was evoking nationalist fervor at the same time he was ingesting world-class journalism. I proposed to myself the notion of the "private subversion of a public good" and began to notice that many Catalans relied on this strategy. For example, they voted to require Catalan as the medium of instruction for public education, and then they enrolled their children in a private English-language school. Buying the story of the ethnic entrepreneurs was only a partial truth, one hiding a more political one.

Each new fieldwork venture reminded me of the importance of navigating markets as a sign of basic competence. In the face of language movements roiling the former Soviet Union, I moved my research focus from Catalonia to the Soviet periphery to learn whether the national projects of the then Union Republics would prevail. In my first trip to the USSR, before I spoke competent Russian, I rented a tiny room in downtown Narva (in today's Estonia) on the eleventh floor of a decaying *Khrushchevka* apartment. I chose Narva as my research site because it bordered on Russia, and nearly the entire population had cultural roots in Russia. My research question was how these populations—living in what the Russian state authorities called the "near abroad"—would react politically to their situation as an ethnic minority in a nationalizing state. On my first foray into an open-air market, there were queues behind every truck carrying goodies. I stood in the back of a line where I could see vegetables for sale. All of a sudden a new truck pulled up, and masses of consumers rushed to gain early access, and I followed them. It turned out that no one knew what would be offered, and the line suddenly contracted. Answering my question (in English) about what was for sale, someone informed me that it was dog bones. Meanwhile the vegetable truck was depleted, as were my culinary aspirations. After the Soviet collapse, national currencies became a new market. In a visit to Ukraine, I quickly became a multimillionaire, alas in *kuponis*. The new Estonian government issued the *kroon*. When I was investigating a more permanent place to reside in Narva, I was invited for a sauna in the coastal village of a leading Russian politician, a former member of the Estonian Soviet before it was disbanded. He had family on both sides of the border with Russia. How he would position himself in the new Estonia was in microcosm the big question motivating my research. I looked down at the tray behind the shift lever and noticed that he had exchanged his rubles for Estonian bills. For him, the market price of *kroons* was a bargain. He was betting on Estonian stability. You can't sauté currency as you can onions, but understanding local markets remains a key to understanding wider political currents. More usefully, I developed skill in distinguishing produce sold in Estonian open-air markets that was imported from the Chernobyl zone of Ukraine, and despite its glorious colors, I knew to keep away.

Colleagues often ask me to spell out the implications of developing local competence in a world of big data (coming from text analysis, night light readings from satellites, and MTurk samples) and experiments relying on randomized controlled treatments. These new data sources permit us to focus on mechanisms driving consequential outcomes at the micro level. These data-intensive approaches should not harden the boundaries between qualitative fieldwork and quantitative analysis. Quite the reverse, and I have long sought to undermine what John Dewey would have exposed as this untenable dualism.[1] Once we are working at the micro level, we need all the more to provide interpretations of our statistical models by asking ourselves why our subjects responded to treatment as they did. Living among the folk who are our subjects enables us to provide plausible and credible reasons for their behavior. These reasons cannot be considered explanations; rather, they are conjectures that should be put to systematic test. In other words, adhering to the onion principle enables us to induce higher-quality conjectures from those whose behavior we seek to understand.

Yoruba market women and cab drivers are probably more strategic than everyday politicians and bureaucrats, the folk we political scientists rely on for local context. Nonetheless, nationalist politicians are notorious for selling researchers a line of popular solidarity. Of course, we know that we are subject to all sorts of manipulation by those we interview; but if we abide by the onion principle, we will know better in which way, and for what reason, we are being made the fool. When you demonstrate to local informants that you are sensitive to their incentives—and aware of their manipulations— you are likely to get more reliable interpretations from them.

David D. Laitin *is the T. Watkins IV and Elise V. Watkins Professor of Political Science at Stanford University.*

PUBLICATIONS TO WHICH THIS FIELDWORK CONTRIBUTED:

- Laitin, David D. *Politics, Language, and Thought: The Somali Experience*. Chicago: University of Chicago Press, 1977.
- ——. *Hegemony and Culture: The Politics of Religious Change Among the Yoruba*. Chicago: University of Chicago Press, 1986.
- ——. *Identity in Formation: The Russian-Speaking Populations in the Near Abroad*. Ithaca, N.Y.: Cornell University Press, 1998.

NOTE

1. James D. Fearon and I have shown how qualitative and quantitative work is at best mutually dependent and not dichotomous; see James D. Fearon and David D. Laitin, "Integrating Qualitative and Quantitative Methods: Putting It Together Again," in *The Oxford Handbook of Political Science*, ed. Janet Box-Steffensmeier, Henry Brady, and David Collier (Oxford: Oxford University Press, 2008), 756–76.

25

THE INTOXICATION OF FIELDWORK

OBTAINING AUTHORIZATIONS IN BURKINA FASO

JOHN F. McCAULEY

▶ FIELDWORK LOCATION: BURKINA FASO

Dolo, the beer brewed from millet in villages across Burkina Faso, is different from the beer one might enjoy in Western contexts. Different in taste, of course, and different in presentation, but most importantly, different in social meaning. As the opaque, honey-colored brew served warm in large calabash gourds goes down by the liter, and village elders express their satisfaction in words you cannot understand, a process surprisingly central to conducting field research unfolds.

My familiarity with that beer is part of a story about obtaining authorization to field a population-based survey in the village of Boussoukoula. Quite apart from the tedium of completing forms from my computer at home, I learned in Boussoukoula that the authorization process can also require long days and nights drinking with village elders.

Researchers interested in gathering data from human subjects via surveys, for example, should be well acquainted with the institutional review board requirements at their home institutions. Those guidelines protect the subjects of our research from unethical treatment, in keeping with the 1979 "Belmont Report." In addition, researchers working abroad must be aware of any additional expectations from in-country. In the West African countries where I do research, this often means making a good-faith effort to share research designs with a national ethics office. In some places, approval must also be obtained at a subnational, provincial level. Although our formal obligations as researchers often stop there, gathering data may never get off the ground without the blessing of authorities in the localities where we work. And, from my experience working in West Africa, it's hard to say ahead of time what that might require.

As a graduate student, I conducted field research in four sites located on each side of the Burkina Faso–Côte d'Ivoire border, and this research was later published with my advisor (and fellow contributor to this book), Dan Posner. Using a cross-border research design that he and others popularized,[1] I aimed to gauge individual-level attachments to religious versus national identities, via surveys, in different political contexts situated in very close proximity (to minimize potential confounding factors). Two of the locations—Niangoloko in Burkina and Ouangolodougou in Côte d'Ivoire— could be classified as towns, a short drive from the border on the main road running between the two countries. The other two—Boussoukoula on the Burkinabé side to the north and Kalamou on the Ivoirian side to the south— are nestled on the eastern part of the border fairly close to a third frontier with Ghana. Boussoukoula and Kalamou are very small, remote, rural villages with predominantly Lobi ethnic populations and are connected by a dirt path and separated by only about seven kilometers. Depending on the security context at any given time, one may not even notice the international border on the path between the two.

My fieldwork started in Boussoukoula where, as in many other small, rural villages in the region, customary traditions remain firmly entrenched. To give a sense of Boussoukoula's insularity and attachment to traditional culture, the first churches and mosques—markers of social influence from outside—did not arrive until the 1990s. Given its size of only several dozen households, it is also quite impossible for outsiders to arrive and leave unnoticed. Of course, that is particularly true for Westerners.

I was accompanied to Boussoukoula by two research assistants and a research coordinator, my longtime friend Ollo—the son of a Lobi chief whose name indicates his place as the third son born to his mother. On arriving, we were met by the delegate to the chief of Boussoukoula. There must have been a local government official appointed to the village, but we were never introduced nor made aware that such introductions would be important or necessary. That is not where local power lies in Boussoukoula. The delegate took us to our accommodations and let us know that we'd be welcome for as long as we needed to stay.

This was the first indication I received that the fieldwork plans I had made would, shall we say, evolve. Our research team had planned to stay in the nearby town of Batié, where we had found paid accommodation knowing that no such accommodation existed in Boussoukoula. Our intention was simply to drive out in the mornings and return in the evenings until the data collection was complete. Instead, however, we were graciously given our own mud hut with a concrete floor, plastic mats for sleeping, and a kerosene lantern. As guests, we were deeply grateful, particularly because we were able to avoid the bumpy back-and-forth ride to Batié. As a researcher, I have to admit that I had other concerns. First, we spent our nights lighting and relighting mosquito coils because we were in the middle of the rainy season in a porous mud hut with a small window but obviously no screening. I was often awake to manage that task because the rolled up t-shirt that served as my pillow quickly lost its efficacy, and I never figured out a sleeping position suitable for a thin plastic mat on a concrete floor. Needless to say, I was not well rested during the week we spent in Boussoukoula. I had also planned to spend some time entering data as it came in daily from the research assistants who served as enumerators. That proved entirely impossible: there was no way to charge my computer's battery, little light to review the data in the evenings, and just too many interpersonal expectations to make the solitary task of data entry feasible.

The conditions were not new to me. Prior to graduate school, I had been a Peace Corps volunteer in a different part of Burkina Faso, also in a small village with no electricity or running water, and I like to think I'm pretty comfortable in such environments. Yet in doing research and collecting data that I hoped would eventually be published in political science journals and contribute to our collective knowledge, I guess I thought that my workspace and working environment would need to be orderly and controlled. I should not have assumed this, and they were not.

Once we were settled, the delegate—a quiet, earnest man of middle-age who had the obvious respect of community members—showed us around the village. We passed the chief's compound, the rudimentary health clinic, the primary school, and the main well around which women were gathered to fetch water, and he introduced us somewhat informally to families along the way. People greeted us warmly in Lobiri, the local language in which the enumerators would conduct the surveys, and children stared and often tagged along. Eventually, we wove our way back to the chief's compound, which was a somewhat more elaborate set of huts, and took up seats on wooden benches under a large tree just outside. It was late morning at this point, and the sun was high in the sky; we were pleased to be sitting in the shade and vaguely aware that introductions were starting to become more formal.

The delegate waved to the brewing station a stone's throw away, and two women brought over several liters of dolo, in jugs like the ones in which gasoline is sold on the informal market around small villages like this one. I am certainly not the first to note the central role of beer in conducting local research—in 1934, Monica Hunter described her attendance at "beer meets" as part of her observational data collection among the Bantu in South Africa[2]—but I hadn't even begun the research yet. Our calabash gourds were filled, and other members of the chief's cabinet and the council of village elders gradually joined us. We explained the very general contours of the research, talked about where we were from, and asked questions about Boussoukoula, pausing in between for translations between French and Lobiri. The elders described their roles and shared stories from local life in the past, which did not seem very different from the present. They filled their own calabash gourds, and the women brought more jugs of dolo. At some point, we were presented with trays of meat that I later learned included sheep brain, a local specialty. At a later point, the sun sunk beyond the horizon, and a few young dancers did an informal but lively performance for us, accompanied by a version of a xylophone. More dolo was served, and at a time of night that, in the absence of electricity, felt very late, the small group began to thin out and we stumbled back to our hut.

Any semblance of control I thought I might have over the agenda was thoroughly dispelled by the morning. To be honest, I was unsure if we had actually received permission from the elders to go forward with the data collection. So Ollo, the research assistants, and I just went with the flow when we were first brought a porridge breakfast and then met by the delegate for another walk around the village, figuring that at some point we would have the opportunity to map out our sampling frame and start working. The walk happened earlier in the day on that second day, but it led to the same place: sitting outside the chief's compound, drinking bottomless gourds of dolo, conversing with the elders, and nodding along to the conversations that either went untranslated or were lost to intoxication. Finally, as night again fell, the chief came out to briefly greet us, and afterward the delegate explained that we were invited to carry out our research beginning the next day. Any assistance we needed would be readily forthcoming.

To recap, we spent over a day and a half drinking dolo, the significance of which only became clear at the end of that process. I ate very good food that I sometimes could not identify, and our conversations with elders ranged from the mundane to the profound, with plenty of quiet drinking or awkward silence in between. Mostly, we invested time with these keepers of tradition, culture, and respect in Boussoukoula. I felt perpetually drunk and had spent those two days not even touching my planned research, but the time on those wooden benches outside the chief's compound was well spent. It was the required local authorization process that we needed to undergo to successfully carry out our work.

I took one concern and three important lessons away from this experience in Boussoukoula, which was repeated to some extent in Kalamou, although less so in the larger towns of Niangoloko and Ouangolodougou. My concern was that the time spent in Boussoukoula prior to beginning the data collection might somehow bias the outcome of our research. Community members were well familiar with the research team by the time the enumerators showed up at their homes to conduct the surveys. I personally attended few surveys beyond the pilot phase to avoid translation difficulties and potential enumerator effects (as the lone Western enumerator), but respondents all associated the research with me, the foreigner who had come to visit. If that familiarity had bred expectations about our survey outcomes, the time spent in Boussoukoula prior to the data collection could have exacerbated concerns regarding social desirability bias. In hindsight, the key outcomes of interest—individuals' primary modes of self-identification—were not likely to have been affected by my presence, and other researchers have certainly spent far more time in localities prior to collecting quantitative data, even if those localities differ in size and insularity from Boussoukoula. So I have no reason to suspect the introduction of additional bias, but it is nevertheless worth keeping in mind how our presurvey engagement with communities might affect the outcomes we wish to measure. In a separate research project I conducted in northern Côte d'Ivoire during the period in which the rebel *Forces Nouvelles* controlled the territory, I was assigned a rebel soldier who accompanied me and the research assistants to households. In that case, I made a deal with the soldier to keep his distance from households when we entered so as not to influence respondents.

Regarding lessons learned from the research in Boussoukoula, the first is that the time we allot for our field activities while sitting in the comfortable confines of our home universities rarely corresponds to the unexpected twists that arise in the field. There are simply too many things that we cannot foresee. In my research in Boussoukoula, only two days were "lost," although to even think of them as such is to overlook their importance to the research process. I have since dealt with hang-ups over authorization at the national level in Chad, imprisoned enumerators in Niger, delays in questionnaire translations in Burkina Faso, and other issues that have cost significantly more time. I now try to build in extra time that can serve as a buffer or, if all goes well, be used for additional soaking and poking, qualitative data collection, and building familiarity with my research context (which we should prioritize in any event to convey the expertise that is expected in talks and papers).

The second lesson learned is that the notion of consent can be complex and ambiguous in the field. Our IRB protocols emphasize the fair treatment of individual subjects and mandate that we obtain voluntary consent from each of them to go forward with a survey interview. In Boussoukoula, however, I learned that consent may be perceived as village-wide, and that traditional leaders have much to do with the consent that any one village member might extend. Lee Ann Fujii noted that it is reckless to attempt data collection in the developing world without authorization from local authorities, and their importance in the issuing of consent is a critical reason for this.[3]

Finally, we are inclined to think of ourselves as researchers and the participants in our research as "subjects." But on that trip to Boussoukoula, I learned that the local people see us first as foreign visitors, with all the good and bad that that entails. Before we can expect to take, we must first develop a level of trust with those whom we expect to give. This can mean long sessions of drinking with elders, eating unfamiliar foods, and demonstrating sincere interest in local community members as partners, particularly in small or tightknit localities. I recognize that some researchers may be unwilling or unable to consume alcohol or meat, and that female researchers may face additional barriers when it comes to building these relationships. I think it would have been possible to avoid certain aspects of the "authorization process" had I not been comfortable, but in that case it would be doubly important to have a competent and culturally informed colleague like Ollo to manage expectations.

I have not been back to Boussoukoula since that project was completed, but the authorization process we went through there remains among my fondest memories as a researcher . . . at least what I can remember of it in between the dolo.

––––––

John F. McCauley *is associate professor of government and politics at the University of Maryland.*

PUBLICATIONS TO WHICH THIS FIELDWORK CONTRIBUTED:

- McCauley, John F., and Daniel N. Posner. "The Political Sources of Religious Identification: A Study on the Burkina Faso–Côte d'Ivoire Border," *British Journal of Political Science* 49, no. 2 (2019): 421–41.
- ––––. "African Borders as Sources of Natural Experiments: Promise and Pitfalls," *Political Science Research and Methods* 3, no. 2 (2015): 409–18.

NOTES

1. Daniel N. Posner, "The Political Salience of Cultural Difference: Why Chewas and Tumbukas Are Allies in Zambia and Adversaries in Malawi," *American Political Science Review* 98, no. 4 (November 2004): 529–45, https://doi.org/10.1017/S0003055404041334.
2. Monica Hunter, "Methods of Study of Culture Contact," *Africa* 7, no. 3 (July 1934): 335–50, https://doi.org/10.2307/1155494.
3. Lee Ann Fujii, "Research Ethics 101: Dilemmas and Responsibilities," *PS: Political Science & Politics* 45, no. 4 (October 2012): 717–23, https://doi.org/10.1017/S1049096512000819.

26

FIELD RESEARCH AND SECURITY IN A COLLAPSED STATE

WILL RENO

▸ FIELDWORK LOCATION: MOGADISHU, SOMALIA

hree scholars and I teamed up to travel to Somalia's capital, Mogadishu, for several weeks in 2015 to conduct research into various aspects of the intriguing politics in that country. We four foreigners were there to interview political, military, and community leaders and to observe what we could. This was my third trip to Mogadishu, having previously conducted fieldwork there in 2012. All members of our team had been in Somalia before. One had visited Mogadishu previously, and another had lived in the city for over a year.

Many foreign diplomats claimed that this city was becoming more secure and prosperous, but we knew that their statements were aspirational at best. Their statements validated their support for the African Union's peacekeeping force that drove al-Shabaab fighters from Somalia's capital city in 2011, as well as the intense international effort to build a new Somali government. The reality was that the security situation in the city had deteriorated, a fact that I could plainly see in comparisons with previous visits. Car bombs, drive-by assassinations, and coordinated attacks were a regular feature of Mogadishu life, and they had intensified alongside new construction, government reform plans, and sunny official statements. These facts also contributed to the intriguing political puzzle that had drawn me to this place: What kind of politics of contemporary warfare in this collapsed state allows for an armed government presence with such intense insurgent infiltration, and even apparent collaborations between those who fought one another?

I believed I had a good understanding of how personal security works in this environment. In previous visits, we met a few Western foreigners in Somalia in scattered and otherwise very unlikely places who seemed to have worked out their local security. We also had studied the local political scene to learn what lessons we could. Ultimately, these observations and experiences taught us that security definitely is about much more than firepower or other forms of physical protection. Security is deeply socially contextualized here, as it is in most environments. Who we knew and how we were perceived was critically important for managing our security environment. All of this requires a good network of people, such as local hosts, journalists, NGO workers, and other informed people.

The first step to figuring out the security puzzle is to answer two questions: Why would a Somali host protect a foreign researcher if a foreigner has considerable value as a kidnap victim? How can the researcher know whether the immediate environment is safe? As for most things political in Somalia, the key to a realistic assessment lay in an accurate understanding of the intricate relationships and logic behind the facade of organizational charts, official pronouncements, and policy reports. One has to have enough knowledge of these connections to understand why a particular host would value the guest's well-being over selling the guest to a criminal gang or jihadists for several tens of thousands of dollars. This knowledge is also necessary to determine whether the host's armed retinue really is strong enough to protect guests from those who may wish them ill. (In our case, this assessment was not made more cheerful by the decision of one research team member to fill his laptop video library with films such as *Captain Phillips* and other chronicles of piracy and kidnapping, accompanied by uplifting documentaries such as *The Act of Killing*.) The key to figuring out what would deter a host from selling the guest to criminals or terrorists is to understand who supports the host and who might get angry if guests went missing. This involves identifying the real local and foreign sources of military assistance to the host (who also must have his own private army) and his past and present political connections.

The second step is to figure out who might see reputational benefits from successfully hosting foreigners. Successful hosting can convince observers that the host is strong and is a desirable associate for others who need to risk it in Mogadishu's unstable and dangerous environment. Conversely, the loss of a guest is seen as a sign of weakness, the kind of signal that no one who is important in a rough place such as Mogadishu would want to send.

For this trip and others, the ideal host is a businessman, preferably one with a small army that is used for commercial and political purposes. The presence of this security serves as a deterrent to those who may harbor ill-intent toward visitors. A strong host shares information widely and has many sources of information—an important element of the politics I had come to study—and is able to explain to insurgents what the foreigners are doing, while also deterring insurgent action. It is a truism that one does not pay a host for protection, as monetizing that relationship sends a signal of weakness and brings with it the suggestion that the guest is far more valuable as a hostage.

Assessing the neighborhood is the third step. Is the neighborhood destroyed from periodic bouts of fighting since the collapse of Somalia's central government in 1991? A wrecked neighborhood is inhabited by people whose often heavily intertwined kinship and political and business networks can't protect them from predators if they eventually rebuild their houses. The businessmen in nicer neighborhoods have protection—from insurgents as much as from other armed businessmen and politicians.

This protection, as well as excellent fresh produce from the Somali coast, proved essential for our work. We were able to spend considerable hours with Somali government officials, experts and notables in the local security scene, knowledgeable observers, journalists, and others. Venturing outside the gates required help from members of the small private army and care to avoid venturing off the recently paved and well-swept streets, which carried a low but present risk of IEDs. These hours, along with the task of figuring out our own security arrangements, produced a wealth of information and critical insights into the interconnected logics of violence and information in Somalia's complex political environment, which defied in important ways much conventional wisdom about violence and information in other conflicts.

Eventually it was time to return to Mogadishu's Aden Adde International Airport. This was a task of some import because this was a flight we could not miss! Experience from past visits heightened the sense of anxiety. For example, one trip to the airport involved running out of fuel near Villa Somalia. As the car rolled to a stop and the driver said "no benzin, no benzin," the clock started ticking. The crowd started to form, and cell phones came out. This level of interest in foreigners was concerning. Fortunately, that host had a small detachment two minutes away. Armed protection (in addition to those we already had) appeared on the scene, and we made our flight.

This time the ride was more relaxed, so why not stop at Jazeera Hotel to have lunch with an international reporter on the way to the airport? Lunch was delightful, and the journalist was informative. I checked out the hotel as a potential base. After all, it was only two hundred meters from the airport gate into the secure Green Zone with its AMISOM peacekeepers. The hotel's roof provides one of the most panoramic views of Mogadishu. We stepped into the elevator, the only working one we know of in the whole city, and it promptly became stuck between floors! After about twenty minutes, the elevator began to move, and we got our view and our photos, arriving at the airport and the flight not to be missed with little time to spare.

The value of this field research lay in the stark contrast between reality on the ground in Mogadishu and reports by international organizations and government agencies. We met foreign and Somali agents involved in assistance to Somali security forces and government whose stories were very different from the official versions. We came to understand how armed groups can collude and collaborate at the same time that they fight each other, and how the politics of state collapse had created an environment of interlocking, yet competing, networks in which leaders of most armed groups hedged their bets by inserting their agents in as many networks as possible—foreign NGOs, the government, al-Shabaab, private security firms, local militias, and security forces. These insights helped me to frame the logic governing uses of violence, how violence is seen by observers in this context, and how information flows and is shared. This work was important for understanding how the processes of state collapse are connected to this distinct logic of violence. Being there also helped me map the actual outcomes of foreign intervention to assist Somalia's government and to fight al-Shabaab, much of which stands in contrast to official plans and reports.

The value of this research outweighed the risks, at least from my perspective in 2015. I have not returned to Mogadishu. Shortly after our visit to the rooftop of Jazeera Hotel, the hotel was targeted in a car bomb attack. The host of that 2015 visit and about forty other people were killed two months after the Jazeera bombing in a coordinated suicide car bomb and follow-on attack that raged for several hours. Mogadishu has become less secure each year, with more bombings and drive-by shootings. The nighttime gunfights in 2015 were a clear signal. Then, in October 2017, the city experienced one of the most deadly terrorist attacks since 9/11 when a massive truck bomb blast killed almost six hundred people. Our precautions, protocols, and institutional review board and Office of Risk Management guidelines could not (and should not) cope with this degree of risk. A risk worth taking in 2015 has become a far greater risk today; even the precautions outlined here would not be sufficient for research today in Mogadishu.

My approach to risk is that it cannot be eliminated but must be managed; even a researcher encased in bubble wrap might get jarred in transit. This means taking concrete steps to reduce risk, such as not traveling at night on Kenyan highways renowned for gruesome crashes, actually taking the malaria pills, and not riding (helmetless) on convenient motorcycle taxis even when Kampala traffic is gridlocked. Mogadishu, however, is a war zone, despite the denials of an international community desperate to make its intervention succeed. Violence is not random, and it is possible to reduce the risk of harm. But a field researcher really should not be explaining to loved ones a strategy for avoiding truck bombs and IEDs, or why some people who were killed were somehow in very different situations.

The benefits of research—mine at any rate—are currently clearly not worth the risks of that worsening situation, which is one very good way to know when it is time to stay away. If one cannot go to the original site, there are alternatives. For those who want to study conflict in the field, conflict is recent history in plenty of places, and many methods are available to get at the information you need. Then you can worry about the traffic and leave the IEDs to others.

_____

Will Reno *is professor of political science at Northwestern University.*

PUBLICATIONS TO WHICH THIS FIELDWORK CONTRIBUTED:

- Reno, Will, and Jahara Matisek. "A New Era of Insurgent Recruitment: Have 'New' Civil Wars Changed the Dynamic?" *Civil Wars* 20, no. 2 (2018): 1–21.
- Reno, Will. "The Politics of Security Assistance in the Horn of Africa," *Defence Studies* 18, no. 3 (2018): 1–16.
- ——. "The Importance of Context When Comparing Civil Wars," *Civil Wars* (forthcoming).

27

BUILDING FIELD NETWORKS IN THE ERA OF BIG DATA

AMANEY JAMAL

▸ FIELDWORK LOCATION: JORDAN

"What do you mean, you've all been picked up by security forces?" I asked frantically, as three of my researchers called me while I was conducting interviews in Amman, Jordan. That day we had decided to divide the interview schedule. I would stay in Amman, and three other researchers would travel to small towns and villages outside the capital.

"We're all being interrogated," said Fatima. "They are accusing us of instigating incitement against the regime."

"How is that?" I asked. Nothing in our interview questionnaire was directly critical of the current regime. We were very careful in developing our questions to ensure safety and security for ourselves and for respondents.

"Well, I don't know, but I don't want to stay here," Fatima said. "They say we can't leave the station. Help us get out!"

We were conducting research on my book project, *Of Empires and Citizens*. We were interested in how citizens viewed authoritarianism and democratization in the larger context of regional and international politics. How did they understand these relationships? Were there aspects about democracy they prized? What did they appreciate about the current leadership and style of rule? How did they view the role of external actors in shaping current political dynamics in Jordan? As citizens, what role did they see for themselves in these relationships? And how did this influence their views about their regime? These were some of the questions we tackled in the questionnaire. Clearly, they were directly political, but we were careful not to suggest that the regime wasn't democratic. We allowed respondents to elaborate on whether they believed the regime was sufficiently democratic, or not.

I knew what had started out as a very pleasant, almost too pleasant, research day was going to be jinxed! Two interviewees showed up to the interviews, and although one of them was terribly late, we had an excellent exchange. Now three members of the research team were in jail. What should I do?

Well, I had been working in Jordan for quite a while. I have an extensive research network of colleagues, NGO leaders, students, researchers, and contacts in government. I immediately contacted a good friend and colleague, who is also well-connected. A bit hysterical and out of breath, I explained the situation.

"Don't worry," he said. "There must be a misunderstanding. In Jordan, researchers aren't arrested."

"But they are," I exclaimed.

"And certainly, they wouldn't arrest your colleagues," he said assuredly. I think that statement was designed to make me feel better, and I probably would have felt better if three members of the research team (!), all of whom had lives and loved ones waiting for them, weren't in jail!

"Give me one hour and I will call you back," he comforted me.

If they didn't get out, surely the security forces would dispatch others to pick me up, I started rambling to myself. Rule number 1, when your research materials (or researchers!) get seized by the government, what does one do? Secure the months of fieldwork already conducted. Upload your electronic research materials; delete your computers and hide hard copy research materials. As I began to execute rule number 1, I completely forgot rules 2 through 10 (or something like that). I think these rules included one to contact my home institution, another to contact the U.S. consulate, and so forth.

Then the phone rang. "They are all on their way back to Amman."

"Wow, you mean they were released?"

"Yes," said my colleague. "I told you it was a misunderstanding. We don't arrest researchers."

"*Shukran, shukran*" (thank you, thank you), I kept saying.

Almost a decade later, the moments of that day are still quite vivid. I remember the fear, the anxiety, the apprehension, and the worry. And relatedly, for this essay, I also recall how easy it was to get in touch with my "accessible" colleague, who was and still is part of a network of colleagues and friends I have built in the Middle East through conducting fieldwork. Not a month goes by that I am not reminded of the value of my field networks. Whether training students, conducting my own research, or participating in conferences, workshops, talks, and university visits, my fieldwork has been the doorway through which I have accumulated outstanding networks in the region. Indeed, these networks are one of my most prized academic and intellectual accomplishments.

In recent years, however, colleagues and friends in my research networks in the region have pointed out that the nature of U.S.-based research is shifting. Fieldwork traditionally entails researchers spending significant time in the field acquainting themselves with the context and people before they begin their data acquisition. This involves some mundane groundwork: reading daily newspapers, meeting other students, conducting interviews, and talking with contacts about current dynamics as they relate to one's project. Wendy Pearlman captures it well in her essay (see chapter 22) when she says she was just "hanging out" and through that process learned a whole lot about her research site. Paul Staniland echoes this insight by labeling the field immersion process as "fieldwork by foot" (see chapter 23).

Then there's the more deliberate work: visiting NGOs and organizations that might be working on similar themes, figuring out who else has written on the topic in the field country, and working on the process of data acquisition itself. However, today's researchers seem to have prized data acquisition over fieldwork. What does this mean? Well, not all data collection strategies are similar. In fact, there is a stark distinction between *fieldwork-based data acquisition* and the *acquisition of data from the field*. Is this about semantics? Absolutely not. This is about process, knowledge accumulation (and not solely data accumulation), integrity, and network building, which includes intellectual and academic reciprocity.

Merriam-Webster's definition of fieldwork is "work done in the field (as by students) to gain practical experience and knowledge through firsthand observation." By definition, gaining "practical experience and firsthand observation" necessitates getting to know one's research site and the people, culture, and community, along with their contextual nuances. Yet data acquisition per se does not require fieldwork. Data can be downloaded, administered in the form of a survey or experiment from a distance, discovered by research colleagues on the ground, or simply picked up from the field. Data collection can entail very little on-the-ground fieldwork.

Of course, different research questions mandate different data collection strategies. I am not going to impose normative boundaries on what is considered good or bad data, or good or bad practices. But I will say the following: Our discipline is moving in a direction that incentivizes data acquisition from the field rather than fieldwork-based data acquisition, and this momentum not only has consequences for how we conduct research—and for how our colleagues in the field perceive our research— but also deprives our discipline of some of the positive externalities linked to fieldwork, such as network building.

Two disciplinary transformations highlight the potential disincentivization of (conventional) fieldwork. The first is the "big data revolution" that is sweeping the social sciences and continues to grow.[1] Big data sets, multiple data sets, "cool" data sets, experimental data sets, social media analyses, and bulk data are all part of this data renaissance. For the social scientist, the new and innovative ways to think about data and data analyses are profound. As the discipline increasingly prizes big data, this push is not necessarily accompanied by efforts to enhance fieldwork funding and research training to meet the associated empirical demands. The incentives for the researcher are to secure data first, rather than use fieldwork as a means of securing data. And because the data demands on students are increasing, this affords very little time and effort for fieldwork. Students are at risk of simply "following the data."

A second development that encourages data collection from the field— and not fieldwork as a means of securing data—is the current funding structures of PhD programs. The five-year funding project (which includes two to three years of coursework) leaves very little time for prospectus development, research design, case selection, and language training, let alone adequate fieldwork.[2] The funding structure encourages students to work quickly, find data, and move toward writing empirically rich papers (oftentimes at the expense of theoretical rigor).

This is an era that mandates rapid data accumulation and publications before entering the market. Chasing down data becomes the sole purpose of field visits, and fieldwork is considered both a luxury and a penalty. It is a luxury because only those who can afford to spend time in the field can do fieldwork. And it is a penalty because the five-year format provides little time for fieldwork. Students are expected to write and research more expeditiously, but it is hard not to see that which is painfully obvious: these demands mandate that students spend less time in the field. And as such, there are trade-offs between conducting significant fieldwork and meeting the demands dictated by a fast-moving field.

At risk then is fieldwork itself and the positive externalities it cultivates. For instance:

1. The continuing evolution of epistemological paradigms depends on accurate context-based research (fieldwork) and not merely data acquisition, as David Laitin reminds us in his essay (see chapter 24): "And when you demonstrate to local informants that you are sensitive to their incentives . . . you are likely to get more reliable interpretations from them."
2. Academic networks are built through fieldwork. Students often take advantage of the networks their advisors have built, and in return they should build new networks for their own students.
3. The academic enterprise and building social science capacity, both here in the United States and abroad, depends on active engagement and intellectual reciprocity often facilitated by scholars while they are conducting fieldwork.
4. Treating fieldwork as research "laboratories" risks reproducing and exacerbating global academic and intellectual disparities and inequalities.

My ability to call on my networks in my moment of need was not based on any academic or other entitlements. Rather, years of investment and nurturing these intellectual bonds were vital. Following the new data acquisition mantra within specified funded time periods may very well render fieldwork an "old-fashioned" mode of data collection to the detriment of the creation and transmission of knowledge at the foundation of social science.

Solutions? The problems I outline aren't zero-sum issues. Structural and institutional solutions to these prevailing challenges are available.

First, PhD programs have to get ahead of the curve. The five-year funding program for students conducting significant fieldwork, including data acquisition and language training, simply does not work. Programs need to recognize that students conducting fieldwork require an additional year of funding. Furthermore, fieldwork grant and fellowship programs should recognize that the costs of conducting fieldwork in an era of big data are shifting as well. Big data are more costly. Traditional funding packages are great at getting students into the field but less beneficial for data collection. The trade-offs students are making are to replace fieldwork with data collection. PhD programs need to disincentivize these trade-offs by allocating more resources to funding packages. The traditional model to get PhD students into the field doesn't go very far if a rigorous data collection requirement is linked to projects.

These discussions and solutions will require proponents of fieldwork and big data to come together to advocate solutions that will simultaneously benefit both camps, and in the end strengthen the overall discipline. Training and mentoring future generations of graduate students requires that we have the vision and the determination to insist that the field doesn't lose sight of the importance of fieldwork to strengthen our knowledge about our own discipline and guarantee that students are developing the requisite network capital so important for the social sciences more generally.

There's a risk, however, that this debate will devolve into yet another polarized cleavage in our subfield, with each camp lobbying for its optimal position at the expense of the other. If this were to happen, I worry that fieldwork-based approaches will be compromised and fewer incentives will be provided to allow students to spend sufficient time in the field. This outcome would be quite unfortunate.

———

Amaney Jamal *is the Edwards S. Sanford Professor of Politics at Princeton University.*

PUBLICATION TO WHICH THIS FIELDWORK CONTRIBUTED:

- Jamal, Amaney. *Of Empires and Citizens: Pro-American Democracy or No Democracy at All?* Princeton, N.J.: Princeton University Press, 2012.

NOTES

1. Gary King, "The Social Science Data Revolution" (Horizons in Political Science Talk, Harvard University, 2011), https://gking.harvard.edu/files/gking/files/evbase -horizonsp.pdf.

2. Rina Agarwala and Emmanuel Teitelbaum, "Trends in Funding for Dissertation Field Research: Why Do Political Science and Sociology Students Win So Few Awards?," *PS: Political Science & Politics* 43, no. 2 (April 2010): 283–93, https://doi .org/10.1017/S1049096510000156.

VI

SEEING AND
BEING SEEN

IDENTITY IN
THE FIELD

28

RESEARCHING AN OLD CIVIL WAR CLOSE TO HOME

LAIA BALCELLS

▶ FIELDWORK LOCATION: SPAIN

I n the preface of my book, *Rivalry and Revenge*, I wrote about my family. The story of my ancestors, and especially that of my paternal grandmother, had brought me to study the Spanish Civil War when I went to graduate school. I wrote that preface before sending the book to press because I felt compelled to say a few words about my background to the readers, who would later find a rather analytical and perhaps "cold" approach to the bloody civil war that affected my country in the 1930s. I think the difference between the preface and the rest of the book illustrates the two faces of a researcher who decided to study a case that felt very close to home.

I had been nervous about studying the Spanish Civil War for my PhD research because it is a polarizing topic in Spain and in Catalonia, my original home. The topic is polarizing partly because of the lack of a thorough transitional justice process after General Francisco Franco's dictatorship ended in 1975, which has made the past a difficult place to (re)visit. The approach to the past is heavily influenced by propaganda from the left and the right, peripheral nationalists and state nationalists, political parties, trade unions, and even the Catholic Church. Few people are able to speak about the bloody past of Spain without falling into propagandistic messages, and those who try not to fall into this trap are easily accused of being supporters of one side or the other. Being in the United States as a graduate student probably helped me decide to study the civil war in

Spain. Although I had a lot of emotions about the Spanish Civil War—my grandmother was an orphan of the war and her life had been marked by it—the physical distance was useful and allowed me to study the war from an analytical point of view. When I went back to live in Spain for several months to do fieldwork, the physical distance was removed, and I had to make a strenuous effort to stay analytical and neutral as a researcher. I honestly believe that I managed to do it, but this required being alert throughout the entire time I was in the field.

THE INTERVIEWS

I conducted more than nine months of fieldwork in Spain, which involved archival and bibliographical research, as well as semistructured interviews with survivors of the civil war in different provinces throughout the country.[1] In this chapter, I will discuss the interviews, although I conducted them in conjunction with the archival research. For example, when I visited local and regional archives, I sought potential interviewees through local historians and local archive workers. These people, together with friends and acquaintances, were crucial points of contact during fieldwork. Indeed, most of my interviewees were selected through a snowball approach, whereby one interview "snowballed" into others via their personal connections.

The interviews I conducted with civil war survivors in Spain were among the most fulfilling and enlightening exchanges in my professional life. From these witnesses, I learned a lot about the civil war that I had not grasped from the dozens of history books I had read on the conflict.[2] However, my pool of interview participants presented particular challenges. I interviewed people who were teenagers or adults during the Spanish Civil War, which took place between 1936 and 1939. Because I conducted the interviews in 2007, my universe of cases were people no younger than age seventy-seven; the average age of my respondents was eighty-four. Of course, interviewing people of this age was not an easy task; it required time and patience. I could not jump straight to the key questions for my research, most of which referred to the distant past. One of the best pieces of advice I received before carrying out my interviews was from Juan Linz, then a Yale professor emeritus, who told me to ask the interviewees about something they remembered about their lives before the beginning of the civil war: How was their kitchen arranged? How was their bedroom set up? What was their street like? This was a starting point for a conversation that enabled people to mentally situate themselves at that moment in time.

I was initially worried that my interviewees would not be able to remember much about the prewar period, the civil war, and the immediate postwar years, which were so far in the past. But most of them surprised me. Perhaps their short-term memory was vanishing, but their long-term memory was remarkably lucid. The interviews showed me that traumatic events leave a clear imprint on people, and they do not easily forget these events and everything surrounding them. Getting to the meat of the interviews frequently took several hours of conversation, which I enjoyed most of the time. I have always relished the company of older people, so I did not mind the long chats.[3]

That said, sometimes interviews were exhausting, especially if I was conducting a handful of them back-to-back. (I did this when visiting villages or cities outside Barcelona, on short trips during which I conducted several interviews in a few days.) The logistics of these long interviews were difficult, but it was also strenuous to hear the stories about neighbors or relatives being killed, raped, or thrown in a mass grave, or about ancestors escaping Spain as refugees only to be killed in a Nazi concentration camp a few years later. I remember those months of fieldwork as some of the most wonderful months of my life, but I also feel that those stories left a little scar inside of me. They made me feel the reality of the civil war that had torn my country apart, including my own family. At the same time, I do believe that the lessons from that fieldwork period stayed with me, aiding me in conducting research in other conflict-torn places such as Chile, Argentina, or contemporary Catalonia.

Historically, there have been political tensions between Catalonia and the rest of Spain, mostly due to the deficient accommodation of national minorities within the Spanish state. Also, although there were many Francoist supporters in Catalonia, this territory has often been associated with the Republican side during the civil war, as it was one of the places where the left was strongest, and one of the last regions to fall into Francoist hands. Being a Catalan researcher helped me to relate and connect with interview subjects from Catalonia, but it did not help that much in other parts of Spain or with interviewees who sympathized with the Francoist side. Outside Catalonia, friend and acquaintance networks were useful; once people had a point of reference (I was coming on behalf of X), it was easier for them to open up and interact and share stories with me.

On a few occasions, the interviews were not successful because people did not want to talk or felt threatened or scared about sharing too much. Quite strikingly, some people in Spain are still afraid of possible reprisals for recounting things that happened during the civil war or for sharing their political views. Having a university researcher stamp from an American university was helpful on some occasions because it reassured people that this interview was part of a serious investigation. During the interviews, I learned a lot about what could be asked and what could not be asked about the Spanish Civil War and the Francoist dictatorship, and about how things could be asked in a different kind of format (i.e., closed-ended survey). Indeed, this learning process was extremely helpful for a nationwide survey I designed (together with Paloma Aguilar and Héctor Cebolla) in April 2008.[4] For example, in this closed-ended survey, we asked about individual and family victimization during the Spanish Civil War and the Francoist dictatorship, a pioneering question in Spanish survey research that people have later used in other post-conflict settings. We included this question despite the fact that some people were skeptical about its success, and we did obtain a decent rate of response. I learned about the feasibility of this question—and about the best way to format it in a closed-ended questionnaire—during my interviews. Conducting fieldwork is a learning process that has positive externalities. In this case, the process of conducting the interviews helped me design a survey.

In the *Politics & Society* article that came out of this research, I wrote the following:

> Although the semi-structured interviews might involve some measurement problems (e.g., backward projection of current political preferences, report bias), the advantage of this method is that it allows the researcher to engage in deep conversations with the respondents and to access what Fujii calls "meta data" (information that goes beyond the interview itself). In this particular case, the interviews put me in a key position to ask about sensitive issues such as political loyalties and wartime experiences, and they allowed me to assess feelings, sensations, and/or attitudes. In fact, the interviews were accompanied by the expression of a myriad of feelings: some interviewees were initially reluctant to talk about that period, some expressed deep emotions when talking

about their experiences (e.g., crying), and some did not let me record their testimony due to shame or fear of reprisals.[5]

It is important to note that those on the losing side of the Spanish Civil War had not had many opportunities to speak about their traumatic experiences in the aftermath of the conflict. That was the case for both the dictatorship (1939–1975) and the democratic period (1977–present) due to the "pact of forgetting" that accompanied the transition to democracy in Spain. Among my interviewees, these people were generally more reluctant to be interviewed and to speak about the war, but some of them ended up being very happy to share their experiences with me. They often thanked me for listening at the end of the interview. I still remember an interviewee who burst into tears after the interview and told me, "you are the first person to whom I have ever recounted this." In a way, some of these interviews were a kind of therapy for the subjects, and I wished I had had more training on how to handle them. I believe that I was only able to conduct this kind of fieldwork because I had a deep knowledge of the case, as well as of the social reality and the feelings that accompanied the remembrance of the civil war and the dictatorship in Spain.

ETHICAL CHALLENGES

My interviews did not have major ethical challenges because I was studying an old civil war in a liberal democracy, and despite the fears of some individuals, people could no longer be punished or prosecuted for their actions during the conflict. Nonetheless, I did follow the necessary ethical procedures to make sure nobody could be harmed in any way, and I protected the anonymity and privacy of the interviewees. Quite unexpectedly, I did face one ethical challenge a few years after finishing my PhD when I received an email from the grandchild of one of my interviewees. This person wanted access to the recorded interview I had conducted with his grandfather, who had recently passed away. However, I was not in a position to share that interview, and I did not do it. This was a major disappointment for the grandchild of my interviewee, but I was backed by my university's institutional review board (IRB) committee, and the issue was resolved with relative ease. This made me realize how important it is to design IRB protocols that will protect subjects even after their passing.

CONCLUSIONS AND GENERAL RECOMMENDATIONS

Doing research on an old civil war may seem less exciting than doing fieldwork in places with ongoing conflicts. I am conducting research on the current conflict in Catalonia now, and I find this somewhat more challenging. Even if the events today are less severe than those that occurred in the 1930s, some people are afraid to talk due to fear of judicial prosecution. I therefore have more constraints in my fieldwork; avoiding risks to subjects is paramount. Nonetheless, doing research on a conflict that occurred in the distant past is not free of challenges, starting with the age of the human subjects and ending with all the measurement issues related to the passage of time.

I recommend that future researchers prepare themselves to be versatile and open-minded. Every case and every fieldwork experience will be different and require a different set of skills. For me, doing fieldwork in Spain, a case that was emotionally very close, took a toll that I did not experience in Chile or Argentina, for example. At the same time, this proximity gave me several advantages: access to people through my social networks; knowledge of the local culture; and being particularly aware and sensitive of how different topics and questions could be addressed in the interviews. It also gave me training and insights that I have later used in other places and projects where I did not have the advantage of the "proximity to home" asset. Doing fieldwork close to home might be emotionally and politically complicated, but it also carries many advantages that facilitate the field investigation and contribute to the success of the research project.

Laia Balcells *is Provost's Distinguished Associate Professor of Political Science at Georgetown University.*

PUBLICATIONS TO WHICH THIS FIELDWORK CONTRIBUTED:

- Balcells, Laia. *Rivalry and Revenge: The Politics of Violence During Civil War*. New York: Cambridge University Press, 2017.
- ——. "The Consequences of Victimization on Political Identities: Evidence from Spain," *Politics & Society* 40, no. 3 (2012): 309–45.

NOTES

1. The research was approved by Yale University's FAS Human Subjects Committee under IRB protocol number 0704002514. For transparency purposes, the interview protocol has been posted on my website, and interested readers can access it through this link: http://www.laiabalcells.com/wp-content/uploads/Online-Appendix-PS.pdf. Anonymized details on the interviewees are also provided in Table A.4.12 of my book: Laia Balcells, *Rivalry and Revenge: The Politics of Violence During Civil War* (New York: Cambridge University Press, 2017).

2. Some classics on this conflict are Antony Beevor, *The Spanish Civil War* (London: Penguin Books, 1982); Stanley G. Payne, *The Spanish Civil War, the Soviet Union, and Communism* (New Haven, Conn.: Yale University Press, 2008).

3. A book written by a journalist, Montserrat Roig, on Catalan survivors of the Nazi camps, was a reference for me at that time. Roig had interviewed advanced age survivors and managed to collect incredible details of their experiences in the camps: Montserrat Roig, *Els catalans als camps nazis* (Barcelona, Spain: Edicions 62, 2017).

4. "Study 2760" (Centro de Investigaciones Sociológicas [CIS], 2008). See Paloma Aguilar, Laia Balcells and Héctor Cebolla, "Determinants of Attitudes Towards Transitional Justice", *Comparative Political Studies* 44, no. 10 (2011): 1397–1430.

5. Laia Balcells, "The Consequences of Victimization on Political Identities: Evidence from Spain," *Politics & Society* 40, no. 3 (2012): 309–45, at 317.

29

POSITIONALITY AND SUBJECTIVITY IN FIELD RESEARCH

ENZE HAN

▸ FIELDWORK LOCATIONS: XINJIANG AND INNER MONGOLIA

T he first time I felt how deeply intertwined one's personal identity and field research experience can be was during my doctoral studies on ethnic politics in China. In 2008, I spent a year in various regions in China where large numbers of ethnic minorities reside, including Inner Mongolia, Xinjiang, and the southern parts of Yunnan province. The purpose of the study was to understand the political logic behind different patterns of ethnic identity construction and explain varying responses to Chinese nation-building policies.[1] Contrasting experiences in different ethnic regions in China for the first time made me keenly aware of the crucial role identity plays in field research. I am an ethnic Han Chinese (the majority and dominant group in the country), which inevitably played a key role in my relations with research subjects, affected my access, and influenced my research findings.

My first stop was Inner Mongolia where, through contacts arranged at a university in Beijing, I stayed with a Mongolian family outside Baotou and traveled easily with a local guide on a motorcycle to visit various herding families. At the time, the Chinese government was implementing a settlement scheme for Mongolian herders. The goal was to move these nomadic communities to urban or suburban areas so they could be better managed—all supposedly done in the name of environmental protection of the overgrazed grassland. With such a large-scale resettlement project, strong grievances arose about the amount of compensation, the methods of resettlement, and corruption in the local government. Although my host Mongolian families and their social circles were aware that I came from the outside—and so must be a Han Chinese—locals were more interested in whether I knew people in Beijing and could help them petition the Chinese government about their grievances regarding the resettlement scheme. In their view, as someone who came from Beijing and as an educated PhD student, I must have the knowhow or the connections to help them. Although people acknowledged our cultural or ethnic differences, I was never made to feel sensitive about being a Han Chinese, nor told that this could complicate my relations with the local Mongolian community.

However, after I left Inner Mongolia and arrived in Xinjiang, the ethnic marker between me and the Uyghurs became a highly sensitive issue. Instead of simply being treated as an outsider, I was equated with the enemy. It started to dawn on me that being a Han Chinese doing research among the Uyghurs was almost impossible. From the Chinese state's perspective, the two most politically prominent and volatile ethnic regions in China are Xinjiang and Tibet. From the perspective of many Uyghurs, the Chinese state has engaged in a hardline approach in Xinjiang to repress their separatist political aspirations as well as their desire for more religious and cultural autonomy, but to no avail. Even people who do not hold such political views are more often than not treated the same, and repression breeds more resistance. Resistance by the Uyghurs is not simply toward the Chinese state but also carries with it a strong animosity toward anything Chinese. In Xinjiang, interethnic division between the Uyghurs and the Han Chinese runs very deep because the latter are often presumed to be agents of the state or colonizers who have come to settle on "Uyghurs' land."

I was in Xinjiang's capital city, Urumqi, in the summer of 2008, hoping to gain access and interview Uyghur people for my research. I had a list of names given to me by some Western contacts who had previously conducted research in Xinjiang, but I soon came to the realize that the interethnic division between the Uyghurs and the Han Chinese was too large a hurdle for me to cross. Even though I was a PhD student studying in a North American university, as a Han Chinese, the "oppressor" group for the Uyghurs (or at least perceived as such), I was treated with strong suspicion and even open hostility. Many Uyghurs simply refused to talk to me, either because they suspected I was a spy for the Chinese state or because they held grudges against the Han Chinese for denying their dream of cultural and political autonomy. Everywhere I went, I could feel hostile looks that made me uncomfortable. At the same time, I witnessed how easy it was for Caucasian researchers, particularly those from the United States, to access the community. I believe this was the case either because of Uyghurs' self-perception of their own Caucasian identity or because the Uyghurs believed the United States could help check the power of the Chinese state and even help them realize their political dream of independence. Such disparity in our field research access highlighted the differences between me and those Western researchers, even though we both might be doing our PhD in North America.

This was the first time I faced the crucial role of one's identity in field research. It had never occurred to me that one's identity and phenotypical traits could have such a strong impact on research access. I also began to understand the co-constitutive nature of the researcher's own identity and his or her research findings. I recognized the difficulty of remaining objective when conducting field research on a topic that may be personal. Because of the difficulty of access and the rejection and hostility I received from the Uyghur community, it was inevitable that these negative experiences colored my emotional reaction to them.

In the end, these negative experiences proved to be useful for my understanding of the political grievances and demands made by the Uyghurs toward the Chinese state. Indeed, my personal experience of the tense interethnic relations in Xinjiang meant that I was not at all surprised by the violent riot in Urumqi in 2009, in which Uyghur mobs violently attacked and killed more than two hundred Han Chinese civilians. The violence prompted a harsh crackdown by the Chinese state, and that vicious cycle has continued in Xinjiang to this day. It was difficult for me to develop a sense of empathy toward the Uyghur cause due to my own ethnic background and, perhaps, nationalistic sentiment. The ease of access to the community and the type of reception one gets influences researchers' personal affect toward their research subjects in many ways, and certainly also may influence the research conclusions.

The contrast between my research experience in Inner Mongolia and Xinjiang has led me to question the issue of positionality and subjectivity in ethnographic field research. In the discipline of political science, an extraordinary amount of emphasis has been put on objectivity and the search for the truth. Using good methods, it is expected that scholars can discern patterns of power contestation and the causal logics of political phenomena. We are warned about the pitfalls of cognitive biases that may arise from our own gender, racial, ethnic, and class backgrounds, but few have discussed at length the possibility of the interactive relationship between the researcher and the research subjects. Sociologists and anthropologists have written at length about positionality[2] and how researchers' identities can yield different outcomes in the research process. But this sensitivity has not been taken as seriously in the positivist discipline of political science. Or, at least, someone like me who was trained as a positivist political scientist had not been sufficiently forewarned to be conscious of the potential hazards of such a relationship.

I have thought hard about the lessons I learned doing field research on China-related issues as an ethnic Han Chinese. Despite all the debates on research objectivity and replicability, what if our research results are inherently co-constituted by who we are? Because I am from the dominant majority group in China, my access to the repressed Uyghur community was significantly curtailed due to the structural antagonistic relations that I simply could not escape. Furthermore, the hostile responses I received also colored my perception toward the Uyghurs. I received a cold and aggressive response and concluded that the problems in Xinjiang seemed to be rooted in the entrenched intercommunal boundary and animosity between the Uyghurs and Han Chinese.[3] Western scholars who conducted research on the same topic may have concluded that the Uyghurs are friendly, passionate, and innocent and that the violence in Xinjiang reflects the Chinese state and its repressive measures. In fact, this is a case of "one person's freedom fighter is another person's terrorist."

So where do these different experiences leave us? Was I more biased than my Western counterparts? Or is all of our research essentially biased in different ways depending on who we are? I believe there is a need to engage in more reflexivity in our fieldwork, recognizing our own subjectivity and positionality and how that shapes our research findings. I do not think there is a need to despair that one's research is more or less biased than that of others. What matters most is to clearly acknowledge this issue rather than proclaim a universalist objectivity. If researchers from different backgrounds communicate and collaborate more and juxtapose and contrast our different perspectives, our findings may generate a fuller picture of the truth.

I later shifted my research focus from domestic ethnic politics in China to Chinese foreign relations with Southeast Asia, and I was more conscious of the effect of my personal identity in my research. I started to appreciate that the research findings I collected through interviews in Southeast Asia were "situated knowledge" due to my identity as a Chinese national. Scholars from other parts of the world would not necessarily be able to replicate my experiences, nor to reach similar conclusions. When I interview government officials and ordinary people about their perceptions of the Chinese migration or Chinese investment in a particular Southeast Asian country, being Chinese inevitably affected their response. An American scholar working on the same topic might be given different responses because of the perceived competitive foreign policy goals of the United States to counter China's expansion of influence in the region.

Informants often say different things to people depending on which perceived identities are at work. Indeed, no two researchers have the same fieldwork experiences because no two researchers are identical, and it is natural that our research is heavily influenced by who we are.[4] Rather than presenting my findings as objective "truth," it is more honest to state that my research findings are heavily influenced by my national identity as Chinese. Likewise, I would appreciate other researchers being more conscious and explicit about their own identities. It is important to realize the effects of subjectivity and positionality in our approach to field research so we make more modest claims in our search for "partial truths." By doing so, we might have a better understanding of the complexities of the world and our place in it.

———

Enze Han *is associate professor in the Department of Politics and Public Policy at the University of Hong Kong.*

PUBLICATION TO WHICH THIS FIELDWORK CONTRIBUTED:

- Han, Enze. *Contestation and Adaptation: The Politics of National Identity in China.* New York: Oxford University Press, 2013.

NOTES

1. Enze Han, *Contestation and Adaptation: The Politics of National Identity in China* (New York: Oxford University Press, 2013).

2. Patricia Ticineto Clough, *The End(s) of Ethnography: From Realism to Social Criticism* (Newbury Park, Calif.: Sage, 1992); Richard Tewksbury and Patricia Gagné, "Assumed and Presumed Identities: Problems of Self-Presentation in Field Research," *Sociological Spectrum* 17, no. 2 (April 1997): 127–55.

3. Enze Han, "Boundaries, Discrimination, and Interethnic Conflict in Xinjiang, China," *International Journal of Conflict and Violence* 4, no. 2 (November 2010): 244–56.

4. Vasundhara Sirnate, "Positionality, Personal Insecurity, and Female Empathy in Security Studies Research," *PS: Political Science & Politics* 47, no. 2 (April 2014): 398–401.

30

RACE AND THE STUDY OF A RACIAL DEMOCRACY

MELISSA NOBLES

▶ FIELDWORK LOCATION: RIO DE JANEIRO, BRAZIL

I first became interested in the racial dimensions of Brazilian politics as an undergraduate student studying the comparative history of slavery. Brazil was one of the largest slave-holding societies in the Americas and the last to end slavery in 1888. Yet even with this history, Brazil had enjoyed the reputation, at least at the time I began my dissertation research, as a country without significant racial inequalities, animus, or violence. Not only had Brazilian slavery ended peacefully without a civil war, but post-slavery Brazilian law and society did not institutionalize legally sanctioned racial discrimination or segregation, as was done in the United States. Like scholars before me, I wanted to better understand these historical trajectories and how they might help to explain the different meanings and consequences of racial identification in Brazil when compared to the United States. In contrast to conventional wisdom, I found that socioeconomic stratification by race was a significant feature of Brazilian society.[1] I also discovered through personal experiences that race mattered in ways not dissimilar from those in the United States.

Before beginning my fieldwork in 1992, I had worked for the Ford Foundation as a summer intern in 1990 in their Rio de Janeiro office. This intern experience, as an assistant to the program officer, allowed me to do a number of things. First, and most practically, it allowed me to practice my Portuguese. I studied the language while an undergraduate and in graduate school, but this job was my first opportunity to live in the country. Second, it allowed me to become more knowledgeable about important political, economic, and social issues in Brazil. The Ford Foundation was well connected to a range of Brazilian institutions in government, private, and non-profit sectors, and I was often invited to meetings and conferences. Indeed, it was through this internship that I was exposed to an activity that became part of my dissertation, and then my first book. Third, I became aware that my identity as an African American would probably affect my fieldwork experience in both negative and positive ways. While working at the Ford Foundation, my exchanges with Brazilians were filled with reminders of the privileged position I occupied, even as an intern. The people with whom I interacted were often seeking new or continued financial support from the Ford Foundation. Although conversations were engaging and productive, they were also stilted. People would typically shape the conversations in the ways they expected or hoped would be most advantageous to them. This was all quite predictable and understandable. My experiences changed when I was no longer the Ford Foundation intern but a young, African American woman living in Rio. There I learned that my identity mattered in ways often similar to my experiences in the United States, although sometimes not.

MY FIELDWORK EXPERIENCES

The idea for my dissertation stemmed from my internship experience at the Ford Foundation. That summer several organizations explicitly organized around a black racial identity were seeking support for a public campaign targeting the 2000 census. They intended to urge Brazilians to choose a darker identity on their census forms. As they saw it, their political claims would be better substantiated if they could convince Brazilians not to see themselves as "white" or "brown" but as "black." A word of explanation: the terms used on the census were "white," "brown," and "black," but the Brazilian term used for brown (*pardo*) is not used in common parlance. A much more commonly spoken term is *moreno*, but demographers considered *moreno* too capacious and ideological for the social scientific and official process of census taking. Similarly, the census term for black (*preto*) is also a complicated word. It is often used to describe objects, not persons. Nonetheless, an alternative term (*negro*), preferred by black organizations, was viewed by demographers as too ideological and therefore unsuitable for the census.

My internship at the Ford Foundation prompted me to think more deeply not only about the campaign itself but also about why its organizers chose the census, of all institutions, to target. I realized that the campaign provided me with a way to think about how state institution and identity were linked. This connection proved especially important in thinking about a comparative study of racial politics because other institutions (such as the law) were not nearly as instructive or conceptually rich. Black organizations had long existed in Brazil—dating back to the early twentieth century—but they were historically limited in their reach and efficacy. Also important, they could not properly be called "mass movements" because the presumed constituency of black people did not see themselves as such.[2] Hence, according to the organizations approaching the Ford Foundation, the campaign was needed to influence the way Brazilians viewed their racial (or color) identity and how they reported that identification to census takers.

There is serendipity in fieldwork. I knew I wanted to study the racial dimensions of Brazilian politics and society, but I was unsure about choosing a specific topic. My work with the Ford Foundation provided an idea that I was able to marshal and use. My dissertation prospectus was based on my thinking backward and forward about the census campaign. Two years later, in 1992, I returned to Brazil, this time by way of a travel grant from the Institute for World Politics. I conducted archival research at the National Library of Brazil in Rio de Janeiro, the libraries of Brazil's Census Institute (*Instituto Brasileiro de Geografia e Estatística—IBGE*), and Getúlio Vargas Foundation (*Fundação Getúlio Vargas*), one of Brazil's most influential think tanks. This archival research allowed me to reconstruct the history of color categorization in the Brazilian census, and I used this history as a case for probing the larger question of how official categorization on the census (such as race or color categories) can both reflect and shape politics. Drawing on several archives, not just that of the Brazilian Census Institute, proved especially fruitful. Several informative but unpublished academic manuscripts were kept at the National Library and at the Getúlio Vargas archives. In conversations with two former IBGE officials, I also learned that missing and relevant documents were held in the private libraries of former officials. Although I reached out to one former official, inquiring about the veracity of this assertion, I was unable to confirm it.

This fieldwork also revealed to me how my identity mattered. It provided a better understanding of why black organizations thought it necessary to influence identity choices on the census. As a researcher, I asked for photocopies of all documents, and library staff performed these tasks. I was meeting one afternoon with a Brazilian doctoral candidate in economics who also worked on the research staff at the IBGE. The library employee copying our documents overheard our conversation and shared his view of his own identity and the category he intended to check on the census. I do not recall his answer, but I vividly recall how he responded when I asked how he would categorize me. He looked at me and became profusely apologetic, saying he did not mean to insult me as he did not (or could not) know how I would receive his response. Then he told me that he viewed me as *negra* (black). That was it. I did not disagree; nor was I insulted. But because of the negative meanings of "black" in Brazil, he viewed it as an insult, for which he felt the need to apologize.

That exchange crystallized the central paradox of Brazilian society and, by extension, Brazilian politics. Brazil was the purported "racial democracy" with no racial discrimination, but no one wanted to be seen or treated as "black." How could Brazilians organize politically to combat racial discrimination if few would publicly assert a black identity? My experiences of being black in Brazil can only rightly be termed "inconveniences," and this was usually remedied when I spoke in English, thereby demonstrating that I was not Brazilian and exempting me from the "black Brazilian" treatment. For example, I recall one day going to the bank to exchange U.S. dollars for Brazilian currency. At the time, the exchange rate was quite volatile, making it advisable to change currency frequently because the U.S. dollar could become significantly more valuable over the course of a week. I went to a nearby bank, and as I entered the door (which opened automatically), I was immediately approached by the bank's police officer, who stopped me. Her first words to me were, in a whisper, "What are you doing here?" I knew in that instant that I needed to respond in English. I acted as though I did not understand the question or its underlying assumptions. Once I spoke in English, she became friendly and allowed me to fully enter the bank and conduct my business.

I am certain my skin color and her view of it were the determining factors in that encounter.

One larger lesson that emerges from this example is that researchers, whether we care to admit it or not, are participants, not detached observers. Our social position and perceptions thereof travel with us. I am confident a white male graduate student would not have been approached in the same way I was in that bank. But let's take that proposition one step further: Would he be as skeptical or critical of the view of Brazil as a racial democracy in the absence of such an encounter, for example? As social scientists, we are expected to rely on data and evidence when drawing conclusions—and we do. But we also rely on our own experiences and observations. We may not theorize as deeply or clearly identify our own subjectivity as anthropologists do. However, all of us are subjects: not just the black woman scholar whose racial and gender identity are explicit dimensions of the scholar's fieldwork experiences but also the white male scholar whose identity often affords invisible (at least to him) privileges and conveniences.

My identity did provide me with easier access to leaders of the census campaign. They assumed (rightly, I should add) that I too was critical of the idea of Brazilian racial democracy and that I understood the aims of their efforts. My one-on-one interviews with leadership were important in allowing my interviewees to elaborate on the different ideological approaches that underlay their overall collective actions. As is true for most social movements, there were competing understandings of the nature of racial identification and politics in Brazil. There were also different assessments of the campaign's probable efficacy. Not surprising, my interviewees were most candid about these differences when speaking privately with me. An important lesson, then, was that one-on-one interviews yielded more authentic data.

I took and continue to take steps in subsequent fieldwork to ensure my personal safety as a matter of course. I am thankful that my one-on-one interviews in Brazil were positive experiences. However, at least in Brazil, I heeded the warnings to only take "radio" taxis to my destinations. Radio taxis are private car services. Although simply hailing a taxi would have cost less and been more convenient, it was decidedly more dangerous for a woman. I was told stories and had heard one news report of a taxicab driver sexually assaulting a passenger. My point is that the vaunted view of fieldwork carried out by the intrepid researcher bears an incomplete resemblance to the lived experiences of women scholars. "Risk" often takes on different meanings and can include ordinary tasks, such as hailing a cab, for example.

LESSONS LEARNED

My subsequent research and fieldwork has been profoundly shaped by my first major research project in Brazil. In my ensuing work, I have learned that being an African American woman researcher matters to the people with whom I interact, in ways both expected and not. Although I am not an anthropologist, awareness of my own subjectivity has been a central feature of my research experiences. There were other more general research lessons as well. Over the years, I have tried to correct for the mistakes made in Brazil, which I only realized once I was back in the United States. Although I tried to carefully organize my documents and note taking, I realized there is always room for improvement. Namely, I could not simply collect documents at the archives or conduct interviews. I also had to constantly engage and think about the information obtained through the documents and interviews in real time. This observation is indifferent to methodology. Technologies and other research tools today greatly assist in organization and obtaining primary sources and secondary documents. However, technologies in organization are no substitute for discernment and continued engagement. Engagement seems obvious, but it is often easier said than done precisely because the desire to maximize time in the field—arranging and conducting interviews, finding documents, and the like—runs counter to stepping back and taking the big view while still in the field.

Finally, I conclude these comments with a robust declaration in support of fieldwork. If you are reading this book, you probably do not need to be convinced, but I still want to offer words of affirmation and encouragement. The ease with which written materials (journal articles, books, magazine and newspaper articles), surveys, and other types of data can be obtained without ever leaving your office makes this affirmative statement necessary. There is no easy substitute for the human experience of visiting a place and interacting with the people. As a researcher, you are changed and informed by these experiences in ways that extend far beyond what you learn from texts or what you may write. When I finished my field-work in Brazil, I knew I was not leaving a racial democracy. In addition, I left with more knowledge about, deeper interest in, and greater appreciation for a range of issues in Brazilian politics and society, including and extending beyond race. As my example and those of my colleagues in this book amply show, fieldwork not only generates original scholarship but also broadens and deepens your intellectual and personal perspective.

Melissa Nobles *is Kenan Sahin Dean of the School of Humanities, Arts and Social Sciences and professor of political science at the Massachusetts Institute of Technology.*

PUBLICATION TO WHICH THIS FIELDWORK CONTRIBUTED:

- Nobles, Melissa. *Shades of Citizenship: Race and the Census in Modern Politics.* Palo Alto, Calif.: Stanford University Press, 2000.

NOTES

1. Mala Htun, "From 'Racial Democracy' to Affirmative Action: Changing State Policy on Race in Brazil," *Latin American Research Review* 39, no. 1 (2004): 60–89; Mala Htun, *Inclusion Without Representation in Latin America: Gender Quotas and Ethnic Reservations* (Cambridge: Cambridge University Press, 2016).
2. Michael G. Hanchard, *Orpheus and Power: The Movimento Negro of Rio de Janeiro and São Paulo, Brazil 1945–1988* (Princeton, N.J.: Princeton University Press, 1998); Tianna S. Paschel, *Becoming Black Political Subjects: Movements and Ethno-Racial Rights in Colombia and Brazil* (Princeton, N.J.: Princeton University Press, 2016).

31

"WHY ARE YOU INTERESTED IN *THAT?*"

STUDYING RACIAL INEQUALITY IN THE UNITED STATES FROM THE OUTSIDE

DESMOND KING

▸ FIELDWORK LOCATIONS: WASHINGTON, D.C. AND U.S. PRESIDENTIAL LIBRARIES

I judged racial divisions to be one of the most important features of American politics and society, but this view was not widely shared by political scientists in the 1980s and 1990s. Although there were important historical studies on racism and segregation, there were few efforts to analyze how the federal government's own policies purposefully contributed to racial inequalities and how lawmakers designed institutions such as federal labor market policy to create, maintain, or expand racial segregation. My expectations were confirmed in this research, and working from a non-U.S. university was an advantage. Notably, while pursuing this research, the most persistent and increasingly irksome questions I encountered as a non-American undertaking fieldwork in the United States were "How did you become interested in racial politics in the United States?" and "Why do you think that is important?"

Whether undertaking archival research across numerous presidential libraries (those of presidents Roosevelt, Truman, Eisenhower, Kennedy, Johnson, and Carter), in the National Archives in downtown Washington, D.C., or interviewing bureaucrats and politicians generous enough to meet with me, I learned to craft polite responses to these inevitable queries. I explained that taking a historical American political development approach to U.S. politics, elections, and public policy outcomes required understanding how constitutive racial divisions and politics are to the political system's organization and outcomes. And I explained how enduring many divisions were and how consequential and purposeful federal policy was in shaping racial patterns in the United States. I would make the same claims today.

My years spent analyzing racial inequality in the United States taught me not only universal lessons about how best to conduct archival research and interviews but also how studying America's most sensitive subject as an outsider could both raise suspicions and open doors in the field. For the most part, the suspicious stance was disarmed, but not always.

MY QUESTIONS

I conducted periods of research in Washington, D.C. and presidential libraries over ten years beginning in the mid-1980s. My interest was to investigate whether and, if so, how the federal government shaped racial segregation in its policy interventions in American society and within its own bureaucratic structures. The period of research interest was from the Pendleton Act of 1882, which introduced a system of merit exam–based entry in the federal civil service, through the early 1970s, when the effects of civil rights legislation began to materialize. Although many scholars of African American politics and history had a loose understanding of this issue, few had undertaken any detailed study of how and why federal bureaucracies segregated their employees and program—and the effects of this policy. Moreover, most still held the view that segregation was a southern phenomenon only.

WASHINGTON, D.C. AS A RESEARCH CENTER

In an era before the widespread use of mobile phones, digital cameras, and internet access, organizing visits to physical archival sources was necessary for any study with a historical perspective. Several centers were available.

First, and most important, were the records available in the National Archives and Record Administration on Pennsylvania Avenue. In this era, all the national archives were available in this building. Most records have since been relocated to the University of Maryland College Park dedicated site, a good hour's shuttle from downtown Washington.

The National Archives were an exceptional resource; they were open until 10 P.M. four evenings a week and until 5 P.M. on Saturdays. I was able to conduct interviews often during the day and spend the evenings and Saturday working with primary documents in the National Archives. However, identifying and calling up records was not unproblematic in a number of respects. Archivists were weary and skeptical of the many "researchers" who trailed through their building, and they had to be convinced that your research inquiry reflected a real research interest rather than a family or genealogical obsession. Furthermore, it took several hours for the records to appear. Once requested, a trolley with twelve to fifteen boxes would eventually appear, and a trolley load could be ordered ahead of time and be ready to be consulted. Photocopying was liberally available. Somewhat dauntingly, the reading room was monitored by an armed police officer who checked readers IDs at the entrance and scrutinized materials on exit. It was not an arduous process of entry and exit, but it was a meticulously controlled one.

The contrast with the second center, the Manuscript Division in the Library of Congress, which was located nearby, was huge. This is a small archive with specialist collections and a high ratio of archivists to researchers. Requested material—for me the huge records of the NAACP—appeared with alacrity, and copying and note taking was undertaken in a comfortably spacious reading room.

Third, most government agencies had their own libraries and record centers containing invaluable records. Access to these sites was variable, often depending on goodwill. Being a non-U.S. citizen was commonly an advantage in persuading archivists and librarians to permit access, and many gave of their time generously to assist in research questions. First, there was genuine courtesy toward a visitor to the country who was undertaking serious research. Second, I inferred that many archivists assumed that the fruits of my research would probably not reach back into the United States because I was based at a university elsewhere (this was not true, of course, as my books are published through U.S. presses), and that they could therefore be more candid in identifying sources and noting the significance of some of them. As civil servants, archivists and librarians work under strict federal regulations about fraternizing and responding to the public; this approach relaxed a little with outsiders. This is a hypothesis only, but I have heard similar reflections from other non-U.S.-based scholars. Last, many were liberals who understood the significance of racial divisions in U.S. politics, and others—notably keepers of labor records—were keen for me to recognize the importance of the records they treasured. For example, I came to place more emphasis on the role of a senior AFL-CIO figure in making labor market policy because of the research materials I was directed toward by an enthusiastic archivist.

ARCHIVAL DISCOVERIES

The vastness of U.S. federal archives and multiple potential sources of information about government policy had some advantages. First, it was possible to cast a research net widely; for example, in addition to calling up records on individual government agencies, the records of congressional committees responsible for overseeing them were also available. This created many opportunities to confirm and cross-reference sources. It could also turn up gems such as unpublished memoranda, long forgotten or mislaid congressional reports on specific topics (such as the hiring of black workers in federal agencies), and correspondence about discrimination in dusty folders.

Second, archival records generated puzzles. For example, one of the main senior personnel I was tracking in the deeply segregated U.S. Employment Service (USES), created as a federal-state system in 1933, disappeared abruptly from his position running the USES. A small newspaper clipping in a folder referred casually to this departure and the reason behind it. This source provided a valuable clue to his role as a facilitator of further segregation in the employment service.

This experience of unexpectedly finding important primary material resonates with the recollection in Stathis Kalyvas (see chapter 4) of finding "tens of unopened, huge bags full of papers rotting away" in the basement of a provincial court building. These records proved important to how Kalyvas conceptualized and studied violence in Greece's civil war for his influential book on political violence, and the documents I found proved similarly valuable in my own work.

Third, noticing that the U.S. Bureau of Prisons was created only in 1927 and was a driver of racial segregation in federal prisons, I tracked the bureau's archives to the Department of Justice rather than to the National Archives. These agency archives provided a treasure trove of records with detailed minutes from the annual meeting of federal prison governors, including discussion about how they would grapple with the looming desegregation implied by the Supreme Court *Brown* decision in 1954. These records, in particular, encouraged me to think about how segregation existed across the whole federal government and about who maintained it.

ARCHIVAL FOOTPRINTS

Replicating the archival sources identified by scholars in their studies is a fruitful way to begin researching topics in archives. My surprise in using this strategy was the inaccuracies in primary source referencing in many existing scholarly publications. At the AFL-CIO archive in Washington, D.C.—another separate collection—the archivist could only locate the material I was seeking to examine by referring to the dates when the scholar had used the facility and the archival records listed under the visit. The reference, as given in the published account, was inaccurate, and such inaccuracy was surprisingly common. To overcome it, readers of my books will find overly long referencing—my intention is that anyone wishing to find the exact source I used to make a point or introduce evidence will be able to do so using my citation.

INTERVIEWING

To examine and investigate the more recent measures in federal agencies designed to tackle racial segregation in the workplace and the federal government's impact on society, I interviewed senior personnel in a range of agencies including the now defunct U.S. Civil Service Commission. Many of the interviewees openly acknowledged that the issues were difficult and contested, and they were willing to discuss aspects of this contestation because they expected the materials to be used in publications outside the United States. An example of these sorts of issues is the post-1964 requirement that every government department and agency create an office of civil rights enforcement as a condition of the 1965 Civil Rights Act. These offices were supposed to conduct annual studies of progress in racial desegregation and racial hiring in their departments and agencies, and to report to the Civil Service Commission. Several departments failed to establish these dedicated offices, and many such offices acted in a desultory fashion despite the urgency of achieving equality of opportunity in employment for previously discriminated against groups. I had useful discussions about the causes of the cross-department variations and the generally slack approach to enforcement.

The historical context is worth recollecting. Progress in alleviating racial inequality took a severe beating during the Reagan years, and although the middle of the George H.W. Bush presidency and opening years of the Clinton administration recorded more positive trends to reduce racial inequalities, there were still searing problems. The Family Support Act of 1988 (although mild compared to its 1996 successor) had further eroded the federal commitment to the least well off, including African American recipients. This era predated mass incarceration.

I also conducted interviews about federal welfare policy, labor market policy, and equal rights with a range of civil servants. Again, many of these interviewees first responded by expressing their surprise that a non-U.S.–based scholar was interested in such issues, but they usually opened up expansively once the interview got rolling. There was variation between white and African American interviewees, the latter less surprised about my research interest. African American professionals were much more aware of the patterns of racialized inequality captured in federal welfare programs and about the barriers to racial equality in education and employment. Many white interviewees also knew the broad trends but wanted to place these beside other important pockets of white poverty and disadvantage. The same question about the source of my interest in racial inequality arose in interviews with interest group and think tank representatives.

LESSONS LEARNED

I learned a good deal from my fieldwork in the United States about both the specific research issues and the practice of research.

I have always preferred semistructured interviews in which I take notes by hand (now on a laptop) rather than recording the conversations. In my experience, especially on sensitive issues such as racial segregation and integration in government departments (or more recently interviewing financial elites in government agencies and banking institutions), *not recording* is essential to reach a useful level of frankness and depth with interviewees. Recorded interviews often become sanitized, or aimless. In the early 1990s, as I conducted this research, I was sufficiently disciplined to write up notes from interviews in detail each evening. This not only helped accuracy but also pointed to other issues and leads to follow as part of the research strategy.

I learned a couple of key lessons from working with primary documents in archives. First, many scholars give poor or inaccurate citations in their reference sections, so it is always worth following up the references and trying to identify the accurate source. Often this source material implies something different than the inference drawn by previous scholars—or at least interpretation of the material is contestable. Second, never hesitate to copy or photograph a source even if you are doubtful about its relevance—researchers rarely have time to physically return to sources, and the memory of which file it is located in is always shaky. Digital cameras now make it easier to record everything. Ideally, a scholar should have months to leisurely sieve through documents, deciding upon relevance and interest; such time is rarely available except perhaps to doctoral students. One of my worst experiences occurred at a presidential library. I was using another archive in the same city, and I missed a day in the presidential records. The archivists had cleared my desk, and I did not have time to find a key document I had been reading. Finally, primary documents will never be fully digitalized, so casting a wide net when consulting them in archives is crucial to stimulating research both for the project at hand and for future projects. As I studied state intervention in the U.S. labor market for my book *Actively Seeking Work?*, the scale of racial segregation of such intervention and of the federal government's positive role in maintaining and fostering that segregation became more and more salient, which helped to define the core argument I developed in *Separate and Unequal*.

CONCLUSION

My preliminary reading about American welfare and labor market policy during the 1930s and 1960s, undertaken before conducting field research, struck me as underestimating the role of racial divisions in shaping federal programs and underplaying the active role of the federal government in fostering segregation. A decade of research in U.S. archival and government sources confirmed these observations. But the scale of this energetic and systematic policy effort to spread and defend racial segregation in American government was far greater than I or other researchers had expected. This takeaway about the value of detailed analysis of primary sources is a lasting one. Doing the research fed my developing ideas about the significance of the federal state in practice, contrary to many standard views about America's "stateless" status.

These findings fundamentally challenged existing scholarship. Most scholars retained the precepts that (a) the federal government merely reflected society's preference for racial segregation; (b) failed to acknowledge its role as an enforcer, facilitator, and creator of swathes of poisonous racial segregation in the United States; and (c) continued to treat racial segregation as a southern phenomenon. Scholarly research after my study has directly picked up on these themes. This work includes Daniel Kryder's study of wartime federal mobilization, Robert Lieberman's book on racial divisions in New Deal welfare policy, Ira Katznelson's innovative study of white versions of affirmative action, Megan Ming Francis's study of how civil rights shaped the American state, Daniel Kato's account of the strong state used to prevent antilynching laws, Kimberley Johnson's work on federal governing of the states, and Debra Thompson's study of census classification and the state.[1] Without archival fieldwork, this conversation in the study of American politics would not have been possible. It is an important conversation for which careful fieldwork will continue to play a key role.

———

Desmond King *is the Andrew W. Mellon Professor of American Government at the University of Oxford.*

PUBLICATIONS TO WHICH THIS FIELDWORK CONTRIBUTED:

- King, Desmond. *Separate and Unequal: African Americans and the US Federal Government*. New York: Oxford University Press, 2007 (1st ed, 1995.
- ——. *Actively Seeking Work? The Politics of Unemployment and Welfare in the USA and Britain*. Chicago: University of Chicago Press, 1995.

NOTE

1. Daniel Kryder, *Divided Arsenal: Race and the American State During World War II* (Cambridge: Cambridge University Press, 2001); Robert C. Lieberman, *Shifting the Color Line: Race and the American Welfare State* (Cambridge, Mass.: Harvard University Press, 2001); Ira Katznelson, *When Affirmative Action Was White: An Untold History of Racial Inequality in Twentieth-Century America* (New York: Norton, 2006); Megan Ming Francis, *Civil Rights and the Making of the Modern American State* (Cambridge: Cambridge University Press, 2014); Daniel Kato, *Liberalizing Lynching: Building a New Racialized State* (Oxford: Oxford University Press, 2016); Kimberley S. Johnson, *Governing the American State: Congress and the New Federalism, 1877–1929* (Princeton, N.J.: Princeton University Press, 2007); Debra Thompson, *The Schematic State* (Cambridge: Cambridge University Press, 2016).

32

NAVIGATING BORN AND CHOSEN IDENTITIES IN FIELDWORK

PETER KRAUSE

▸ FIELDWORK LOCATIONS: ALGERIA, ISRAEL, NORTHERN IRELAND, PALESTINIAN TERRITORIES

"How about those Boston Tapes?"

"*'Ant fil mukhabarat*?"

" 'Krause' is a Jewish name, right?"

"*Comment pouvons-nous faire confiance à un Américain en ce qui concerne notre propre histoire*?"

As I conducted fieldwork for my dissertation and first book on the internal dynamics and effectiveness of four national movements across ten different countries, I was challenged with these four questions (and others like them) on countless occasions by former militia members, politicians, academics, and the general public. At the most basic level, they were all asking me the same thing: *Who are you*? The questioners wanted to know not simply for their own edification but also so they could judge whether I was trustworthy or suspicious, friend or foe, one of "us" or one of "them." They had a right to ask; after all, I was asking them to share their most personal stories, sensitive documents, and precious time with me—all in societies polarized by recent or ongoing violent conflict.

These stories illustrate how I answered those questions, and how my answers shaped how I see and am seen in the field. I learned a great deal because my academic, national, and religious identities placed me in different roles across my four national movements of study: sometimes natural friend, sometimes natural foe, sometimes natural outsider. However,

I also learned that decisions I made about who I am and how I do my work could transcend those differences, and that those selective parts of my identity as a person and a scholar were as important or more important to my relationships in the field and the quality of my research.

HOW ABOUT THOSE BOSTON TAPES?

This question was asked by an elderly taxi driver mere minutes after I had gotten into a cab from the Belfast airport. The question came *before* I had even told the driver that I was from Boston, let alone that I was a professor at the very institution, Boston College (BC), that had given the tapes their colloquial name in Northern Ireland. Sleepy from a red-eye flight, I immediately snapped to attention with a jolt of anxiety as I understood this unprompted question meant that the issue of the "Boston Tapes" was big news for everyone in the area, not simply for former militants and members of my university.

The so-called Boston Tapes (officially called "The Belfast Project") were an oral history collection of more than two hundred audiotape interviews with forty-six former members of the Irish Republican Army (IRA) and the Ulster Volunteer Force (UVF). The idea was that these individuals, many of whom had never given interviews before or admitted their membership in these militant organizations, could speak freely about their role in the Troubles of Northern Ireland (1968–1998), knowing that the tapes would not be released until after their deaths. Unfortunately for most of the interviewees—and a number of others implicated in their confessions—when two prominent individuals died (IRA member Brendan Hughes and UVF member David Ervine) and project director Ed Moloney produced a book and documentary in 2010 based on their interviews, the Police Service of Northern Ireland (PSNI) learned of the project and subpoenaed the remaining tapes. This set off an ongoing legal battle that has involved Moloney and other members of the project, the justice system and governments of Northern Ireland, the United Kingdom, Ireland, and the United States, and Boston College. Although no Boston College faculty members were involved in the project, the fact that Moloney directed it with the support of a BC Irish Studies center and BC's Burns Library (which was expected to serve as the repository for the tapes) gave the university a visible role in the controversy.

The project itself is unfortunately now an infamous case study in how *not* to conduct field research, largely because of the overpromising of anonymity to interview subjects and a misunderstanding of the severity of the criminal and political ramifications of the project. My faculty position had enabled me to learn from BC experts in Irish history, access excellent Irish archives at the Burns Library, and meet with key figures including former Irish President Mary McAleese and her husband (and former senator) Martin McAleese while they were on campus. As I sat in the back of that taxicab from the airport, the question confirmed what I had worried about in the preceding weeks: my Boston College affiliation could hinder rather than assist me for this phase of my book.

To add to my concern, the timing of my visit to Belfast couldn't have been worse. Gerry Adams, then head of Sinn Féin (the former political wing of the IRA and now a leading political party in Ireland and Northern Ireland), was arrested just a few weeks before I arrived based on supposed revelations in the tapes about his alleged time as an IRA leader. The gravity of the issue hit home once again when I was walking to conduct my first interview on the Falls Road in the heart of Republican west Belfast. There on a stone wall in large graffiti letters—underneath a Sinn Féin sign no less—was "Boston College Touts." In this case, "Tout" means "informer," and the fact that the charge was so publicly displayed—and not subsequently removed or covered up—had troubling implications given the weighty historical precedents for political graffiti and the treatment of informants in Northern Ireland.

Nonetheless, from my conversation with the taxi driver to my interviews with former militants, politicians, and journalists, I decided to tell everyone up front that I was a professor at Boston College. I could have presented my research affiliation at MIT and hidden my BC connection, but that is not honest, not safe (as it would endanger me and future researchers who would then be viewed more negatively), and breaks the bonds of trust that had been so severely strained in the Belfast Project. I was ready to accept that my access might suffer a bit in order to secure honestly gotten information and understanding of the Irish national movement.

As I contacted potential interviewees, they relayed understandable concerns, leveled serious questions, and made some less serious jokes at my expense. I explained that I began working at Boston College a decade

FIGURE 32.1 Anti-Boston College graffiti on the Falls Road in Belfast.

after the project began, that I shared their concerns about their reputation and security, and that my goal was to fairly and honestly analyze the actions and effectiveness of their organizations. In part because of my openness about who I was, I not only gained access to almost every person I contacted—the only concession was that the former members of one faction asked for anonymity in my book, which I granted—but I also gained a deeper education about my case than I ever would have received had I concealed my affiliations.

I learned that the Sinn Féin and former IRA members I interviewed were not surprised by the behavior of the Northern Irish justice system, which they believed always had it in for them, nor were they upset about researchers documenting the history of Republican efforts in the Irish national movement. What they truly disliked about the Belfast Project/Boston Tapes was that its Irish directors had focused on interviewing the minority of former IRA members who were anti-Sinn Féin, anti-Gerry Adams, and anti-Good Friday Accords. Their concerns also made clear to me something that most Americans don't understand: Although Northern Ireland is generally understood in the American psyche as a settled conflict successfully brought to a happy end, to those in Belfast the embers of the struggle are still smoldering to the point that the recounting and analysis of recent history can stoke them in dangerous ways. Many of my interviewees looked to honest academics to tell stories they felt were often manipulated by journalists or politicians with an agenda. So their concerns were different than I might have expected, and it was the honest presentation of my situation and my previous record of research without a political agenda that gained me trust and access to key figures in the movement. By refusing to hide the affiliation that I was generally so proud to have, I hoped in some small way to help restore the reputation of Boston College with the Irish community.

For other scholars at home and in the field, your academic affiliations play a key role in your reputation because they are often the first thing people know about you. You have less choice with your home affiliation, but you have significant choice with additional affiliations abroad. Affiliating with a local university or research center can open some doors for you, but potentially close others, so make sure you are aware of local developments before you arrive and know the difference. Think carefully about the values of any potential affiliation and its reputation with local communities because that will become part of your reputation. Remember that it's a two-way street: you represent your affiliations in the field and you have the responsibility to leave it as good or better than you found it. Don't "ruin" the field for others with unethical or unsafe practices. Above all, remember that the basic choice to conduct fair and honest research can take you far, even in sticky situations where trust seems hard to come by.

'ANT FIL MUKHABARAT?

"KRAUSE" IS A JEWISH NAME, RIGHT?

Researchers must choose not only which academic institutions they affiliate with but also to what extent they affiliate with governments. Palestinians in the West Bank, Jordan, Lebanon, and Syria have asked me, "*'Ant fil mukhabarat?*" (Are you in the intelligence services?) The answer was (and is) that I am not a member of any intelligence service, never have been, and never have been approached to join, despite the similar suspicions of friends, family, and fellow students in my Arabic programs who have posed this same question to me many times. But the question and the answer are more complex than that.

It is a serious and understandable question, not just because I am a tall white male with a crew cut, but also because Palestinians, as a people without a state, face significant suspicion and repression everywhere they reside. Therefore, they have interactions with intelligence and security officials at a far higher rate than most populations. It is a question not just about bias but also about safety and security, and I am cognizant and respectful of that as a researcher.

Israelis—some indeed part of the intelligence services—ask me a different question with similar intent. Those who have flown out of Ben Gurion airport have experienced the "exit interview," in which young, trained security officials ask numerous questions to ascertain how much of a threat you pose from their perspective. The one thing they have never asked me directly is if I'm Jewish; instead, we engage in a somewhat amusing but nonetheless serious game of Taboo in which they ask many other questions to find out the same thing: "Do you speak Hebrew? Even Alef Bet? Do you have family here in Israel?" In my experience, Israeli citizens have no such qualms, and a majority of them have asked me directly at one time or another if I'm a member of their tribe. Sometimes they suspect this based on how I look—which is apparently "somewhat Jewish"—but also based on my last name. Krause is indeed a somewhat "Jewish name," but as the son of a Catholic mother and Protestant father, I am decidedly not Jewish—although I do in fact have some Jewish ancestors.

Their interest in this aspect of my identity is understandable given how important Judaism is to being Israeli and how often Israelis perceive issues of security, bias, and personal interactions—especially on my topics of study—through this lens. It is also such a small religion population-wise that many Jews are excited to meet another one of the fifteen million, just in general, or because they want to play the name game and introduce me to other relatives and friends.

My answers to these and related questions from Palestinians and Israelis mean that I am not one of "them," but I am also not one of their enemies in their long-running conflict. Instead, I am apparently the somewhat rare non-Jewish, non-Muslim, non-Arab, non-intel officer, non-activist scholar studying Israeli-Palestinian politics these days. Some of those aspects of my identity are chosen for me by my heritage; others I've chosen myself. There is no doubt that I have seen some of the glimmer in the eyes of Israelis and Palestinians dissipate when they learn that I am not an active member of their tribe, ethnically or politically. However, as with my experience in Belfast, choosing the long view on my relationship with these communities has paid dividends.

At home and certainly in the field, I try to lead my interactions with passionate inquisitiveness rather than cemented opinions, whether I am talking to those who committed violent acts or to politicians of all national and political stripes. My openness and commitment to as much objectivity as possible has taught me to see each society with more depth and nuance than I would have learned to do otherwise. I am open and honest with myself and others about how my given identity shapes how I see and am seen. But I've also found that these chosen aspects of my identity—maintaining an open-mind longer than I naturally would, developing empathy (if not sympathy) for those I study, learning to speak and understand their language, and building trust through multiple interactions in which I am not always the one leading the discussion—have helped me build relationships and carry out even-handed research on sensitive topics, from "price-tag" violence by Israeli settlers to bombings by Palestinian armed groups. When you are interacting with those who believe truth is on their side if only others would listen to them, fairly presenting yourself as someone who seeks to help find said truth without a separate agenda makes you a welcome partner in that effort, even if you are not a conventional ally.

COMMENT POUVONS-NOUS FAIRE CONFIANCE À UN AMÉRICAIN EN CE QUI CONCERNE NOTRE PROPRE HISTOIRE?

"How can we trust an American when it comes to our own history?" I had faced versions of this question in other countries, implicitly or explicitly, but this time it was posed directly by an administrator of the Algerian National Archives. I had been warned by peers and mentors about doing fieldwork in Algeria: "The first country in North Africa you want to do fieldwork in is *Algeria*!?" But I had been warned the previous year not to go to Northern Ireland during the Boston Tapes controversy, and I had been warned in graduate school to avoid focusing on the Israeli-Palestinian conflict altogether if I wanted to have any professional future. Those experiences had nonetheless worked out. Unfortunately, sometimes even the most honest attempts to analyze history are met with unsympathetic, bureaucratic brick walls. As I learned in Algeria, the best responses to such obstacles are clear-eyed persistence and a viable Plan B (especially if you are working on Middle East politics these days, where, as Marc Lynch points out in chapter 35, the basic necessities of fieldwork—visas, archival access, survey approval, and interviewees—are far from given or secure).

Before arriving in Algeria for the first time, I took two steps that paid enormous dividends: securing a scholarly affiliation and talking to scholars who had previously conducted fieldwork in the country. First, after setting up a meeting at a conference with its director, Robert Parks, I pursued and was granted an affiliation with Le Centre d'Études Maghrébines en Algérie (CEMA) in Oran, which is the *only* foreign research center in Algeria. Parks was incredibly generous in helping me navigate the process of acquiring a visa on multiple occasions (no easy task), as well as the even more onerous and time-consuming process of submitting a dossier to gain access to Algeria's National Archives. This process involved filing the dossier during my first visit to the country, followed by a return visit months later, by which time the decision on my application should have been made. Unfortunately, when I arrived in Algeria for my second stay, I proceeded to the archives only to be told by the archivist that I did not yet have access. So began a weeks-long process during which I called, emailed, and finally resorted to walking in person to various Algerian ministries to plead my case, which required use of my semipassable

French (given that the Arabic I can speak is of little use in the Maghreb). After days upon days of failure and seeing my time in Algeria slip away, I encountered a kind female official in the Ministry of Foreign Affairs who found my application and discovered that it had been approved weeks ago! Frustrated but relieved, I showed up triumphantly at the archives the next day and happily handed a copy of my approval to the archivist.

"Yes," she noted, "you now have access to the archives. You now must complete this form to request specific documents." Unlike in most other archives, however, the form would then be taken under consideration by "The Committee," who would render its ruling on my access at some unspecified time. Feeling a bit like an optimistic Sisyphus, I nonetheless eagerly awaited their decision. Of the seventeen documents I requested on colonial Algeria in that first form (I had to make up for lost time!), they granted me access to precisely two. I had thoroughly researched the archive and thought I understood the restrictions, so I was incredulous and questioned why I had been denied access to so many documents. The archivist responded that living people were written about in those documents, and so I could not see them for their safety. I then provided chapter and verse on how we could be quite certain that for the vast majority of the documents—which were on average over sixty years old—every person named in them was dead. The archivist was unmoved, and after a bit more back and forth she challenged me with the question of why they should trust me, an outsider, an American, with their history.

To be fair, I don't think it was the archivist who was driving the stonewalling. I knew how sensitive revolutionary history was in Algeria, and how challenging the infamous Algerian bureaucracy was to navigate, even for native Algerians. I therefore did not feel entitled to view their documents, but I certainly was frustrated that I had spent months of my limited time away from home trying to gain access, only to be seemingly thwarted at the gates.

Nonetheless, I did not let my frustration get the best of me. Instead, I persisted. I requested ten documents the next day; I got three. The following day I requested fifteen documents; I got six . . . and so on. My relationship with the archivists improved when they realized that much of my research told a version of the Algerian government's favorite story: how and why they gained independence from France. Unfortunately, I did not have multiple additional months to turn these drips into a reliable stream of information, so I needed to supplement my evidence elsewhere. That is when my affiliation with CEMA and my legwork before my arrival paid off yet again.

I had sought out scholars who had done work in Algeria before I arrived, most notably William Quandt, who had done serious fieldwork in Algeria in 1966, just four years after the revolution. Not only was Quandt kind enough to share contact information for some prominent Algerian leaders—who I reached out to and interviewed while I waited for my archival dossier approval—but he also granted me full access to his fifty-year-old interview notes from prominent Algerians of the revolution. Realizing they were housed at CEMA, I took a train from Algiers to Oran and was overjoyed at the treasure trove of information I found there. Quandt had interviewed the vast majority of Algerians I would have wanted to talk to, most of whom were now deceased. He kept excellent notes on his questions (which were often similar to mine) and their answers. I used the time I wasn't squeezing blood from a stone at the National Archives to pore over these interviews and set up more of my own with current and former members of the National Liberation Front (FLN) and other revolutionary groups.

All in all, my experience in Algeria was the most challenging and least productive of the countries in which I did significant fieldwork for my book, but it was still incredibly valuable and far from a disaster because of an extraordinarily helpful institutional affiliation, support of generous scholars, and my decision to persist while pursuing multiple research avenues simultaneously.

WHERE OBJECTIVITY AND SUBJECTIVITY MEET

Comparing my fieldwork experiences across countries and contexts, a few themes emerge. I gained tremendous insight into national movements and political violence by studying cases in which my national and religious identity made me at different times a potential supportive member, a target, or a distant bystander of both the movement and the states they struggled against. This is where objectivity and subjectivity met; observing the shifting perspectives of both myself and those around me allowed me to better research and analyze the dynamics of national movements.

In addition to these inherent aspects of my identity, it was important for me to recognize the significant impact that the more flexible aspects of my identity—from affiliations and language skills to humility, honesty, and empathy—had on how I was received, how I did my research in the field, and how I began to construct who I am as a scholar. I don't believe there is any one ideal combination of these chosen aspects of one's identity, and it's true that not everyone has the same ability to choose. Nonetheless, I prize the pluralism of political science in how scholars seek knowledge, and I hope that our field continues to have a healthy mix of positivists and interpretivists, activists and observers, and even more scholars in the gray areas in between. We learn things we would collectively otherwise miss, and we are stronger for it.

――――

Peter Krause *is associate professor of political science at Boston College and research affiliate in the MIT Security Studies Program.*

PUBLICATIONS TO WHICH THIS FIELDWORK CONTRIBUTED:

- Krause, Peter. *Rebel Power: Why National Movements Compete, Fight, and Win.* Ithaca, N.Y.: Cornell University Press, 2017.
- ――. "The Structure of Success: How the Internal Distribution of Power Drives Armed Group Behavior and National Movement Effectiveness," *International Security* 38, no. 3 (Winter 2014): 72–116.
- Krause, Peter, and Ehud Eiran. "How Human Boundaries Become State Borders: Radical Flanks and Territorial Control in the Modern Era," *Comparative Politics* 50, no. 4 (July 2018): 479–99.

VII

BEING ETHICALLY
ACCOUNTABLE

33

ON RESEARCH THAT "MATTERS"

ERICA CHENOWETH

▶ FIELDWORK LOCATION: GLOBAL

Many political scientists think the questions we ask are important, and we want our research to matter.[1] But my formal training as a political scientist gave me very little preparation to deal with two unexpected preoccupations over the past few years: (1) the professional and ethical responsibilities of engaging with people who were trying to apply my research findings to their current contexts; and (2) the politicization of my research findings. This essay is a cautionary tale about the risks of engaging extensively with public audiences about the practical implications of our research when these audiences may not understand the limitations of our work. It is also a story about how accepting U.S. government funding—particularly from defense and intelligence agencies—can make people skeptical about the researcher's intentions and the reliability of the research findings. This is not a story about fieldwork specifically, but these lessons can apply to those conducting research using any method. I conclude by discussing my experience developing an informal ethical practice regarding engaged scholarship, and I offer some considerations for others who many wish to do the same.

First, a bit of background. While completing my doctoral research on terrorism and political violence, I developed a parallel interest in the strategic effects of nonviolent resistance. With my colleague Maria Stephan, we published an article titled "Why Civil Resistance Works," in *International Security* in 2008. In it we argued that nonviolent campaigns with maximalist goals were twice as likely to succeed as violent ones between 1900 and 2006. In our book of the same title, we put forward a series of arguments explaining why this was the case, and we detailed the ways nonviolent resistance achieved what armed insurrection couldn't in four cases in the Middle East and Southeast Asia.

When the book was published in the spring of 2011, our findings joined a much larger set of discussions about the value of people power movements and nonviolent action. These debates had garnered much renewed interest within the United States and internationally because of current events: the Arab Spring was in full swing, and Occupy Wall Street was about to take off in the United States. In the years that followed, I developed new research projects on the dynamics of nonviolent resistance, and I also gave talks, workshops, and lectures on the topic in over a dozen countries. I began to publish more regularly in newspapers, blogs, and public outlets to discuss extensions and applications of my research to current events. My visibility on these topics has led people to begin to reach out to me directly—often with heartrending accounts of their struggles—requesting public endorsements, advice, or support for organizing their campaigns. Although connecting my research with real-world problems has always been important to me, I had to learn on the fly how to navigate some unforeseen challenges that come along with engaged scholarship.

ENGAGED SCHOLARSHIP AND THE MORAL HAZARD PROBLEM

Political scientists—especially those of us working in policy-oriented schools—are regularly exhorted to conduct research with an impact. Institutional review boards (IRBs) instruct us in how to protect our subjects during the research process, but there is little to no institutional, administrative, or ethical oversight when it comes to sharing the implications of our scholarship with those in the real world. Thus we are unprepared for the ways in which our findings might be used in unanticipated ways—sometimes harmful ones.

For example, one of the findings I derived from the Nonviolent and Violent Campaigns and Outcomes (NAVCO) data set is that no dictatorships had defeated a mass uprising whose participation rate surpassed 3.5 percent of the population. I called this the "3.5 percent rule" in a TEDx talk that circulated widely on YouTube. Later, organizers and activists in many countries seized on the 3.5 percent rule alongside many other symbols and slogans to galvanize support.

Surprising and inspiring descriptive statistics can give audiences a false sense of cause and effect as well as predictive power. Often what gains traction—whether in a twelve-minute TEDx talk or in an op-ed—does so specifically because it is not weighed down with caveats and nuance. Putting the full transcript of my TEDx talk online, with links to references, did nothing to counteract this fact. In addition, I did not fully appreciate how public deference to perceived "experts" and "authorities" can lead people to embrace and apply research findings with unbridled confidence.

Unlike the healing professions, social scientists do not take a Hippocratic oath. Academics' perceived authority on their subjects compels them to take special care not to overstate their confidence in their findings, or to motivate people to take undue or misinformed risks. When engaging with such audiences, I came to appreciate the crucial practice of remaining modest about the claims we can make based on the empirical evidence, carefully distinguishing correlation from causation, identifying caveats and limitations of available data, and providing what information we can without emboldening people to take risks beyond those they would otherwise take.

This dovetails with the classic moral hazard problem that economists often face—the tendency to support certain policy interventions or programs that carry risks of failure without assuming any of those risks themselves.[2] For instance, I try to follow a principle of not offering specific tactical or strategic advice to activists or movements in which I am not personally involved. This is because I don't see myself as qualified to comment on foreign contexts and also because I would assume none of the risks and bear few of the burdens of any strategic errors.

POLITICAL SCIENCE IS POLITICAL

As research gains traction, it becomes increasingly likely—and potentially increasingly costly—for it to become politicized. Because my research on nonviolent resistance was seen to "matter," other previously irrelevant aspects of my work were swept up into new narratives aimed at discrediting both the findings and my motives in disseminating them.

Since I was a doctoral student, I have been part of several teams funded by the U.S. Department of Homeland Security and the Department of Defense's (DoD) Minerva Initiative to study counterterrorism, terrorism, and political violence. When I began my career, conversations about the potential risks or conflicts of interest with government research funding were only just beginning in my academic circles. In the mid-2000s, many security studies scholars viewed ethics conversations as largely applying to human subjects research rather than to secondary data collection. When discussions around ethics did occur, they typically focused on accuracy: the importance of high data quality, transparency, and replication. Some conversations about the potential *political* implications of federal funding were indeed happening,[3] and I knew some scholars who would accept funds from the National Science Foundation but not from the DoD. However, these colleagues typically framed their choices as arising from their personal political leanings.

I, too, approached much of my work as a critic of U.S. foreign policy. But my thinking was that it was reasonable to spend taxpayer dollars conducting research on topics that mattered to the public, as long as I subjected my work to peer review and made the data and related findings publicly available. Researchers accepting federal funds exercised considerable independence and autonomy when it came to the research questions, designs, and interpretation of results, even when they arrived at conclusions that critiqued U.S. government foreign policy and security policy. As one of relatively few young female security scholars at the time, it felt important to have a seat at the table when opportunities arose to contribute to collaborative research projects and initiatives.

Unlike my terrorism research, the research behind the book *Why Civil Resistance Works* was funded exclusively by private foundations and university funds, and subsequent iterations of the NAVCO data set have never received any U.S. government funding.[4] But once organizers and activists began citing the book's findings in their struggles, the compartmentalization of funding sources for my different research projects became politically irrelevant. Regardless of my intentions and expectations, my associations with various U.S. government agencies—although wholly unrelated to the research supporting the book—became the subject of conspiracy theories. Outside the United States some saw proponents of nonviolent action, including me, as peddling a theory that reinforced American hegemonic ambitions by supporting "regime change" abroad. Such theories were particularly potent among those who sympathized with a narrative accusing the United States of supporting "soft coups" in authoritarian regimes by backing color revolutions. The theory was empirically tenuous but highly popular in Russia, Iran, Venezuela, Turkey, and among some critics in the United States. As a consequence, my limited and indirect associations with the U.S. government were parlayed into conspiratorial narratives.

Even within the United States, skeptics on the left and right have regularly attacked proponents of nonviolent action. Critics on the left argue that advocates of nonviolent resistance benefit the U.S. government by promoting a "passive" population over a militant revolutionary one. Others suggest that the government has co-opted proponents of nonviolent action, who either help the U.S. government better suppress these movements or actively discourage oppressed populations from properly defending themselves against their oppressors, thereby "pacifying" them in the face of incredible injustice. On the right, critics suggested that my coauthor and I had manufactured our findings because of opposition to the Second Amendment of the U.S. Constitution. We argued that unarmed civilians had historically confronted and overthrown oppressors more successfully than armed insurrectionists, so our study threatened the narrative that Americans needed to remain well armed to deter and confront tyranny.

Regardless of what one makes of these different narratives, many people at home and abroad justifiably perceive U.S. defense, foreign policy, and security agencies—and some private foundations—as directly at odds with their own aspirations for justice, dignity, and rights. The fact that I sought and accepted funds from such groups to support various research projects in the past cannot be undone. But transparency necessitates full disclosure,[5] and the political reality of guilt by association presented a major risk for activists approaching me with questions about how to use nonviolent resistance in active conflicts.

For example, on one occasion when giving a lecture in a semiauthoritarian country, a minder approached me during the reception and asked whether I was there because I intended to bring a color revolution to her country. This interaction did not make me fearful for my own safety, but it did make me anxious for the welfare of the many activists who attended the lecture. (One person in attendance later met me at a separate event in the United States, where she was pursuing a graduate degree; she told me that she and her family had experienced a forceful interrogation and routine police harassment after attending the lecture.) I've had similarly worrying encounters in academic fora such as public lectures live-streamed on various social media platforms, and over unencrypted email. As a scholar visibly active in public engagement regarding the findings of my work, I have little ability to convey risks to people who voluntarily reach out to me with sensitive information on public or surveilled channels that could put them in jeopardy in their countries of origin. This issue was particularly troubling in the case of Syria, where in the early days of the uprising, those seen to reach out to American or European academics for support were singled out for brutality by the Assad regime as traitors and conspirators. Similar issues have arisen for activists who have reached out to me from Venezuela, Russia, and elsewhere.

I was unprepared to fully appreciate and recognize the ways in which my public interactions with various research users and audiences would become political acts—with or without my intention or forethought. I wanted to conduct research that "matters," but I have had to jettison the illusion that research findings can ever be apolitical. The choices that we make about what questions to study, how, and with which supporters are all relevant to someone's political agenda at some point in time.[6] This reality can establish a perceived or actual conflict of interest between the source of our research funding and consumers of our research more broadly.

ON RESPONSIBLE ENGAGED SCHOLARSHIP

Needless to say, the question of how to conduct responsible engaged research has remained paramount in my mind. I am convinced that it is unrealistic and naïve to think that *disengaging* from diverse audiences relieves us of our ethical responsibilities. Refusing to engage in the major questions of our time, or obscuring them in paywalled academic journals, is not a responsible or viable solution, nor will it prevent people from using published work for their own purposes. We cannot control the way people use our work once it is published, whether or not we engage with various constituencies. As such, the question is not whether to engage but how to engage, with whom, and to what ends.

My response to these ethical and moral dilemmas has been to put together a personal code of conduct for my own research practices. I first did this in 2013 as I became increasingly aware of how wide-ranging the dilemmas and considerations of engaged scholarship could be. I was not trying to create a formula for perfection or absolution. Instead, my aim was to formally reflect on the values and principles that animate my work, establish a baseline of minimum standards for my own conduct, and develop a written commitment to consult widely if I were unsure of any case. I also wanted to build a path to accountability to others, which I did by obtaining feedback on the code from colleagues over the course of 2013 to 2015, and by establishing a small group of trusted advisors who were willing to talk through any questions or issues upon request. My advisory group includes people whose moral and ethical instincts I trust, who have no personal or professional reason to withhold critical feedback, and who can keep a confidence. I've relied on their support and my evolving ethics code to make many decisions about professional opportunities in the years since.

Core questions inform my personal code of ethics and provide a process for staying true to it day by day. I share some of these questions here in hopes that they help others prepare for the moral and ethical conundrums inevitably present in engaged and political research.

On Core Values

- What values are most important to me?
- What is my primary purpose for my life? In my profession?
- What problems do I want to help to solve, and what are my guiding assumptions about how such problems originate? Have I contributed to such problems, wittingly or unwittingly?
- What sacrifices am I willing to make—professionally, financially, and otherwise—to stay true to these principles?
- Who are the intended audiences for my research? Why?

On Potential Intended and Unintended Consequences of Engaged Scholarship

- How can I best communicate regarding the limitations of the claims I am able to make based on empirical evidence, the identification of various caveats, and the role of uncertainty in applying results to current or future contexts?
- What are some potential unintended audiences for my research?
- Are any of the potential audiences—intended or unintended—in conflict with one another?
- Could my research findings be harmful to anyone? Could they motivate action that could harm others?
- Could my research embolden people to take risks beyond those they would otherwise take?
- Can I take steps to ensure that appeals for advice or public endorsements are treated with the utmost confidentiality and care?

On Funding, Research Partnerships, and Associations

- What steps will I take to ensure transparency about my associations, past and present?
- From whom am I willing to accept funding to support my research? Are any of my intended audiences in conflict with these funders?
- Am I able to engage with any people within the U.S. government in limited ways that can be helpful? Are there people in foreign governments with whom I am willing to engage? Might my association with such people put anyone at risk, now or in the future?
- Am I willing to conduct research if the results are proprietary?
- If and when I choose to engage with various audiences, am I willing to refuse to cooperate in and openly challenge activity I view as immoral or at odds with my primary purpose, even if doing so comes at a professional cost?
- Am I comfortable collaborating with scholars who do not share my own core commitments? At what point during a potential collaboration should I approach this topic with them?
- How do I involve students and research informants in my research? Do I provide my students with as many opportunities as possible to participate

in this research? Do I credit my students, collaborators, and research informants accurately for their contributions?

On Accountability to My Ethics Code

- What personal processes do I follow for reflection, self-examination, and building moral courage? What will I do when I have doubts about whether I am following my ethics code?
- Have I invested time in building a community of like-minded colleagues and confidantes who hold me accountable to my principles?
- Do I have an open mind regarding potential further refinements or revisions to my core principles and a willingness to constantly improve my effectiveness in fulfilling my primary purpose?
- How can I set an example for others regarding how to engage with various audiences on difficult or sensitive topics?
- Am I willing to talk and write about my experiences, both positive and negative, so that they can benefit others?
- Am I willing to constructively challenge and encourage my colleagues, professional networks, and students to think deeply about their own moral and ethical commitments—and to develop guiding principles and codes of conduct for themselves?

This is surely not an authoritative or exhaustive list of questions one ought to ask, but they flowed directly from experiences that I've found morally troubling. I am still an amateur ethicist. But I can say that following a systematic process, putting my principles on paper, and building a small group of professional and personal confidantes who are willing to hold me accountable to my ethics code have provided more opportunities for personal and intellectual growth than I could have anticipated. I am grateful to the editors of this book for providing all researchers with an opportunity to share best practices, including those regarding an issue that we rarely discuss—the ethical dilemmas of producing research that "matters" in unanticipated ways.

———

Erica Chenoweth *is the Berthold Beitz Professor in Human Rights and International Affairs at Harvard Kennedy School.*

PUBLICATIONS TO WHICH THIS FIELDWORK CONTRIBUTED:

- Chenoweth, Erica, and Maria J. Stephan. *Why Civil Resistance Works: The Strategic Logic of Nonviolent Conflict.* New York: Columbia University Press, 2012.
- Chenoweth, Erica. "Nonviolent and Violent Campaigns and Outcomes Data Project," Harvard University, 2019. https://www.navcodata.org/.
- Stephan, Maria J., and Erica Chenoweth. "Why Civil Resistance Works: The Strategic Logic of Nonviolent Conflict," *International Security* 33, no. 1 (Summer 2008): 7–44.

NOTES

1. I thank Zoe Marks, Jessica Stern, and the editors for their invaluable comments on this chapter.
2. Thanks to George DeMartino for this insight from an economist's perspective.
3. See, for instance, the Social Science Research Council's exchange on the ethical dimensions of the Minerva Initiative, http://essays.ssrc.org/minerva/.
4. After the Arab Spring, I did receive various federal grants to develop different data on mobilization—a development that, in hindsight, likely reinforced these issues.
5. The fact that transparency can often lead to unintended risks for informants is an issue taken up in the Qualitative Transparency Deliberations that have taken place over the past decade. See the various working papers available at https://www.qualtd.net/. However, here the discussions relate mostly to risks to informants and less to the risk to people who take up published research findings to support their own political struggles.
6. On the issue of finding oneself in the midst of power relations that are both unexpected and difficult to fully understand, see Cathrine Brun, " 'I Love My Soldier': Developing Responsible and Ethically Sound Research in a Militarized Society," in *Research Methods in Conflict Settings: A View from Below*, ed. Dyan Mazurana, Karen Jacobsen, and Lacey Andrews Gale (Cambridge: Cambridge University Press, 2013), 129–48; Elisabeth Jean Wood, "Reflections on the Challenges, Dilemmas, and Rewards of Research in Conflict Zones," in *Research Methods in Conflict Settings: A View from Below*, ed. Dyan Mazurana, Karen Jacobsen, and Lacey Andrews Gale (Cambridge: Cambridge University Press, 2013), 295–308.

34

THE FIELD IS EVERYWHERE

ZACHARIAH CHERIAN MAMPILLY

▶ FIELDWORK LOCATIONS: SOUTH SUDAN, COLOMBIA

THE FOREIGN RESEARCHER

I entered the space warily. My trusted guides, members of a minority tribe in country X had warned me that members of the majority community were unlikely to recognize, or even acknowledge, the country's history of brutal ethnic conflict. This despite a long history of ethnonationalism that culminated in a devastating civil war. Members of the minority community had been systematically marginalized from economic and political power, and political elites openly espoused explicitly ethnonationalist views. Yet, I reasoned, my foreign origins and the fact that this was an academic gathering of relatively liberal members of the majority meant this would be a more welcoming space than my guides had suggested.

I was wrong. Everyone in the room was from the majority tribe, despite the condition of the minority being the topic of discussion. After filling my plate with strawberries and cinnamon rolls, I struck up a conversation with two conference attendees. My ancestors are Dravidians from South India. We bear a superficial resemblance to members of the minority tribe, and these two young academic stars were intent on guessing my origins. They informed me that they had been debating which specific tribe I called my own. I explained that I was an American citizen but that my parents hailed from the Indian subcontinent. They seemed perturbed that

I would choose to study African politics instead of my ancestral homeland. They asked me to name my hosts, and I mentioned the names of academics from the minority tribe who had welcomed me. Many of these were leading intellectuals, some of whom shared academic departments with figures in the room. They nodded politely but only seemed to grow more dubious of my presence.

We assumed our positions around a long table. At the head, a world renowned economist from the majority tribe pontificated on the challenges of national integration. A former top economist at the International Monetary Fund and a noted curmudgeon, he inveighed against development schemes pushed by technocrats that overpromised and underdelivered. During the Q&A, I meekly raised my hand and asked whether his models considered that existing development programs largely favored the majority community. Having read my Amartya Sen, I wondered whether this might mask and even entrench the systemic inequality between the country's tribes. He eyed me warily, unsure if I was a plant sent by the country's troublesome minority intellectuals, many of whom had raised similar questions in the past, but who, in this space, were completely absent. His discomfort about my ethnic allegiances was revealed as he dismissed my question with a curt "no."

After the conference ended, I walked back to my West Los Angeles apartment in the still bright southern California sun. As I reflected on the monochromatic group of experts who had been debating African development at UCLA, I felt unsettled. Although we were all American citizens, I couldn't shake the feeling that my brown skin rendered me an infiltrator, a figure of suspicion whose very presence threatened to undermine the scholarly consensus that pervaded the room.

THE RESEARCHER IN FOREIGN LANDS

A few years later as a newly minted PhD, I traveled to South Sudan with a white American colleague. I speak passable Kiswahili, and everywhere I went people assumed I hailed from the East African coast. This is not an unfamiliar reaction. In Tanzania, where I lived for two years, locals were dubious of my claim to Indian origin and would often reject the idea that I was an American. Against my mild protestation, they would decide that I was a half-caste, a person of mixed racial origins in the local parlance.

Honestly, I've used that confusion (obsession?) with my identity in advantageous ways while conducting fieldwork. In the Democratic Republic of Congo, I told soldiers from the national army that I was Kenyan shortly after Indian peacekeepers had been accused of running a prostitution ring. It seemed easier, and less risky, than trying to convince them that I am a hyphenated American.

Being confused for someone from the region is common for me when I conduct research in the Global South, just as I am confused for a foreigner in the Global North. In Colombia, people assume I hail from the north coast and chide me for my piss-poor Spanish. In Sri Lanka, Sinhalese assume I am from the Tamil minority. But it is in East and Central Africa, historically regions of tremendous ethnic mixture, that I feel most invisible. It is not the same for my white colleagues.

My travel companion in South Sudan was a bearded American photographer who would not look out of place in a Patagonia catalog. It had been almost seven years since the beginning of the War on Terror, and its tentacles stretched deep into the newly emerging country. American contractors, fresh from years "rebuilding" Iraq and Afghanistan, were arriving in droves now that the Obama administration had begun to cut off the tap of U.S. government funds. They wore Carhart pants with their army issued combat boots, revealing that many had recently left the U.S. military to take on far more lucrative work as private contractors. It also made plain how thin the membrane between private and public, and between postwar reconstruction and war-making, had become during eight years of the Bush administration.

My companion and I experienced two different worlds in South Sudan. Among South Sudanese, I was treated as a person from the region. When my ethnicity came up, my Indian-ness received far more attention than my American-ness, which most denied. In contrast, my friend was viewed suspiciously. Much to his chagrin, he was assumed to be working for the CIA or the DoD, or to be an ex-military private contractor. At the hotel bar, it was my turn to be a figure of suspicion. We mixed with a variety of contractors, UN employees, and NGO workers and, as my companion revealed to me later, the assumption was that I was a Somali or Kenyan businessman. The reason for which this vast expatriate world had been assembled was to protect South Sudanese from my nefarious designs on their country.

QUESTIONING THE MYTH OF THE
OBJECTIVE RESEARCHER

I offer these anecdotes not to protest my treatment but to acknowledge a basic reality—the field is everywhere. As social scientists, we do not don protective clothing to enter a pristine laboratory cut off from the outside world, as do some of our colleagues in the natural sciences. Instead, the power relations that shape the political phenomena we study are simultaneously embedded within our bodies, our language, and our minds in ways that directly shape our research practices and findings. Yet the colonial myth of the objective Western researcher entering the field to scientifically interrogate the lives of foreign peoples untouched by outsiders remains.

At a conference a few years ago, I mentioned that there was little value in assuming that our research subjects are unaware of who we are as researchers. I pointed out that as academics we are expected to maintain a robust online presence with personal biographies, archives of our writing, and even snapshots of our personal lives. Our digital footprints make it easy for anyone with internet access to learn far more about us than we know about them. This raises the question: Who is studying whom? Even if we pretend to be the objective researcher experimenting on the natural world, our interlocutors are likely to view us through their own subjective lens, through which we are far from unbiased and are active players in constructing their social realities. My fellow panelists were aghast. They questioned my adherence to scientific rigor and openly challenged as postmodern gobbledygook my emphasis on issues such as positionality, subjectivity, and agency.

A few months later I was in Bogotá, Colombia, to research the recently concluded civil war. I had managed to arrange an interview with some representatives of the Revolutionary Armed Forces of Colombia (FARC) through a friend who had made the trip a few months earlier. To secure the meeting, I was asked to share my writings on rebel groups so FARC members could vet my political bona fides. As the target of numerous American interventions, whether as part of the War on Communism, the War on Drugs, the War on Terror, or some combination of all three, they were suspicious that I could be a CIA plant.

They were right to be concerned. The money flowing into my field of conflict studies from three-letter agencies probably surpasses the combined total of all other funding sources. Many leading scholars studying political violence see no conflict of interest in taking funding from the Department of Defense's Minerva Research Initiative, which is designed "to improve DoD's basic understanding of the social, cultural, behavioral, and political forces that shape regions of the world of strategic impor- tance to the U.S." Political scientists at almost every top department in the United States are on the intelligence and defense dole. Most receive grants of one to two million dollars annually through a process that does not require peer review. This is far more than the tens of thousands available from private foundations or the National Science Foundation, with their often onerous application processes.

Yet few of these studies—which range across disciplines and include studies of rebel organization, conflict dynamics, and terrorist attacks— critically interrogate their own role in shaping U.S. government policy.[1] This is equally true for studies that avoid examining direct military tactics in favor of a focus on subjects such as climate change, reconstruction, peacekeeping, music and culture, and even nonviolent resistance, which are treated as self-evidently positive and hence unworthy of critical reflec- tion. Instead, scholars hide behind their imagined adherence to the sci- entific method, pooh-poohing anyone, usually foreign intellectuals, who question their reliance on counterinsurgency funding to "objectively" study resistance in foreign lands.

But is objectivity possible when our largest donors explicitly state their intentions to use our findings to inform their strategic agenda? Shouldn't the rigor with which we approach the study of foreign peoples, the pre- sumed objectivity we aspire to as we administer surveys, conduct inter- views, or review archival documents, also shape our engagement with potential donors to our work? Is the DoD or the CIA funding research merely out of an interest in supporting basic science, with no direct impli- cations for their own actions in the countries that we arrive in as ostensibly objective researchers?

Accepting that the field is everywhere means that we should no longer embrace the uncritical laboratory model of social science research. The field is not over there, isolated and immune from our actions over here. They are mutually constituted. Dismissing our subjects as paranoid cra- zies for imagining all white Americans as CIA agents neglects our own complicity in allowing the U.S. defense and intelligence establishments an outsized role in our intellectual production.

> You know the truth I did not want to tell you much because I thought you were a spy of the company...I am disappointed of all those who come to take advantage of our needs ... because they come with a single objective to seek their purposes. pisoteranos ... I could have told you many more things but I had to first know who you were the Americans hate, because they are involved in all the problems of the world ... they lead to conflicts, they create problems, they condemn us and then they kill us. because they are a power that only buts in these Third World countries their intyeresese. riches that affirms their power to them. as a country power ... they go through all the needs of the people, they are not interested in hunger n and the misery of anyone ..

👍 Like   💬 Comment   ↪ Share

FIGURE 34.1 Facebook message from Colombian "campesino."

This was brought home to me during my most recent trip to Colombia in March 2019. On a visit to a town recently controlled by the FARC rebellion, I met a self-identified "campesino" who warily shared with me tales of his life under rebel control. As the interview concluded, he asked if we could keep in touch. I offered first my email address and then my phone number, but he had neither. Instead, he asked if I was on "Face." The next day the message shown in figure 34.1 was pasted on my Facebook wall.

What would it look like if instead we start with the assumption that no conflict is bounded and that the factors that shape the trajectory of any specific conflict are equally likely to be externally derived, as many academic studies have argued?[2] What if we recognize that the millions flowing into academic departments from the intelligence and defense communities—money that funds professor salaries, graduate fellowships, field work expenses, survey research, and so much else—shape the same political dynamics that we seek to interrogate?[3]

RECOVERING RESEARCHER SUBJECTIVITY

My own approach is to start from the assumption that researchers possess their own political position, whether acknowledged or not. I'm not saying that we should never engage with the military or intelligence community. Rather, we should apply the same skepticism regarding the motives and behaviors of actors in the "field" to everyone we encounter throughout the research process, especially the institutions and organizations that make that process possible in the first place. Instead, we reserve our suspicions for those who are identifiably different from us.

This is especially relevant for the discipline of conflict studies. The growing clandestine footprint of U.S. military action means that few conflicts exist free of American involvement. Regardless of our individual politics, we are implicated in these dynamics. We do not abandon our national or other identities as we enter the "field." Instead, these identities shape the nature of our engagement with our interlocutors in ways that directly affect our eventual findings.

Acknowledging our own subjectivity opens up the possibility of interrogating entire systems that produce the dynamics we wish to uncover. Rather than disengaging, what would it look like for researchers to treat the U.S. government as an integral subject of their analysis? How can a researcher of Colombia or South Sudan (or for that matter, Israel/Palestine, Iraq/Syria, or Afghanistan/Pakistan) study these countries' wars without critically exploring the motivations and effects of American policy, both public and covert? Instead, as with most donor-grantee relationships, we too often absolve the U.S. government, and ourselves, from the rigorous interrogation to which we subject our foreign interlocutors.

Beyond the potential bias in our scholarly findings, recognizing our own positionality allows us to grant our field subjects the basic dignity they deserve. Foregrounding our own racial, gender, national, ideological, and other identities, beyond the meaningless disclosure statements required by institutional review boards or grant-making agencies, can facilitate a more substantive dialogue that makes space for nuance, contradiction, and fluidity, the same characteristics we demand that others recognize in us.

This broader view will enable us to ask the larger questions about how systems of power function and how our own positionality shapes the framing and interpretation of our field data. These are not difficult to see. The entire field of "terrorism" studies broke away from the study of political violence in the aftermath of the 9/11 attacks, not due to substantive intellectual differences but because terrorism studies set as its objective the production of "policy relevant" research that shapes the basic questions and overall worldview that researchers adopt.[4] It is impossible to

284 BEING ETHICALLY ACCOUNTABLE

separate these epistemological choices from both the political economy of research funding and the individual subjectivity of terrorism researchers.

As a scholar of color, I am certainly more sensitive to these dynamics than most. I acknowledge that it can be challenging for me to separate the research findings of an individual scholar from their specific identity characteristics. When I see a white American male scholar championing the idea that indiscriminate violence can be an effective strategy of counterinsurgency, or that insurgents in Africa are greedy criminals in pursuit of profit above all else, or that women fighters lack agency and are mere tools of powerful male commanders, I admit that I connect these to their maleness, American-ness, or other identities, and I devalue their analysis accordingly. I'm sure this goes both ways. As a dark skinned, bearded scholar of violent movements who tries to take seriously the politics of actors whose behavior I too find heinous, I have been accused of working to legitimize terrorists despite my pacifist leanings. But at least I own my political positions. Do you?

Zachariah Cherian Mampilly *is Marxe Chair of International Affairs at the School of Public and International Affairs, CUNY.*

PUBLICATIONS TO WHICH THIS FIELDWORK CONTRIBUTED:

- Branch, Adam, and Zachariah Cherian Mampilly. *Africa Uprising: Popular Protest and Political Change.* London: Zed Books, 2015.
- Gowrinathan, Nimmi, and Zachariah Cherian Mampilly. "Resistance and Repression Under the Rule of Rebels: Women, Clergy, and Civilian Agency in LTTE Governed Sri Lanka," *Comparative Politics* 52, no. 1 (October 2019): 1–20.
- Mampilly, Zachariah Cherian. *Rebel Taxation: Between the Moral and Market Economy* (Book manuscript in progress).

NOTES

1. Scholars in the natural sciences often seem more aware than social scientists of how their research may be shaped by U.S. military priorities. Competitors in the Defense Advanced Research Projects Agency (DARPA) Grand Challenge, for example, suffer no illusions that the self-driving vehicles they design will

eventually be retooled for deployment by the military in various conflict scenarios and potentially nonconflict policing purposes as well. Faced with such realities, some employees at Google and Microsoft have threatened to walk off the job if their work on artificial intelligence is sold to the Pentagon to improve drone targeting.

2. Kristian Skrede Gleditsch, "Transnational Dimensions of Civil War," *Journal of Peace Research* 44, no. 3 (2007): 293–309, https://doi.org/10.1177/0022343307076637.

3. Catherine Lutz, "Selling Our Independence? The Perils of Pentagon Funding for Anthropology," *Anthropology Today* 24, no. 5 (2008): 1–3, https://doi.org/10.1111/j.1467-8322.2008.00608.x.

4. For example, see articles by contributors to Richard Jackson, Marie Breen Smyth, and Jeroen Gunning, eds., *Critical Terrorism Studies: A New Research Agenda* (Abingdon, UK: Routledge, 2009). As Magnus Ranstorp notes in his contribution, in 2001 only about one hundred studies on terrorism were published in academic journals; by 2007 that number had jumped to 2,300.

35

THINGS CHANGE

PROTECTING YOURSELF AND YOUR SOURCES IN UNCERTAIN TIMES

MARC LYNCH

▸ FIELDWORK LOCATION: EGYPT

In the days and months following the 2011 overthrow of Egypt's president Hosni Mubarak, activists were eager to talk. They had played a pivotal role in bringing about an almost unthinkable political change against incredible odds, and they were eager to have their stories told. Activists could be forgiven for being intemperate in their remarks. After all, the dictator had been removed, the wall of fear had been broken, and few could conceive of the old order returning. In those months, I was one of hundreds of researchers interviewing them, publishing articles based on their insights and experience, and helping to curate their diverse stories into a coherent analytical narrative.

Political scientists who are aware of the fragility of democratic transitions might have been more wary about the potential for Egypt to relapse into authoritarianism. But in those heady days, this was very much a minority view. Activists came forward with astonishing stories of bravery and creativity—and also with stories and opinions that might later prove damning when restored regimes went looking for revenge. With Mubarak gone, why be coy about stories of outsmarting the security services through less than legal methods? With the Muslim Brotherhood entering openly into the political fray, ultimately winning both majorities in Parliament and the presidency, what danger could there be for Brotherhood members in revealing the organization's internal divisions and controversies to foreign researchers?

In July 2013, Egypt's democratic transition ended with a bloody military coup. The new military regime deemed the Muslim Brotherhood a terrorist organization, the source of all of the country's problems, and unlicensed public protests a criminal act. Activist accounts of contacts and cooperation with the Brotherhood or of their daring protest plans, seemingly so harmless in 2011, suddenly took on a more sinister tone. Indeed, they became the foundation for arrests, imprisonment, and worse. In the years following the coup, one after another of my Egyptian sources and contacts—Brotherhood and non-Brotherhood activists alike—went to prison, fled into exile, or were killed.

Did any of my articles lead to their being identified as Brotherhood supporters or other threats to the new regime? Did the attention of Western academics such as me put a target on their backs? I hope not, but it's possible. Issues of privacy, informed consent, and risk do not vanish during moments of political opening. These issues apply over a longer time frame than those revolutionary contexts, and they affect the reputation and safety of researchers and activists alike. Even if local contacts are thrilled to talk during those moments, the researcher should err on the side of caution and responsibility—because things change.

For more than a decade before the uprising in 2011, I studied and wrote about the Muslim Brotherhood in Egypt and across the Middle East for various academic and policy publications. At that time, the Brotherhood was still technically an illegal organization, but it was easy to find and meet with its leadership and members. By 2005, eighty-eight Brothers were members of Parliament, and the Brotherhood's office in downtown Cairo was well known by most taxi drivers.

In 2006, after years of interviewing Brotherhood members at various ranks (including Mohammed el-Morsi, a workmanlike member of the Guidance Council later elected president), I finally was given the chance to interview Mohammed Mehdi Akef, then the Supreme Guide. I did not learn a great deal from this brief conversation that I had not gleaned from the interviews with lower ranking members, but it served a validating function for my research and provided some useful quotes that I used in relevant publications. A photo taken by the Brotherhood's media attaché of me shaking hands with Akef during that nearly decade-old interview (which I had happily posted to my own Facebook page) eventually showed up in Egyptian newspaper articles (and right-wing U.S. websites) as evidence denouncing me as an apologist for terrorism.

I published several articles in those years exploring the argument that the Muslim Brotherhood might serve as a firewall against violent terrorism, an issue of both policy and theoretical importance, and the focus of a small but lively academic debate. But the anti-Brotherhood fever that consumed Egyptian politics in 2013 turned those academic debates into something quite different. The coup was followed by a full-spectrum attack on the Brotherhood, with many Gulf states labeling the organization a terrorist group.

This went beyond analytical disagreements among scholars. Writings deemed sympathetic to a declared terrorist movement could be grounds for far worse than a letter to the editor or a hostile blog post. An official rebuttal to an article I had written about the Brotherhood for the *Washington Post* was released under the name of the Egyptian ambassador to the United States. At least one well-known Egyptian scholar of Islamist movements was arrested upon returning to Egypt to visit family, and that scholar remains in detention today. Would I be arrested for supporting a terrorist organization if I tried to return to Egypt? Would my students be safe?

Once again, something that had seemed safe and appropriate at the time became dangerous later when politics changed. I am now grateful that I did not publish a full list of my dozens of interviews with Brotherhood members or other Egyptians who commented favorably upon them in the name of transparency, as is increasingly demanded from some corners of political science, including the editors of many of the field's leading journals. Transparency that seems like a reasonable scholarly practice at one time can end up being incriminating evidence in a state security court within only a few years—because things change.

In 2005, I sat down in a crowded Cairo café with one of the young bloggers pioneering political uses of the internet. Alaa Abdelfattah was already well known within the global network of bloggers and internet activists, and by the time I met him, we already had more than a dozen common friends and acquaintances. I have never forgotten his answer when I asked why he blogged under his own name rather than trying to cover his tracks with a pseudonym. Secrecy was pointless in an Egyptian context, Alaa told me. If the authorities wanted to know who he was, they would find out. Attempted secrecy would be an admission that he had something to hide, and in his view the whole point of online activism at that moment was its public nature. Putting independent ideas out into the online public under his own name defined his political agency, and he would not succumb to fear of repression or surveillance. Alaa became a leading figure in the Egyptian revolution, and a key source for the many journalists and academics who knew him.

After Mubarak's fall, Alaa continued on a revolutionary path even though many other activists opted-in to the transitional system. He ended up in prison over alleged violence during a protest and remained there for years despite support from all of his international friends. I used my blog and Twitter feed, and my platforms at *Foreign Policy* and the *Washington Post*, to draw attention to his case—and to the plight of many other activists, academics, and citizens languishing in Egypt's prisons. It seemed to do little good, and I feared that it might be doing more harm by making the authorities even more stubborn. Years later, however, I heard from several other old contacts about whose cases I had written frequently during their time in prison. Each told me that he very much appreciated those efforts, public and private. It was important to know they had not been forgotten. But I still wondered if they might have been released sooner without the glare of publicity.

I have spent many hours reflecting on that balance between helplessness and ways my writing could help individuals on the margins. Indeed, we have an ethical obligation to do what we can, however small, to defend those who have given us their trust, telling us their stories and sharing their insights. We are not helpless to respond—even when things change.

Young scholars will rarely hear more consistent advice than that they should carefully listen to their local interlocutors, and privilege those voices over the voices of outside analysts. At one level, this is excellent advice. Good political science requires, or should require, a deep understanding of political context and local issues. A premium should be placed on field research, on learning languages, and on deep immersion in the cases we study. Egyptian activists and scholars often complained about "fly-by" scholars, those "revolutionary tourists" who came to Cairo for a week after the revolution, had their local junior colleagues organize a few interviews with English-speaking activists, and emerged as "experts" on Egypt. Most Middle East political scientists versed in the value of field-work, ethical research, and qualitative methodology would sympathize with the Egyptians over those Western analysts.

Egypt's experience offers warnings as well. Local scholars and activists are often deeply involved in the politics being studied, and that strongly shapes both their perspective and the personal networks they might offer up for interviews. Political scientists are keenly aware of these concerns when it comes to snowball survey designs. But it can be far too easy to lose sight of these problems when engaged in qualitative field research. The political scientist should not serve as the vector for projecting the views of a sympathetic group of colleagues and contacts. In a revolution-ary context, however, it seems downright unethical to stand back and offer dispassionate analysis rather than advocate for what "everyone" in the country knows to be right.

Those politically shared horizons frayed as Egypt's democratic tran-sition failed. Many of the secular and putatively liberal Egyptians in the academic networks of American political scientists enthusiastically sup-ported the overthrow of the Brotherhood. Some couched their vocal criticism as a critique of Western political science for imposing incorrect analytical frameworks on the June 30 "Tamarod" protest and the subse-quent July 3 military removal of Morsi. They lambasted political scientists like me for warning of the dangers of a military coup by denouncing our allegedly Orientalist misunderstanding of Egypt and our mislabeling of July 3 as a coup rather than a revolution. Friendships frayed, Facebook connections were severed, and academic meetings became fraught. Schol-ars whose personal and professional identities were deeply bound up in their organic connections with their Egyptian peers were unsettled by suddenly being cast in the role of imperialist villain.

Deferring to the views of local scholars may have seemed like the right thing to do, but analytically it became a disastrous mistake. Sisi's coup was exactly what it had appeared to be. Its repressive effects were mostly what political scientists had predicted rather than the intervention to restore democracy that many Egyptian supporters had claimed to expect. What was the ethical obligation in this case? Would choosing to go along with the enthusiasm for the June 30 protests out of deference to local voices, in the face of the expectations of the political science literature, have been the right course of action? Or were ethical standards of political science best served by presenting political analysis informed by research regardless of local sensitivities? Instead of a restoration of democracy so enthusiastically cheered by many Egyptians, an ever-fiercer repression eventually caught up with them—because things change.

What lessons does this experience offer for political science fieldwork? First, considerations of privacy and risk to research subjects should remain paramount regardless of current political conditions. Activists themselves, caught up in the passions of today, may not be the best judges of what will be safe tomorrow or next year. Be careful about how interviews are used, even if the journalists around you are not.

Second, be aware of the pressures toward data transparency in the discipline. It is all too easy to imagine a journal editor committed to the Data Access and Research Transparency standards insisting that authors publish a transparent list of interviews and identifying information in a context deemed nonthreatening at the moment. But once those interviews are available online, they are always available—even when political conditions change and the once innocent statements become grounds for serious consequences. Protect your interlocutors even if they don't, at the moment, feel that they need to be protected.

Finally, be careful. As other essays in this collection remind us, research that could be done in Egypt over the last few decades—to say nothing of the open environment from 2011 to 2013—is less possible today. The murder of Italian PhD student Guilio Regini and the detention of Waleed Salem, a PhD student from the University of Washington, are only the most publicly visible edge of the new risks of political science research in Egypt. Also worrying is the arrest of a Lebanese tourist over social media postings critical of Egyptian sexual harassment—something many American graduate students might easily post. There are no longer clear red lines about what it is permissible to study, and there is little reason to believe that a Western passport or an academic affiliation will protect researchers from local security services today.

The risks of research in the Middle East are likely to increase, not diminish, in the coming years. Even if conditions do ease at some point, there is little reason to trust that they will stay that way. Political science researchers must begin from the premise that they and their interviewees potentially will be at risk. Hold the line in defending the privacy and safety of those contacts—because things change.

———

Marc Lynch *is professor of political science and international affairs at George Washington University.*

PUBLICATIONS TO WHICH THIS FIELDWORK CONTRIBUTED:

- Lynch, Marc. *The Arab Uprising: The Unfinished Revolutions of the New Middle East*. New York: Public Affairs, 2012.
- ——. *The Arab Uprisings Explained: New Contentious Politics in the Middle East*. New York: Columbia University Press, 2014.

36

ETHNOGRAPHY WITH EXTREMISTS

LIVING IN A FASCIST MILITIA

ALESSANDRO ORSINI

▸ FIELDWORK LOCATION: ITALY

was warned not to write my book, *Sacrifice: My Life in a Fascist Militia*. Sacrifice is a fascist organization that has been involved in numerous incidents of violence in Italy. In some cases, it has been violently attacked by far left organizations. In other cases, Sacrifice members have been the attackers. Many of its militants are in prison for beating up political adversaries or for taking part in various kinds of clashes. But no Sacrifice militant has ever been arrested for larceny or robbery or drug pushing. Violence against people is always the reason for their arrest.

I managed to gain access to two cells in Italian towns (that I call Mussolinia and Lenintown) to understand the cultural significance Sacrifice comrades attribute to violence. The history of this research, recounted in my book, is long and complicated and forced me to live in more than one city. It lasted for five years and was divided into three stages.

The first stage, the "approach stage," took roughly three and a half years. During that time I managed to become friendly with some important Sacrifice militants after taking out a membership in a gym that they own.

The second stage, the "entry stage," lasted for four months, three of which I spent as a full-time militant. During those three months I played the part of a militant day in and day out, including weekends. This stage ended with my expulsion from the group and an explicit warning not to approach any comrade in the future.

The third stage, the "departure stage," lasted a year. Because I could no longer approach the group, I continued to study it through the enormous quantity of documents that the Sacrifice comrades publish on Facebook, and also thanks to a friendship I had developed over five years with a Sacrifice militant who did not live in Mussolinia or in Lenintown. This young man, although a highly respected militant, had begun a deradicalization process after the birth of his son, but he has never spoken about this with his other comrades.

This is what I call "living ethnography."

WARNINGS FROM POLICE AND FAMILY

I received numerous warnings about the dangers and costs of my ethnographic research with fascist militants, but two in particular stuck out: one from a police chief and one from my own mother.

At the beginning of the "entry stage," I asked for and was granted an appointment with the chief of police in Lenintown, who received me in his office. He told me that the Sacrifice militants had been involved in numerous aggressive acts and that a recent beating of a young woman by Leonidas, the local Sacrifice leader, was just one of many episodes. At the end of a very cordial conversation lasting thirty minutes, the chief of police advised me not to conduct research in Lenintown. After confirming that I was still quite determined to study Sacrifice in Lenintown, his tone, until then friendly, suddenly became firm and decisive:

> Professor Orsini, the people you want to study are dangerous and violent, and we might not be able to protect you. If you decide to go ahead with your research, you will have to assume total responsibility for your choice. We have a special unit that deals with Sacrifice and, as I told you, we're conducting our investigation into the fights in which Leonidas is involved. I would also inform you that you could be charged if you break the law. Being a sociologist does not mean having special permission to commit crimes. Bear that in mind.

A few days after the meeting with the police chief, at the end of three and a half years of preparation, I was permitted to enter the Mussolinia and Lenintown cells. I joined at a significant moment in their lives; the police were finishing their investigations on Leonidas after having arrested another group member.

A second warning came soon after from my mother, who helped me to better understand the reality of everyday life in a fascist militia. During a dinner in my parents' apartment in Rome, at which one of my two brothers was present, my mother got up from the table and refused to continue eating after I'd explained what my new research involved. "Alessandro," she said, "I've never been so ashamed in all my life! And if a friend of mine should see you? Or someone who knows your father? Do you realize how much shame you're bringing on your family? Why do we all have to pay the price for your absurd choices?"

Over the next three days, my mother called me three times and sent me eleven messages on WhatsApp accusing me of damaging my family's image, being selfish, and putting myself in serious danger. Then she asked my father—himself a psychology professor—to intervene and convince me to give up my research. In the end, she said she would explain to her friends in Lenintown why I was associated with the Sacrifice fascists. But I asked my mother not to speak to anyone about my research for a number of reasons linked to my personal safety.

NEGOTIATING ENTRY INTO A FASCIST MILITANT CELL

Despite the warnings, I proceeded with my plan to enter the Sacrifice militia. The greatest challenge, which I spent more than three years attempting to overcome, was to gain permission from the group's leadership to be accepted into the militia as a member. As a consequence, I was allowed to participate in all of the activities and meetings of the militia, including the distribution of fascist leaflets in the streets as well as one of the comrades' most popular initiatives, the distribution of food to poor Italians. The militants donate five euros each to purchase the goods whenever the militia leaders decide to launch the program. One of my tasks was to stand in the street, distributing flyers with the Sacrifice symbol, explaining our initiative.

I decided to distribute flyers, rather than simply observing, for two reasons. First, I came to the conclusion that distributing flyers was a good way to increase the level of trust toward me from other group members. Second, I intentionally wanted to run the risk of being insulted or verbally assaulted, something that did happen on numerous occasions. Under-standing what it means to be a fascist militant implies understanding what it means to live surrounded by people who despise you. From my ethnographic perspective, I was not aiding Sacrifice, I was just helping myself better understand the everyday life in a fascist militia.

Near the end of the process, while I was alone in the LUISS University Faculty Room in Rome, I telephoned Marcus, the head of the Mussolinia militia. I answered all his questions on the type of research I intended to carry out. The telephone call lasted forty-six minutes. Marcus said, "I'm sorry to ask all these questions, but we're very paranoid because we're always afraid that someone is trying to damage us. This is why we never give information to anyone and we don't trust anyone."

With these words, he gave me three fundamental items of information I could use to manage my relations with the Sacrifice militants:

1. "We're always very paranoid."
2. "We're always frightened that someone is trying to harm us."
3. "We don't trust anyone."

Marcus said that he was "flattered" that a university professor was interested in his militia. In my ethnographic notes, which I have in front of me as I write these words, I recorded that Marcus treated me with great respect: "His voice seems insecure. It's like the voice of some-one who thinks he's talking to a very important person. Sometimes he doesn't finish his sentences as if he were afraid of getting the construc-tion wrong."

Marcus told me he was in favor of my entering the militia, but he had first to obtain the permission of the national leaders. This was our dia-logue, which I copied onto a piece of paper as it was happening:

MARCUS: My leaders will ask me what Sacrifice will gain from accepting your requests. They'll ask me what . . . Do you see? What you can offer.
ME: What do you think I could offer the national leaders?
MARCUS: The national leaders will certainly want a political gain. That is, it's not about money. I'd like to let you enter the militia but . . . Do you under-stand what I mean?
ME: You want to know what I can offer Sacrifice as a university professor?

MARCUS: Correct.

ME: I think that the Sacrifice national leaders would be interested in increasing their members, entering places where they can't go.

MARCUS: Right! [Marcus laughs]

From that moment on, a negotiation began that allowed me to answer the question that everyone was asking: "Why would a fascist militia like Sacrifice, with such a high level of paranoia, decide to let a sociology professor enter its organization?" The answer is that Sacrifice's national leaders hoped to gain access to my department and use me to launch a strategic penetration of Italian universities.

The cause of my ultimate expulsion was linked to this negotiation, which became more complicated over time. Initially, we agreed on everything; but problems arose later, and I received a demand that I couldn't accept. A Cornell University Press editor and a senior MIT professor—the only people I asked for advice in addition to my father—reminded me that there were rules that I couldn't break.

In an exchange of emails, the MIT professor told me that I would have to abide by two fundamental rules during my research. The first was to respect the people I was studying. I had to reveal my identity and the purpose of my research. The second rule was to respect what Thomas S. Kuhn, in his book *The Structure of Scientific Revolutions*, calls the "scientific community," that is, my colleagues.[1] The MIT professor was also concerned about my personal safety.

The initial negotiation with Marcus ended with this deal. In exchange for the authorization to enter the Mussolinia militia, I agreed to:

1. Urge my students to read my book on Sacrifice after its publication.
2. Invite one of the Sacrifice national leaders to my sociology course so he could talk to my students.

Marcus thought he had closed an excellent deal, but in fact I hadn't conceded anything, for two reasons. First, when I write a book that costs me years of work, I ask my students to read it and discuss it in class. Second, every year I seek out a violent political activist, perhaps even someone who has committed one or more homicides for ideological reasons, to come and talk with my students. On April 8, 2014, for example, I had invited to LUISS University in Rome an extreme-left terrorist who had killed seven people but who, after having served thirty-two years and six months in prison, had become a fervent Catholic. He had never repented publicly for the homicides he had committed, but he had written essays criticizing his role in the Prima Linea terrorist group, of which he had been a leader.

A lengthy exchange of texts, emails, and telephone calls was initiated between me and Marcus. Marcus talked to the national leaders and then told me what they had said. In the end, he said that the national leaders had decided to accept my proposal because they thought it was advantageous for Sacrifice. Then Marcus sent me an email in which he said,

> I told the national leaders that I'm in favor of you entering my militia because, if you were someone who wanted to badmouth us, you could write a pack of lies behind a desk, like the journalists do. Someone who has bad intentions doesn't act like you. He doesn't ask for authorizations, and he doesn't spend his own money renting an apartment in Lenintown.

As time went on, a relationship of trust and respect was created between me and Marcus; it would save me on the night Leonidas expelled me from the Lenintown militia.

A key problem remained, however. Dux, the founder of Sacrifice, who no one was allowed to contradict, said that an eye had to be kept on everything I did and that I should agree to have the manuscript read before its publication. This was the condition that I refused and that, in the end, caused my expulsion.

Augustus, a member of the Sacrifice national executive, visited me at my university to confirm the terms of the deal: having my students read my book, inviting a Sacrifice leader to my class. In addition, I told him that I would show the national leaders those parts of my manuscript in which their interviews appeared, and they would be able to ask for corrections or additions. I later phoned Augustus and, using the language of the Sacrifice militants, told him that I needed to talk to "my leaders" to see if I could accept their request to have the full manuscript read before its publication. In fact, I don't have "leaders" in the Sacrifice sense, but I couldn't explain to Augustus how the scientific world functioned. Augustus told me he was in favor of my research and tried to convince me to accept the request of Dux. This was my response:

> Augustus, I get what you're saying, and I'm very grateful for your help, but like you I also have leaders and I can't do everything I want. I don't believe that my leaders would allow me to accept, but I'll ask them all the same.

Augustus asked me to put myself in his shoes, and I asked him to put himself in mine. Then he asked, "Where are these leaders of yours?"

"They're in the United States."

> I don't understand you. No one will ever know that you let the book be read before publishing it. None of us will ever tell anyone that we've read it. The problem is solved. These guys are in the United States!

I gave Augustus the most fascist answer I could think of:

> Augustus, the problem is that I, like you, even though I'm not a fascist, profoundly believe in honor and loyalty. My leaders are my leaders, and I could never betray their trust. Perhaps they'll never find out that I let you read the manuscript, but I would lose honor, and I could no longer look at myself in the mirror.

Augustus continued to say that he couldn't understand me and repeated that my leaders would never know anything. I continued to be very polite and replied that I had already agreed to show all the parts of the manuscript that quoted Sacrifice leaders, who could ask me to make corrections or additions. Augustus told me that he would try to find a solution, but he didn't tell me that I had to leave the militias. From that moment on, I did the simplest thing in the world: I waited for the day of my expulsion to arrive. I was well aware that neither my contact in the Cornell University Press nor the MIT professor would agree that I should allow my manuscript to be vetted by Sacrifice before its publication. The reason is obvious—it's called self-censorship. Ultimately, I was expelled three months after joining Sacrifice for my refusal to have my manuscript read by the group leadership before publication.

LESSONS LEARNED

The key ethical lesson I learned from my process of entering a fascist militia is that it is crucial to remain in contact with someone who represents the social world to which the ethnographer belongs. The ethnographer needs to stay in contact with a moral world that is different from that of the fascists. After spending almost all of my time with Sacrifice militants, on more than one occasion I realized I was running the risk of becoming a fascist militant from an ethical point of view. Remaining in contact with the MIT professor and my father—a professor of psychology at La Sapienza University of Rome—helped me avoid being completely absorbed by what I termed "the parallel world" of Sacrifice. Unfortunately, my father died from lung cancer during my research, and the MIT professor became my only remaining ethical point of reference. Beyond human supporters, many books helped me understand the ethical risks I ran during my time in Sacrifice, including *Obedience to Authority* by Stanley Milgram.[2]

For a number of reasons, including the fact that I was assaulted by some extreme-left militants for being a Sacrifice militant during my time in the group, I became very obedient to the authority of Leonidas, my "leader" in Lenintown, who was a violent professional boxer. Had the MIT professor not told me that I could not let Sacrifice leaders read the manuscript before its publication, I think I would have let them read it without feeling that I was doing something wrong from an ethical point of view. I am almost sure I would have at least deleted a paragraph or two to retain the trust I had managed to gain during both the approach and entry stages, but also to protect my personal safety. After all, my principal aim was not to be expelled by the militia. I was obsessed with gathering information for as long as possible so I could write a well-informed book.

The fact that I wrote an email asking for advice from the MIT professor demonstrates that I got confused from an ethical point of view. Being a scholar, I should have known that I could not let fascists vet what I had written about them before publication. Becoming a full member of a new community allows for unparalleled insight and understanding, but researchers must maintain connections to their prior scholarly and social communities to reinforce their ethical responsibilities and remain true to themselves and their research.

THE ETHICS OF PARTICIPATING IN A
VIOLENT FASCIST MILITIA

I would like to add a few words about the ethics of my full participation in a violent fascist militia. Ethnographers are split between those who turn to Kantian ethics and the so-called utilitarians. The first group claims that in no case must individuals be considered as a means to an end: concealment, deception, and falsehood must always be rejected, even if the aim to be achieved is that of scientific knowledge.[3] Utilitarians believe it is permissible to hide one's identity and publish confidential information if one's goal is the advancement of knowledge or the exposure of behavior deemed unfair and harmful to the community. In this case, the achievement of a higher aim is used to justify the harm to people who, unbeknownst to them, have been involved in the study, as was the case with the famous experiments of Stanley Milgram,[4] David Rosenhan,[5] and Philip Zimbardo.[6] Before moving to Lenintown, I already had coped with questions of ethics in participant observation during my ethnographic research with extreme-left terrorists who committed several homicides.[7]

My red lines on these ethical issues fall into two categories: academic and personal. On the academic level, my red lines coincided with those of my colleagues at MIT: "Do what MIT allows you to do, according to the highest ethical and professional standards that MIT expects their researchers to carry out in their work." Before making direct contact with the Sacrifice leaders in Mussolinia and Lenitown, a senior MIT professor was very clear with me about what I was allowed and not allowed to do during my time embedded in the cells in Lenintown and Mussolinia. It turns out that my academic red lines were rooted in Kantian ethics.

On a personal level, my red lines were much more practical; namely, I sought to avoid being punched in the face. I have often, but not always, made efforts to avoid being pulled into dangerous or potentially violent situations. I have avoided employing concealment, deception, and falsehood both to comply with the MIT ethical and professional standards and to reduce the risk of being punched in the face one day or another. This was a real concern, especially because I regularly walked with the Sacrifice militants in broad daylight through Lenintown and Mussolinia, two cities where I had friends and the group had enemies. This combination

302 BEING ETHICALLY ACCOUNTABLE

of academic and personal red lines formed the foundation of my ethical approach to my research, keeping me and those around me safe during my time in the field.

———

Alessandro Orsini *is director of the Observatory on International Security at LUISS University of Rome.*

PUBLICATION TO WHICH THIS FIELDWORK CONTRIBUTED:

- Orsini, Alessandro. *Sacrifice: My Life in a Fascist Militia.* Ithaca, N.Y.: Cornell University Press, 2017.[8]

NOTES

1. Thomas S. Kuhn, *The Structure of Scientific Revolutions* (Chicago: University of Chicago Press, 1970).
2. Stanley Milgram, *Obedience to Authority: An Experimental View* (New York: Harper & Row, 1975).
3. Rosaline Barbour, *Introducing Qualitative Research: A Student's Guide* (London: Sage, 2013).
4. Milgram, *Obedience to Authority.*
5. David L. Rosenhan, "On Being Sane in Insane Places," *Science* 179, no. 4070 (January 1973): 250–58, https://doi.org/10.1126/science.179.4070.250.
6. Philip G. Zimbardo, *The Lucifer Effect: Understanding How Good People Turn Evil* (New York: Random House, 2008).
7. Alessandro Orsini, "A Day Among the Diehard Terrorists: The Psychological Costs of Doing Ethnographic Research," *Studies in Conflict & Terrorism* 36, no. 4 (2013), 337–51, https://www.tandfonline.com/doi/abs/10.1080/1057610X.2013.763601; Alessandro Orsini, "Interview with a Terrorist by Vocation: A Day Among the Diehard Terrorists, Part II," *Studies in Conflict & Terrorism* 36, no. 8 (August 2013): 672–84, https://doi.org/10.1080/1057610X.2013.802975; Alessandro Orsini, "Are Terrorists Courageous? Micro-Sociology of Extreme Left Terrorism," *Studies in Conflict & Terrorism* 38, no. 3 (March 2015): 179–98, https://doi.org/10.1080/1057610X.2014.987593.
8. Some material was reprinted from Alessandro Orsini, *Sacrifice: My Life in a Fascist Militia* (Ithaca, N.Y.: Cornell University Press, 2017), © 2017 by Cornell University, used by permission of the publisher.

37

BUILDING TRUST WITH EX-INSURGENTS

EMIL ASLAN SOULEIMANOV

▸ FIELDWORK LOCATIONS: WESTERN EUROPE, TURKEY,
UNITED STATES

My experience with this topic—let's call it fieldwork—dates to the early 2000s. In 2001, as a first-year PhD student of International Relations at Prague's Charles University, I was approached by an owner of a newly established Czech publishing house to write a monograph on the Russian-Chechen conflict. Flattered by the offer, I managed to change the already approved topic of my PhD thesis from a general national security–related issue (favored by the department) to the Russian-Chechen conflict. This ensured that I spent the next three to four years focusing on a single research project. In truth, I had been fascinated by this conflict since the mid-1990s when the war in the North Caucasus began. Our family lived in Moscow at that time, and I barely escaped conscription into the Russian Army as an 18-year-old in 1995–96, when I would have most likely been deployed to Chechnya.

Given my long-term interest in the topic, I wanted to go the extra mile and collect data that was not available in existing open sources. Yet traveling to Chechnya to collect data was not an option in the early 2000s when the war in this tiny republic on Russia's southwestern fringe was at its peak. My early attempts to approach Chechens based in Russian cities outside Chechnya for interviews were rather ineffective as well. Having fled a wartime hell, people were too fearful of Russia's omnipresent intelligence services and police to share sensitive information with an outsider like me. The only way to talk to people was by contacting Chechen diaspora communities in the West; thousands of Chechens fled the war and sought refuge in the safe haven of Europe. In fact, the Chechen diaspora was growing rapidly in the early 2000s, increasing from several hundreds to nearly one hundred thousand within a decade or so.

To access this community, I revived some of my older contacts. As a former student at a Moscow university and an ex-boxer, I had personal connections to dozens of Chechens from many walks of life. Fortunately, some of my friends and acquaintances, having disappeared at the turn of the century, eventually found their way to Europe in the early 2000s. Some of them had participated in the war and had acquired complex knowledge of what was going on in Chechnya. Most important, they were willing to share their knowledge with me. Serving as gatekeepers, they also helped me approach important members of Chechen diaspora communities scattered across western Europe, who then referred me to additional contacts. In the first half of the 2000s, I contacted dozens of eyewitnesses of the ongoing war, including former insurgents, who were based across Europe from the Czech Republic to France.

Ironically, at that time I lacked formal training in how to conduct interviews. A former student of German and law, and a current student of international relations, I had no knowledge of the theory and practice of ethnographic research. Moreover, as a graduate of a social science discipline in a post-Communist country, I had only a vague idea about research designs, research questions, and hypotheses, to say nothing of interview protocols.[1] Having talked to dozens of eyewitnesses and participants in the war—a unique experience given how sensitive the topic was for the newly emerging Chechen diaspora in the West—I was at a loss as to how to use the valuable data I had managed to collect. Therefore, my first work on the project—which also turned out to be my revised PhD thesis—didn't explicitly include interviews. I simply didn't know that I could have made formal use of the data collected during them.[2]

It was not until the fall of 2006—nearly a year after I finished my PhD thesis and months before my book was published—that I learned about ethnographic research in general, and that I could have made great use of my interview material in particular. This realization occurred during my one-year research stay as a Fulbright-Masaryk fellow at Harvard University's Davis Center for Russian and Eurasian Studies. I met interesting people at Harvard, MIT, and Boston University and learned—as a postdoc!—about the principles of qualitative social science research. I also took advantage of my access to Harvard's libraries to familiarize myself with the most up-to-date literature on armed conflict. Two things struck me. First, the mainstream literature on armed conflict focused on macro-level explanations that neglected what I had gathered from discussions with eyewitnesses of the Russian-Chechen conflict. It was not political discrimination, nationalism, or economic deprivation—or any "large" phenomenon—that drove individuals to violence in Chechnya. Rather, violence there had grassroots motivations such as revenge (grievance), honor (social sanctions), and problems with a neighbor (selective incentives). In fact, many former insurgents I had talked to ultimately joined the insurgency not *because* of political issues (for example, support for the idea of Chechen independence) but rather *in spite of* political issues (for example, animosity toward separatist Chechen elites). Second, I stumbled onto *The Logic of Violence in Civil War*, a new book by (fellow contributor) Stathis Kalyvas that had just arrived in Widener Library. Focused on micro-level violence, it was much more in line with the insights I had gained during the five years of my own research—and it was based, among other sources, on interview material, which was thrilling and inspirational!

In mid-2007, I returned to Europe—and back to interviews. But now I was more knowledgeable about what I wanted to do, and I was able to conduct my interviews in a systematic way, organizing them along the lines of my research questions.[3] Looking back to the early 2000s, my lack of formal training seemed like a blessing of a kind—or I at least I pretend to think so. Because I was not driven by certain theoretically informed perspectives, I was open to various strands of information and their cardinally varying interpretations. Instead of moderating discussions, I let them flow freely, allowing my respondents to give me as much information—and from as many perspectives—as they deemed necessary. Being a rather altruistic friend, a sympathizer, and a listener—instead of a researcher taking notes—I was seen, I assume, as a more trustworthy and ingratiating person, asking questions in an intuitive and nonbinding way. Of course, this was a time-consuming endeavor, and fortunately for me, I had the necessary time and honestly enjoyed the friendship and hospitality of Chechen families and friends. Yet it also enabled me to gain the trust of the respondents—the biggest asset in ethnographic research[4]—which ultimately paid off, particularly in the later stages of my research.

"ARE YOU HIDING SOMETHING?":
COPING WITH ETHICAL CHALLENGES

From the outset of encounters with respondents, a number of ethical issues—in a larger, supraformal sense—made their way into my research. The major concern of many Chechen émigrés, most of them asylum seekers or individuals who had been granted political asylum in western Europe, concerned whether I worked for Russian intelligence, pro-Moscow Chechen authorities, or Western asylum-delivering authorities. This was dismissed fairly easily, however; my close contacts with some reputed members of the Chechen diaspora community helped to ease the tension. That I was an academic working on the Russian-Chechen conflict also eased my entry into these rather introverted communities; I was seen as a researcher driven by a relatively clear and neutral objective. But was my objective truly neutral, and should it have been neutral? For most respondents who had suffered from the war, having lost their relatives, homes, and homeland, my research was not seen as an unbiased initiative. Quite the contrary, as a person visibly sympathetic to the Chechen cause, I was expected to show the world the sufferings of the Chechen people and the injustice inflicted upon them by the Russian Army. For some, this was the ultimate reason they consented to see me in the first place and were willing to share their gruesome experiences with an outsider.

Initially I sought to explain the unbiased nature of my research, but I soon realized that was doing more harm than good. Particularly in the post-2007 context of my research, my theoretically informed questions about the nuances of civilian targeting, pro-insurgent support, and honor-centered obligation to retaliate were in sharp contrast to the politically flavored motivations of some respondents. They wanted to use me as a channel of communication to the outside world about the war crimes committed by Russia in Chechnya, or about the Chechens' efforts to obtain and defend their independence from time immemorial. I will never forget a verbal challenge by a sixty-year-old respondent, formerly a highly positioned officer in the ranks of the separatist Chechen Army, about whether I was going to "theorize on the suffering of his people." This line was indeed painful, having known my respondents for years and having befriended many of them. Against this background, the very idea of using their experience to "build a theory"—and ultimately advance my academic career—resurfaced in my thoughts frequently, challenging the intrinsic ethics of what I was doing.

I decided to somewhat alter the mission of my research as I presented it to the respondents. Instead of looking into how collective violence against Chechen village communities instigated retaliation, motivated pro-insurgent support, or sparked anti-insurgent activism, I reframed my research around the motivation for the indiscriminate violence used by Russian forces against the ethnic Chechen civilian population. This was a small trade-off; after all, this was part of the story. Having known many respondents since 2001, and only having refocused my research on specific and quite sensitive issues since 2007, I managed to reduce the level of controversy involved in my "theory-building" questions. Moreover, my long-term contact with respondents—and their trust—eventually enabled them to move beyond nationalist clichés and to talk about other things, such as Chechen infighting.

My personal background has often led others to perceive me as (dis) loyal or as culturally and politically proximate (or alien) to my interviewees. Being of Armenian descent on my maternal side and of mixed Turkic-Jewish descent on my paternal side—and having grown up in Yerevan and Moscow—it was not easy for me to clearly introduce myself in ethnic terms. This was something that Chechen respondents, with their standard post-Soviet politicization of ethnicity, clearly expected. To make things even more complicated, my paternal grandparents were of Noghai origin, having moved centuries ago from the Crimean Khanate-held areas of the northwestern Caucasus to the Yerevan Khanate and having culturally assimilated into the local then-majority Turkophone Turkish-Azerbaijani population. Whether I introduced myself—or was identified by my respondents—as a Turk, Azerbaijani, Armenian, Noghai (Chechens usually expected ethnicity to be defined patrilineally), or as a Muslim, a Christian, or an atheist had profound implications for how respondents viewed me, and whether, to what extent, or with which "sauce" they wanted to share their experiences with me. For instance, a former brigadier general repeatedly expressed fascination with Israel and Jews. Willing to get him on my side, I was quick to mention the ethnic origin of my late grandmother—a piece of information that then, thanks to the interconnectedness of the Chechen diaspora, spread to several other respondents. Shortly thereafter I was characterized as a "Jewish boy" by a segment of the community, and some respondents lost interest in talking to me or questioned my trustworthiness on ethnic grounds. Some went so far as to refer to my mixed-ethnic background as a "mess"; others found me suspicious on the ground of my Noghai origin. As one respondent told me, "You don't look as a Mongol. Are you hiding something from us?" Upon learning about my mother's ethnic background, another respondent challenged my "loyalty" to the Chechen cause on the simple ground that Armenians were Russia's allies. Ever since, I have sought to avoid conversations about my ethnic and religious background, hiding or "correcting" somewhat "controversial" parts of my personal identity to make sure my trustworthiness is not questioned.

Trust, as we all know, is at the core of good ethnographic research. Having carried out interviews with dozens of former fighters, I have come to realize that many reiterate politically held beliefs to justify their past deeds in front of outsiders and, most important, in front of themselves. Usually, during initial interviews, respondents provide "big" motivations for going to war, such as struggle for the sake of Islam or Chechnya's independence. It took multiple meetings, sometimes over the course of many years, to build the necessary trust for some respondents to admit that their actual trigger was not political or ideological but deeply personal, such as a commitment to avenge a relative's murder or rape.[5] In some cases, my role seemed to be more of a psychiatrist than of a social scientist. It was striking to see how many former insurgents and civilian eyewitnesses of the war had for years sought to push away deliberations on their deeds, hedging against the past to protect themselves emotionally. I recall a tough war veteran who burst into tears telling me a story of a personal loss. In fact, it was only during the interviews that some respondents spoke out and let the burden of the past fall off their shoulders.[6] Needless to say, this was made possible by the trust between the respondents and the researcher—something that takes years to cultivate but is easy to lose.

Since the beginning of my odyssey, security has been an enormous concern for nearly all respondents. In fact, some Chechen émigrés returning to Chechnya—or their relatives—have been detained, tortured, and killed in Chechnya by the pro-Moscow Chechen authorities. The Kremlin-backed regime of Ramzan Kadyrov has monitored the activities of the Chechens residing in western Europe. The regime has employed violence against the relatives of those leaving "disrespectful comments" toward Kadyrov and his family on social media or elsewhere and has targeted Kadyrov's personal enemies along with ex-insurgents. In recent years, the situation has been aggravated by the exodus of dozens to hundreds of Western Europe-based Chechen youngsters to Syria, where they joined locally operating jihadist groups. Many Chechen families have grown fearful of Western intelligence and authorities. Years ago, many respondents consented to being interviewed upon finding out that my papers would be published in English-language scholarly journals and monographs—and not in Russian-language dailies accessible by pro-Moscow Chechen and Russian authorities. Today they have become increasingly uncomfortable with the former option as well.

Against this backdrop, conducting research on sensitive topics in the diaspora has become an increasingly tough challenge. Respondents have long routinely refused to sign consent forms, to be audio- or videotaped, or even to give researchers a green light to take notes during interviews, but some have recently asked me *not* to use data they provided months or years ago. Others have asked me to take extra measures to disguise information that could help identify them. Some respondents have grown increasingly paranoid about communication channels being monitored, about me being critical of or unjust to their cause, or even about me not being entirely reliable. They have distanced themselves from me in an effort to improve their and their families' security—even to the point of claiming they don't know me. Despite these challenges, I manage to stay in touch with dozens of respondents and discuss important issues related to my ongoing research, although the openness of my respondents has generally decreased. Because of these changes in the political environment, I no longer provide information in my publications on the cities and times when interviews were conducted, and I have gradually reduced the specific information on the locations of interviews and may provide no location information whatsoever. With the current trend in leading journals to follow the Data Access and Research Transparency Initiative standards, which demand greater data transparency, my interviews may soon come to an end to protect both my contacts and myself. This would be a blow to my work and that of others, but ethical issues regarding the safety of interviewees are larger concerns than whether my next article will be published.

Emil Aslan Souleimanov *is associate professor at the Institute of International Relations, Prague.*

PUBLICATIONS TO WHICH THIS FIELDWORK CONTRIBUTED:

- Souleimanov, Emil Aslan, and David Siroky. "Random or Retributive?: Indiscriminate Violence in the Chechen Wars," *World Politics* 68, no. 4 (2016): 677–712.
- Souleimanov, Emil Aslan, and Huseyn Aliyev. "Blood Revenge and Violent Mobilization: Evidence from the Chechen Wars," *International Security* 40, no. 2 (Fall 2015): 158–80.
- Souleimanov, Emil Aslan. "An Ethnography of Counterinsurgency: Kadyrovtsy and Russia's Policy of Chechenization," *Post-Soviet Affairs* 31, no. 2 (2015): 91–114.

NOTES

1. It is horrible to admit that PhD students lack training on these issues and that our university libraries are not equipped with basic textbooks, but it is unfortunately the truth.
2. Emil Souleimanov, *Endless War: The Russian-Chechen Conflict in Perspective* (New York: Peter Lang, 2007).
3. Of course, my initial theoretical assumptions were often disproved by the facts presented to me by respondents, which led me to constantly revise my research questions.
4. I generally consider my work ethnographic because of the usual combination of in-depth interviews with participant and nonparticipant observation. During the fifteen years I worked with Chechen individuals and families, I was immersed in the everyday banalities of my respondents' lives while focusing on the meanings they constructed around themselves and their narratives. Wherever I had an opportunity, I juxtaposed information acquired from some respondents, for example, former insurgents, to information provided by their family members, neighbors, or other individuals with firsthand knowledge of phenomena. In many other instances, circumstances allowed me only to carry out semistructured or in-depth interviews. This kind of research, although fully legitimate in itself, cannot be defined as ethnographic research per se. See, for instance, Edward Schatz, "What Kind(s) of Ethnography Does Political Science

Need?," in *Political Ethnography: What Immersion Contributes to the Study of Power*, ed. Edward Schatz (Chicago: University of Chicago Press, 2013), 1–22.

5. It is intriguing to note that had I accepted my respondents' initial explanations, the findings of my research would have been completely different! But how many political scientists do we know who spend years building trust—and repeatedly meeting with their interlocutors?

6. An important clarification must be made here. During my interaction with respondents, eyewitnesses, or veterans of violent conflicts, my role was not that of a psychiatrist. Although respondents occasionally try to treat researchers as such, unless formally trained in counseling or a related discipline, social scientists should be aware of their ability to do immense damage—unwittingly—by trying to act as aspiring psychiatrists. I am grateful to an anonymous reviewer for pointing out this important issue. See, for instance, Cyanne E. Loyle and Alicia Simoni, "Researching Under Fire: Political Science and Researcher Trauma," *PS: Political Science & Politics* 50, no. 1 (January 2017): 141–45, https://doi.org/10.1017/S1049096516002328.

38

ON BEING SEEN

ORA SZEKELY

▸ FIELDWORK LOCATION: LEBANON

O n a rainy night in February 2009, I got into a taxi in Beirut with a journalist friend and headed for the southern suburbs known collectively as the Dahieh. Through my friend's extensive local connections, she had gotten permission for us to attend a public event being held by Hezbollah.[1] It was my fourth year of graduate school, and I was in Beirut to conduct dissertation research on Hezbollah, among other nonstate organizations. Their public outreach was a major focus of my project, and I was delighted to have the opportunity to attend one of their events.[2]

The event in question did not disappoint. When we arrived, after first mistakenly trying to get in through the regular women's entrance, we were politely redirected to the press entrance where we lined up under a tent erected to protect us from Beirut's wintry drizzle while our names were checked against a list. We were then admitted to a massive space that looked like a cross between an arena and an airplane hangar, full of people waving flags, posing for photos, and in some cases, posing their children for photos in front of the pack of journalists in the press enclosure in the center of the room to which we were directed.[3]

The press pen had an excellent view of the rest of the space, which was divided by gender, with men on one side and women on the other. The event was a commemoration of the death the previous year of Imad Mughniyeh—one of Hezbollah's founders and a central architect of its military strategy—and was therefore attended, as far as I could tell, mostly by party members and active supporters. The front rows were filled with party dignitaries and a few political allies. Despite the somewhat grim official focus of the event, there was a festive atmosphere, and many of the attendees seemed to have brought their own flags. We were given commemorative sashes, (one of which I still have) in the distinctive shade I still think of as "Hezbollah yellow," that were printed with the faces of three of the group's leaders who had been killed by the Israeli military or intelligence services.

The event began with a series of speeches by various party leaders, interspersed with videos on a massive screen at the front of the room celebrating Hezbollah's military exploits as well as performances by Hezbollah's (all male) choir and their backup band in front of an elaborate stage set. The main event was an address—conducted live via video from a presumably safe location—by Hezbollah's leader, Hassan Nasrallah. Overall, the event felt like a cross between a political rally and a Broadway show, and it gave me exactly the insight I'd been looking for into Hezbollah's propaganda apparatus. I found the entire event fascinating.

For many of the journalists sitting around us, though, the evening was apparently a bit too long to sit through. Although a few stayed for the entire event, as the evening wore on, the seats around us began to empty. We were relatively close to the front of the room, and these vacancies soon proved irresistible to some of those in the men's section behind us, who hadn't had seats nearly as good as ours. Eventually, the "press section" became just another seating area.

This change in seating arrangements had somewhat unanticipated results (or at least, results that were unanticipated by me). Hezbollah's public events are almost always covered by its satellite TV channel, Al Manar. This was no exception, and there was an enormous camera boom hovering over the room. It had largely avoided filming the press section when it was full of journalists, photographers, and cameras from rival news organizations, but by the end of the evening most of those people had trickled away. The camera began swinging in over our heads, filming the section in which we were sitting, now surrounded by regular rally attendees.

The next day, when my friend walked into work, her coworkers delightedly informed her that they'd seen both of us on Al Manar the night before—the cameraman had even zoomed in on us a couple of times. My friend and I, who both have red hair, had been instantly recognizable to her coworkers, and they had a great time teasing her about it at the office. But when she shared this with me, I felt deeply uncomfortable, although I also had to admit that it was pretty funny. Appearing on television in the audience at a Hezbollah rally (even if only briefly) seemed like it probably violated some basic rule of field research, even if I wasn't sure which one. Wasn't I supposed to be the observer rather than the observed? In the end, there were no real consequences (at least none that I know of), but it did leave me with a sense that I wanted to avoid similar experiences in the future if at all possible.

As it happened, this became relevant only a few months later. I returned to Beirut that spring for the 2009 election campaign and was invited by a member of one of Lebanon's Christian political parties to attend a televised debate against a rival Christian party that was being aired on Al Manar (again). When we arrived at the venue, which turned out to be essentially an empty parking lot in downtown Beirut, I was invited to sit with some other members of the party—right behind the podiums where the debate was being held, and right in front of the cameras. I think the offer was made without any particular agenda, but the prospect of appearing on camera immediately set off some internal alarm bells, so I politely excused myself and sidled off to the back of the lot where I struck up a conversation with the crew from Al Manar who had come to film the event. Once they figured out I wasn't a journalist from a rival outlet, they gave me some good insights into how the campaign was going. That felt like a much better point from which to observe events.

My reactions in these instances will probably feel familiar to many other researchers. At the most basic level, I don't particularly enjoy appearing on television or video. When I've done so in the past, I rarely watch myself afterward. (I delegate that to my husband, who then reassures me that, no, I didn't have anything in my teeth.) But these episodes also highlight what is, at least for me, a tension in the research process: the need to balance the academic researcher's role as an ostensibly objective outside observer, on one hand, and the human relationships we develop with those we study, on the other. In the case of research that I've done involving (sometimes violent) political organizations, this has been overlaid with a tension between the need to develop trust with my research subjects and a responsibility not to misrepresent myself as a partisan supporter of their particular organization, even if I may be sympathetic to the human suffering of their civilian supporters. All of which is to say that I'm relatively certain no one who knows me would see me on Al Manar and assume I'd joined Hezbollah, but I wasn't comfortable with the idea that I might be passing myself off as a movement supporter to people who might then be more likely to tell me things they otherwise wouldn't.

Reflecting on these experiences leads me to raise the following questions (some of which are also addressed elsewhere in this book): To what degree are we responsible for how we are seen by the communities, organizations, and individuals who are the subjects of our research? How do we balance the need to develop trust with those we study with the need to be transparent about our position as researchers and, perhaps, our personal beliefs? How do we (and should we) draw that line when working with those to whom we are politically or personally sympathetic? Conversely, how do we negotiate these issues when studying organizations or individuals whose actions we do not support or condone? And when there is a power imbalance between researchers and those we study—based on colonial legacies, structural hierarchies of race and gender, current political relationships, or some combination thereof—how does that complicate these issues?[4]

One obvious response is methodological; in formal interviews, at least, some of these questions become moot because these interviews are often much clearer interactions in which both the interviewer and the person or people being interviewed understand their roles. But even in an interview, questions can arise about how the interviewer feels, personally, about the subject at hand, which can sometimes be difficult to answer. Interview participants may also simply assume that the interviewer is in some way "on their side," leading them to share more than they otherwise might. Although this might sometimes be the case—after all, many of us are drawn to particular research subjects as a result of our own personal and political attachments—it isn't always, which for me, at least, can sometimes feel a bit deceptive.

The best way I've found to deal with these challenges, beyond trying to keep myself as invisible as possible in the research process, is a combination of transparency and compassion: transparency about my role and my research, and compassion for my research participants as human beings, if not necessarily sympathy for their political objectives or their methods of pursuing them.

Transparency—that is, being open with our research participants about who we are and what we are doing—not only means that our interview subjects have the chance to say "no" but also means they know what they're saying "yes" to. It means being open about our positions as researchers, how their data will be used, who will see it, and in some cases, the limits of our ability to protect that data. (My personal rule of thumb is to tell my interview subjects that if there's something they don't want printed in a book—including their names—I don't need to know it, and I certainly won't write it down or record it.)

This does not have to mean engaging in lengthy disclaimers about our personal political views—indeed, it probably shouldn't. But it does mean being honest about who we are and what we're doing there. Above all, it means not trying to get away with anything. Not only is this safer for all concerned, it also feels most intuitively comfortable to me. If I'm going to be seen, I want to be seen accurately. I'm more or less fine with being filmed in the press enclosure at a political event or being seen talking to the camera guys—I'd just rather not be mistaken for a movement adherent, either by outside observers or by party members themselves.

Perhaps the trickier problem, though, is how to gain our research participants' trust without conveying the idea that we have taken a side. I try, as much as possible, to separate my own political preferences and sympathies from the research process, while still engaging with those I'm interviewing with compassion and empathy. But this has been easier in the context of some research projects than others. Maintaining some objective distance has generally been much easier in the case of the armed groups I've studied than with noncombatant refugees or women's rights activists, for instance. Hearing stories of personal loss and trauma over and over again can make it difficult to remain entirely dispassionate, and it probably should. This is made doubly difficult when those conversations are followed by conversations with those responsible for, or even just supportive of, those same atrocities. I have at times found myself interviewing people on different sides of the same conflict who have both suffered significantly, and I have been moved by both conversations. Perhaps most confusingly, I have at various points found myself at public events where I was somewhat unsure myself whether I was there as a researcher or as a participant. At vigils for political prisoners, memorials for those killed in violent conflict, or commemorations of past atrocities, it isn't always possible to separate myself emotionally, and frankly, I hope it never will be. I suspect the same is true for many of my colleagues as well. If we are filmed at such events, and assumed therefore to be less than fully objective, that may be a fair assessment, and perhaps a reasonable trade-off.

For many of us, the process of doing field research is about balancing a number of competing imperatives: to understand others' points of view while remaining objective, to listen without judging, and to be a witness without being a partisan. None of this is easy, but it is easier for me when I am standing behind the camera—rather than in front of it.

Ora Szekely *is associate professor of political science at Clark University.*

PUBLICATIONS TO WHICH THIS FIELDWORK CONTRIBUTED:

- Szekely, Ora. *The Politics of Militant Group Survival in the Middle East.* New York: Palgrave Macmillan, 2016.
- ——. "Hezbollah's Survival: Resources and Relationships," *Middle East Policy* 19, no. 4 (Winter 2012): 110–26.

NOTES

1. The event was held at Sahet al Shehada (Martyrs Square) in the heavily Shiʿite southern Beirut neighborhood of Dahieh. There are actually two (or possibly more) Sahet al Shehadas in Beirut. Getting cab drivers from Christian East Beirut to drive to the Sahet al Shehada in Dahieh, rather than the one downtown, often required explicitly stating that, yes, I meant the one in Dahieh, and, no, I would not prefer to go to the Sahet al Shehada in central Beirut, regardless of how nice the cafés might be, and, yes, I was sure I knew where I was going.
2. A great deal of excellent work has been done on Lebanon in general and Hezbollah in particular, including by several contributors to this volume. A much abbreviated selection includes Nicholas Blanford, *Warriors of God: Inside Hezbollah's Thirty-Year Struggle Against Israel* (New York: Random House, 2011); Augustus Richard Norton, *Hezbollah: A Short History* (Princeton, N.J.: Princeton University

Press, 2007); Kamal Salibi, *A House of Many Mansions: The History of Lebanon Reconsidered* (London: I. B. Tauris, 2003).

3. I later realized that Christopher Hitchens, no fan of Hezbollah, was sitting a few seats away from us. That still may be the single oddest thing I've ever encountered during field research.

4. For further reflections on research ethics in the context of participant observation, ethnography, and interview-based research, see Lee Ann Fujii, "Five Stories of Accidental Ethnography: Turning Unplanned Moments in the Field Into Data," *Qualitative Research* 15, no. 4 (2015): 525–39; Lee Ann Fujii, *Interviewing in Social Science Research: A Relational Approach* (Abingdon, UK: Routledge, 2017).

VIII

STAYING SAFE
AND HEALTHY

39

CONDUCTING SAFE FIELDWORK ON VIOLENCE AND PEACE

SARAH ZUKERMAN DALY

▸ FIELDWORK LOCATION: COLOMBIA

"A LO MEJOR NO PASA NADA"

ME: Is it safe to travel to Murindó en el Chocó?
FRIEND: A lo mejor no pasa nada.

This phrase is the response I received every time I sought to determine the safety of a place to which I hoped to travel within Colombia. It translates as "hopefully" or " maybe nothing will happen." It put the onus on me, the recipient of this advice, to determine what "a lo mejor" meant. Did it mean "hopefully" there was only a 10 percent chance that something would happen, or "maybe" a 50 percent chance? It required assessing the risk tolerance of the person providing the advice. In a country in which violence stretches as far back as anyone can remember, violence at times seems to loom in the future as well, and violence has touched nearly everybody and everywhere, the phrase "a lo mejor" comes to mean something different. And then I had to assess, what is my own risk tolerance? Will I travel somewhere if it is a 50 percent chance, but not a 60 percent chance, that something might go wrong? What would change that calculation?

I began researching Colombia in 2003 with a project on the onset and dynamics of the Revolutionary Armed Forces of Colombia (FARC) insurgency. While in the field, paramilitary organizations that fought against the FARC began to sign peace agreements, disarm, demobilize, and follow puzzlingly divergent postwar trajectories. Some of the organizations dissolved. Others remained strongly cohesive. Some maintained governance roles and authority over civilian life, and others played anemic roles in their communities. Some silenced their guns, and others returned to organized violence. Explaining this variation brought me back to the field for several years to conduct surveys and interviews of ex-combatants, their families, psychologists, recipient communities, and victims for my dissertation and first book. I have continued to conduct fieldwork in conflict areas across the world to study the outcomes and dynamics of postwar elections for my second book on why citizens vote for political actors who used violence against the civilian population. One of the key aspects and challenges of my fieldwork is navigating safety concerns, which is the focus of this chapter.

QUIÉN MANDA POR ACÁ

It is difficult to know when you are safe because the correct answer to the question *Quién manda por acá* (Who is in charge?) may be illusive. Here are a few examples.

I enter the ominous, cement cinder block building, hollow on the inside, daunting on the exterior. I progress through the security checks, and they stamp my forearm with an invisible stamp, only decipherable under ultraviolet light that indicates "I am just visiting . . . I may be released." I wonder what would happen if it rubs off, or if, in the heat of the midday sun, I sweat it off. As I wonder, I emerge into the bright light of the patios on the inside of Bellavista prison. I am in the patios of the former Autodefensas Unidas de Colombia (AUC), the paramilitaries. FARC has their own patios. Different gangs have their own patios.

After interviewing paramilitaries for several hours, I have to go to the bathroom. I am a woman in an all-men's prison. I ask the person in charge. He met me at the prison entrance. He has accompanied me around the prison. He arranged the interview room. He helped keep everything orderly during my meetings. He is a prison guard. He says, "of course," and proceeds to lead me down a long, dark corridor. Through the musky gloom I make out men's cells on either side. At the end of the corridor is a closet-sized bathroom. I am trapped. My companion points out his cell. I realize that he is not a prison guard, but a prisoner. He is de facto in charge; roles appear reversed here. My heart begins to race, and my inner thoughts ping-pong between "everything will be OK, everything will be OK" and "you are an idiot, you are an idiot." I did emerge unscathed, but I did not know who was really in charge inside the prison.

ROLE REVERSAL

On another day inside the prison, I interviewed a paramilitary commander who had been responsible for extorting all buses and taxis for the entire metropolitan area of Medellín, Colombia's second largest city—a massive operation. He was guilty of countless crimes and was sentenced to a combined forty-five years in prison. He had not shaved in what looked like months and had barely bathed in as long. He exuded a stench. During our conversation, he seemed distracted and kept staring at my hands. I moved them out of sight, below the desk. His eyes continued to look down. Finally, he blurted out, "I cannot believe that you did not get a manicure." I was taken aback. We were discussing the extortion racket, victimization, and coercive governance, and he was concerned about my cuticles! Over the course of our interview, he continued to return to his utter disbelief at the disrepair of my nails, which seemed ironic given his present physical condition and the gravity of his crimes. Weeks later, I found myself in a nail salon, getting a manicure. I thought to myself, "quién manda por acá?" Role reversal.

On other occasions, I incorrectly assessed who was in charge. It was at these moments that I felt less secure. I visited a "high-security" prison in Tierralta, at which many of the masterminds of the paramilitary phenomenon in Colombia were gathered. I assumed that the commanders would be in cells. Instead, only a low hedge separated these human rights abusers from liberty. The commanders explained to me that they were there of their own volition and therefore did not need cells or barbed wire. When I interviewed several of the top FARC commanders, including Pastor Alape, Marco Calarcá, Carlos Antonio Lozada, Sandra Ramírez, and Rodrigo Granda, there were guards outside their doors, but it was unclear if the guards were protecting them or me. I had to recalibrate my understanding of quién manda.

I frequented a restaurant in Apartado that had my favorite juices: feijoa and uchuva. A magnetic woman usually held court at a table next to mine. She alternated between hushed whispers, barked orders, and boisterous

324 STAYING SAFE AND HEALTHY

merrymaking. I later learned that she was the sister of Carlos Mauricio García Fernández, alias "Doble Cero," an infamous paramilitary commander in Urabá and Córdoba. Quién manda por acá?

Figuring out who is in charge and who you can trust is essential for ensuring your safety during fieldwork, but it requires that you allow roles to be reversed, and assumptions and priors to be popped. Risk assessments during fieldwork are complicated by a number of other factors as well.

THE STORY BEHIND THE NUMBERS

For the past fifteen years, I have tracked violent events in Colombia, beginning with those in 1964 and continuing to the present. This added a numeric probability to violence in different places at different times. On one hand, it made me aware that almost nowhere was "safe," and on the other hand, it demonstrated that the likelihood of anything happening in X location at exactly X moment in time was very low.

The benefit of being in the field is that there is a story behind every number, and you can learn that story. The numbers sometimes can abstract from the story, but other times they fail the reality. For me, the qualitative and quantitative diverged one evening in Aguachica, a small city in northeast Colombia. In thick, saturated air, I sat at a desk opposite a FARC guerrilla in the courtyard of a school, abandoned since classes had let out several hours earlier. I began the section of a survey I was enumerating on why he had joined an armed group. He answered that the most important factor in his decision to join the FARC was "wanting money, land, and food." I asked him to tell me the story of how he joined. He descended into a narrative of how the paramilitaries had come into his town and had killed his family. That was when he decided to join the FARC guerrillas. Fieldwork provides the opportunity to marry the numbers with real stories. In this case, it helped me understand the multiplicity of motives underlying recruitment and the challenges of using blunt survey questions to reveal these complex motives.

QUOTIDIAN LIFE DURING WAR

Adding to the complexity of deciding whether a place is safe for fieldwork is the false sense of security and the quotidian nature of life during war.

Even in the most active combat areas in a war, violence does not happen every day, or even every week, nor everywhere. Violence is episodic. When I traveled to Tibú in the Colombian region of Catatumbo, near the Venezuelan border, people told me it was "very caliente" (meaning combustive and dangerous). But that did not mean that I saw anything violent or experienced anything of the sort. In fact, quite the opposite, because daily life usually goes on, no matter how dangerous a place is. People drank *tinto*, sat about chatting, walked this way and that, worked, laughed, and shouted. The fact that life looks very normal during war makes it highly challenging to assess danger because you usually cannot see it.

Compounding this is the false sense of security that extended time in the field creates. It is psychologically exhausting to live in fear, and for this reason we have coping mechanisms. We create a sense of security in an unsafe environment, and our risk tolerance increases because we crave and need a semblance of normalcy. Understanding these factors, which render assessments of security blurry in conflict zones, is also important to keeping oneself safe in such environments.

Situations morph constantly and quickly on the ground in conflicts: one day a place might be deemed safe, and the next, dangerous. Before traveling to "complicated" parts of Colombia, I sought input from people I knew high up in the military intelligence services and would seek their advice the night before I traveled. I mapped the local violence patterns down to the neighborhood level, knowing that one *vereda* might lie above my risk threshold and the adjacent one below it.

If you are studying political science because you care about the real world, then you will enjoy, and even love, fieldwork. Allow yourself to "muck around," to have the field complicate and revise your view of the issues and processes, and to have the realities and voices on the ground marinate before imposing theoretical order on them. But for fieldwork to be productive and enjoyable, you must prioritize your safety. Find trusted people who can help you assess security risks in the moments before you travel, learn the stories behind the numbers, be wary of the quotidian life during war and a false sense of security, and always seek to know quién manda.

––––––

Sarah Zukerman Daly *is assistant professor of political science at Columbia University.*

PUBLICATIONS TO WHICH THIS FIELDWORK CONTRIBUTED:

- Daly, Sarah Zukerman. *Organized Violence After Civil War: The Geography of Recruitment in Latin America*. New York: Cambridge University Press, 2016.
- ——. "Voting for Victors: Why Violent Actors Win Postwar Elections," *World Politics* 71, no. 4 (October 2019): 747–805. https://doi.org/10.1017/S0043887119000091.
- ——. "The Dark Side of Power-Sharing: Middle Managers and Civil War Recurrence," *Comparative Politics* 46, no. 3 (April 2014): 333–53.

40

YOUR SAFETY AND THEIRS

INTERVIEWING SEX-TRAFFICKERS

CARLA B. ABDO-KATSIPIS

▸ FIELDWORK LOCATION: LEBANON

O n March 27, 2016, Lebanese Internal Security Forces raided the Chez Maurice and Silver brothels in search of seventy-five Syrian women who had been brought across the Lebanese border and coerced into prostitution.[1] Both establishments were run by the same group, whose senior traffickers were Maurice Jaajaa, a Lebanese national, and Imad Rihawi, a Syrian national.[2] These women were trafficked during the Syrian Civil War and were brought to Lebanon under the pretext of either work or marriage. When the defendants were formally accused on April 16, 2016, it became clear that this would be the first ever case to test the 2011 law, No. 164, Punishment for the Crime of Trafficking in Persons,[3] and it would be doing so under the backdrop of armed conflict. This case was heavily covered by the media, garnered significant public interest, and was the primary case study in my research on sex-trafficking of Syrian refugees in Lebanon.

I had completed the rigorous, full institutional review board (IRB) review process over the previous two months and had already been asked a lot of questions related to interviewing vulnerable populations, specifically those linked to criminal activity:

- How would I react to participants telling me about participation in former crime?
- How would I protect participants' identities?

- Did I have a legal duty to report their testimony?
- How could I get the information I wanted and still be sensitive to the subject matter?

Some of my research had been inspired by Howard Becker's study of the behaviors of drug addicts in his book *Outsiders: Studies in the Sociology of Deviance*. Working as a dance musician, Becker first interviewed fellow dance musicians who were marijuana addicts. These participants led him to others outside of the profession through personal referral. Becker's method of collecting data was participant observation—he worked with the addicted musicians he studied.[4]

In contrast, I had no plans to participate in the industry of the interviewees. So I decided that the best way to gather information was through targeted interviews by referral. As Lee Ann Fujii indicates in *Interviewing in Social Science Research: A Relational Approach*, I wanted to appear nonthreatening, to actively listen, to treat the participants with respect no matter what, and to give participants the lead in the conversation.[5] However, the practical aspect of finding people with access to the sex-trafficking ring was more uncertain than I liked, and I knew there was an element of chance in finding either traffickers or victims who were willing to speak with me. Approaching vulnerable populations was markedly different from any of my previous research on voting behavior. I was excited but anxious about the fact that I would have less control over this process than I had had in other research endeavors.

DEVELOPING A NETWORK

I began my research by developing an affiliation with the Arab Institute for Women at the Lebanese American University.[6] Through their expertise and generous referral process, I began interviewing academics, journalists, attorneys, police, judges, and civil society activists; and I attended the public hearing of victim testimony. These were professional interviews, and those who agreed to be interviewed openly gave me their time and knowledge. Through this network, I learned that the trial would be held on July 7, 2017,[7] and that the gallery was public. This would be my chance to see the legal process in action. I attended—unsure of what to expect. Would I hear victim testimony again? Would I meet traffickers here? What would the outcome be?

Having arrived early to the courtroom, only two men were present, one was dressed in a formal attorney's cloak reserved exclusively for the courtroom. The attorney approached me and asked the purpose of my presence there. In broad strokes, I told him that I was a researcher interested in the Chez Maurice sex-trafficking case. He introduced himself as one of the defense attorneys in the case, volunteered to speak to me, and gave me his card and phone number. Good start, I thought. I will talk to him, and he can refer me to others.

Then Issam[8] approached me.

INTERVIEWING SEX-TRAFFICKERS

Issam sat next to me and chatted about the weather and the day he was having. As the conversation progressed, he said he had overheard my conversation with the defense attorney. He indicated that he had worked in the Chez Maurice trafficking ring as a guard and, like the others accused of sex-trafficking in this case, was released on bail. He asked me questions about my intentions and learned that I was approaching this matter scholastically and without judgment. Hearing this, he said he wanted to share his experience, and he gave me some practical advice:

> Look, what you are trying to research isn't easy. Let me talk to you and find others who will. You won't be able to get them to speak to you any other way, OK? We all went through a lot in prison, and we have a hard time trusting anyone. You might step on other people's toes—I don't want anything to happen to you.

Although he did not clarify what "anything happening to me" actually meant, I felt that this was a fair warning. No one in the sex-trafficking ring had a reason to trust me without someone to back me up, and poking around blindly could backfire. I thanked him for his support in my research, feeling both grateful and a little anxious as I did so. I reasoned that at least part of the rationale for Issam's willingness to assist me in finding interviewees was to monitor how much access I had to information, but without him I would have very little access at all. Wasn't access to traffickers what I wanted? But what was I really getting myself into? Could I trust him—after all, wasn't he also accused of criminal activity? Had my fieldwork studies prepared me for this?

Shortly after Issam offered to assist me, the court gallery started to fill. Easily recognizable through media coverage, Imad Rihawi, one of the senior traffickers of the ring, sat down a few seats away on the same bench.

"Issam, is that . . . " I asked.

"Yes, that's him," Issam responded before I could finish my sentence.

"Can I talk to him?"

"I really wouldn't advise you to. We all have trust issues from prison, and I don't think he will."

"I don't mean to push, but can you just ask him, please? If he says no, I won't ask again."

"OK, but I do not think he will agree." Issam spoke to Rihawi, and came back to me, looking a bit nervous. "Carla, he agreed. Keep it short, don't ask him tough questions, and don't look him in the eye. He is extremely violent."

Aren't we in a public court gallery? I thought. What could he do? Before I could process this information further, Rihawi and Issam had exchanged seats. As instructed, I looked straight ahead and did not turn my head. I then asked him if he could tell me his narrative about the case.

"All of these are lies; someone has an interest in prosecuting me. I treat these girls better than people did where they came from." Rihawi quickly turned his head, leaned into my physical space, and gave me a piercing glare that scared me badly. I ended the interview and thanked him for speaking to me. He returned to his spot, and Issam came back to sit next to me.

"How did it go?" Issam asked. I exhaled slowly, preparing to answer, when Issam said,

> I thought so. Carla, again—let *me* figure out who you can speak to. Don't take this the wrong way, but you seem really innocent. I know you have read about the case, but you don't seem to fully realize what some of them are capable of.

Them, I thought. Does he perceive himself as being different? Is that why he wants to help me?

Privately, Issam discussed the possibility of conversations with other members of the ring, came back to me, and indicated that he had arranged two meetings with fellow sex-traffickers. Some were similarly accused of detaining victims; others were accused of both physically abusing and detaining victims. Both meetings were slated for only a few hours later in the day. The first meeting was with female traffickers, and the second with male traffickers. He would accompany me to the meeting with the male traffickers, but I would be on my own with the women. Issam arranged for both meetings to be in separate public places.[9] "So that everyone is comfortable," he said.

I had imagined the process of speaking to the accused traffickers being in a quiet room reserved for research at my university. However, one thing had become clear to me—they would speak to me, but on their terms. I would have to be flexible about this.

During my meeting with the female traffickers, most of the women began by indicating complete innocence on their part as well as that of their senior traffickers—Imad Rihawi in particular. Seemingly primed, they said that the victims had come willingly, and they unpacked aspects of their defense before I started to ask questions. As the conversation progressed over the course of two hours, the women spoke more candidly about their work, largely as guards, in the sex-trafficking ring.[10] Toward the end, an admission that they too had been trafficked as minors surfaced, and one woman gave me a clear-cut complete confession. After wrapping up my meeting with them, thanking them for their time and honesty, and reassuring them of anonymity, I made my way to the meeting with the male traffickers.

Issam was already there, and as he introduced me to the men, I found that he was right—I needed someone on the inside to vouch for me and would not get candid answers otherwise. Unlike the female traffickers, the men had quite a few questions for me, and Issam heavily shielded me from most of them. He also sat next to me the entire time. He seemed a little worried about my safety around the male traffickers.

"So, Carla—where are you from? What is your last name?" asked Faudel,[11] one of Issam's colleagues.

"Don't ask her that," Issam answered—before I could. He did not know the answers to those questions either, but it became clear to me that he did not want my identifiable information revealed to anyone in the ring.

"Why are you interested in this case?" asked Salim, another trafficker who had agreed to participate.[12]

"She is doing research on it and wants to hear what we have to say," Issam answered, once again before I could.

"Research for what? For whom? Issam, you're an idiot! Why do you trust her so much? How well do you know her? How do you know that everything you say won't be all over the news by tomorrow? What do you know about her, anyway?" Faudel raised his voice with each question, and Issam responded in a surprisingly neutral tone.

"Stop screaming, you're upsetting her! Can't you tell she just wants to talk? Besides, why did you come? You talk to her and tell me why I trust her!" He turned to me and said, "I'm sorry, we all have trust issues from prison—don't panic, he didn't mean to yell."

Faudel looked me in the eye and apologized for raising his voice. I reminded him that I only wanted to know what happened, and that anything he said would remain anonymous. He then took a deep breath and began telling me about how much money he made, how long he had worked for the sex-trafficking ring, his role as a guard, the duration of his shifts, and other matters. As he and Issam spoke with me candidly, so did the other men in the group. Unlike the female traffickers, none of the men spoke in defense of their senior traffickers—or even in defense of themselves. I strongly suspected that this was a function of Issam's presence. Not only had Issam vouched for me, but the other men knew he had already spoken to me about sex-trafficking; there was no use engaging in either defense or denial. This meeting also took approximately two hours. I thanked them for their time, their candor, and reiterated my promise of anonymity.

I was elated with the openness that both groups displayed. However, I reminded myself not to get too excited. I had to think about matters of safety—not only theirs but also mine. Both groups were talking to me in public—couldn't I have been seen, and if so, couldn't I have been followed? I didn't know for sure, but I wanted to take precautions. I took a bus to a town located in the opposite direction from where I lived and spent two hours milling around in a random restaurant there. Then I took another bus to a secondary town, spent an hour or so in their clothing shops, took a taxi to a third town (neighboring my own), and then walked the rest of the way home.

By the time I arrived home, I felt that I had taken appropriate precautions. Fortunately, Issam had shielded me from all questions about my identity except for my first name. I did not feel that any of the people I spoke to had enough information to put me in danger. Mindful of their safety as I typed my notes, I made sure to exclude information concerning their names, nationalities, regions of origin, the locations of the interviews, and only indicated their testimony through the use of a pseudonym.

I called the defense attorney a few days later and asked for a meeting. He said he was busy and that he would prefer not to speak to me anymore. I told him I understood and hung up.

As I continued my research, I asked myself about Issam's motivation in helping me and why his fellow traffickers were willing to participate. Everyone had reported the experience of ostracization due to the charges. By speaking to me, they had someone willing to listen to their story with the promise of anonymity—and without judgment. It was through this process that I learned the full value of attentive listening.

This research project taught me a valuable lesson. If I wanted to interview vulnerable people, I needed to get someone to vouch for me, adapt to the needs of my subjects, and be flexible about the logistics. Above all, I needed to listen actively and to be mindful of their safety as well as my own.

——

Carla B. Abdo-Katsipis *is visiting assistant professor of government in the College of Social Studies at Wesleyan University.*

PUBLICATIONS TO WHICH THIS FIELDWORK CONTRIBUTED:

- Abdo-Katsipis, Carla B. "The Rise in Sex-Trafficking Among Syrian Refugees and Its Legal Challenges" (Article under review).
- ——. *Victims and Perpetrators: Women in Conflict* (in preparation).

NOTES

1. Rania Hamzeh, "Women Trafficking in Lebanon: The Torture Chambers of Chez Maurice," *The Legal Agenda*, April 14, 2016, http://legal-agenda.com/en/article.php?id=3137.

2. As of publication, Maurice Jaajaa is still at large, and Imad Rihawi has been arrested. Document of Accusation No. 2211, 2016.

3. Document of Accusation No. 2211, 2016.

4. Howard Saul Becker, *Outsiders: Studies in the Sociology of Deviance* (Glencoe, Ill.: Free Press of Glencoe, 1963), 83–85.

5. Lee Ann Fujii, *Interviewing in Social Science Research: A Relational Approach* (Abingdon, UK: Routledge, 2017), 1–8.

6. During the time I was affiliated with them, the name of the organization was the Institute for Women's Studies in the Arab World.

7. The trial was postponed during this hearing.

8. Issam is a pseudonym for a lower-level trafficker who was arrested in the Chez Maurice case and was charged with detaining the victims. He agreed to speak to me under conditions of anonymity.

9. Owing to the promise of anonymity to the interviewees, I cannot reveal the exact locations of our meetings.

10. These women were mostly charged with detaining victims.

11. Faudel is a pseudonym for a lower-level trafficker who was also arrested in the case. He was charged with detaining victims. He agreed to speak to me under conditions of anonymity.

12. Salim is a pseudonym for a lower-level trafficker who was also arrested in the case. He was charged with detaining victims. He agreed to speak to me under conditions of anonymity.

41

SHINGLES ON THE CAMPAIGN TRAIL

RAVI PERRY

▶ FIELDWORK LOCATION: OHIO, USA

When Barack Obama was preparing for the Democratic National Convention, where he would make history as the first black major party nominee for president, I was in Toledo and Dayton, Ohio, conducting field research for my dissertation. My research involved interviewing elected officials, area community members, campaign organizers, and the media. I wanted to capture their conception of how advocacy for policies and programs for blacks in majority white cities can be effective in producing substantive outcomes for black communities, as well as substantial crossover support of white liberals for black candidates (in this case, for mayor).

At that time, Ohio had five black mayors—one in each of its major cities—and each city was majority white. I traveled to Toledo and Dayton to conduct more than one hundred interviews of mayors, city officials, campaign staff, media personnel, and community leaders. Toledo is my hometown, so familiarity with the city was not a concern. Also, my niece was born and raised in Dayton, so my ability to navigate that city was not too difficult. These two facts became critically important later, when my comfort with my surroundings helped me navigate a personal crisis, the first inklings of which were documented in my field note journal:

It is 6 PM on Wednesday July 9, 2008 and I am here in thrilling Toledo, Ohio! I, again, had an excellent interview and I am constantly reassured of my project's pending success. The more my name is thrown around lately, the more requests I get to apply for jobs (who knew?). I also went to the emergency room today. I was suffering from some kind of break out on the right side of my neck that spread to my shoulder, chest and back that I could not explain since none of my habits have changed.

I came down with an unexplained illness while conducting interviews in Toledo in June and July 2008. I was twenty-six years old. The sudden episode was immediately debilitating and required me to go to the emergency room where I was admitted. The staff there was also surprised to see such a young person in this condition. They attributed the outbreak to a combination of factors, all centering around stress.

> Well, it's shingles. Evidently it is common to get at some point that is random for anyone who has ever had chicken pox, which I have had. But, it may be induced by stress, over exhaustion, the sun, etc. So, I guess I need to take a few deep breaths!:)

Throughout this period of delay in the hospital, I was also courting the person who would later become my husband. My daily emails to him documented my field experience with shingles. I took extensive notes in my interviews, but I did not take further notes on my outbreak. In my emails, I described the pain, the concern, and the aspiration to complete the field research so I could begin my planned predoctoral fellowship in August 2008 in Rochester, New York. But to get there, I first needed to complete my interviews! I was frustrated and nervous and in severe pain:

> I'm annoyed that [having shingles] means taking an additional 5 pills a day for the next ten days. . . . I was highly nervous last night as I read more about the condition as well and its potential effects. I am confident, though, that I caught it in time. It only has appeared on a small localized spot on the left (or right?) side of my body. A small rash on the bottom of my neck, shoulder blade/back, and chest. The meds appear to be working. I must admit, though, I was extremely uncomfortable last night and to add to the pain I had a moment where I was cold and shaking. So, I turned off the air. This occurrence has re-awakened my heightened emotional sensitivity to my health condition. I don't like it and I'm not

happy about it. It serves as a reminder of what I have. I am aggressively searching for a doctor to check on me while I'm here in Ohio and it has encouraged me to not even think about not setting up with one in Rochester once I arrive there.

As this email attests, I was concerned about multiple conditions—adding shingles to my preexisting conditions was just too much. This experience awakened me to the fact that I had no plan for doctor's visits away from campus while in the field. Meanwhile, I found myself having to stop my interviews and reschedule appointments.

> [The doctors had] me on Acyclovir (Zovirax) 800 mg orally five times daily for 10 days and Vicodin as needed. I'm 26 years old. This should not be happening.

These sudden symptoms revealed to me that I was not prepared for any health emergency.

After my Toledo experience, which ultimately delayed my interview schedule by over a week, I then traveled to Dayton to conduct the same kinds of interviews there. I was still reeling from the episode in Toledo with shingles. I was feeling better, but I was still in severe pain as I tried to complete my field research. Ultimately, I had to wait to see another doctor, so I went to Dayton to begin my second round of interviews.

> I am feeling better. (I'm looking better too!) My shoulder area did begin to kill me when I was out earlier at church and people kept hitting me on my shoulder to say hello, though. Very painful. They say the sores go away within weeks, the pain can last longer though. I hope that isn't the case. Hence, a pending doctor visit. I'm up now after a nap to do some writing and to organize some phone calling. I'm on my way to another interview. I think I am making progress on my goals for the day. I contacted my doctor whose next available appt. is 7/31. I am trying to get that pushed a week earlier; however, for now, that's where it stands.

As fate would have it, I found myself in the hospital again battling a sudden kidney stone—this time in a city I didn't know very well (except for some visits there to see my niece!). While confined to a hospital bed in Dayton due to a sudden severe pain, I vividly recall being annoyed that I received no calls of support from the guy I called a boyfriend at the time. (We were married a couple of years later, but we ultimately divorced.) I also vividly recall curling in a fetal position for hours while screaming loudly to absorb the excruciating pain—it didn't help. It wasn't shingles this time; it was a kidney stone that felt like the size of a boulder. Vicodin didn't help much either, and the nurses kept telling me there was nothing they could do because "these kind of things just have to pass on their own," not exactly a comforting message. After several days of the worst pain I have ever experienced, the kidney stone "passed," and I was able to return to the field in Dayton to finish my interviews—slower, weaker, but present.

These experiences—shingles and kidney stones—taught me to have a personal plan of action to protect my health while on field research. Looking back on it now, I should have treated that field research like an international excursion to an unknown destination with all of the complexities that requires. That way, I would have planned for these episodes. At the same time, I don't know if planning would have done much. I did nothing, per se, to cause both shingles and a kidney stone while conducting field research, but perhaps there was something I could have done to decrease the likelihood of an occurrence. Who knows?

These episodes taught me one major lesson in conducting research in the field: slow down. I was so excited by the "getting done" aspect that I did not adequately prepare for or enjoy the experience while I was there. I regret not preparing better. One's health can surely stop whatever research is ongoing. Without your health, all of your other goals are out of reach.

I am thankful that my health improved, I wrote my thesis, and I graduated. The human relations approach—the framework of my dissertation—was coined by Cornel West in *Race Matters* and is best defined as governing directed with and by an explicit appeal to people's common humanity.[1] Perhaps it was my brush with two health scares while on the interview trail that encouraged me to take a similar approach to how I engage with the discipline as a scholar-activist. While in graduate school, in particular, my father (a sociologist) admonished me to be mindful that without my health none of my academic goals would be possible. His gentle advice prioritized my humanity and our common experience above the pressure to finish.

To this day, my research, teaching, and community engagement—my politics—are focused on improving the lived conditions of people. How can we serve the constituencies with the most need and everyone else simultaneously? How can my research inform these efforts? This framework has afforded me the rich opportunity to be more fully human. Attention to your health and to the improved health of community members can help you successfully merge your personal and professional identities.

Ravi Perry *is chair and professor of political science at Howard University.*

PUBLICATION TO WHICH THIS FIELDWORK CONTRIBUTED:

- Perry, Ravi. *Black Mayors, White Majorities: The Balancing Act of Racial Politics.* Lincoln, Neb.: University of Nebraska Press, 2014.

NOTE

1. Cornel West, *Race Matters* (Boston: Beacon Press, 2001).

42

DRINK THE TEA

VIPIN NARANG

▸ FIELDWORK LOCATION: INDIA

"**W**ould you like some tea?" asked the retired three-star Indian Army general.

"Thank you sir, that would be wonderful," I replied.

Although I am not usually a tea drinker, and neither wanted nor needed tea given the Delhi summer heat—where the morning temperature was already over one hundred degrees—this was the first senior Army general with whom I had scored an interview during my doctoral research. I did not want to be rude, and knowing that refusing tea and biscuits is potentially insulting to a host, I readily accepted.

After beginning the interview on Indian conventional military strategy and its evolving nuclear weapons program, the general's aide brought the tea and biscuits. I politely took a sip and immediately knew I would be in trouble. It was barely lukewarm. As a lifelong visitor to India, even I still abided by three rules, especially in the summer: no unboiled water, no ice, no raw vegetables. I was quite sure the water for the tea had never reached a boiling temperature, which is critical to make the water drinkable. What to do? Leave the rest of the tea and risk insulting the host, or continue drinking it and risk an infamous bout of Delhi Belly (at which I was a seasoned pro)? I already had taken in a decent amount (sunk cost fallacy!), so how much more damage could I do? I decided to drink the rest of the tea.

A couple of hours later, I paid the price. I was in the car, stuck in Delhi traffic, heading to another meeting when I started getting the shakes and my body started aching. I immediately knew the culprit and thought, this isn't going to be good. I powered through my next meeting, which was my last of the day, and headed straight back to the house where I was staying. Things were deteriorating fast, and I couldn't hold anything down, or in. This was going to be bad. My usual strategy of filling myself with Imodium was going to be insufficient, so I made the decision to nuke the bacteria with antibiotics, hoping I could keep them down long enough to start being effective. Due to the overprescription of antibiotics in India, many antibiotics—such as Cipro—that used to be prescribed for such situations are no longer effective. I had to take my chances on Azithromycin, which I had carried with me from my U.S. doctor for precisely this scenario. Long story short, I was out of commission for about three days.

Was it worth it? Absolutely. As a fourth-year nobody graduate student just getting off the ground, it required a lot of effort to get contact information for someone who knew anything about Indian conventional military and nuclear strategy. The Indian military and government are very opaque about these matters. They tend not to keep written archives that one can consult, nor do they publish regular "posture reviews" as is done in the United States. The only way to get credible information about Indian security thinking is to go to the field and meet as many people in the system as possible to try to triangulate developments—and then sift through the misinformation, misdirection, accusations of being a CIA spy, and so forth. This is complicated by the adage that "those who know don't speak, and those who don't know speak too much." This is all too true in South Asia.

Through a random series of events and circuitous contacts, my first substantive interview was with the retired Army three-star general, someone who had just left the military and had experience with India's experiment with the so-called Cold Start conventional strategy to redesign India's military strategy. This had deep implications for India's nuclear strategy and its attempt to escape the paralysis of Pakistan's nuclear threat, which was critical and also germane to my dissertation. I suffered through the tea (and what I still think was a mild bout of dysentery) to discover that India's purported Cold Start strategy was frozen and would never materialize—and that the Army was frustrated at its isolation from civilian leaders regarding integration of its conventional and nuclear strategies. The general also gave me a set of invaluable introductions and contacts for officers who had recently left India's Strategic Forces Command—a set of contacts that were impenetrable without his introduction. If it took a bout of dysentery for the general to vouch for me as someone worth meeting—and not a

CIA spy as is usually the suspicion for those trying to get details on India's or Pakistan's most sensitive secrets—so be it. To be fair, I was young, healthy, and probably a little too cavalier about it. I certainly paid a heavy price for this information. It is obviously not worth risking life, limb, or stomach, but illnesses can happen when doing fieldwork. I learned a valuable lesson for the future: "pretend" to drink the tea. (Make the slurping noises, but don't consume any! There is a good chance the host won't notice.)

The snowball interviews proved to be invaluable for my dissertation—which later became my first book. I believe I had collected the most detailed and novel data on India's evolving nuclear posture to that point in time. None of the details had been written down anywhere previously. Although the officers sometimes spoke elliptically, I was able to piece together crucial procedures and facts that painted the picture of a nuclear force increasingly different—more responsive, more ready, more mature—than anyone had previously thought. I had to go to Delhi—and maybe get dysentery—to get these details.

Nor were health issues the only risks I faced while conducting field research. At some point, I even made the mistake of flying to Simla (rather than going by train and road, a combination which is statistically more dangerous in India, for what that's worth) to interview an officer at India's doctrine development command. It was only after my trip that I learned that Simla is one of the world's ten most dangerous airports to fly into; it has one of the shortest certifiable runways allowed for civilian aircraft and sits on top of a mountain, with cavernous valleys on either side. I held on for dear life as we dipped into one of those valleys after takeoff, trying to gain speed and altitude. Never in my life had I been so happy to safely land back in Delhi.

Between the increasing pollution; water and food issues, especially in the summer; and the chaotic traffic during the day and the dangerous speeds at night, I try to be off the road before midnight. One certainly has to be careful in Delhi, as in any large developing city. Lest you think fieldwork in Delhi is only hazardous to one's health, I also fall in love with India all over again when I arrive. The sights, the sounds, and the food are nothing like you've ever experienced before. If you think you've had Indian food at your neighborhood curry house, you haven't had anything until you've tried HaveMore on Pandara Road, Karim's in Old Delhi, or the classic Moti Mahal. I literally have dreams about a fresh butter naan out of a tandoor, done right. Or the food shacks in Goa en route to the

Naval War College, or a detour to Kerala where the food is so different and spiced so purely that it could be from a different country than what we are used to in North India.

Delhi is an assault on the senses, one's patience, and occasionally one's stomach. There is nothing more frustrating than being stuck in two hours of traffic in the monsoon rain just to go two kilometers because of the combination of impassable roads and the congestion of cars, rickshaws, and goats; or braving that chaos to show up at the appointed time for a meeting only to be stood up because the person forgot, or something better came up. Everyone operates on Indian Standard Time, where 7 P.M. dinner means 10 P.M., and where "would you like some tea?" really means "drink this tea"—or at least pretend to—come hell or high water (or dysentery!). One summer, many years after my first research trip, protestors had literally destroyed the lone canal that feeds Delhi its water. We had our young son with us, so I was terrified. No water? What the heck does that even mean? But everyone else was nonchalant, including my Punjabi mother-in-law, for whom it didn't even register because, as she said, she was a daughter of Partition—they had lived through far worse. What I viewed as existential crises were not even minor nuisances for Delhi residents. And sure enough, through some creative *jugaad* (the Hindi word for creative "hacking"), they managed to divert water and repair the canal to avoid a disruption.

Somehow, through all the chaos, India works. Once I experienced Delhi like this—one can never fully understand or learn it—I had a much better appreciation for India's lumbering, seemingly sclerotic, and dysfunctional security strategy. India faces social, economic, and political challenges far worse than foreigners can imagine, all while operating on Indian Standard Time; but somehow, through it all, it gets the job done. Without countless trips to Delhi, lukewarm tea in the summer that occasionally comes with a side of dysentery, I would never have understood that.

Vipin Narang *is associate professor at the Massachusetts Institute of Technology.*

PUBLICATION TO WHICH THIS FIELDWORK CONTRIBUTED:

- Narang, Vipin. *Nuclear Strategy in the Modern Era: Regional Powers and International Conflict.* Princeton, N.J.: Princeton University Press, 2014.

ONE LAST THING BEFORE YOU GO . . .

LAIA BALCELLS

Chapter 28: Researching an Old Civil War Close to Home

Try to **stay neutral even if you have political opinions about the case**, and even if you have personal connections to one of the sides in a conflict, to victims of a conflict, or to key political actors. Exercise being an objective observer and self-correct when you feel you are not being analytical enough. At the same time, do not forget that you are human, and **be kind to yourself**: find outlets after intense or traumatic interviews and healthy ways to cope with them. Stay flexible and open-minded, and adapt as much as possible to the context, including the human characteristics of your subjects. Be patient during fieldwork because things do not always work out immediately, and **be ready to implement the skills acquired during one project to a future one**. Work hard, but also be appreciative of your time doing fieldwork as much as possible.

MIA BLOOM AND AYSE LOKMANOGLU

Chapter 19: Conducting Fieldwork in a Virtual Space

Like traditional field research, **we recommend keeping a research journal**. Journaling is essential to take note of observations, to highlight the similarities or differences, or to document anything that appears to be out of place. Furthermore, a research journal for virtual research becomes a secondary source of data and is not redundant. Journaling may prove to be essential for recognizing patterns and pinpointing research topics that demand further investigation. Because we paired screenshots with a research journal, we spotted the differences in how ISIS published its official magazines, such as when they moved publication from Fridays to Thursdays. We could emphasize which districts in Iraq or Syria generated the greatest numbers of eulogies and correlate this with events on the ground. Journaling was a critical tool that contextualized the data.

MATTHEW FRANKLIN CANCIAN AND KRISTIN E. FABBE

Chapter 13: "You Don't Know What You're Getting Into"

Trust but verify! Survey data is a powerful way for us to understand political phenomena, but the process of conducting a survey is messy. Scholars are vulnerable to paying for data that is allegedly collected in a certain area and in a certain way but that may have been gathered at a convenient central location or even manufactured wholesale. **Electronic tools should be used by all researchers to monitor their survey enumerators and to be able to prove that the survey was collected as intended.** Survey software like Qualtrics can record valuable metadata, such as the time elapsed for each survey. Sharing photos of enumerators in action over WhatsApp can be both fun and provide early warning of malfeasance. GPS location, where cell service is available, provides a way for scholars to conduct unannounced site inspections. Setting up these precautions in advance will prevent scholars from being taken for a ride when conducting surveys in the field.

ERICA CHENOWETH

Chapter 33: On Research That "Matters"

Before pursuing grants from security, military, or intelligence agencies in the government, ask yourself the following questions:

1. Am I willing to disclose this funding source publicly (i.e., on my personal website) for the rest of my career?
2. Might people I have met or would like to meet in the field be put in danger by my association with this particular agency?

3. Are there people from whom I would want to conceal my association with this particular agency?

If the answer is yes to 1 and no to 2 and 3, you're probably good to go. But if your answer is hesitant or ambivalent about any of them, or you're worried that your associations might put your research informants at risk in the field, **talk to a number of scholars in the field**—including those who have never accepted funding from such sources—**to help you come to an informed decision about whether and how to proceed**.

FOTINI CHRISTIA

Chapter 8: Navigating Data Collection in War Zones

The most robust lesson I have learned from my fieldwork is that **the field holds a lot of richness and opportunity just waiting to be discovered**. While doing largely observational dissertation-related research on civil war alliances in Afghanistan and Bosnia, I noticed some excellent conditions for field experiments on local governance and development lurking in the background. I was aggressive in pursuing these opportunities in both settings, resulting in some exciting projects and journal articles. Focus first and foremost on the fieldwork for the specific inquiry at hand, but keep your eyes and ears open for other research opportunities, as well as for potential collaborations on the ground. Closely following local developments and talking to policy experts and journalists while in the field can help highlight such opportunities for original research design and innovative measurement strategies that are bound to pay high research dividends.

SARAH ZUKERMAN DALY

Chapter 39: Conducting Safe Fieldwork on Violence and Peace

Fieldwork, at times, may present an ethical and personal challenge: **being a chameleon**. I interviewed people who had done bad things and people with whom I strongly disagreed. I found that I had to maintain a chameleon personality and show empathy for all viewpoints. I had to somehow show empathy not only for the victim who had lost his or her entire family in a brutal massacre but also for the commander who had orchestrated the massacre. I had to listen with an open mind to people from the whole range of the political spectrum. Everything in the field comes through personal connections. If people believed I was neutral, they would share their stories, information, connections, and access with me. To gain an unvarnished story and to remain safe required that I withhold judgment. However, being a chameleon can be trying on a personal and ethical level. When it is, **make sure to give yourself time and space to process your interactions, and maintain trusted friends with whom you can be a more immutable version of you**.

KEITH DARDEN

Chapter 18: My Stint as a Ukrainian Taxi Driver

Always remember that in the field, **the subjects of your research are not your friends—they are the gatekeepers to the information you need**. To get them to open up, you need to find a set of keys specific to that context. You may have to strategically take on a slightly different persona, or create a slightly different personal history of yourself, or stress some things from your true past and suppress others. Much is out of your hands or restricted by institutional review board standards. **You have the most control over the image of yourself that you present and the settings in which you present it**. If you are creative and strategic in your selection of both your persona and the settings, you are more likely to secure the information you are seeking.

CHRISTINA M. GREER

Chapter 5: Conducting 1,500 Surveys in New York City (With Great Uncertainty and a Limited Budget)

When conducting interviews, **arrive early and expect to stay later than anticipated**. For almost every interview I have ever conducted, I was told that my subject had thirty minutes maximum to dedicate to me and my project. You may only receive thirty minutes from your interview subjects, but in the event that they want to give you more time, do not overbook yourself. If the conversation is going well and they understand the necessity of your research, a thirty-minute conversation can extend into an invitation to join them at a meeting or an event as they conclude with you. **Allow flexibility in your schedule** so you can accept new opportunities that may arise.

And as you are concluding, **ask your interview subject to suggest someone else with whom you should speak**. Don't leave until you have a name (and contact information) so your snowball sample can continue to grow.

NADYA HAJJ

Chapter 9: Let Go and Let Ali

Read widely and deeply in your area of study before heading into the field. Let the literature inform your *first* round of interview questions. However, interviewing is a dynamic process, and there will be numerous iterations of research questions as you gain experience in the field. **Develop rapport with respondents by interviewing multiple times, actively listening, and asking for feedback**. Always end an interview by asking, "Is there anything I should have asked you that I didn't?" An offhand remark at the end of an interview may lead to the most interesting revelations that connect a case to a broader theory in political science.

ENZE HAN

Chapter 29: Positionality and Subjectivity in Field Research

Be aware of your own positionality and subjectivity when conducting field research. Even when using good methods, the potential interactive relationship between you and your research subjects is sometimes difficult to overcome. Either ignoring it or pretending it never exists is not honest. **Confront your own "baggage" and engage more reflexivity in your fieldwork** by recognizing how your own identity—such as race, gender, class background, and nationality—can or does shape your research access and findings. Do not worry that your research is more or less biased than others'; everyone's research access will be different and presents different perspectives. What really matters is clearly acknowledging this issue rather than proclaiming a universalist objectivity.

AMELIA HOOVER GREEN

Chapter 14: Successful Fieldwork for the Fieldwork-Hater

If you can possibly manage it, **give yourself an initial, nonresearch (or barely research) field visit to get your bearings**. Plan for a few weeks of slow, exhausting, potentially exhilarating logistics. Scope out neighborhoods, interview potential research staff (translators, fixers, research assistants), and figure out the (literal) lay of the land. You'll figure out quickly whether some parts of your plan need discarding, and when you return, you'll know exactly where to go for phone minutes, Imodium, and bottled water. More important, you'll return with a plan in place. In my experience as a field-work-hater, "getting my bearings" is a never-ending process; the fact that it never ends means that—if you're so inclined—it can be drawn out forever, crowding out actual research. Don't do that! It feels terrible.

AMANEY JAMAL

Chapter 27: Building Field Networks in the Era of Big Data

There is no substitute for fieldwork. **We need to work hard to safeguard fieldwork access and immersion**. Research is better informed by fieldwork, and the mentorship and development of future scholars requires access to adequate fieldwork. Institutional tools can be implemented to guarantee that fieldwork doesn't become a second- or third-order priority for the training of graduate students. As a collective discipline, I hope we urge our respective institutions and funding agencies to value this fundamental aspect of the training and development of future generations of political scientists.

STATHIS N. KALYVAS

Chapter 4: Fieldwork by Decree, Not by Design

Fieldwork is a unique opportunity to correctly characterize a social and political process, discover how people on the ground really behave, and equally important, what they believe about their behavior. **Be open to what the "field" has to teach you**, particularly—and this is the hardest part—when it forces you to radically revise what you thought you knew about the question you are asking.

CARLA B. ABDO-KATSIPIS

Chapter 40: Your Safety and Theirs

It is imperative to **start research on risky populations with expert interviews**—this will help you "get your feet wet" and become more famil-iar with your research topic in fieldwork terms. **Interviewing vulnerable populations requires flexibility and a willingness to adapt to new**

developments. Particular attention should be made to considerations of personal safety and to the safety of your subjects. **Meet in public during the daytime, avoid asking or sharing too much identifiable information, and use transportation that will not be traced back to you.** I say this not to encourage distrust, but to accommodate the reality of a situation in which those you are interviewing have access to resources made available through high-risk networks. Under these circumstances, both you and your subjects are under heightened scrutiny.

DESMOND KING

Chapter 31: "Why Are You Interested in That?"

When using archival sources, it is essential to **physically go to the archives and read broadly in them**. Despite the rise of digitalization of archival sources (which is an extremely valuable development), visiting primary sources is important for understanding how sources connect and to prompt other searches. It is important also to **look for multiple archival sources**—many organizations and institutions have their own collections in addition to what is available in national sources. Returning to sources that other scholars have purportedly consulted also often pays dividends.

When conducting interviews, it is important first to **undertake pilot interviews in which you test questionnaires in a couple of trial runs**, and then make decisions about whether to tape-record or not. If your subject matter is contentious and nuanced, as was my interest in racial equality, getting interviewees to speak more openly and usefully may necessitate taking down the interview by hand.

Finally, both archival research and interviews are often frustrating—boxes of records may have no interesting content or interviewees may provide excessively careful replies. **Perseverance will yield interesting materials and conversations** that will be rewarding for your research project.

PETER KRAUSE

Chapter 32: Navigating Born and Chosen Identities in Fieldwork

I never truly understood this T. S. Eliot quote until I started to conduct fieldwork: **"We shall not cease from exploration, and the end of all our exploring will be to arrive where we started and know the place for the**

first time." Coming home, I recognized not simply what was different about Boston from whatever city or village I lived in, but also what was different about the way I behaved while abroad. When doing fieldwork, I often lived in more working-class areas, and I devoured the local news. I had more quality, noninstrumental interactions with those around me, and I felt part of communities in ways that I didn't when at home. Doing fieldwork is an amazing privilege whose benefits extend far beyond your research. **Prepare for the possibility that it will change you**. When you return home, things may look different, and you may start to know them, and yourself, for the first time.

BETHANY LACINA

Chapter 12: Crossed Wires

Write while you are in the field. Try to formulate an argument based on what you have seen so far. This exercise will bring up issues you can address before you leave the field. Also, consider writing some of the material that will eventually be a "background" section giving readers context for your research. That material is particularly easy to access while in the field because the specifics of the narrative—proper nouns, dates, events—are on your mind every day.

DAVID D. LAITIN

Chapter 24: The Onion Principle

Although armed with your preanalysis plan, don't be afraid to take advantage of your experience in the field to go beyond it. You'll **label the new stuff you learn "exploratory"**; no shame in that. As with all lab scientists, take the lead from Doc Watson: I'm a goin' fishin 'cause everybody's fishing / And I'm a goin' fishing too.

IAN S. LUSTICK

Chapter 1: Fieldwork and Emotions

Studying politics in the field is inevitably fraught. What is of concern to the researcher is competition for resources in contexts within which the stakes are much higher for the protagonists than are the rewards of telling the truth to academic researchers. This means that a great deal of responsibility is placed on the interviewer to abide by whatever promises of confidentiality and anonymity are made. But it also means that **the credibility of whatever you are told in an interview is open to question**. One rule of thumb I have used is to not quote or cite interviewees as corroboration of a claim unless what they tell me was manifestly against their interest for me to know or to be made public. This does not mean that I do not learn from interviewees who tell me things that serve their interest, or that I do not in fact believe them. In part because of the weight of evidence, and in part due to the relationship between what they say and my theoretical assumptions, I may be profoundly convinced that their account is exactly correct. These beliefs may shape my research strategies, the questions I ask others, and the kinds of sources I will consult, but they will not, per se, be the evidentiary basis for the validity of those claims.

A corollary of understanding the highly political nature of an interview in the field is that **once the political interests of the interviewee are established, it is possible to use them as leverage**. For example, when interviewing members of a large bureaucratic apparatus about a sensitive subject, it is best to (1) start from below and work upward; (2) encourage interviewees to see the interviewer as a potential resource in the battles they are most concerned with—battles with other bureaucrats; (3) use the information interviewees offer about their bureaucratic adversaries to establish credibility in subsequent interviews with those adversaries; and (4) learn from what these other bureaucrats say, in their excited defense against their rivals, about substantive matters of interest.

MARC LYNCH

Chapter 35: Things Change

A great deal of the value of field research is simply being there: observing, meeting people, road testing assumptions, discovering new sources of data. But it's easy to get fooled into thinking that you are doing more than you actually are. **Be very careful about getting trapped in bubbles of like-minded contacts**, especially if you've met them through other scholars working on the same topic. When the same three people end up being the anonymized sources for a dozen dissertations—and, as often as not, for the journalists producing contemporary media accounts that might seem like independent checks on the validity of the information—it can create an artificial impression of a rigorous consensus formed by multiple scholars. Meeting more people won't help if they are all from the same social and political networks. **You need to diversify your contacts, not just proliferate them**. Try to find new people relevant to your topic through means other than referral by your initial points of contact so that you don't unintentionally represent the views of a single social network as something larger.

ZACHARIAH CHERIAN MAMPILLY

Chapter 34: The Field Is Everywhere

"The field is everywhere" is a mind-set, a worldview, and an epistemological reckoning. It suggests that we as researchers are not isolated from power dynamics but are integral to their functioning. It is not a call for resignation, however. Like our own research subjects, we do not lack agency. We may not always choose our ascriptive identities, yet how we wield them is consequential in both the intellectual and policy domains. Recognizing that **no actor, including ourselves as well as our donors, is neutral**, and that all are worthy of ethical and critical engagement, can prevent either implicit or explicit bias from infecting our work, bolstering the quality of our scholarly findings.

How to do this may appear overwhelming for most of us raised within a positivist epistemology that emphasizes researcher objectivity and scholarly detachment. Yet **recognizing subjectivity does not negate the intellectual rigor of our work**. Indeed, as anthropologists, sociologists, and scholars working within other interpretive traditions have already demonstrated, scholarly research on political violence is only deepened when the researcher acknowledges the distinct effects of various forms of identity on knowledge production. The best work in conflict studies has never been siloed within a specific disciplinary or epistemological tradition. As scholars working on politically sensitive subjects, it is incumbent on us to engage with these works in meaningful ways, including taking seriously the ethical, epistemological, and political concerns they raise about the entire research process.

ZOE MARKS

Chapter 2: Cooking Soup and Killing Chickens

Stepping outside of our known networks and embedding ourselves in new realities comes with anticipated physical and emotional risks. Yet we rarely anticipate the ways **intensive fieldwork can change our ideas, thinking, and worldview, and sometimes also profoundly shape our personalities, personal lives, and coping strategies**. As a result, the culture shock and isolation of returning home can be a more jarring and difficult adjustment than that of going into "the field." In researching Sierra Leone's civil war, I was prepared for fieldwork to be challenging and anticipated secondary trauma or fear (neither of which came to pass) from listening to hundreds of war stories. What I did not expect was that in Sierra Leone I would find strength and solidarity in other people's courage and survival; that showing up to hold their pain, or hold their child, or help with daily tasks would bolster my ability to bear witness to the harms they had experienced. Coming back to idyllic Oxford, I felt cracked open—alone with and overwhelmed by the narratives I had been given. Trappings of wealth, simple pleasures like hot showers, and silly pastimes horrified me, whereas nibbling down my Sierra Leonean friends' homemade farewell foodstuffs and walking two miles to buy plantains and yams from the Caribbean minimart comforted me. It provided sensory familiarity as I typed field notes, or more often sat staring at archives and testimonies wondering why it needed academic translation at all. Eventually I found companionship in two friends studying contemporary history who had done emotionally equivalent research on political violence. **I could not have known in advance who would be my support network**, or what new habits and hobbies would bring solace and familiarity, **but I wish I had known I would need it**. I wish someone had told me that there would be a valley between the question "How was fieldwork?" and feeling understood in whatever answer I could provide— and I wish I had known that that valley could take years (and yams) to cross.

JOHN F. McCAULEY

Chapter 25: The Intoxication of Fieldwork

Build in extra time for unexpected delays, and **be prepared to invest in sometimes personal and unexpected ways to establish trust with local**

authorities. Relatedly, I have learned lessons regarding the choice of research sites. Keep in mind, first, the importance of choosing research sites (whether nationally or subnationally) that allow for the testing of key hypotheses and alternative explanations. There is a temptation to go to the places we know, we like, where we are comfortable, or where we have good friends, but those factors do not advance the research. That said, it is important to have a trusted local institutional partner, however informal, as well as acquired familiarity with the terrain. In addition, multiple country contexts mean a multiplication of administrative hurdles; it is often worth the cost, but those choices should be made with care. Finally, all things equal, **be bold and choose to study the places we know less about**.

KRISTIN MICHELITCH

Chapter 11: Radio Gaga

Calculate your budget and add an additional line item of 10 percent for contingencies. If the donor/foundation does not accept contingency as a line item, then inflate everything by 10 percent and plan to spend the budget *without* contingency. **You will need that contingency money for contingencies**! Also, be careful on donkey carts.

VIPIN NARANG

Chapter 42: Drink the Tea

Double and triple check the visa requirements for your fieldwork country—and always apply for the correct category, don't play games with the categories. **Always have an exit plan no matter where you are going**.

RICHARD A. NIELSEN

Chapter 3: Recite!

We don't like to admit it, but the ability to spend years living in foreign places is correlated with wealth, health, and status. Fieldwork is not equally accessible; it's easier with money, free time, and few obligations. For those of us with kids, it's especially galling that fieldwork grants almost never pay for your family to accompany you. **If you find yourself in a position that doesn't allow the traditional "fieldwork year" in graduate school,**

don't despair. Get to the field for short, focused visits and make the most of that time. Go for a few weeks, come home, process what you experienced, and then go again for a few more weeks. Repeat as possible. Aim for grants that will cover multiple plane tickets. Use the wonders of the digital age to stay immersed while you're not there. Your fieldwork may look different from other people's, but you can still do great research.

MELISSA NOBLES

Chapter 30: Race and the Study of a Racial Democracy

Language preparation is an obvious objective if you are researching in a non-English-speaking country. This is true even if English serves as a second language for those you intend or expect to interview. For me, language preparation became important in ways I had not fully appreciated before visiting Brazil. Studying Portuguese and Brazilian history and culture prepared me well for the social interactions that enveloped my research. In other words, you cannot approach every part of your fieldwork preparation instrumentally. Learning the language, reading the great literature in that language, listening to the music, and studying the art and history both introduces you and reminds you of the joy and excitement of learning something new. It is often easy to lose sight of this fundamental joy of fieldwork, especially when you're focusing on politics. This knowledge also provides oil for your social interactions. In some situations, your expertise on a particular topic may well exceed that of those around you. However, fieldwork experiences are often more productive and enjoyable if you are broadly knowledgeable.

ALESSANDRO ORSINI

Chapter 36: Ethnography with Extremists

When it comes to establishing direct contact with unrepentant violent militants on either end of the political spectrum, the ethnographer—who wants to base the research on participant observation—should not involve anyone else in the process of making contact. **Doing research with diehard terrorists or with violent, extreme-right militants is dangerous,** especially when it relies on participant observation in unpredictable circumstances. Although the ethnographer should shield others from the risks that he or she is undertaking, **the ethnographer should provide all of the information about his or her research to a trusted person**—including the real names of the individuals and where and when the researcher meets with them. This confidant can assist in an emergency and potentially contact the proper authorities in case of imminent danger.

LINDSEY O'ROURKE

Chapter 17: Details in the Doodles

Sometimes embarking on a new major research project can feel like an insurmountable task, and it can be hard to get your wheels rolling on it. In these situations, I have found it helpful to **temporarily ignore the big picture and instead focus on manageable daily goals**: write X number of words, read X number of articles/chapters, or commit to X hours of background research. Even if you do not reach your daily goal, you will gradually build momentum. As long as you make some forward progress every day, the project will feel less and less intractable. To quote the wise jogging baboon from Bojack Horseman: "Every day it gets a little easier, but you gotta do it every day. That's the hard part. But it does get easier."

WENDY PEARLMAN

Chapter 22: On Field-Being

Do not underestimate the value of spending time in fieldwork sites outside the auspices of formal fieldwork. Months or years of simply "being" in field sites is a crucial step in acquiring foreign language proficiency. It allows you to play diverse roles other than "researcher," each of which give you a different perspective on the communities you seek to understand. **It invites you to follow rather than guide the disclosure of information, which exposes you to things for which you might not even think to search.** Finally, it hones analytical intuitions that help you to discern questions that are worth researching and make sense of what you gather in pursuit of answering them. For students seeking to understand a part of the world different from their own, **think of every trip as an installment or investment in a long-term career in the production of knowledge.** Everything you learn can enhance your understanding, even when you are not actively and intentionally engaged in research.

RAVI PERRY

Chapter 41: Shingles on the Campaign Trail

I never learned how to write good notes, but the approach I use while con-ducting field interviews presumes that good notes are taken. For many years I just assumed the "good notes" would come. But they won't just come unless you work at it. **Take notes immediately after interviews**. If necessary, pull over to the side of the road—or better yet, don't pull away right after the research is finished. **Before you leave, make sure you are satisfied with the notes you have taken**. You will need the notes and you will need to under-stand them later when the interview is no longer fresh in your memory.

DANIEL N. POSNER

Chapter 10: Be Prepared (To Go Off Script)

Buy and read the local newspaper every day when you are in the field. Many newspapers in the countries you study may be available online these days. But you can learn a huge amount from the parts of the newspaper that are usually not included in the online versions: advertisements, human interest stories, "news from the districts," and even personals and want ads. Seeing which international wire stories the local editors choose to reprint (or not) is also often illuminating. In addition, **familiarity with local news provides entry points for conversations** that can lead to useful insights.

Field work can be exhausting—especially in places with poor security. Having a safe, comfortable retreat at the end of the day (with a mosquito net if malaria is endemic in the area) is essential for your well-being. **Don't skimp on lodging**.

WILL RENO

Chapter 26: Field Research and Security in a Collapsed State

Reliable and timely information about conditions is invaluable. Those who travel to places like Somalia for field research should read offi-cial reports of the security situation with a critical eye. Foreign minis-try reports sometimes reflect the state of political relations between the issuing government and the country being evaluated. Many of these reports are general and follow formats that are not entirely appropriate for conditions in failed states and very complex conflicts where there is no clear government or rebel side. Risk management services for businesses can provide detailed information, but these are very expensive unless the university library or risk management office provides access to these services (as mine does). **There is no substitute for information from one's own network of researchers, journalists, NGO workers, and relevant government officials** (preferably ones with critical perspectives on their work) who can provide guidance.

Experience helps. In my case, the most relevant experience was gained in Iraq and Afghanistan, but this isn't a practical or helpful plan for others. One can benefit (as I did) from the experience of others on a research team, including people who are from the place where one conducts research or has experience living in conflict conditions of a similar sort.

Figure out what you will do with requests for assistance. In Somalia, this has included requests for help getting a family member into university. These are serious and sometimes genuinely plausible prospects. I have helped people get into universities simply by using the knowledge I have about the intricacies of funding and acting as a cultural interpreter and coach for application essays. This sort of thing can be fairly easy for the researcher but quite difficult for someone who is otherwise very worldly and intelligent and well-prepared. Responding to this sort of request is a sign of respect. Many have put aside their time for my benefit and have helped in all sorts of ways. It's the least I can do.

Switch on your communications device tracking setting. Take photos and send them to friends; these photos come with embedded coordinates so people will know where you are! **Expect contacts to Google you and Google again**. Expect that they will ask other people about you. Some will insist that you "friend" them on Facebook, so expect that they will be able to see your other associations. This is a trust issue: Will you share and let them see with whom you hang out? The trend away from Facebook and toward LinkedIn and other social media means these requests tend to broaden.

ROBERT ROSS

Chapter 21: Learning from Foreign Colleagues

Interviews in China benefit from establishing a personal relationship with Chinese colleagues. Sharing meals and drinks with Chinese colleagues is an agreeable requirement for professional development. Chinese colleagues appreciate your efforts to become "accustomed" to China and to dining on delicacies such as sea cucumber, eel, pig's knuckle and pig's ear, stewed pork belly, hundred-year-old eggs, jelly fish, and the spiciest Sichuan cuisine, as well as to enjoy drinking full-strength *baijiu* (e.g., mao-tai). **Sharing food and liquor also opens windows** onto Chinese culture and enriches our travels with enjoyable and relaxed moments shared with Chinese friends.

STEPHEN M. SAIDEMAN

Chapter 7: When the Linguistic Lightweight Goes Abroad

Rent a cell phone at the airport as you arrive. **Get cash out of bank machines—they have the best rates** (except for the illegal money changes in places like Argentina, and that can be scary). You may have to visit these machines often to get cash if you are paying your assistants in cash, as I did. Trying to transfer money to pay translators/assistants proved to be more difficult than paying in cash—globalization is overrated. Get travel advances if you can because fieldwork can be very expensive.

You can eat cheaply in expensive cities while still eating very well—smaller restaurants in alleys were just as good, if not better, and certainly much less expensive than bigger restaurants or those in hotels. I never spent much time enjoying the nightlife in the places I visited—I **use evenings to transcribe** my interview notes.

EMIL ASLAN SOULEIMANOV

Chapter 37: Building Trust with Ex-Insurgents

As researchers, we are often expected to keep our emotional distance from "human subjects," avoiding close personal contact to make sure research is done in a mostly sterile way. Yet you cannot keep your distance, pursue sensitive information that could compromise your respondents, and be insensitive to them at the same time. In ethnographic research, in general, and in research on civil war, in particular, there is no sterile environment. Your aim is to **gain the trust of the people so they are comfortable sharing sensitive information** that could, hypothetically speaking, hurt them or those close to them. With the strict exception of the security of the respondents, certain trade-offs are simply unavoidable.

VALERIE SPERLING

Chapter 20: All the Signs Are There

When doing interviews, don't talk too much. You might relate to what your interviewee is saying, or you might be tempted to chime in to show that you're familiar with what the interviewee is describing. You might suspect that the two of you could be fast friends, so you might want to share your own experience and talk about yourself. Resist the urge; let them talk. The flip side of this advice is that some of your interviewees (because they are human) will provide long, vague responses to your questions. My very first interviewee (when I was doing my dissertation fieldwork) was such a person—kind, eager to help, and terrifically wordy. Our interview lasted for nearly three hours, and as time went by, I realized with growing anxiety that I wasn't getting actual answers to my queries. As I learned later, this frustrating situation can usually be cured by interjecting with a simple question: "Could you give me a concrete example?" Finally, **try to do something for your interviewees**. They are donating their time to you; ask if there's something you could do for them.

PAUL STANILAND

Chapter 23: Fieldwork on Foot

Get out of your hotel or guesthouse room and don't spend too much time emailing and reading the news from home. Go to the local bookstores and coffee shops, buy newspapers, find ways to meet people other than interviewees, and make yourself conversant in the key political and social issues being discussed in the public sphere. Pick up the basics of how to buy food like something of a local, what taxi fares you should be paying (though I am happy to pay more because I have more, I like to know the baseline), and inexpensive places to have fun. **Don't only associate with expats**—they can be great, but they're not why you are there. Don't worry about losing a day or two to feeling lazy, wanting to do some writing instead of fieldwork or going to tourist sites. But don't let a couple of days turn into a week or two. It will get harder to do extended fieldwork as work and family obligations grow. **Learn how to cold-call**—it still gives me a pit in my stomach, but it's gotten a little easier with experience.

JESSICA STERN

Chapter 15: How to Interview a Terrorist

Consider learning to meditate—both to learn how to focus and to bring yourself back to psychological and spiritual stasis. Spending time with violent people can be deeply disorienting.

Empathy is an important skill. Fieldwork helps you develop that skill, which benefits not only your work life but also your personal life.

ORA SZEKELY

Chapter 38: On Being Seen

There are a couple of basic logistical choices that can make travel for research in places with complicated politics just a little easier. If you can, **mail anything that might raise eyebrows at an international border (political propaganda, leaflets, books, etc.) to yourself or a friend at home**, preferably using DHL or a similar service. It'll probably get there just fine, and this can help avoid awkward conversations if your luggage is opened.

Also, always **wear comfortable shoes**.

MARC TRACHTENBERG

Chapter 16: Stumbling Around in the Archives

Before you do archival work, especially if it's in a foreign country, **learn what you can about the rules before you go**, and plan your trip accordingly. This applies especially to the rules about photocopying, to the number of boxes you can see in a day, to whether you can order boxes in advance, and to whether you need special permission to consult various collections. You should also set yourself up with a good camera connected to a laptop.

Do as much as you can before you leave your home base. It is amazing how much material is currently available online or on microfilm, and finding aids are now often posted on the websites maintained by various repositories.

Finally, **get in touch with people who have recently returned from the places you're planning to go** and talk about various practical aspects of doing this kind of work (housing, etc.). When you arrive, be sure to talk with the archivists about the work you're doing—about what sources you might use (some of which might not even be listed in the finding aids), and about other people who have been working on similar topics. You'd be amazed by how helpful they can be.

KRISTA E. WIEGAND

Chapter 6: Hezbollah Will Take Your Data

Even though you will not know at the outset who you will interview during field research, it is helpful to lay the groundwork as much as possible before traveling abroad. First, make sure you receive **proper training and apply for IRB approval as early as possible**. If you are a graduate student, make sure your advisors are completely on board with your project. Second, **do online research** for people you would like to interview, and contact as many people as possible before your trip. Third, at the end of your interview, **ask for names of other people you should interview**, so you can use them as referrals to open doors that would otherwise be difficult to open. Fourth, both **record and write your interview notes in case one is lost or incomprehensible**. Finally, **thank your interviewees graciously for their time** and follow up with a thank-you note.

CONCLUSION

WHAT DOES IT MEAN TO DO FIELDWORK?

PETER KRAUSE AND ORA SZEKELY

What does it mean to do fieldwork?

If we thought we had the answer to this question before we began editing this book, our understanding of the concept has been both broadened and deepened in the course of our work on it. The stories included in this volume cover a lot of ground, both literally and metaphorically, from rural Inner Mongolia to urban Cairo, and from participant observation with Italian fascists to digging through the U.S. National Archives. As Zachariah Cherian Mampilly puts it in chapter 34, "the field is everywhere." The enormous range of subjects covered herein reflects both the theoretical richness of political science as a discipline and the methodological creativity of researchers in the field. We feel privileged to have had the chance to bring their reflections on their research together in one place.

When we set out to put this book together, we did not have an explicit list of issues we wanted to cover beyond a general desire to include a range of thematic topics and geographic regions. We quickly listed a number of themes we hoped to see addressed—logistics, ethics, methods, and the importance of researchers' personal identities—but we didn't have a specific checklist of the subjects we wanted to see discussed. We believe that much of our discipline's strength is in its pluralism. After all, we could not have predicted that we would be able to include chapters on how to handle contracting shingles in Toledo, Ohio, during election season and what to do when your car breaks down on a highway in Chile.

As chapter submissions began to come in, a clear set of themes emerged. Indeed, despite the enormous theoretical range and methodological variety of field-based research being done in political science, one of the most interesting takeaways from this book is that some elements of the research experience remain relatively constant across a wide range of contexts, topics, and methodologies. Interviewing human traffickers in Lebanon is very different from interviewing retired generals in India, but lessons from one experience can be usefully applied to the other, and vice versa.

One of the strongest common threads that runs throughout the chapters is the sheer unpredictability of the research experience. A researcher can schedule a solid week of interviews, only to have a sudden political event or freak snowstorm leave her with nothing but free time. Chance encounters—a conversation on a bus, an exchange with a friendly waiter, an invitation to a dinner party—can provide important insights and unexpected opportunities. Although planning is obviously tremendously important to successful field research, flexibility—as Nadya Hajj puts it, to "let go and let Ali"—is crucial.

We hope that reading about our contributors' struggles and failures, the mistakes they made and the challenges they faced in the field, as well as the emotional responses these experiences elicited, will inspire readers to feel that they can surmount such obstacles as well. We also hope these stories serve as a reminder (and perhaps a reassurance) that when things go wrong, sometimes it can represent a new opportunity. Field research is the beginning of the research process, not the end of it. Even very experienced scholars find themselves rethinking their research projects in the midst of field research, or reframing their ideas substantially based on their findings. A chance encounter can lead not only to new findings but to an entirely new project, with new field research to do.

In a similar vein, we were struck by the remarkable creativity displayed across the various stories. Good field research often relies on careful scheduling and organization, scrupulous note taking, and above all, attention to detail, but creativity is also profoundly important. Finding new and interesting ways to build connections with possible informants (for instance, cooking groundnut soup with militants' wives in Sierra Leone or learning to recite Qur'an to build rapport with Islamist activists in Egypt) not only makes research more successful but also makes it far more enjoyable. We hope these stories inspire readers to develop their own innovative research designs and methodologies.

A second overarching theme is that interpersonal dynamics matter a great deal. Having a strong rapport with a particular local official can be tremendously helpful in opening doors leading to new information or new contacts, whereas an interview with someone with whom you simply do not gel can make an hour feel like a week. Interpersonal relationships are not everything, but the stories collected here demonstrate that they are tremendously important. At the same time, they are no substitute for careful planning, preparation, and the other practical components of fieldwork.

With no end in sight to the scholarly arms race to publish more, faster—and gather ever-more data to do so—our contributors remind us that research can be most productive when a long-term vision accompanies short-term demands. Many of the best (and happiest) researchers lay down deep roots in the communities in which they work, and as Wendy Pearlman points out, that process starts early and is developed over the course of a career. Amaney Jamal demonstrates that fieldwork is far more than data acquisition, and that building professional networks via "active engagement and intellectual reciprocity" is the key to improving both one's own research and that of our international community of scholars. In an era when students and professors are continually pushed to publish their next paper as soon as possible, the experience and impact of these contributors demonstrate the tremendous value of "slow scholarship."

A corollary to this, of course, is that the individual researcher is far from invisible in the research process. Most academic researchers strive for objectivity, in the sense that we try to figure out what's true based on evidence, not what we wish were true or what someone else wants to convince us is true. But no one goes into the field (or the lab) as a blank slate. We all bring our individual histories, preferences, and perceptions with us when we do research, whether we are interviewing Al Qaeda members or seeking to understand the Brazilian census. An awareness of our own subjectivity is a tremendously important feature of the research process. Moreover (and this is another clear theme here), the experience we bring with us can be an asset or a disadvantage in the research process. Our own identities, both as we ourselves understand them and as they are perceived by research participants, can make it easier or more difficult to work in certain communities, meet with certain informants, or even sit alone comfortably in a café reading the newspaper.

A third theme that arose from the stories collected here is a real concern with the ethics of field research. What do we owe our research participants? How do we ensure maximal intellectual honesty and theoretical rigor while conducting research under sometimes unpredictable circumstances? How can we hold ourselves accountable to both of these principles at the same time? Who are we ethically responsible to, what are we responsible for, and what does that responsibility mean in practice?

For many researchers, the human connections created through the research process do not necessarily end with the end of research. Researchers may develop moral commitments and emotional attachments to their research sites; indeed, these may have influenced their choice of research topic in the first place. Some of the contributors chose their field sites for methodological or empirical reasons, and others chose theirs based on prior experience, personal or family connections, or political commitments. Regardless of the original impetus behind the choice to do field research in a particular place, the experience itself can create both an incentive and an opportunity for researchers to give back to the communities who have shared their insights and experiences with us. Such engagement can take a range of forms, from political advocacy, to using relevant language skills in volunteer work in one's home community, to fund-raising, to bringing a little-discussed issue to public attention through public talks, op-eds, and other media engagement. But what if such engagement—because of security, political allegiance, or some other complicating factor—is either impossible or undesirable? There is, after all, a substantive difference between doing research in a civilian community and interviewing warlords. What do we owe research participants who have done things that we personally may find troubling? These are not easy questions. Some of the chapters tackle them directly, and others reference them in passing, and not all of us approach these issues in the same way. It is our hope that this book can contribute to a fruitful discussion of these issues in the discipline.

The stories, reflections, and insights collected here demonstrate that field research, for all its variation, is at its core a human experience. To "do field research" means to go somewhere—whether that is a community meeting at the YWCA in one's own neighborhood, a Telegram channel frequented by ISIS members, or a refugee camp in Lebanon—to learn something about the experiences and beliefs of those involved in a particular phenomenon. It may involve working with a team of researchers and enumerators, long hours of participant observation at protests and rallies, or many solitary hours painstakingly transcribing and translating interviews. It can be exciting, tedious, joyful, heartbreaking, and terrifying, sometimes all at once. It almost invariably involves discovering something strange, unexpected, and fascinating. It can involve long plane flights, long bus trips, and long walks. It can require learning a new language, relearning how to buy vegetables, figuring out how not to get kidnapped, or learning to see one's own neighborhood in an entirely new light. What defines field research is not the location itself but our relationship with a particular context and our engagement with the people involved.

What, then, is "the field"? It can be anything—or anywhere—we want it to be. We hope this book has expanded and enriched your conception of the field, challenged your assumptions about fieldwork, given you new ideas for research questions and methodologies, made you reconsider pressing ethical issues, and inspired you to think about your own identity and its impact on your research. If reading these stories and their related lessons did even some of that for you—with a laugh, a tear, a cringe, or a smile of recognition along the way—we will have succeeded.

INDEX

Note: Page numbers in *italics* indicate illustrations.

National Science Foundation (U.S.), 270, 281

NATO nuclear strategies, 137–38

Nazi Germany, 227, 231n3

neo-Nazis (U.S.), 128

Netherlands, 132–33

networking, 210; Abdo-Katsipis on, 328–29; anonymous contacts versus, 154–55, 161–62; Balcells on, 227; with expatriates, 75–76, 361; Jamal on, 215–20, 349, 366; Lynch on, 352–53; Stern on, 128, 130

New Deal policies, 252

New Institutional Economics, 85

Nielsen, Richard A., 6, 36–43, 355–56

Niger, 207

Nigeria, 196–98, 200

9/11 attacks, 129–30, 132. *See also* War on Terror

Nobles, Melissa, 9, 238–44, 356

Nonviolent and Violent Campaigns and Outcomes (NAVCO) data set, 268–70

Northern Ireland, 188, 190–91, 255–58, *257*

nuclear weapons, 127–28, 137–38, 340–41

Obafemi Awolowo University, 197

Obama, Barack, 335–39; Russian sanctions of, 169–71, *170*

Occupy Wall Street movement, 268

Office of Radio and Television in Mali (ORTM), 93–100

Office of Risk Management guidelines, 213

"onion principle," 9, 196–200, 351

oral histories, 13, 226–29, 255–58

Orientalism, 21, 290

O'Rourke, Lindsey A., 8, 106, 142–49, 357

Orsini, Alessandro, 10, 293–302, 356–57

Ottoman Empire, 151–52, 154

Padgett, John, 50

Pakistan, 128–31, 341–42

Palestine, 15–22, 184, 259–60

Palestinian National Front, 20

Palestinian refugee camps, 83–87, 368

Paris, 135–37, 188

Parks, Robert, 261

PATRIOT Act, 68. *See also* War on Terror

Peace Corps, 196, 204

peacekeeping soldiers, 281

Pearlman, Wendy, 8–9, 173n2, 183–87, 217, 357, 366

Pendleton Act (U.S., 1882), 246–52

Pentagon Papers, 144

people power movements, 268, 271–72. *See also* Arab Spring

Perry, Ravi, 11, 335–39, 358

Petersen, Roger, 50–51

Philippines, 69

Polish-Lithuanian Commonwealth, 151–52, 154

"political correctness," 177

Portes, Alejandro, 83

positionality of research, 228; Han on, 234–36, 348; Krause on, 9–10, 254–64, 351, 366–67; Mampilly on, 280–84, 353; Nobles on, 241–44; Szekely on, 9–10. *See also* subjectivity

positivist political science, 40–43, 115, 235

Posner, Daniel N., 3, 7, 88–91, 203, 358

posttraumatic stress disorder (PTSD), 133, 162, 227

Prima Linea (terrorist group), 298

principal-agent theory, 73

prison system: Colombian, 322–24; United States, 248–49

privacy. *See* confidentiality concerns

property rights, of Palestinians, 85–87